BLOOD & ROSES

The Vampire
in 19th Century Literature

Edited by
Adèle Olivia Gladwell & James Havoc
for
CREATION PRESS

BLOOD & ROSES
The Vampire in 19th Century Literature
A. Gladwell & J. Havoc
(Editors)
A Creation Press Artefact
Creation Classics III
Published by
CREATION PRESS
1992

CREATION PRESS
83, Clerkenwell Road
London EC1
Tel/Fax: 071-430-9878

CONTENTS

Introduction

THE EROGENOUS DISEASE

The vampire - perfect incarnation of Eros and Thanatos, whose coming ruptures the hymen of midnight, corrupts the virtuous virgin and de-enlightens the sexual morals; illuminating the eclipsed subconscious, and embodying archetypes of the sexual imagination. A vampire's spectre augurs erotic deliria: carnal debilitation, autoerogenous metempsychosis, fetishism and lesbianism, necrophiliac dementia, auto-symbolic incest, masturbation. As the Shadow's avatar, the vampire represents the anima or animus of manifest desire and dread, born of the right side of the brain; opening the body's blood-gates, flooding the repressed psyche with wonder and disgust.

The male vampire is a catamenial harbinger supping blood from the newly violated throat (neck) as menses discharge through the cervix (neck of womb) from the rawly-opened uterus. He is the psyche's first lover, supping on the purpled maidenhead. The Prince of Darkness, with his waxing and waning crescent fangs, is the over-riding animus of menstruation prevalent in late 19th Century and modern mythology. An anathema abalienated from the recesses of the "imaginary". Appearing at the "dark" time or tenebrose side of the cyclical female calendar, he conveys the impression he is witholding esoteric knowledge and an animalistic magnetic instinct. The sexual lycanthropy of the dream-mind. Like a religious master. Frightening but unbelievably exciting. Lupine, bestial, yet often serene. He liberates his lady (his hostess). Her Victorian bustles and corsets unravel, and she swiftly cavorts in a white shroud encrimsoned with bloody maculations; utterly unhampered. Gone is her ascetic pallor as her full sexuality is embraced by her very own "dark lover" and "alternative husband". The one who relishes, feeds upon the side of herself ordinarily denied her by patriarchal Victorian standards. The *accoucheur* of the sexual antinomian. Worshipping the raw eternal wound.

And the vulva can be a flower. The overly lush orchid or narcotic opiate poppy. Blooming, blossoming, expanding and opening. Or stifled. And menstruation can be the flower; the bloom of power and possibility. The flow-er. The Olde English flower; a posy of roses; red, red roses; *blood and roses*. And as a flower mysteriously holds within it the promise of future fruit or not, so can she. Only she is forced into being passively maternal, and so the flower becomes a threat and not a promise. For it is a symbol of non-procreation, and the women turn inwards during their bleeding - towards their dreams and the multi-aspects of their deep or truer selves. Towards archetypal lovers, animal accomplices, bestial alter-egos and mythological icons.

And to the vampire, strangely internally related and connected to the hostess of blood; de-flowering and marauding in the dead of the night. The blood of de-petalment; the blood of the maidenhead; the cherry blood.

And to all the behavioural phenomena that Victorian women were not allowed to execute or express. All the "female maladies". All the sicknesses and weaknesses of the mind were due to the base, carnal nature of the female flesh, and so they must be punished. The hysteria, the melancholy and the nymphomania. All perverse symptoms of she who would not settle down quietly in her cloistered boudoir - as good Victorian women should. So who was this fearsome male who appeared to encourage the evil lasciviousness and deviancy of her sex? And what of his female counterpart; the lamia? She who all the men dreamt about and slandered.

Areligious, agnostic or unholy, the recusant vampire is repulsed by the crucifix - apt, since it is the blood of Jesus which has most usurped the power from the blood of menstruating and sexual women; like all other misogynistic religions, Christianity forever stands between women, their self-awareness and the ease they fell over their carnality and sexuality.

In dreams blood is a common metaphor for semen; the visitation of a female vampire (or succubus, or lamia) can coincide with a young man's nocturnal ejaculations or masturbation. This can be the first rendezvous with the anima; the first awareness of the archetype inherent in all men. That she may be threatening is synonymous with the perplexing "lovers' games" we can play with the archetypal gender other, or simply the lucifugal essence of sexual elements. The mingling of blood, a two way violation evoking a repressed desire for a circle of cunnilingus/fellatio, oral/genital contact or incestuous indulgence.

While women may welcome the attentions of the thanatoid stranger, like an erogenous liberty, absorbing the proffered gift of undeath in a promissory eternity of small death (*petit mort*) or orgasm, it is more common for men to live and dream in dread of the female vampire's bloody mouth. Disembodied, the genito-features recall congested haematic labia unnaturally champing with fangs. The powerful *vagina dentata*, threatening him with emasculation and loss of his "attribute". The myth of the Gorgon Medusa perfectly illustrates this fear. The snakes undulating on her head (symbols of exuviation, life/death cycles and female sexuality) and the internecine fangs. The "death-stare" that can stiffen men to stone; arouse them to stiff erection, as well as petrify them. The decapitated head with its ensanguined and dripping neck is the bleeding womb neck. Concupiscence and etiolation combine in a variant chiaroscuro scenario of the male psyche.

Moreover, for men the male vampire is a sexual threat with which they cannot compete, being a projection and fantasy of the dominant power of the female imagination. A chaotic and unleashed energy of the mind and body shaking up the rhetorical patriarchal order's definitions of behaviour and morality. As Dracula, the eponymous *anti-hero* of Bram Stoker's masterpiece proclaims: "The girls that you all love are mine."

In **Blood and Roses**, the chosen 19th Century tales of embodied and atmospheric vampirism are enlightening reflections on Victorian sexual ethics and attitudes. Myriad blood-suckings and energy appropriations are covered; the religious or moral fears and subversions are very evident, and highly seminal: "eaten alive by desire" or fending off the threat of being consumed by the immoral "chaos" of an aberrant sexuality, that has little interest in acceptable procreative nuptials. The anthology, arranged chronologically, commences with Polidori's *The Vampyre* - generally accepted as the first prose incarnation of the "traditional" vampire in English - and concludes with extracts from Stoker's *Dracula*, the first book to fully describe the sexually diabolic or fatal concept of castration and subversion born of repression.

The vampires in this collection of stories, prose and poetry fall roughly into four archetypal groups. However, I do not wish to strangle the poetics of any of the works by suggesting too regimented a critical categorisation. That the vampire is essentially a creature of alluring, hypnotic and unknown qualities refutes many attempts at logical dogma.

However it is interesting to note, due to the diverse social situations of the stories and writers, as well as the differing intentions, that parallels and contrasts can be seen between the vampires that were invented.

Whether one reads Freudian theory into vampiric tales - with the allegory of social discontent and childhood disturbance; or Jungian theory with its exposés of suppressed collective unconscious archetypes. Whether one delves into Oedipal theories of oral satisfaction and shame; or interprets the writer's struggle with the vampiric demon in himself as being the essential struggle which the artist must endure to create, as a catharsis. Whether one sees socio-political manifestations of violence, sadism, individual oppression or xenophobia as behind the vampire's metaphor - the four types of vampire still tend to be applicable.

The Satanic, Diabolical Overlord - who is the aristocratic and sexual male figure - comes mainly from the Romantic mythic figure of literature in England. If we consider Lord Byron - rôle model for Polidori's Lord Ruthven - we realise that his own *persona* partially arose from the psychological device of seeing artistic creation as vampiric; Byron's draining of his psyche as he hauled himself and his sanity into a black well of unexplored creative terrains and sexual misdemeanours. The figure of Byron, with his alluring anti-heroic, and slightly cruel, qualities, is synonymous with the Romantic vampire. Through Stoker, this male figure becomes very much the animus, or superhuman male, of the châtelaine or young female subject of the story. He relates directly to her as the hostess, as an embodiment of her own imaginary figment. This erotic possession can answer desires to belong fully to an entity from the dream; of the dreams. She is the object of the attentions of a superior being, one of her own mind's desire. His stunning beauty, mesmeric eyes and sophistication, as well as his overwhelmingly savage lovemaking, are the stuff "bad" dreams are made of.

Moreover, his lovemaking is essentially *all* foreplay, gearing itself to her needs.

It is the stuff "good" girls shouldn't even think about, with their shameful menses, and the virginity they should hold onto like a virtuous prize. The rape connotations of *Dracula* could be born of the fear that this "sex without guilt" means they no longer feel, with this one male manifestation, shame about the "stink" of their menstruation. The thrill of helplessness is the thrill against the "better self", and paradoxically coupled with power, for this demonic force cannot really harm. He is there, after all, to remove the stifled woman from her hot house of repression. He is her desideratum. And as in *Dracula*, the hostess will sup blood (semen) too, something only her alter-ego self will advocate, in this Victorian scenario. The insatiability of the vampire is a superhuman, and somewhat praterhuman, love. Both lupine and reptilian, and instinctive. As his feculent bed chamber mausoleum stinks of rot and death; the anality, too, of his being is as revoltingly enticing as his desire for the overripe ensanguined flower. He will sup, indulge in symbolic cunnilingus, where others will only dominate and impregnate. Feasting at the secret cicatrix of the cervix. The carcanet of bloody dead red droplets. There she will hear the outraged cries of her menfolk trying to pull her back, out of her dream, to annihilate her animus. The luteal phase of a woman's cycle precedes the build-up to bleeding and multi-orgasmic ability; in a context of narcissism, hedonism and non-procreational subversion.

"Ideally, the men should be able to share the experience of this rhythm too. If the men do not bend ... then they will break and carry our world down with them." (*The Wise Wound* - Shuttle and Redgrove)

From all this is born the concept that men's bodies are the norm and women's bodily changes are "problematic". But, whenever the moon signals the vampire will count the 28 days and appear.

Dracula, or the diabolical Lord, can also symbolise a super-father figure. (Because the animus is an archetype he has an inherent relationship with *all* women). Then, it is the insistence on exclusive possession that arises in one who hasn't succeeded in emancipating herself from infantile desires. But in a repressive patriarchal society, how can she? Thus she is his one and only, and he hers. He can turn to the men in the society and through his spine-tingling popysma infer - "She never really belonged to you, because you do not understand her like I do."

He will emerge into the scenario as if into a traditional love story. She will undergo an initiation through contact with him; will be attracted, then repulsed, then attracted again. This sequence signifies her awareness of her own masculinity, the forbidding of this discovery, and her reluctance to turn from this liberty and narcissism. There will be in the story paramount respect for the hunted by the hunter. Consequently, there will be the Victorian scientific approach to "dealing" with the vampire, as in any womanly, hysteric "malady". The fiancé will keep a vigil, and chase out the demon, or lycanthropic beast. From Polidori and Byron onwards, this is very much the consensus on the vampire as Diabolical Lord. Yet only in

Stoker's *Dracula* can one overtly read the sexual threat of the vampire as animus or anima; dream-lover or incubus/succubus.

The Fatal Woman was also conceived initially in a Romantic setting. The female vampire as muse. Draining away the strength and sanity of the male writer (narrator), as she leads him into the *dépassement* of deeper and darker, and ultimately transcendental, waters.

The love affair of writer with pen had to have a woman as metaphor, or instigator. To become literal, to actually encounter the muse, to embody her, led writers such as Baudelaire, Keats and Swinbourne to forever swing between the dawn and dusk of horror and delight. "...For the true artist a woman is his evil destructive demon, she is his vampire" says W.S. Reymont in *Wampir. La Belle Dame Sans Merci*; the beautiful woman more radiant, more superreal, than even the Holy Mother. She could entrance like death herself but then she would, because of the nature of the passion, destroy and emasculate too. She would sup reason as she supped blood (semen) and lifeforce. She would filch the ego. She was the greatest unknown, an extreme experience incarnate. She was the collosus, the Black Goddess and she was, ultimately, death itself; where every terrifying and exciting quest culminates and becomes an entirety in itself. Sometimes she would be projected onto a mortal woman, and then sometimes it could become, unfortunately, a scenario doomed to misogyny and the ruthless destruction of the female "vampire".

The Unseen Force, or Atmospheric vampire, written of by the Irish-American Fitz-James O'Brien and, later and most effectively, by Guy de Maupassant, was a state of losing one's life force, or social standing, to a place, time or non-incarnate extension of self. Maybe an emotional fear, social fear or political fear. Similar, in many ways, to the Folkloric vampires of Europe. Gogol, Toystoy and Turgenev all wrote tales that could clearly be seen as metaphors and analogies of political or social events of the time. Class struggles; the threat of the peasant or the threat of the aristocrat. Struggles against social changes or ideals; socialism and communism, or even, it has been suggested, fascism. Anything that threatened the *status quo* of the time. A xenophobia; the fear of the outsider. The re-emergence of the pariah. The ugly one, or the strangely different one, with differences too dire to accept and too threatening to not destroy. In essence, once more a sexual threat although at the deepest level of sub-conscious.

Gautier's *The Beautiful Dead*, or *Clarimonde*, is the perfect fatal woman tale. Considering the time when it was written, it really is extraordinarily daring, and quite beautiful; but then again it could only have been written at that time. Clarimonde epitomizes the "belle dame sans merci"; she seduces the narrator, a young priest, drawing him away at the dead of night into a fantastical dream-world the very antithesis of his daytime moral duties. Every binary opposition exists here. Male-day and female-night. Order and chaos. Religious order and pagan, even satanic, heresy. Morality and immorality, even amorality. Right hand brain and left hand brain. Symbolic realm and imaginery realm. Appropriation and giving. Ego and superego or id.

What makes the story so remarkable, aside from the poetics of the narrative (here beautifully realised in translation by Lafcadio Hearn), is the nature in which Gautier draws out these polarizations; draws out the oppositions until they are as tightly, tortuously stretched as they can be before the inevitable break down and the emergence of one side as the victor; as must happen with all power polarizations in a similar semantic setting.

Clarimonde is the perfect lamia with all her seductions finely honed. Phantasmagoric and drawn from dream; her aesthetic, and not psychological, appeal epitomizes the sexual fantasy of the repressed or morally restrained. She is the inducer of autoeroticism and wet dreams. She is dangerous but she is not cruel. She is passionate but she is not loving. In other words this is not a nurturing emotion.

For a female writer the lamia or female vampire can represent a repulsive libidinal desire, but for the male the lamia is alluring and paradoxical. Her qualities are reptilian, as the male vampires are lupine. Bestial sexual undertones are the physical basis for vampires, as they manifest the animalism of ourselves as creatures with driving and instinctual needs. The lamia will often have moist or fevered skin, hot breath and contracted or dilated eyes. The hissing poppysma of the vampire is in keeping with these supposed serpent qualities. Moreover the links between the snake and the seductive woman go back a long way. The distrust and the sin adjoin. And in other cultures and contexts, the snake-like shedding of skin, the exuviae, recall the shedding of the lining of the womb. The undulations of the snake are the pulses and sways of the vagina and pelvis. The snake has become female sexuality, in its most threatening sense.

In works such as Coleridge's *Christabel* and Sheridan le Fanu's *Carmilla* there is an entriguing overlap of the mother/lover role of the female vampire. It is as if the lamia has a pact with the real mother which allows her to teach the young girl "naughty" things. Even more interesting is to consider this lamia as being born from the male imagination into this role; from his psyche seductively sways this projection of his libido. An alternative mother/lover to introduce the girl to her sexuality.

The lamia is also in human form, and is therefore a victim of emotion; conversely she is supernatural and a victim of immortality. (In another context we realise she is an archetype of the unconscious and maybe this is what imbues her with this immortal, goddess-like quality). But like the *femme fatale* since time began, we may also see her as a victim of her nature. She cannot help her nature; she hungers (literally) for love but she may destroy that which she loves and which gives her life; because she is *somewhat* human.

Edgar Allan Poe experimented with female protagonists in some of his stories, including *Ligeia*, contained in this collection. But the female vampire is never the narrator. *Ligeia* is wonderfully clever, and essentially vampiric in its atmosphere as well as its characterisations. The story of the lamia is told by someone who could perhaps be a vampire himself. The lamia is dead, and according to the narrator she could be the cause of his debilitation. But we never can assess blame, such is the ambiguity of the recollection. Poe's stories in this vein are mirrors of the disintegration of the conscious, the ego and the objective rationality as two partners attempt to control, consume, seduce and destroy each other. His stories are black metaphors describing human interaction. The female will transubstantiate herself by consuming will (and semen or blood). A life-in-death context. He is death-in-life; drained and emaciated.

But the most enjoyable element of such stories as *Ligeia* is the nature of the narration by the narrator. He is untrustworthy, and addicted to opium. And in the same way one's sense of the truth of a story is thrown if told by one party who has a personal grudge against another party, not to mention a debilitating addiction, so ours is tested here. And so the woman comes across as the perfect lamia in this narrator's eyes. Her serpentine, thanatoid being is truly vampiric. But *both* are vampires. On her death bed a further truth is exposed. Necrophilia - a central element in traditional vampirism. A mating of the death instinct and the life instinct. Eros and Thanatos. Poe's story can actually be read as a far more sophisticated version of "Wake Not The Dead" (c.1800, accredited to Johann Ludwig Tieck), with the same thematic reoccurrence of necrophile obsession between lovers or spouses (Poe's own obsession with dead brides and blood can be traced back to the death of his young wife, who vomited blood from a ruptured artery as she sung to him).

As D.H.Lawrence wrote of Poe's lover-as-vampire phenomenon, as well as his own:

" ... Each individual organism is vivified by intimate contact with fellow organisms...In spiritual love, the contact is purely nervous. The nerves in the lovers are set vibrating in unison like two instruments. The pitch can rise higher and higher. But carry this too far, and the nerves begin to break, to bleed, as it were, and a form of death sets in ... It is easy to see why each man kills the things he loves. To *know* a living thing is to kill it ... For this reason, the desirous consciousness, the SPIRIT, is a vampire."

To lose the mask, the *persona*, the social front in the quagmire of sexual love is to feel the filch, the sup, the love-bite of the lover-as-vampire; and recognise the mythos of these black love stories.

In order to fully execute this angle of the vampire myth Poe did not explicitly utilise the universal lengend of the vampire with all the common traits, habits and settings. It became merely a metaphor for the human condition and desire for perfect sexual love and unity, with all its aspirations and failings. Poe's lovers consume each other in a psychological sense and there is little eroticism, but a leviathan craving for possession and domination, in the face of loss (both of the self and the other). Strains of the succubus/incubus myths of nighttime/deadtime theft and satiation are also apparent.

Included in this collection is a new, free translation by Jeremy Reed of Charles Baudelaire's *Les Metamorphoses du Vampire*. Baudelaire was of course hugely inspired by Poe, and his use of the vampire myth is similar to Poe's; but, of course, it is also well known that Baudelaire was a great, almost masochistic, lover of sexual enervation and energization; adoration and quandary. Here the poet appreciates the vampiric experience, and as his sexual desire is sated and he lays supine and exhausted (drained), so she becomes a symbol of death. An ecstasy that is an agony, as she metamorphoses into a degenerating, skeletal being. Many symbols of orgasm or *petit mort* are apparent, as is the death of reason, the death of sexual vigour and the fatality of the serpent-like female. Moreover, I do not think she is merely a *femme fatale*, but, as so many of his works illustrate, she is Baudelaire's striving for absolutism incarnate. She is nature herself, with death as her main element, and all the cycles of life, birth and destruction inherent. Life instinct, erotic and death instinct. Perhaps she also encompasses his search for something beyond his knowledge, which he knows he will never discover but which still encourages him on; for this is its very nature. The transcendental made literal. The dream personified, as the most colossal desire. Baudelaire often projected onto his muse the mysteries of nature as a mean mistress; a microcosmic vampire; an entity neither understood or possessed, as well as a vampire of the "pith from my bones". Jeremy Reed's translation is fresh with an exciting raw sexual edge, the ineluctable abjection within the sexual act.

Ivan Turgenev also goes beyond the surface qualities of the lamia in his story *Phantoms*. Here, in this beautifully written and complex analogy, there appear to be three-fold vampiric elements at work. The phantom Alice is his nighttime dream lover; a sexual fantasy apparent by the midnight flights of fancy she takes him on. Clearly symbolic of sexual encounters, dreams of sex or onanistic indulgence, the flying represents the sexual expression "to float" or to lose one's footing in sexual ecstasy. Fear of flying soon gives way to enjoyment; the next morning he appears languid, inert, with the dark rings under his eyes symbolising a surfeit of pleasure. Auto-eroticism was regarded a sin, not forgetting, and loss of semen represented loss of vital fluids. Clearly, she is the anima, as shown by the feeling of recognition he feels at their encounters, as one would feel at meeting in dream an archetype of the collective unconscious.

Their flights to far-off places satisfy his desires to surmount the limits imposed by nature and supply a strong link to ancestry, history and how our forefathers floated in the waters of our world's very inception. Falling and drifting without the anchoring restraints of morality.

The leviathan "death" rolling along like a reptilian thundercloud at the end of the story is refered to as feminine. "Here *she* comes". And there is no escaping the huge amorality, the "no-conscience" of death. Death as the (ultimate) vampire too.

At the very end of the story we hear of the peasants' revolt. An uprising of the underclass against the land-owners who for years have bled them dry; yet another aspect of the vampiric references which fill Turgenev's story. Some almost have his empathy; others his disdain. This story is both a tale of a lamia and a folkloric vampire.

Carmilla, the lesbian fatal woman, evokes a complimentary female circle.

In the geographical limbo of Styria - where English manners meet European lores, in fantastical Gothic settings - *Carmilla* is also set. The most famous lesbian vampire story, and beautifully executed in a poetic-turned-prose style with a great deal of erotic collusion on the part of J.Sheridan Le Fanu. The young lady, narrating her story, encountered Carmilla - her pasionate doppelgänger - ten years previously. The bridges between fantasy, dream and reality burn with a lusty fire, but tens years later they are still aflame. This is the story of a narcissistic female relationship; its intentions truly subversive for its time. The obsessive love of Carmilla is uncanny in its fervour, but it is also very real. She speaks of the greatest pinnacle of extreme pleasure - death (orgasm?). Dying and losing oneself in the ecstasy of love. Her tumultous excitement mesmerises her friend. For she is a well-brought up Victorian girl, an innocent, and a passive in the world of the predominant male in the scenario - her father. Carmilla's passion excites the young girl Laura, even as it repulses her. This ambiguity is frequently described. Pleasurable caresses that mingle with the aftertastes of disgust. A growing adoration that also feeds an abhorrence. For such is this unholy threat! Carmilla's breasts rising and falling with the ardour of a lover (for she *is* a lover) unnerve the young girl. The perplexion of the adolescent as she ponders on these passionate events mirrors not only the unknown erotic foreplay of the vampire's nature; but also, importantly, the unknown loveplay of lesbianity. The foreplay that phallocentricity pretends simply cannot exist. Not unlike the vampire's aesthetics of dangerous eroticism; overwhelming sexuality and powers beyond patriarchal understanding. This is not to suggest the lesbian *is* Vampire; rather to highlight the belief in our patriarchal society that women together can really *do* nothing of any great importance (penetration); conversely if they do, it is the greatest subversive act known to mankind; not unlike that of the vampire.

The sexual morals of the time are all too evident, and Le Fanu writes with a remorseless collusion with Carmilla, as far as he possibly can. Carmilla's disgust of the church, and vice versa. The petty hypocrisy, as she sees it, of the fear of death. The non-procreational fatal woman, glittering on the brink of amorality, outside of neat Victorian society, has never been so charming, so intelligent, so gracious and graceful - or so threatening.

From beyond death or un-death, Carmilla seeks the flipside extremes of love and hatred. An exterior extension of Laura's shadow, or alter-ego. On an incestuous or infant behavioural level Carmilla could be read as an epitome of the Mother-figure in Laura's Elektra complex; evident in the absence of the girl's real mother, and the dominance of her father and the lengthy approval-seeking Laura partakes in. Her relationship with Carmilla is a self-contained affair, that shames as it comforts and liberates.

The metaphor of female liberation as a vampiric ambience of the period, similar to the folkloric and atmospheric vampire - the woman who breaks from the bonds of "proper" feminine behaviour is the outsider or dissident, and is treated thus, in a form of xenophobia. As was common at this time, this "female malady", this abberation of the "weak" female mind and flesh was given specifically sexual connotations. That the body and mind were feeble and susceptible to hysteria and unchaste uteromanic behaviour was a very unrelenting and, in fact, enforced belief of Victorian patriarchy. Now, in an era of feminist psychology, we can better understand that a "female malady" or psychological illness can be a *consequence* of the traditional feminine role, not a deviation from it. This is not to suggest that lesbianism be construed in such a context, but that in this 19th Century era any attempt by a female to break from patriarchal ideals was then viewed as an abberation of the accepted behaviour. Then, if melancholy, depression, muteness, alcoholism and hysteria followed then it was *because* of the female flesh, not the society that had enforced the suffering. The weakness of the women's physical beings is frequently reinforced in Carmilla, and it is explained as a symptom of the femininity. Carmilla's supposed fall from a horse, although no apparent damage has been done; faintness, loss of rose-tinted colour, all symptoms of femininity not quite as it should be. Anything socially deviant was an act of madness, and there is a sense of Laura's fear of being the only one to experience and know certain things.

It is very strange indeed to consider that the unchaste, immoral Victorian "madwoman" with her concupiscence, her dishevelled clothing and "emotional" mind - as the essential feminine nature - became such a cultural icon. An icon of fluidity; milk, blood, tears, flowers and all that is mutable and flowing; such as many Romantic heroines. Whilst this romanticised image may be aesthetically interesting, and seminal, it is well to remember that this concept kept women passive. Now, of course, we can view this kind of emotional expression as a protest, in a post-feminist context. We can read it as a subversion from the "norm" and see the Romantically-appropriated Ophelia as heroine. It is indeed shameful that what was termed "female-madness" and abberation then, has taken so long to become a symbol of defiance in our modern times.

The confusion of roles in Carmilla is our confusion also. Mother or lover? It is an erotic love; one of slow gravitation towards sensuality and forbidden terrains, and one that enhances feelings of the mystery of lesbianity and non-penetrative sexual love; also, importantly, of the mother-love inherent in all humans; suppressed, repressed, or not.

Whilst Carmilla is always described by Le Fanu as beatific and captivating, she is also ascribed the feline or serpentine qualities of the lamia. Nocturnal; with a sensual delight in her biting and sucking that is lovingly - lasciviously - detailed. Remembering this is Laura's dream/fantasy, the orality of the breast sucking is highly symbolic. So too is the males' intense gaze upon the bite mark; voyeurism is rampant. So Carmilla is not only Laura's own libidinal desire, incarnate, but also a wet-nursing alternative mother. What therefore fascinates me so much concerning this story is the huge gap there appears to be between the Carmilla whom Laura knows, and the terrible Mircalla/Millarca the menfolk desribe. Even after hearing the General's story and surely (subconsciously) putting the pieces together to deduce that this is the vampire, Laura still smiles and welcomes the "beautiful" Carmilla unto her, only finally convincing herself that Carmilla *is* an evil creature after the men's actions of destruction. Even at the very end of the tale, Laura sits dreading (half hoping ?) to hear Carmilla's step at the door.

The dreaded figure that haunts the margins of 19th Century female writing can be an incarnation of the author's anxiety and rage. More so if, in another light, that figure seems to best resemble the forbidden vampire. In Charlotte Brontë's *Jane Eyre*, we encounter perhaps the only female vampire or lamia as written about by a female writer of that period. Here, however, she is no *femme fatale*. It is as if the author enacts her own desires to escape male houses and texts by the literary incarnation of Bertha Rochester; the first wife of the Jane Eyre's intended spouse. Her sexual suppression manifests as the *madwoman in the attic* (if the wondrous Thornfield Hall, wherein all Jane's joy, sorrow, emotional and sexual birthing takes place, is the body; then the dark semi-obscured attic is surely the mind, where this dark madness has her abode). This female madness *is* protest and defiance. An attempt at escape from female bondage, by subverting the everyday logical run of events.

Bertha is, of course, vastly different from the lamia; she is, in effect, the "other woman". And her crime is emphatically her sexuality; her animalism; her bestial nature. Strangely, the idealized *femme fatale* can be a way of keeping women subservient, and maybe this is a sublimated male desire. The sexual woman is not to be taken home, for she can castrate; and she is not really to be married because she is powerful and threatening to the ego. She can only be fantasy, an object; and here in the case of the young Jane Eyre we see that this female vampire, presented to us by a female writer, becomes the object of threat, jealousy, spite and scorn - despite the case that clearly she *is* Jane Eyre's dark double.

Bertha stands between Jane and her ultimate Victorian happiness - marriage. It is Jane's animal aspects, suppressed sexuality and id and, most of all, unsocialized female-ness incarnate as Bertha that prevent the nuptial bonding with Mr. Rochester. So, Bertha is locked away. A psycho-sexual predator; who may appear, to Jane, an actual vampire. Bertha becomes almost mythic because she is this projection of sublimated sexuality, whilst still retaining human qualities. Her attacks occur on nights of a full, blood-red moon (the symbols of the female cycle are not difficult to spot) - and we could postulate that at such times Jane comes face to face with her sexual, bestial self through an oneiric mirror.

Bertha is perhaps the only violently sexual woman in Victorian literature.

Her sexuality costs her her humanity, as she carries the full brunt of Jane's desires, propensity to passion, and is the *flesh* of it all. (Interestingly, twenty years ago, prior to feminist beliefs, Bertha would have been seen as a projection of Rochester's; not Jane's. It is fascinating to consider Bertha as Rochester's suppressed anima, perhaps. All the more terrifying and vampiric to his sanity, the more he quoshes his female aspect.)

In the end, however, Bertha has to "end" in order for the happiness to ensue. Jane's libidinal surreal hybrid, of symbol and actual force, stops. The fallen woman falls, and in a removed context (second-hand) Jane learns her vampire is no more.

Another strange, almost mediated, female vampire is featured in Charles Nodier's *Smarra, ou les Démons de la Nuit*. Heavily influenced by Polidori's *The Vampyre*, Nodier was later to write a melodramatization of the classic tale. In this weird story, a nightmare within a nightmare, Méroé, Demon Queen of the Night, sends to her hapless victim a vampiric creature in the shape of a incubus: Smarra, a rictus-mouthed, griffin-like, flying monstrosity based on the beast in Fuseli's painting "The Nightmare". This bizarre tale is narrated by a young man who tells of his dream of a friend's horrific dream, wherein Méroé unleashes the Smarra, her demon lover, to torture the young men. "The most beautiful of all the beauties of Thessaly", she sends her incubus off from her enchanted stone ring; as it falls onto her breast, growling, directing it to the young warrior Polemon in his nightmare (*as a nightmare*). Petrified, the narrator, Lucius, watches Polemon's torture from within his dream, unable to assist. The story is the most extraordinary concoction; a veritable hallucination of the dream-space that defines the essence of vampirism, impotence, nightmarish paralysis and powerlessness. Nodier has captured the spirit of the vampire by realising the dream setting so well. The incubus/succubus manifestations set forth by the sorceress aptly describe the sexual drainage of nocturnal-emission dreams of dread and desire. The beautiful Méroé epitomises the dreadful nature of the power of sexuality and the unconscious, in her ability to evoke nightmares in men, and this idea of the nightmare vampire is both sophisticated and superreal.

In a different vein, somewhere else, another vampire is trancing a woman to the point whereby the "lovebite", the "kiss of deathlessness" can be issued. His mephitic body will disappear before light, but will court her by night. The male vampire; more complicated in literary history than the lamia. The male vampire we know best was born forth from the Romantic era. Byron's demonic figure of poetry was an early awareness of energy transfer. A similar discovery of devilishly, seductive and dangerous characters was made by the Brontës; both in *Jane Eyre* (as aforementioned) and *Wuthering Heights* (consider Heathcliffe and Cathy's libidinal desires). These sorts of characterisations went on to become the blood-suckers, rather than the dangerous lovers, in the form of Gothic novels and tales of horror.

But it was Byron and Shelley who were the personifications of the exiled man. Poets and wretched dreamers; they were outcasts yet still dependant;

lovers who were incapable of loving; supermen with weaknesses. Byron really was the metaphoric vampire, and he wrote about himself when he invented the anti-hero. The Gothic Don Juan; Milton's Satan; the Romantic artist himself. A psychic vampire who's self-perpetuation depends on the destruction of others. The solipsist gone awry. The Great Abject Lover. In the early 19th Century the Bryonic anti-hero already manifested many of the mythic qualities of the vampire. The melancholy libertine with his hypnotic eyes and obsession with the *thanatos* in *eros*; the nihilism of love and desire. Byron was more powerful than other men (a "talked about" ladies man) but he was blighted by his power.

There is a strong link confessed by Byron himself. An incestuous relationship with a half-sister and the spillage of hymeneal blood; the blood of the maidenhead. Clearly evident in his work was this fascination with a certain kind of blood and energy appropriation. The central motif of defiled blood suggests a coupling of incest and vampirism. As if we have the superhuman, overly-desirous male and the young woman who cannot absorb this terrific power.

The woman will become the thing she hates; shamed, she will have to share in the sins of the recounted "father". The two central fluids - blood and semen - used in Byron's work signify the eroticism (and evil) of blood-letting or rupture, or an attack on male virility; with an emphasis on blood-letting as death. A moral *cul-de-sac* in which the poor woman suffers for sins projected onto her. This is the start of the classic male vampire.

When John Polidori, not to mention others in his wake, came to write tales of vampirism born from these very real aspects of Victorian sexuality and subversion, several aspects remained, necessarily, structurally constant. The sense of conspiracy and collusion between the vampire and victim, always apparent. With Bram Stoker's *Dracula* this takes on an exciting new slant and we shall go into this, in greater depth, later. Stoker was well aware of the whole issue of fantasy and dream, on the part of the female character - probably from reading *Carmilla*. However, for earlier works there is a definite indication of the victim subconsciously inviting the attacker, possibly by fantasising the attack. Not unlike current ignorant social undertones that suggest the rape victim subconsciously invites the attacker; and a concept that owes absolutely nothing to post-feminist knowledge of female fantasy and female desire in reality. But interestingly enough, considering the sexual subversiveness of the female and vampire relationship, some writers clearly do set their story in the realm of dream/fantasy, in an attempt to comment on sexual strait-jackets imposed on both sexes in this era.

And it is the fact that these "victims" are never wantonly destroyed; they are indeed often preordained and even adored, giving a sense of this very much being a figment of the female's imagination - and consequently a threat to her menfolk at the same time. Is the vampire then "invited" by the female psyche; and is she not consumed by a sensual desire for forbidden pleasures rather than overwhelmed by an unwanted intruder? He is a figure from the nightime; a dim world somewhere between sleep and wake - a dreamspace. Often he is a deceased or lost alternative spouse, or companion.

The repeated themes of death, or more specifically *undeath*, and the recurring blood and fluidity symbols (so menstrual in their re-occurrence and unharm) recall the Christian transubstantiation of drinking Jesus' blood, and are therefore a great threat to the Church, having as their protagonist a blossoming young woman.

There is of course the simple cultural analogy of the threat of the Devil to the Church, Paganism or Satanism (with its carnality), or even the xenophobia-inducing threat of the East or of Islam.

Yet the most important element, for me, is that this is the realm of the night, the unconscious, and the one place we cannot control. The threat of the succubus; the threat of the female imagination. The suffocation of the nightmare with the child-fears it evokes in all. It cannot be fought in the same manner a carnate enemy can.

Polidori's Lord Ruthven was clearly modelled on Byron, and *The Vampyre* was indeed the first of its genre. Not only inspired by Byron, it evoked public interest only because the public thought it was also written by him, clearly seeing that the Ruthven character *was* him. Ruthven is a rakehell and a ladykiller, metaphorically and literally; we recall Byron's indiscretions as corrupter and romancer. Polidori manages to convey this vampire as a handsome and striking demon-lover to the ladies, as well as a vampiric sponge to the young male companion (a role Polidori clearly identified with concerning himself and Byron). Ruthven has a *penchant* for young society ladies, upon whom he casts his fatal dead grey eye. Different in many respects from Dracula, this cool, aloof, enigmatic character is highly more nefarious, destructive and wanton. He might be seen to prefigure the sociopathic narrator in Lautréamont's *Maldoror* in this respect, by being a harbinger of wanton, unbridled evil to whom guilt is unthinkable. In contrast to Count Dracula, who is a "slave to his thirsts", Polidori's vampire will also corrupt souls - for the hell of it. Ultimately, *The Vampyre* is perhaps most remarkable for being the only story in which the "hero" perishes, and the vampire triumphs - an audaciously nihilistic ending.

Polidori's anti-hero Ruthven bears much similarity to Heathcliffe in *Wuthering Heights* - incidentally written the same year as *Jane Eyre*. Considered then an amoral, scheming devil, Heathcliffe is now considered a tragic hero and wretchedly romantic lover. But he too has the slightly supernatural qualities of the vampire. A little ghoulish; a little other-worldly. In *Wuthering Heights*, Cathy and Heathcliffe in effect "vamp" off each other to the point where Cathy claims - "I am Heathcliffe." This goes back to Poe's stories of the passionate ferocious lovers, their pernicious flux of energy exchanges. She dies and he feels, in his emaciation, that she has taken part of his life with her. So, he prowls around at night, not eating, white in the face. He visits her grave; he wanders the moors. His tight-stretched, marcid body trembles; his eyes are strangely glassy. He becomes the living dead/undead. What little blood he has runs cold in his veins; the fire has gone out and he searches for her for replenishment.

In Lautréamont's *First Song of Maldoror*, we find the persona of the vampire, and its associated imagery, used to present a creature of pure amorality; the ultimate outsider. Maldoror makes a pact with prostitution and mates with female sharks. He cannot believe he is even of human parentage, deeming himself "more". Graveyards, home of the dead, are his chosen haunt; he sees corpses arise, bloodied, from their graves. He has reveries of slashing children with razors, of drinking their blood. This wild cruelty and amorality - recalling de Sade - combined with Lautréamont's bizarre imagistic juxtapositions, make *Maldoror* the first piece of genuine proto-Surrealist writing.

Maldoror himself is, in a theoretical sense, society's worst enemy, embodying everything we don't understand about nature. Everything beyond nature; all the unexplained amorality that nature hides behind her rank, fatalistic skirts. Supernature. He is an almost notional figure who rarely figures in the realms of the literal, so continuing the theme of the dream/unconscious space that is the greatest vampire of all. He can also be seen as a plague metaphor; an apocalyptic vortex that defies all rationality and all consciousness; having no parameters, no conscience and no egoism - like nature in our worst dreams.

This concept of something that will sweep over us and destroy us (a familiar Romantic notion) and that we cannot control or even fully conceive of nor understand, also occurs in other works. There is a plague metaphor, an apocalyptic vision in Wilde's *The Picture of Dorian Gray*; Huysmans' *La-Bas*; Polidori's *The Vampyre* and Turgenev's *Phantoms*, among others.

Varney the Vampire - or, *The Feast of Blood* - by J. Malcolm Rymer was a "penny dreadful", thrilling and redundant in turn. But it had considerable influence on many mid-century stories (between Romanticism and Stoker at the end of the century), and it is still influential today (compare Rymer's chilling description of Varney with Klaus Kinski in Herzog's *Nosferatu the Vampyre*). Once read, who can forget the scene where Varney first visits the young lady in her bed chamber. It really has all the elements to its structure, which reads in a bizarre fashion - with surrealistic tense changes and descriptions - like a love story of sorts. The initial encounter between vampire and female, and the compelling attraction. The repulsion and anxiety. The rebirth of attraction. The initiation or consummation through sex, symbolised by blood-letting (could be menstrual, hymeneal blood or semen). The discovery by the menfolk, and their quasi-medical/scientific explanations. The midnight vigils. The gathering together to chase the intruder out, and his ultimate destruction. The vampire, of course, is of an impeccable background, powerful, learned and threatening. Usually his accent is strangely unplaceable but veering towards Eastern Europe. In Varney's case he is an English lord. Tall and gaunt; as his blood-lust increases so does his animalism, until he becomes quite grotesque and repellant. He becomes a true outsider, a terrible pariah. His blood-less moon face; with fangs a-glint and claws to match; his stealthy gait and his terrible eye that completely holds her immobile; she considers he is not an inhabitant of this earth and, of course, he is not.

In Count Stenbock's *True Story of a Vampire*, we again encounter the traditional figure of the aristocratic vampire, except for one twist - the effete Vardalek is clearly homosexual. Apart from his feminacy he is, we learn, rather serpent-like; almost like a lamia. His victim is a young, lively, beautiful (shades of *Death in Venice*?) "gazelle-like" boy. The two strike up a loving relationship. The homosexuality of the story is obvious; the homophobic hysteria of the time symbolically recounted.

As well as the sexual tones of the story and the considered "corruption" of the lad, there is a parallel of the old sucking life from the young. A metempsychosis of sexual energy and vigour. The two-way encounter is beautifully told. The boy does not seem to struggle with defiance, but falls in a languid (post-orgasmic) swoon. The romance of the relationship is also devoid of terror and there is a beautiful and musical seduction.

Ultimately, the tale must be seen as a plea for sympathy with the outsider - the vampire as allegory for the homosexual. Vardalek is sorrowed by his predations, but nonetheless must follow the call of his unorthodox yearnings. Appropriately, the vampire is not killed or destroyed; he simply disappears of his own accord. Stenbock's final irony is to set the tale in Styria - home of *Carmilla*.

In Huysmans' *La-Bas* we encounter literal vampirism as a sexual perversion. A "religious" obsession with death. As in *Maldoror*, there is an apocalyptic space. A space that defies reason. A plague space. There can also be seen a reflection between the macrocosm of this turmoil and the microcosm of the quagmire of the mind with all its unconscious inevitabilities and tortures. The fact that one cannot fully comprehend the nature of the unconscious is externalised by the amoral chaos of the protagonist's misdeeds. The vampirism on the sanity, and the draining of the soul by moral restraints and immoral yearnings. Everything to excess with no reasoning, just like a chaotic apocalypse. The vampire is, of course, Gilles de Rais, the aristocrat and one-time soldier; the narrator is Durtal, the historian (thus Huysmans). His predilection for the consumption of his victims' flesh, and the drinking of their blood makes Gilles de Rais a vampire in the real sense; a cannibal, set in a world of threatening, inverted morality and truly corrupt, perverse religious mania.

Huysmans also emphasises de Rais' "pathetic" urge to atone for his sins, in much the same way as does Oscar Wilde's protagonist in *The Picture of Dorian Gray*. Wilde's book was written in the same year, and it is believed that Huysman's earlier *A Rebours* - the definitive Decadent text - was his inspiration. *The Picture of Dorian Gray* features a very definite type of vampirism, much recognised by the Romantics: the artist as vampire, or the artistic experience as vampiric. Although Wilde's story is a complex and skilled amalgamation of many analogies and intentions, the comments he makes about the process of creation are integral as the pivot. The awareness of the artist and his inner self, and the energy abalienations involved become the starting point for the vampiric experience. There can be catharsis and rejuvenation; enervation and emaciation also. And above all there will be a charge; a circuit.

Essentially, Dorian Gray is a vampire in a folkloric sense. Bringing with him ruination like a plague (cf. *Maldoror* and *The Vampyre*). The vampirism arises from the artist Basil Hallward's attempts at Realism. He wants to make his art "mirror" life, exactly. He in fact makes it superreal; more real than Dorian, the subject. Instead of the art simply being "illusionistic" - a falsehood that suggests the truth - the art becomes the reality. Dorian becomes the un-reality; the deathless person. Now created, the monster, Dorian, corrupts all who come into contact with him in his limitless desire for death. He creeps around at night; a fatal, sybaritic and destructive being. In the final chapter, included herein, he is remorseful, and seeks absolution; at one point actually describing the "living death" of his own soul. He is a two-dimensional illusion of a person, a shadow; meanwhile, the painting mirrors his "true" self. His end is caused by him knifing the horrible visage of himself in the painting; an image that illustrates the grotesque vampire he has become. The knifing and the crumbling to dust, as his years and sins catch up with him at last, anticipating the demise of Count Dracula by six years.

In some respects Arthur Machen's *The Inmost Light* is reminiscent of Wilde's story in intent. It involves a doctor's scientific experiments into occultism, and the vampiric force instigated by his unrelenting curiosity regarding the unseen elements. A large and glorious gem-stone is the vampiric mediator; soaking up the soul of the doctor's wife; in the place of her spirit a demonic energy too-terrible-to-believe enters, transmuting her brain into that of something "not human". Whilst the stone is the spirit appropriator, it is the process of scientific exploration into dark waters, perhaps those considered taboo, which brings about this horrific energy exchange. Dr. Black steals his wife's soul; his own energy is then gradually sucked by the stone too. In attempting to enter the forbidden and dark zone of the "other world" for never-before-glimpsed-knowledge, he sacrifices his most valuable attribute in this world. And the sacrifice persists.

A classic example of the "atmospheric vampire" is Guy de Maupassant's *The Horla*, a tale that recalls Nodier's *Smarra* in its evocation of the "reality" of vampirism in the form of the plaguing paralysis that affects us in our vulnerable sleep. The time when daylight's lucidity is replaced by the hazy penumbras that our strabismic vision cannot make sense of. The impotence; the nightly terrors; the time when anything is possible because, and only because, it is our unconscious' space. The one place that has no reason; nor explanation. The only thing to fear is fear, and this summarises the illusions, the delusions of an over-active imagination. Especially when, in the case of *The Horla*'s narrator, it seeps into his wakening reality and is made almost tangible by the extent of our convictions: his sense of being preyed upon by an unseen creature finally drives him to madness and inadvertent murder.

The externalisation of internal fear epitomises the base of much horror; and it is a telling state of affairs that the narrator considers this vampiric "visitor" - this Horla - to actually have taken over his mind and sanity.

Seldom examined in the context of vampire fiction, yet pre-dating *The Horla* by some 25 years in its treatment of an atmospheric, debilitating evil, is Edward Bulwer-Lytton's *The Haunters and the Haunted* - often known by the more knowing title *The House and the Brain*. Though displaying few ostensible hallmarks of the traditional vampire story, it remains one of the most outstanding - and most disturbing - examples of a tradition of 19th Century romantic occult fiction which can be traced directly back to Polidori's *The Vampyre*. An old house is here the object of possession by the murderous spirit of a Black Magician who has achieved an immortality of sorts by means of a powerful malediction. Lytton hints at a matrix of violent murder, betrayal and sadism linked to an erotic covenant, whose instigators and victims alike have lost their very souls to this demonic figure's "vampiric" power.

Finally, the house itself comes to represent the bodily casing of the magician's spirit, and is seemingly bent on draining the will, and the energy, of the narrator by a terrifying display of apparitions. Such spectral *revenants* doubtless require the vitality of the living to sustain substance. As in *The Horla*, the manifestations of the shadowy reason-suppers may also be seen as projections of the imagination; a "waking nightmare", the literal vampire born forth from our own dreads. Indeed, interestingly, Lytton's frequent use of the term "Shadow" prefigures its use as a psychological signifier for alter-ego or anti-social immoral self.

The outcome of the story is reassuringly familiar: armed only with a sobering volume of practical essays - his equivalent of the traditional vampire hunter's silver crucifix - the narrator (narrowly) retains his sanity, survives his night in the house, and returns to break the malediction. Within his tale, Lytton also broaches a point made in both *The Horla* and *Carmilla* - that everything is natural, and all that proceeds from Nature is of that context; and therefore nothing can be Supernatural, or surpass the cosmos. In short, it is the mysteries of our natural world which may appear phantasmagoric or inexplicable (ie vampiric). Carmilla herself makes the point that everything on earth or in heaven lives as nature ordains - we know that in this she includes her own kind. This perhaps leads on to the telling (sub-) title of the story; the house and the brain - which is "real", and which "imaginary"?

The version included here is one abridged by Lytton to remove a particular plot quirk he was later to reprise more fully in his *A Strange Story*.

Chronologically last in this collection, and very much the crowning example of the genre, is Bram Stoker's famous *Dracula*. Written just before the turn of the century, this novel admittedly owes much to many previous vampire tales; none, however, in my mind, go so far into the seminal mythology as Stoker's classic. It really does encompass not only the most culturally recognised male vampire that literature, and consequently film, has ever produced; but also one of the most fascinating characterisations of the lamia (especially sexually-subversive and powerfully symbolic); as well as a folkloric element and the fœtid *ambience* of plague metaphor.

Whilst one can point out myriad psycho-sexual relevances and apply many theories, one cannot fully clarify all that Dracula is about. One cannot capture its essence; for its essentialism is based in the nature of filigree psycho-sexual ambiguities, ambivalency, shadow, myth, taboo, and the oneiric labyrinth that is the vampire creature's true abode. The fact that one can suggest, but not claim, didactic definitions is what makes Dracula so compelling, and still, today, so seminal.

Whilst it may seem ironic that Dracula returns to folklore (in lieu of its significant psycho-sexual content) perhaps it is because little stress has been placed on the literary side of the novel. In fact, the writing is a little clumsy and not particularly sophisticated; and the work came to light too late to be a Gothic- or Romantic-linked work. Despite being misplaced, its unexplained nature and the wonderful tension it evokes with its subject matter ensure it will remain of great significance.

Stoker used such strong psychological violence there was little need for gruesome physical extremes, or too much action that would have been easier to explain. Instead we are left with innumerable questions of the vampire's reasons, motives or origins, to be pieced together from diverse diary entries; all of which highlight Dracula as an unexplained myth.

We have the basic structure of Dracula's meeting with the Harkers; his pursuit of Lucy; the staking of Lucy; the staining of Mina and the final pursuit of Dracula. We have Van Helsing's absurd accent and incredulous medical qualifications, and we have a group of honest, loyal and exceedingly dull young men. With these ingredients Stoker deliberately set out to make us shocked and also, importantly, jealous. No vampire is more alluring (a great deal is obviously owed to the Bryonic trad. here) than Dracula. He has unlimited power with no responsibilities; he knows all the right people but has no need of friends; he is violent, predatory, but feels no guilt; he has life without death and he has sex with no shame. His only "disadvantage" is his appetite.

And so the men rally round, under the wise eye of Van Helsing, to rid their place of the one who has ravaged their women. This articulate, intelligent being is too sexually potent to be tolerated. Strangely, there is no real mention of his erotic power - but Stoker cleverly makes us very much aware of it. Hints of sado-masochism, anality, orality and other secret vices abound. Dracula is charming and enigmatic, but he also reeks of animalistic sexual depravity; bearing an "anal charisma" of graveyard eroticism.

Count Dracula, in Freudian terms, is a super father figure. He is undermining the young men by keeping all the young ladies to himself, and in order to continue with their genetic lines and sexual expression they are compelled to destroy him. Conversely, Van Helsing is another father figure; a "good" father figure; but he does not have the sexual potency or the strong "family" set-up - actually an inverted mockery of the "nuclear" family - that Dracula has. However, it will be Van Helsing's knowledge which finally destroys this "demon-father".

All of the human central figures are models of chastity, but this is what makes Dracula and his women so fascinating. In the first description, of Harker and the female vampire, the salacious intensity is boundless. The sense of anticipation; and the depiction of the female vampire's salivating lips (or labia) suggesting the act of fellatio (for Harker's head and neck read the head and shaft of the penis). The temptation and threat combine. Dread and lust. This masturbatory fantasy is classic lamia/anima projection.

The young giggly neophyte Lucy becomes a *femme fatale* after her "initiation" by Dracula, and the consequent liberating sexual act: the symbolic de-flowering, the virginal blood of which Dracula drinks. (Conversely, the blood here could also be menstrual blood, from her menarche and blossoming, which he drinks from her genito-face as the animus of menstruation.) Lucy is then sustained by drinking from the boys - an obvious sexual act of intercourse or fellatio, intimating a circle of blood-(semen-) letting and drinking. The sexual inference of this, considering the Victorian era, is a most revelatory erotic expression and quite unsurpassed in any other "legitimate" literature of the time. When Lucy is destroyed, her vampiric emancipation is squashed by a stake - a clear phallic symbol, issued by her fiancé. These sexual analogies cause Van Helsing many a perplexing time also; what could be the significance of the blood-letting Lucy performs upon him, when she was almost like a daughter to him? His guilt and shame almost cause him a breakdown.

The most sexually liberated female is Mina. A strong intellect, good with language and pen, but, unfortunately by social standards, suddenly a sexual wanton. Mina drinks directly from Dracula; she's quickly given up on the young boys. The symbolic fellatio, and the symbolic cunnilingus Dracula performs on her, forms another circle that has elements of blood, semen and even milk inherent. If Dracula is such an archetypal figure of the female unconscious and if he is drinking her cervical blood, then surely he is the greatest threat to patriarchy and the boys as could be conceived. He is not threatened by a bleeding vulva, or prone to believe that her vagina holds within it castrating fangs (and that the blood is really the blood of his penis); nor is he only interested in the ovulation and the procreation. He is welcomed as an old lover; in the same way some of the male narrators felt they knew the lamia from somewhere, so the female will recognise the male vampire as her animus.

The "deviant" liberation manifested is also what gives rise to the plague metaphor. Those who have been in contact, become "infected" and the panic to stop this "sickness" spreading is sadly reminiscent of cultural beliefs about sexuality and illness. Add to that the considered unholiness and ensuing punishment, and we can see how today we have made little social progress. Equally shaming is our social inability to remove the "romantic" element of an apocalyptic implication when it applies to reality.

Ultimately, Count Dracula is destroyed by the scientific and religious virtues of the menfolk. Yet it is never the menfolk we remember, but always Dracula's cool and mesmerising visage; his magnetic presence and sexuality that stays in our minds: drawing us back, time after time, to his legend.

Adèle Olivia Gladwell

FELICIEN ROPS (1833-1898) was already a well-known artist in his native Belgium when, in 1862, he encountered Charles Baudelaire. He subsequently followed the poet back to Paris and, under his sway, entered his "Satanic" period. Always fascinated with prostitution, he now also became haunted by the visions of Death which populate his later works. Condemned as a pornographer during his lifetime, he may now be much admired for his obsessive juxtapositions of Eros/Thanatos.

THE VAMPYRE

John Polidori

It happened that in the midst of the dissipations attendant upon a London winter, there appeared at the various parties of the leaders of the *ton* a nobleman, more remarkable for his singularities, than his rank. He gazed upon the mirth around him, as if he could not participate therein. Apparently, the light laughter of the fair only attracted his attention, that he might by a look quell it, and throw fear into those breasts where thoughtlessness reigned. Those who felt this sensation of awe, could not explain whence it arose: attributed it to the dead grey eye, which, fixing upon the object's face, did not seem to penetrate, and at one glance to pierce through to the inward workings of the heart; but fell upon the cheek with a leaden ray that weighed upon the skin it could not pass. His peculiarities caused him to be invited to every house; all wished to see him, and those who had been accustomed to violent excitement, and now felt the weight of *ennui*, were pleased at having something in their presence capable of engaging their attention. In spite of the deadly hue of his face, which never gained a warmer tint, either from the blush of modesty, or from the strong emotion of passion, though its form and outline were beautiful, many of the female hunters after notoriety attempted to win his attentions, and gain, at least, some marks of what they might term affection: Lady Mercer, who had been the mockery of every monster shewn in drawing-rooms since her marriage, threw herself in his way, and did all but put on the dress of a mountebank, to attract his notice -- though in vain; when she stood before him, though his eyes were apparently fixed on hers, still it seemed as if they were unperceived; even her unappalled impudence was baffled, and she left the field. But though the common adultress could not influence even the guidance of his eyes, it was not that the female sex was indifferent to him: yet such was the apparent caution with which he spoke to the virtuous wife and innocent daughter, that few knew he ever addressed himself to females. He had, however, the reputation of a winning tongue; and whether it was that it even overcame the dread of his singular character, or that they were moved by his apparent hatred of vice, he was as often among those females who form the boast of their sex from their domestic virtues, as among those who sully it by their vices.

About the same time, there came to London a young gentleman of the name of Aubrey: he was an orphan left with an only sister in the possession of great wealth, by parents who died while he was yet in childhood. Left also to himself by guardians, who thought it their duty merely to take care of his fortune, while they relinquished the more important charge of his mind to the care of mercenary subalterns, he cultivated more his imagination than his judgement. He had, hence, that high romantic feeling of honour and candour, which daily ruins so many milliners' apprentices. He believed all to sympathize with virtue, and thought that vice was thrown in by Providence merely for the picturesque effect of the scene, as we see in romances: he thought that the misery of a cottage merely consisted in the vesting of clothes, which were as warm, but which were better adapted to the painter's eye by their irregular folds and coloured patches. He thought, in fine, that the dreams of poets were the realities of life. He was handsome, frank, and rich: for these reasons, upon his entering into the gay circles, many mothers surrounded him, striving which should describe with least truth their languishing or romping favourites: the daughters at the same time, by their brightening countenances when he approached, and by their sparkling eyes, when he opened his lips, soon led him into false notions of his talent and merit. Attached as he was to the romance of his solitary hours, he was startled at finding, that, except in the tallow and wax candles that flickered, not from the presence of a ghost, but from want of snuffing, there was no foundation in real life for any of that congeries of pleasing pictures and descriptions contained in those volumes, from which he had formed his study. Finding, however, some compensation in his gratified vanity, he was about to relinquish his dreams, when the extraordinary being we have above described, crossed him in his career.

He watched him; and the very impossibility of forming an idea of the character of a man entirely absorbed in himself, who gave few other signs of his observation of external objects, than the tacit assent to their existence, implied by the avoidance of their contact: allowing his imagination to picture every thing that flattered its propensity to extravagant ideas, he soon formed this object into the hero of a romance, and determined to observe the offspring of his fancy, rather than the person before him. He became acquainted with him, paid him attentions, and so far advanced upon his notice, that his presence was always recognized. He gradually learnt that Lord Ruthven's affairs were embarrassed, and soon found, from the notes of preparation in _____ Street, that he was about to travel. Desirous of gaining some information respecting this singular character, who, till now, had only whetted his curiosity, he hinted to his guardians, that it was time for him to perform the tour, which for many generations has been thought

30

necessary to enable the young to take some rapid steps in the career of vice towards putting themselves upon an equality with the aged, and not allowing them to appear as if fallen from the skies, wherever scandalous intrigues are mentioned as the subjects of pleasantry or of praise, according to the degree of skill shewn in carrying them on. They consented: and Aubrey immediately mentioning his intentions to Lord Ruthven, was surprised to receive from him a proposal to join him. Flattered by such a mark of esteem from him, who, apparently, had nothing in common with other men, he gladly accepted it, and in a few days they had passed the circling waters.

Hitherto, Aubrey had had no opportunity of studying Lord Ruthven's character, and now he found, that, though many more of his actions were exposed to his view, the results offered different conclusions from the apparent motives to his conduct. His companion was profuse in his liberality; the idle, the vagabond, and the beggar, received from his hand more than enough to relieve their immediate wants. But Aubrey could not avoid remarking, that it was not upon the virtuous, reduced to indigence by the misfortunes attendant even upon virtue, that he bestowed his alms; these were sent from the door with hardly suppressed sneers; but when the profligate came to ask something, not to relieve his wants, but to allow him to wallow in his lust, or to sink him still deeper in his iniquity, he was sent away with rich charity. This was, however, attributed by him to the greater importunity of the vicious, which generally prevails over the retiring bashfulness of the virtuous indigent. There was one circumstance about the charity of his Lordship, which was still more impressed upon his mind: all those upon whom it was bestowed, inevitably found that there was a curse upon it, for they were all either led to the scaffold, or sunk to the lowest and the most abject misery. At Brussels and other towns through which they passed, Aubrey was surprised at the apparent eagerness with which his companion sought for the centres of all fashionable vice; there he entered into all the spirit of the faro table: he betted, and always gambled with success, except when the known sharper was his antagonist, and then he lost even more than he gained; but it was always with the same unchanging face, with which he generally watched the society around: it was not, however, so when he encountered the rash youthful novice, or the luckless father of a numerous family; then his very wish seemed fortune's law -- this apparent abstractedness of mind was laid aside, and his eyes sparkled with more fire than that of the cat whilst dallying with the half-dead mouse. In every town, he left the formerly affluent youth, torn from the circle he adorned, cursing, in the solitude of a dungeon, the fate that had drawn him within the reach of this fiend; whilst many a father sat frantic, amidst the speaking looks of mute hungry children, without a single farthing of his late immense wealth, wherewith to buy even sufficient to satisfy their present craving. Yet he took no money from the gambling table; but immediately lost, to the ruin of many, the last gilder he had just snatched from the convulsive grasp of the

31

innocent: this might but be the result of a certain degree of knowledge, which was not, however, capable of combating the cunning of the more experienced. Aubrey often wished to represent this to his friend, and beg him to resign that charity and pleasure which proved the ruin of all, and did not tend to his own profit; but he delayed it -- for each day he hoped his friend would give him some opportunity of speaking frankly and openly to him; however, this never occurred. Lord Ruthven in his carriage, and amidst the various wild and rich scenes of nature, was always the same: his eye spoke less than his lip; and though Aubrey was near the object of his curiosity, he obtained no greater gratification from it than the constant excitement of vainly wishing to break that mystery, which to his exalted imagination began to assume the appearance of something supernatural.

They soon arrived at Rome, and Aubrey for a time lost sight of his companion; he left him in daily attendance upon the morning circle of an Italian Countess, whilst he went in search of the memorials of another almost deserted city. Whilst he was thus engaged, letters arrived from England, which he opened with eager impatience; the first was from his sister, breathing nothing but affection; the others were from his guardians, the latter astonished him; if it had before entered into his imagination that there was an evil power resident in his companion, these seemed to give him almost sufficient reason for the belief. His guardians insisted upon his immediately leaving his friend, and urged, that his character was dreadfully vicious, for that the possession of irresistible powers of seduction, rendered his licentious habits more dangerous to society. It had been discovered, that his contempt for the adultress had not originated in hatred of her character; but that he had required, to enhance his gratification, that his victim, the partner of his guilt, should be hurled from the pinnacle of unsullied virtue, down to the lowest abyss of infamy and degradation: in fine, that all those females whom he had sought, apparently on account of their virtue, had, since his departure, thrown even the mask aside, and had not scrupled to expose the whole deformity of their vices to the public gaze.

Aubrey determined upon leaving one, whose character had not yet shown a single bright point on which to rest the eye. He resolved to invent some plausible pretext for abandoning him altogether, purposing, in the mean while, to watch him more closely, and to let no slight circumstances pass by unnoticed. He entered into the same circle, and soon perceived, that his Lordship was endeavouring to work upon the inexperience of the daughter of the lady whose house he chiefly frequented. In Italy, it is seldom that an unmarried female is met with in society; he was therefore obliged to carry on his plans in secret; but Aubrey's eye followed him in all his windings, and soon discovered that an assignation had been appointed, which would most likely end in the ruin of an innocent, though thoughtless girl. Losing no time, he entered the apartment of Lord Ruthven, and abruptly asked him his intentions with respect to the lady, informing him at the same time that he was aware of his being about to meet her that very night. Lord Ruthven answered that his intentions were such as he supposed all would have upon such an occasion; and upon being pressed whether he intended to marry her, merely laughed. Aubrey retired; and, immediately writing a note to say, that from that moment he must decline accompanying his Lordship in the remainder of their proposed tour, he ordered his servant to seek other apartments, and calling upon the mother of the lady, informed her of all he knew, not only with regard to her daughter, but also concerning the character of his Lordship. The assignation was prevented. Lord Ruthven next day merely sent his servant to notify his complete assent to a separation; but did not hint any suspicion of his plans having been foiled by Aubrey's interposition.

Having left Rome, Aubrey directed his steps towards Greece, and crossing the Peninsula, soon found himself at Athens. He then fixed his residence in the house of a Greek; and soon occupied himself in tracing the faded records of ancient glory upon monuments that apparently, ashamed of chronicling the deeds of freemen only before slaves, had hidden themselves beneath the sheltering soil or many-coloured lichen. Under the same roof as himself, existed a being, so beautiful and delicate, that she might have formed the model for a painter, wishing to portray on canvass the promised hope of the faithful in Mahomet's paradise, save that her eyes spoke too much mind for any one to think she could belong to those who had no souls. As she danced upon the plain, or tripped along the mountain's side, one would have thought the gazelle a poor type of her beauties; for who would have exchanged her eye, apparently the eye of animated nature, for that sleepy luxurious look of the animal suited but to the taste of an epicure. The light step of Ianthe often accompanied Aubrey in his search after antiquities, and often would the unconscious girl, engaged in the pursuit of a Kashmere butterfly, show the whole beauty of her form, floating as it were upon the wind, to the eager gaze of him, who forgot the letters he had just decyphered upon an almost effaced tablet, in the contemplation of her sylph-like figure. Often would her tresses falling, as she flitted around, exhibit in the sun's rays such delicately brilliant and swiftly fading hues, as might well excuse the forgetfulness of the antiquary, who let escape from his mind the very object he had before thought of vital importance to the proper interpretation of a passage in Pausanias. But why attempt to describe charms which all feel, but none can appreciate? -- It was innocence, youth, and beauty, unaffected by crowded drawing-rooms and stifling balls. Whilst he drew those remains of which he wished to preserve a memorial for his future hours, she would stand by, and watch the magic effects of his pencil, in tracing the scenes of her native place; she would then describe to him the circling dance upon the open plain, would paint to him in all the glowing colours of youthful memory, the marriage pomp she remembered viewing in her infancy; and then, turning to subjects that had evidently made a greater

33

impression upon her mind, would tell him all the supernatural tales of her nurse. Her earnestness and apparent belief of what she narrated, excited the interest even of Aubrey; and often as she told him the tale of the living vampyre, who had passed years amidst his friends, and dearest ties, forced every year, by feeding upon the life of a lovely female to prolong his existence for the ensuing months, his blood would run cold, whilst he attempted to laugh her out of such idle and horrible fantasies; but Ianthe cited to him the names of old men, who had at last detected one living among themselves, after several of their near relatives and children had been found marked with the stamp of the fiend's appetite; and when she found him so incredulous, she begged of him to believe her, for it had been remarked, that those who dared to question their existence, always had some proof given, which obliged them, with grief and heartbreaking, to confess it was true. She detailed to him the traditional appearance of these monsters, and his horror was increased, by hearing a pretty accurate description of Lord Ruthven; he, however, still persisted in persuading her, that there could be no truth in her fears, though at the same time he wondered at the many coincidences which had all tended to excite a belief in the supernatural power of Lord Ruthven.

Aubrey began to attach himself more and more to Ianthe; her innocence, so contrasted with all the affected virtues of the women among whom he had sought for his vision of romance, won his heart; and while he ridiculed the idea of a young man of English habits, marrying an uneducated Greek girl, still he found himself more and more attached to the almost fairy form before him. He would tear himself at times from her, and, forming a plan for some antiquarian research, he would depart, determined not to return until his object was attained; but he always found it impossible to fix his attention upon the ruins around him, whilst in his mind he retained an image that seemed alone the rightful possessor of his thoughts. Ianthe was unconscious of his love, and was ever the same frank infantile being he had first known. She always seemed to part from him with reluctance; but it was because she had no longer any one with whom she could visit her favourite haunts, whilst her guardian was occupied in sketching or uncovering some fragment which had yet escaped the destructive hand of time. She had appealed to her parents on the subject of Vampyres, and they both, with several present, affirmed their existence, pale with horror at the very name. Soon after, Aubrey determined to proceed upon one of his excursions, which was to detain him for a few hours; when they heard the name of the place, they all at once begged him not to return at night, as he must necessarily pass through a wood, where no Greek would ever remain, after the day had closed, upon any consideration. They described it as the resort of the vampyres in their nocturnal orgies, and denounced the most heavy evils as impending upon him who dared to cross their path. Aubrey made light of their representations, and tried to laugh them out of the idea; but when he saw them shudder at his daring thus to mock a superior, infernal power, the very name of which apparently made their blood freeze, he was silent.

Next morning Aubrey set off upon his excursion unattended; he was surprised to observe the melancholy face of his host, and was concerned to find that his words, mocking the belief of these horrible fiends, had inspired them with such terror. When he was about to depart, Ianthe came to the side of his horse, and earnestly begged him to return, ere night allowed the power of these beings to be put in action; he promised. He was, however, so occupied in his research, that he did not perceive that daylight would soon end, and that in the horizon there was one of those specks which, in the warmer climates, so rapidly gather into a tremendous mass, and pour all their rage upon the devoted country. He at last, however, mounted his horse, determined to make up by speed for his delay; but it was too late. Twilight, in these southern climates, is almost unknown; immediately the sun sets, night begins; and ere he had advanced far, the power of the storm was above -- its echoing thunders had scarcely an interval of rest; its thick heavy rain forced its way through the canopying foliage, whilst the blue forked lightning seemed to fall and radiate at his very feet. Suddenly his horse took fright, and he was carried with dreadful rapidity through the entangled forest. The animal at last, through fatigue, stopped, and he found, by the glare of the lightning, that he was in the neighbourhood of a hovel that hardly lifted itself up from the masses of dead leaves and brushwood which surrounded it. Dismounting, he approached, hoping to find some one to guide him to the town, or at least trusting to obtain shelter from the pelting of the storm. As he approached, the thunders, for a moment silent, allowed him to hear the dreadful shrieks of a woman mingling with the stifled, exultant mockery of a laugh, continued in one almost unbroken sound; he was startled: but, roused by the thunder which again rolled over his head, he, with a sudden effort, forced open the door of the hut. He found himself in utter darkness: the sound, however, guided him. He was apparently unperceived; for, though he called, still the sounds continued, and no notice was taken of him. He found himself in contact with some one, whom he immediately seized; when a voice cried, "Again baffled!" to which a loud laugh succeeded; and he felt himself grappled by one whose strength seemed superhuman: determined to sell his life as dearly as he could, he struggled; but it was in vain: he was lifted from his feet and hurled with enormous force against the ground -- his enemy threw himself upon him, and kneeling upon his breast, had placed his hands upon his throat -- when the glare of many torches penetrating through the hole that gave light in the day, disturbed him; he instantly rose, and, leaving his prey, rushed through the door, and in a moment the crashing of the branches, as he broke through the wood, was no longer heard. The storm was now still; and Aubrey, incapable of moving, was soon heard by those without. They entered; the light of their torches fell upon the mud walls, and the thatch loaded on every individual straw with heavy flakes of soot. At the desire of Aubrey they searched for her who had attracted him by her cries; he was again left in darkness; but what was his horror, when the light of the torches once more burst upon him, to perceive the airy form of his fair conductress brought in a lifeless corpse. He shut his eyes, hoping that it was but a vision arising from his disturbed imagination; but he saw again the same form, when he unclosed them, stretched by his side. There was no colour upon her cheek, not even upon her lip; yet there was a stillness about her face that seemed almost as attaching as the life that once dwelt there: upon her neck and breast was blood, and upon her throat were the marks of teeth having opened the vein: to this the men pointed, crying, simultaneously struck with horror, "A Vampyre! a Vampyre!" A litter was quickly formed, and Aubrey was laid by the side of her who had lately been to him the object of so many light and fairy visions, now fallen with the flower of life that had died within her. He knew not what his thoughts were -- his mind was benumbed and seemed to shun reflection, and take refuge in vacancy; he held almost unconsciously in his hand a naked dagger of a particular construction, which had been found in the hut. They were soon met by different parties who had been engaged in the search of her whom a mother had missed. Their lamentable cries, as they approached the city, forewarned the parents of some dreadful catastrophe. To describe their grief would be impossible; but when they ascertained the cause of their child's death, they looked at Aubrey, and pointed to the corpse. They were inconsolable; both died broken-hearted.

Aubrey being put to bed was seized with a most violent fever, and was often delirious; in these intervals he would call upon Lord Ruthven and upon Ianthe -- by some unaccountable combination he seemed to beg of his former companion to spare the being he loved. At other times he would imprecate maledictions upon his head, and curse him as her destroyer. Lord Ruthven chanced at this time to arrive at Athens, and, from whatever motive, upon hearing of the state of Aubrey, immediately placed himself in the same house, and became his constant attendant. When the latter recovered from his delirium, he was horrified and startled at the sight of him whose image he had now combined with that of a Vampyre; but Lord Ruthven, by his kind words, implying almost repentance for the fault that had caused their separation, and still more by the attention, anxiety, and care which he showed, soon reconciled him to his presence. His lordship seemed quite changed; he no longer appeared that apathetic being who had so astonished Aubrey; but as soon as his convalescence began to be rapid, he again gradually retired into the same state of mind, and Aubrey perceived no difference from the former man, except that at times he was surprised to meet his gaze fixed intently upon him, with a smile of malicious exultation playing upon his lips: he knew not why, but this smile haunted him. During the last stage of the invalid's recovery, Lord Ruthven was apparently engaged in watching the tideless waves raised by the cooling breeze, or in marking the progress of those orbs, circling, like our world, around the moveless sun; indeed, he appeared to wish to avoid the eyes of all.

Aubrey's mind, by this shock, was much weakened, and that elasticity of spirit which had once so distinguished him now seemed to have fled for ever. He was now as much a lover of solitude and silence as Lord Ruthven; but much as he wished for solitude, his mind could not find it in the neighbourhood of Athens; if he sought it amidst the ruins he had formerly frequented, Ianthe's form stood by his side; if he sought it in the woods, her light step would appear wandering amidst the under-wood, in quest of the modest violet; then suddenly turning round, would show, to his wild imagination, her pale face and wounded throat, with a meek smile upon her lips. He determined to fly scenes, every feature of which created such bitter associations in his mind. He proposed to Lord Ruthven, to whom he held himself bound by the tender care he had taken of him during his illness, that they should visit those parts of Greece neither had yet seen. They travelled in every direction, and sought every spot to which a recollection could be attached: but though they thus hastened from place to place, yet they seemed not to heed what they gazed upon. They heard much of robbers, but they gradually began to slight these reports, which they imagined were only the invention of individuals, whose interest it was to excite the generosity of those who they defended from pretended dangers. In consequence of thus neglecting the advice of the inhabitants, on one occasion they travelled with only a few guards, more to serve as guides than as a defence. Upon entering, however, a narrow defile, at the bottom of which was the bed of a torrent, with large masses of rock brought down from the neighbouring precipices, they had reason to repent their negligence; for scarcely were the whole of the party engaged in the narrow pass, when they were startled by the whistling of bullets close to their heads, and by the echoed report of several guns. In an instant their guards had left them, and, placing themselves behind rocks, had begun to fire in the direction whence the report came. Lord Ruthven and Aubrey, imitating their example, retired for a moment behind the sheltering turn of the defile: but ashamed of being thus detained by a foe, who with insulting shouts bade them advance, and being exposed to unresisting slaughter, if any of the robbers should climb above and take them in the rear, they determined at once to rush forward in search of the enemy. Hardly had they lost the shelter of the rock, when Lord Ruthven received a shot in the shoulder, which brought him to the ground. Aubrey hastened to his assistance; and, no longer heeding the contest or his own peril, was soon surprised by seeing the robbers' faces around him -- his guards having, upon Lord Ruthven's being wounded, immediately thrown up their arms and surrendered.

By promises of a great reward, Aubrey soon induced them to convey his wounded friend to a neighbouring cabin; and having agreed upon a ransom, he was no more disturbed by their presence -- they being content merely to guard the entrance till their comrade should return with the promised sum, for which he had an order. Lord Ruthven's strength rapidly decreased; in two days mortification ensued, and death seemed advancing with hasty steps. His conduct and appearance had not changed; he seemed as unconscious of pain as he had been of the objects around him: but towards the close of the last evening, his mind became apparently uneasy, and his eye often fixed upon Aubrey, who was induced to offer his assistance with more than usual earnestness -- "Assist me! you may save me -- you may do more than that -- I mean not my life, I heed the death of my existence as little as that of the passing day; but you may save my honour, your friend's honour." "How? Tell me how? I would do any thing," replied Aubrey. "I need but little -- my life ebbs apace -- I cannot explain the whole -- but if you would conceal all you know of me, my honour were free from stain in the world's mouth -- and if my death were unknown for some time in England -- I -- I --- but life." "It shall not be known." "Swear!" cried the dying man, raising himself with exultant violence, "Swear by all your soul reveres, by all your nature fears, swear that for a year and a day you will not impart your knowledge of my crimes or death to any living being in any way, whatever may happen, or whatever you may see." His eyes seemed bursting from their sockets: "I swear!" said Aubrey; he sunk laughing upon his pillow, and breathed no more.

Aubrey retired to rest, but did not sleep; the many circumstances attending his acquaintance with this man rose upon his mind, and he knew not why; when he remembered his oath a cold shivering came over him, as if from the presentiment of something horrible awaiting him. Rising early in the morning, he was about to enter the hovel in which he had left the corpse, when a robber met him, and informed him that it was no longer there, having been conveyed by himself and his comrades, upon his retiring, to the pinnacle of a neighbouring mount, according to a promise they had given his lordship, that it should be exposed to the first cold ray of the moon that rose after his death. Aubrey was astonished, and taking several of the men, determined to go and bury it upon the spot where it lay. But, when he had mounted to the summit he found no trace of either the corpse or the clothes, though the robbers swore they pointed out the identical rock on which they had laid the body. For a time his mind was bewildered in conjectures, but he at last returned, convinced that they had buried the corpse for the sake of the clothes.

Weary of a country in which he had met with such terrible misfortunes, and in which all apparently conspired to heighten that superstitious melancholy that had seized upon his mind, he resolved to leave it, and soon arrived at Smyrna. While waiting for a vessel to convey him to Otranto, or to Naples, he occupied himself in arranging those effects he had with him belonging to Lord Ruthven. Amongst other things there was a case containing several weapons of offence, more or less adapted to ensure the death of the victim. There were several daggers and yagatans. Whilst turning them over, and examining their curious forms, what was his surprise at finding a sheath apparently ornamented in the same style as the dagger discovered in the fatal hut; he shuddered; hastening to gain further proof, he found the weapon, and his horror may be imagined when he discovered that it fitted, though peculiarly shaped, the sheath he held in his hand. His eyes seemed to need no further certainty -- they seemed gazing to be bound to the dagger; yet still he wished to disbelieve; but the particular form, the same varying tints upon the haft and sheath were alike in splendour on both, and left no room for doubt; there were also drops of blood on each.

He left Smyrna, and on his way home, at Rome, his first inquiries were concerning the lady he had attempted to snatch from Lord Ruthven's seductive arts. Her parents were in distress, their fortune ruined, and she had not been heard of since the departure of his lordship. Aubrey's mind became almost broken under so many repeated horrors; he was afraid that this lady had fallen a victim to the destroyer of Ianthe. He became morose and silent; and his only occupation consisted in urging the speed of the postilions, as if he were going to save the life of someone he held dear. He arrived at Calais; a breeze, which seemed obedient to his will, soon wafted him to the English shores; and he hastened to the mansion of his fathers, and there, for a moment, appeared to lose, in the embraces and caresses of his sister, all memory of the past. If she before, by her infantine caresses, had gained his affection, now that the woman began to appear, she was still more attaching as a companion.

Miss Aubrey had not that winning grace which gains the gaze and applause of the drawing-room assemblies. There was none of that light brilliancy which only exists in the heated atmosphere of a crowded apartment. Her blue eye was never lit up by the levity of the mind beneath. There was a melancholy charm about it which did not seem to arise from misfortune, but from some feeling within, that appeared to indicate a soul conscious of a brighter realm. Her step was not that light footing, which strays where'ere a butterfly or a colour may attract -- it was sedate and pensive. When alone, her face was never brightened by the smile of joy; but when her brother breathed to her his affection, and would in her presence forget those griefs she knew destroyed his rest, who would have exchanged her smile for that of the voluptuary? It seemed as if those eyes, that face were then playing in the light of their own native sphere. She was yet only eighteen, and had not been presented to the world, it having been thought by her guardians more fit that her presentation should be delayed until her brother's return from the continent, when he might be her protector. It was now, therefore, resolved that the next drawing-room, which was fast approaching, should be the epoch of her entry into the "busy scene". Aubrey would rather have remained in the mansion of his fathers, and fed upon the melancholy which overpowered him. He could not feel interest about the frivolities of fashionable strangers, when his mind had been so torn by the events he had witnessed; but he determined to sacrifice his own comfort to the protection of his sister. They soon arrived in town, and prepared for the next day, which had been announced as a drawing-room.

The crowd was excessive -- a drawing-room had not been held for a long time, and all who were anxious to bask in the smile of royalty, hastened thither. Aubrey was there with his sister. While he was standing in a corner by himself, heedless of all around him, engaged in the remembrance that the first time he had seen Lord Ruthven was in that very place -- he felt himself suddenly seized by the arm, and a voice he recognized too well, sounded in his ear -- "Remember your oath." He had hardly courage to turn, fearful of seeing a spectre that would blast him, when he perceived, at a little distance, the same figure which had attracted his notice on this spot upon his first entry into society. He gazed till his limbs almost refusing to bear their weight, he was obliged to take the arm of a friend, and forcing a passage through the crowd, he threw himself into his carriage, and was driven home. He paced the room with hurried steps, and fixed his hands upon his head, as if he were afraid his thoughts were bursting from his brain. Lord Ruthven again before him -- circumstances started up in dreadful array -- the dagger -- his oath. -- He roused himself, he could not believe it possible -- the dead rise again! -- He thought his imagination had conjured up the image his mind was resting upon. It was impossible that it could be real -- he determined, therefore, to go again into society; for though he attempted to ask concerning Lord Ruthven, the name hung upon his lips, and he could not succeed in gaining information. He went a few nights under the protection of a matron, he retired into a recess, and there gave himself up to his own devouring thoughts. Perceiving, at last, that many were leaving, he roused himself, and entering another room, found his sister surrounded by several, apparently in earnest conversation; he attempted to pass and get near her, when one, whom he requested to move, turned round, and revealed to him those features he most abhorred. He sprang forward, seized his sister's arm, and, with hurried step, forced her towards the street: at the door he found himself impeded by the crowd of servants who were waiting for their lords; and while he was engaged in passing them, he again heard that voice whisper close to him -- "Remember your oath!" -- he did not dare to turn, but, hurrying his sister, soon reached home.

Aubrey became almost distracted. If before his mind had been absorbed by one subject, how much more completely was it engrossed, now that the certainty of the monster's living again pressed up his thoughts. His sister's attentions were now unheeded, and it was in vain that she entreated him to explain to her what had caused his abrupt conduct. He only uttered a few words, and those terrified her. The more he thought, the more he was bewildered. His oath startled him; -- was he then to allow this monster to

40

roam, bearing ruin upon his breath, amidst all he held dear, and not avert its progress? His very sister might have been touched by him. But even if he were to break his oath, and disclose his suspicions, who would believe him? He thought of employing his own hand to free the world from such a wretch; but death, he remembered, had been already mocked. For days he remained in this state; shut up in his room, he saw no one, and ate only when his sister came, who, with eyes streaming with tears, besought him, for her sake, to support nature. At last, no longer capable of bearing stillness and solitude, he left his house, roamed from street to street, anxious to fly that image which haunted him. His dress became neglected, and he wandered, as often exposed to the noon-day sun as to the mid-night damps. He was no longer to be recognized; at first he returned with the evening to the house; but at last he laid him down to rest wherever fatigue overtook him. His sister, anxious for his safety, employed people to follow him; but they were soon distanced by him who fled from a pursuer swifter than any -- from thought. His conduct, however, suddenly changed. Struck with the idea that he left by his absence the whole of his friends, with a fiend amongst them, of whose presence they were unconscious, he determined to enter again into society, and watch him closely, anxious to forewarn, in spite of his oath, all whom Lord Ruthven approached with intimacy. But when he entered into a room, his haggard and suspicious looks were so striking, his inward shudderings so visible, that his sister was at last obliged to beg of him to abstain from seeking, for her sake, a society which affected him so strongly. When, however, remonstrance proved unavailing, the guardians thought it proper to interpose, and, fearing that his mind was becoming alienated, they thought it high time to resume again that trust which had been before imposed upon them by Aubrey's parents.

Desirous of saving him from the injuries and sufferings he had daily encountered in his wanderings, and of preventing him from exposing to the general eye those marks of what they considered folly, they engaged a physician to reside in the house, and take constant care of him. He hardly appeared to notice it, so completely was his mind absorbed by one terrible subject. His incoherence at last became so great, that he was confined to his chamber. There he would often lie for days, incapable of being roused. He had become emaciated, his eyes had attained a glassy lustre; -- the only sign of affection and recollection remaining displayed itself upon the entry of his sister; then he would sometimes start, and seizing her hands, with looks that severely afflicted her, he would desire her not to touch him. "Oh, do not touch him -- if your love for me is aught, do not go near him!" When, however, she inquired to whom he referred, his only answer was "True! true!" and again he sank into a state, whence not even she could rouse him. This lasted many months: gradually, however, as the year was passing, his incoherences became less frequent, and his mind threw off a portion of its gloom, whilst his guardians observed, that several times in the day he would count upon his fingers a definite number, and then smile.

The time had nearly elapsed, when, upon the last day of the year, one of his guardians entering his room, began to converse with his physician about the melancholy circumstance of Aubrey's being in so awful a situation, when his sister was going next day to be married. Instantly Aubrey's attention was attracted; he asked anxiously to whom. Glad of this mark of returning intellect, of which they feared he had been deprived, they mentioned the name of the Earl of Marsden. Thinking this was a young Earl whom he had met with in society, Aubrey seemed pleased, and astonished them still more by his expressing his intention to be present at the nuptials, and desiring to see his sister. They answered not, but in a few minutes his sister was with him. He was apparently again capable of being affected by the influence of her lovely smile; for he pressed her to his breast, and kissed her cheek, wet with tears, flowing at the thought of her brother's being once more alive to the feelings of affection. He began to speak with all his wonted warmth, and to congratulate her upon her marriage with a person so distinguished for rank and every accomplishment; when he suddenly perceived a locket upon her breast; opening it, what was his surprise at beholding the features of the monster who had so long influenced his life. He seized the portrait in a paroxysm of rage, and trampled it under foot. Upon her asking him why he thus destroyed the resemblance of her future husband, he looked as if he did not understand her; -- then seizing her hands, and gazing on her with a frantic expression of countenance, he bade her swear that she would never wed this monster, for he -- But he could not advance -- it seemed as if that voice again bade him remember his oath -- he turned suddenly round, thinking Lord Ruthven was near him but saw no one. In the meantime the guardians and physician, who had heard the whole, and thought this was but a return of his disorder, entered, and forcing him from Miss Aubrey, desired her to leave him. He fell upon his knees to them, he implored, he begged of them to delay but for one day. They, attributing this to the insanity they imagined had taken possession of his mind, endeavoured to pacify him, and retired.

Lord Ruthven had called the morning after the drawing-room, and had been refused with every one else. When he heard of Aubrey's ill health, he readily understood himself to be the cause of it; but when he learned that he was deemed insane, his exultation and pleasure could hardly be concealed from those among whom he had gained his information. He hastened to the house of his former companion, and, by constant attendance, and the pretence of great affection for the brother and interest in his fate, he gradually won the ear of Miss Aubrey. Who could resist his power? His tongue had dangers and toils to recount -- could speak of himself as of an individual having no sympathy with any being on the crowded earth, save with her to whom he addressed himself; -- could tell how, since he knew her, his existence had begun to seem worthy of preservation, if it were merely

42

that he might listen to her soothing accents; -- in fine, he knew so well how to use the serpent's art, or such was the will of fate, that he gained her affections. The title of the elder branch falling at length to him, he obtained an important embassy, which served as an excuse for hastening the marriage (in spite of her brother's deranged state), which was to take place the very day before his departure for the continent.

Aubrey, when he was left by the physician and his guardians, attempted to bribe the servants, but in vain. He asked for pen and paper; it was given him; he wrote a letter to his sister, conjuring her, as she valued her own happiness, her own honour, and the honour of those now in the grave, who once held her in their arms as their hope and the hope of their house, to delay but for a few hours that marriage, on which he denounced the most heavy curses. The servants promised they would deliver it; but giving it to the physician, he thought it better not to harass any more the mind of Miss Aubrey by, what he considered, the ravings of a maniac. Night passed on without rest to the busy inmates of the house; and Aubrey heard, with a horror that may more easily be conceived than described, the notes of busy preparation. Morning came, and the sound of carriages broke upon his ear. Aubrey grew almost frantic. The curiosity of the servants at last overcame their vigilance, they gradually stole away, leaving him in the custody of an helpless old woman. He seized the opportunity, with one bound was out of the room, and in a moment found himself in the apartment where all were nearly assembled. Lord Ruthven was the first to perceive him: he immediately approached, and, taking his arm by force, hurried him from the room, speechless with rage. When on the staircase, Lord Ruthven whispered in his ear -- "Remember your oath, and know, if not my bride today, your sister is dishonoured. Women are frail!" So saying, he pushed him towards his attendants, who, roused by the old woman, had come in search of him. Aubrey could no longer support himself; his rage not finding vent, had broken a blood-vessel, and he was conveyed to bed. This was not mentioned to his sister, who was not present when he entered, as the physician was afraid of agitating her. The marriage was solemnized, and the bride and bridegroom left London.

Aubrey's weakness increased; the effusion of blood produced symptoms of the near approach of death. He desired his sister's guardians might be called, and when the midnight hour had struck, he related composedly what the reader has perused -- he died immediately after.

The guardians hastened to protect Miss Aubrey; but when they arrived, it was too late. Lord Ruthven had disappeared, and Aubrey's sister had glutted the thirst of a VAMPYRE!

SMARRA

Charles Nodier

...While I was struggling against the terror which had seized me, and trying to pluck from my breast some curse that might arouse the vengeance of the gods in heaven:

"O wretched one," cried Méroé, "may you be punished for ever for your insolent curiosity! Ah! You dare to violate the enchantments of sleep... You speak, you cry out and you see... Well! You shall speak no more but to lament, you shall cry out no more but to implore the hollow pity of the absent, you shall see no more but scenes of horror which will chill your soul!" Thus expressing herself, in a voice more searing and high-pitched than that of a wounded hyena still threatening its hunters, she took from her finger the iridescent turquoise which sparkled with lights as varied as the colours of the rainbow, or as the wave which rears up with the rising tide, reflecting, as it furls upon itself, the mingled hues of the rising sun. She presses the hidden spring, to reveal a golden casket containing a colourless and formless monster, which thrashes and howls and leaps and falls back crouching on the enchantress' breast.

"There you are, my dear Smarra," says she, "sole darling of my amorous thoughts, you whom the hatred of the heavens has chosen amongst all their treasures to wreak despair among the sons of men. I order you to go now, fond, beguiling or terrible spectre, go and torment the victim I have delivered up to you; plague him with tortures as cruel and implacable as my own wrath. Go and sate yourself upon the anguish of his beating heart, count the convulsive poundings of his quickening pulse as it speeds up or grows slow...contemplate his painful death throes and suspend them merely in order to begin again... This is the price, oh faithful slave of love, to be extracted at the gate of dreams before you sink once more upon the scented pillow of your mistress, and embrace the queen of nightly terrors in your loving arms..."

She speaks, and the monster leaps from her burning hand like the rounded quoit of the discobolus; he spins in the air with the speed of those fireworks they launch on ships, spreading his weirdly scalloped wings, rises, falls, swells, diminishes and, like some deformed and gleeful dwarf, his fingers armed with nails of a metal finer than steel, which penetrate the flesh without rending it, and suck the blood from it like the insidiously pumping leech, he clamps himself upon my heart, swells, lifts his great head and laughs. In vain my gaze, frozen with fear, spans the space it can encompass for the sight of some consoling object: the thousand demons of the night escort the fearful demon of the turquoise. Stunted, wild-eyed women; purple-red snakes whose mouths spit flame; lizards poking human faces above a lake of mud and blood; heads newly-severed from their trunks by the soldier's war-axe, but which look at me with living eyes, hopping on reptile's feet...

Translated by
Judith Landry

THE BEAUTIFUL DEAD

Théophile Gautier

Brother, you ask me if I have ever loved. Yes. My story is a strange and terrible one; and though I am sixty-six years of age, I scarcely dare even now to disturb the ashes of that memory. To you I can refuse nothing; but I should not relate such a tale to any less experienced mind. So strange were the circumstances of my story, that I can scarcely believe myself to have ever actually been a party to them. For more than three years I remained the victim of a most singular and diabolical illusion. Poor country priest though I was, I led every night in a dream -- would to God it had all been a dream! -- a most worldly life, a damning life, a life of Sardanapalus. One single look too freely cast upon a woman well-nigh caused me to lose my soul; but finally by the grace of God and the assistance of my patron saint, I succeeded in casting out the evil spirit that possessed me. My daily life was long interwoven with a nocturnal life of a totally different character. By day I was a priest of the Lord, occupied with prayer and sacred things; by night, from the instant that I closed my eyes I became a young nobleman, a connoisseur of women, dogs, and horses; gambling, drinking, and blaspheming, and when I awoke at early day-break, it seemed to me, on the other hand, that I had been sleeping, and had only dreamed that I was a priest. Of this somnambulistic life there now remains to me only the recollection of certain scenes and words which I cannot banish from my memory; but although I never actually left the walls of my presbytery, one would think to hear me speak that I were a man who, weary of all worldly pleasures, had become a religious, seeking to end a tempestuous life in the service of God, rather than a humble seminarist who has grown old in this obscure curacy, situated in the depths of the woods and even isolated from the life of the century.

Yes, I have loved as none in the world ever loved -- with an insensate and furious passion -- so violent that I am astonished it did not cause my heart to burst asunder. Ah, what nights -- what nights!

From my earliest childhood I had felt a vocation to the priesthood, so that all my studies were directed with that idea in view. Up to the age of twenty-four my life had been only a prolonged novitiate. Having completed my course of theology I successively received all the minor orders, and my superiors judged me worthy, in spite of my youth, to pass the last awful degree. My ordination was fixed for Easter week.

I had never gone into the world. My world was confined by the walls of the college and the seminary. I knew in a vague sort of a way that there was something called Woman, but I never permitted my thoughts to dwell on such a subject, and I lived in a state of perfect innocence. Twice a year only I saw my infirm and aged mother, and in those visits were comprised my sole relations with the outer world.

I regretted nothing; I felt not the least hesitation at taking the last irrevocable step; I was filled with joy and impatience. Never did a betrothed lover count the slow hours with more feverish ardour; I slept only to dream that I was saying mass; I believed there could be nothing in the world more delightful than to be a priest; I would have refused to be a king or a poet in preference. My ambition could conceive of no loftier aim.

I tell you this in order to show you that what happened to me could not have happened in the natural order of things, and to enable you to understand that I was the victim of an inexplicable fascination.

At last the great day came. I walked to the church with a step so light that I fancied myself sustained in air, or that I had wings upon my shoulders. I believed myself an angel, and wondered at the sombre and thoughtful faces of my companions, for there were several of us. I had passed all the night in prayer, and was in a condition well-nigh bordering on ecstasy. The bishop, a venerable old man, seemed to be God the Father leaning over his Eternity, and I beheld Heaven through the vault of the temple.

You well know the details of that ceremony -- the benediction, the communion under both forms, the anointing of the palms of the hands with the Oil of Catechumens, and then the holy sacrifice concelebrated with the bishop.

Ah, truly spake Job when he declared that the imprudent man is one who hath not made a covenant with his eyes! I accidentally lifted my head, which until then I had kept down, and beheld before me, so close that it seemed that I could have touched her -- although she was actually a considerable distance from me on the farther side of the sanctuary railing -- a young woman of extraordinary beauty, and attired with royal magnificence. It seemed as though scales had suddenly fallen from my eyes. I felt like a blind man who unexpectedly recovers his sight. The bishop, so radiantly glorious but an instant before, suddenly vanished away, the tapers paled upon their golden candlesticks like stars in the dawn, and a vast darkness seemed to fill the whole church. The young woman appeared in bright relief against the back-ground of that darkness, like some angelic revelation. She seemed herself radiant, and radiating light rather than receiving it.

I lowered my eyelids, firmly resolved not to open them again, that I might not be influenced by external objects, for distraction had gradually taken possession of me until I hardly knew what I was doing.

In another minute, nevertheless, I reopened my eyes, for through my eyelashes I still beheld her, all sparkling with prismatic colours, and surrounded with such a purple penumbra as one beholds in gazing at the sun.

Oh, how beautiful she was! The greatest painters, who followed ideal beauty into heaven itself, and thence brought back to earth the true portrait of the Madonna, never in their delineations even approached that wildly beautiful reality which I saw before me. Neither the verses of the poet nor the palette of the artist could convey any conception of her. She was rather tall, with a form and bearing of a goddess. Her hair, of a soft blonde hue, was parted in the midst and flowed back over her temples in two rivers of rippling gold; she seemed a diademed queen. Her forehead, bluish-white in its transparency, extended its calm breadth above the arches of her eyebrows, which by a strange singularity were almost black, and admirably relieved the effect of sea-green eyes of unsustainable vivacity and brilliancy. What eyes! With a single flash they could have decided a man's destiny. They had a life, a limpidity, an ardour, a light that I have never seen in human eyes; they shot forth rays like arrows, which I could distinctly *see* enter my heart. I know not if the fire which illumined them came from heaven or hell, but assuredly it came from one or the other. That woman was either an angel or a demon, perhaps both. Assuredly she never sprang from Eve, our common mother. Teeth of the most lustrous pearl gleamed in her smile, and at every inflection of her lips little dimples appeared in the satiny rose of her adorable cheeks. There was a delicacy and pride in the regal outline of her nostrils bespeaking noble blood. Agate gleams played over the smooth lustrous skin of her half-bare shoulders, and strings of great blonde pearls -- almost equal to her neck in beauty of colour -- descended upon her bosom. From time to time she elevated her head with the undulating grace of a startled serpent or peacock, thereby imparting a quivering motion to the high lace ruff which surrounded it like a silver trellis-work.

She wore a robe of orange-red velvet, and from her wide ermine-lined sleeves there peeped forth patrician hands of infinite delicacy, and so ideally transparent that, like the fingers of Aurora, they permitted the light to shine through them.

All these details I can recollect at this moment as plainly as though they were of yesterday, for notwithstanding I was greatly troubled at the time, nothing escaped me; the faintest touch of shading, the little dark speck at the point of the chin, the almost imperceptible down at the corners of the lips, the velvety floss upon the brow, the quivering shadows of the eyelashes upon the cheeks, I could notice everything with astonishing lucidity of perception.

And gazing I felt opening within me gates that had until then remained closed; outlets long obstructed became all clear, permitting glimpses of unfamiliar perspectives within; life suddenly made itself visible to me under a totally novel aspect. I felt as though I had just been born into a new world and a new order of things. A frightful anguish began to torture my heart as with red-hot pincers. Every successive minute seemed to me at once but a second and yet a century. Meanwhile the ceremony was proceeding, and I shortly found myself transported far from that world of which my newly-born desires were furiously besieging the entrance. Nevertheless I answered "Yes" when I wished to say "No," though all within me protested against the violence done to my soul by my tongue. Some occult power seemed to force the words from my throat against my will. Thus it is, perhaps, that so many young girls walk to the altar firmly resolved to refuse in a startling manner the husband imposed upon them, and that yet not one ever fulfills her intention. Thus it is, doubtless, that so many poor novices take the veil, though they have resolved to tear it into shreds at the moment when called upon to utter the vows. One dares not thus cause so great a scandal to all present, nor deceive the expectations of so many people. All those eyes, all those wills seem to weigh down upon you like a cope of lead; and moreover, measures have been so well taken, everything has been so thoroughly arranged beforehand and after a fashion so evidently irrevocable, that the will yields to the weight of circumstances and utterly breaks down.

As the ceremony proceeded the features of the fair unknown changed their expression. Her look had at first been one of caressing tenderness; it changed to an air of disdain and of mortification, as though at not having been able to make itself understood.

With an effort of will sufficient to have uprooted a mountain, I strove to cry out that I would not be a priest, but I could not speak; my tongue seemed nailed to my palate, and I found it impossible to express my will by the least syllable of negation. Though fully awake, I felt like one under the influence of a nightmare, who vainly strives to shriek out the one word upon which life depends.

She seemed conscious of the martyrdom I was undergoing, and, as though to encourage me, she gave me a look replete with divinest promise. Her eyes were a poem; their every glance was a song.

She said to me:

"If though wilt be mine, I shall make thee happier than God Himself in His paradise. The angels themselves will be jealous of thee. Tear off that funeral shroud in which thou art about to wrap thyself. I am Beauty, I am Youth, I am Life. Come to me! Together we shall be Love. Can Jehovah offer thee aught in exchange? Our lives will flow on like a dream, in one eternal kiss.

"Fling forth the wine of that chalice, and thou art free. I will conduct thee to the Unknown Isles. Thou shalt sleep in my bosom upon a bed of massy gold under a silver pavilion, for I love thee and would take thee away from thy God, before whom so many noble hearts pour forth floods of love which never reach even the steps of His throne!"

These words seemed to float to my ears in a rhythm of infinite sweetness, for her look was actually sonorous, and the utterances of her eyes were re-echoed in the depths of my heart as though living lips had breathed them into my life. I felt myself willing to renounce God, and yet my tongue mechanically fulfilled all the formalities of the ceremony. The fair one gave me another look, so beseeching, so despairing that keen blades seemed to pierce my heart, and I felt my bosom transfixed by more swords than those of Our Lady of Sorrows.

All was consummated; I had become a priest.

Never was deeper anguish painted on human face than upon hers. The maiden who beholds her affianced lover suddenly fall dead at her side, the mother bending over the empty cradle of her child, Eve seated at the threshold of the gate of Paradise, the miser who finds a stone substituted for his stolen treasure, the poet who accidentally permits the only manuscript of his finest work to fall into the fire, could not wear a look so despairing, so inconsolable. All the blood had abandoned her face, leaving it whiter than marble; her beautiful arms hung lifelessly on either side of her body as though their muscles had suddenly relaxed, and she sought the support of a pillar, for her yielding limbs almost betrayed her. As for myself, I staggered towards the door of the church, livid as death, my forehead bathed with a sweat bloodier than that of Calvary; I felt as though I were being strangled; the vault seemed to have flattened down upon my shoulders, and it seemed to me that my head alone sustained the whole weight of the dome.

As I was about to cross the threshold a hand suddenly caught mine -- a woman's hand! I had never till then touched the hand of any woman. It was cold as a serpent's skin, and yet its impress remained upon my wrist, burnt there as though branded by a glowing iron. It was she. "Unhappy man! Unhappy man! What hast thou done?" she exclaimed in a low voice, and immediately disappeared in the crowd.

The aged bishop passed by. He cast a severe and scrutinising look upon me. My face presented the widest aspect imaginable; I blushed and turned pale alternately; dazzling lights flashed before my eyes. A companion took pity on me. He seized my arm and led me out. I could not possibly have found my way back to the seminary unassisted. At the corner of a street, while the young priest's attention was momentarily turned in another direction, a negro page, fantastically garbed, approached me, and without pausing on his way slipped into my hand a little pocket-book with gold-embroidered corners, at the same time giving me a sign to hide it. I concealed it in my sleeve, and there kept it until I found myself alone in my cell. Then I opened the clasp. There were only two leaves within, bearing the words, "Clarimonde. At the Concini Palace." So little acquainted was I at that time with the things of this world that I had never heard of Clarimonde, celebrated as she was, and I had no idea as to where the Concini Palace was situated. I hazarded a thousand conjectures, each more extravagant than the last; but, in truth, I cared little whether she were a great lady or courtesan, so that I could but see her once more.

My love, although the growth of a single hour, had taken imperishable root. I did not even dream of attempting to tear it up, so fully was I convinced such a thing would be impossible. That woman had completely taken possession of me. One look from her had sufficed to change my very nature. She had breathed her will into my life, and I no longer lived in myself, but in her and for her. I gave myself up to a thousand extravagances. I kissed the place upon my hand which she had touched, and I repeated her name over and over again for hours in succession. I only needed to close my eyes in order to see her distinctly as though she were actually present; and I reiterated to myself the words she had uttered in my ear at the church porch: "Unhappy man! Unhappy man! What hast thou done?" I comprehended at last the full horror of my situation, and the funereal and awful restraints of the state into which I had just entered became clearly revealed to me. To be a priest! -- that is, to be chaste, never to love, to observe no distinction of sex or age, to turn from the sight of all beauty, to put out one's own eyes, to hide for ever crouching in the chill shadows of some church or cloister, to visit none but the dying, to watch by unknown corpses, and ever bear about with one the black soutane as a garb of mourning for oneself, so that your very dress might serve as a pall for your coffin.

And I felt life rising within me like a subterranean lake, expanding and overflowing; my blood leaped fiercely through my arteries; my long-restrained youth suddenly burst into active being, like the aloe which blooms but once in a hundred years, and then bursts into blossom with a clap of thunder.

What could I do in order to see Clarimonde once more? I had no pretext to offer for desiring to leave the seminary, not knowing any person in the city. I would not even be able to remain there for more than a short time, and was only waiting my assignment to the curacy which I must thereafter occupy. I tried to remove the bars of the window; but it was at a fearful height from the ground, and I found that as I had no ladder it would be useless to think of escaping thus. And, furthermore, I could descend thence only by night in any event, and afterward how should I be able to find my way through the inextricable labyrinth of streets? All these difficulties, which to many would have appeared altogether insignificant, were gigantic to me, a poor seminarist who had fallen in love only the day before for the first time, without experience, without money, without attire.

"Ah!" cried I to myself in my blindness, "were I not a priest I could have seen her every day; I might have been her lover, her spouse. Instead of being wrapped in this dismal shroud of mine I would have had garments of silk and velvet, golden chains, a sword, and fair plumes like other handsome young cavaliers. My hair, instead of being dishonoured by the tonsure, would flow down my neck in waving curls; I would have a fine waxed moustache; I would be a gallant." But one hour passed before an altar, a few hastily articulated words, had for ever cut me off from the number of the living, and I had myself sealed down the stone of my own tomb; I had with my own hand bolted the gate of my prison!

I went to the window. The sky was beautifully blue; the trees had donned their spring robes; nature seemed to be making parade of an ironical joy. The *Place* was filled with people, some going, others coming; young beaux and young belles were sauntering in couples towards the groves and gardens; merry youths passed by, cheerily trolling refrains of drinking songs -- it was all a picture of vivacity, life, animation, gaiety, which formed a bitter contrast with my mourning and my solitude. On the steps of the gate sat a young mother playing with her child. She kissed its little rosy mouth, and performed, in order to amuse it, a thousand divine little puerilities such as only mothers know how to invent. The father standing at a little distance smiled gently upon the charming group, and with folded arms seemed to hug his joy to his heart. I could not endure that spectacle. I closed the window with violence, and flung myself on my bed, my heart filled with frightful hate and jealousy, and gnawed my fingers and my bedcovers like a tiger that has passed days without food.

I know not how long I remained in this condition, but at last, while writhing on the bed in a fit of spasmodic fury, I suddenly perceived the Abbé Sérapion, who was standing erect in the centre of the room, watching me attentively. Filled with shame of myself, I let my head fall upon my breast and covered my face with my hands.

"Romuald, my friend, something very extraordinary is going on within you," observed Sérapion, after a few moments' silence; "your conduct is altogether inexplicable. You -- always so quiet, so pious, so gentle -- you to rage in your cell like a wild beast! Take heed, brother -- do not listen to the suggestions of the devil. The Evil Spirit, furious that you have consecrated yourself for ever to the Lord, is prowling around you like a ravening wolf and making a last effort to obtain possession of you. Instead of allowing yourself to be conquered, my dear Romuald, make to yourself a cuirass of prayers, a buckler of mortifications, and combat the enemy like a valiant man; you will then assuredly overcome him. Virtue must be proved by temptation, and gold comes forth purer from the hands of the essayer. Fear not. Never allow yourself to become discouraged. The most watchful and steadfast souls are at moments liable to such temptation. Pray, fast, meditate, and the Evil Spirit will depart from you."

53

The words of the Abbé Sérapion restored me to myself, and I became a little more calm. "I came," he continued, "to tell you that you have been appointed to the curacy of C_____. The priest who has charge of it has just died, and Monseigneur the Bishop has ordered me to have you installed there at once. Be ready, therefore, to start to-morrow." I responded with an inclination of the head, and the Abbé retired. I opened my breviary and began reading some prayers, but the letters became confused and blurred under my eyes, the thread of the ideas entangled itself hopelessly in my brain, and the volume at last fell from my hands without my being aware of it.

To leave to-morrow without having been able to see her again, to add yet another barrier to the many already interposed between us, to lose for ever all hope of being able to meet her, except, indeed, through a miracle! Even to write to her, alas! would be impossible, for by whom could I despatch my letter? With my sacred character of priest, to whom could I dare unbosom myself, in whom could I confide? I became a prey to the bitterest anxiety.

Then suddenly recurred to me the words of the Abbé Sérapion regarding the artifices of the devil; and the strange character of the adventure, the supernatural beauty of Clarimonde, the phosphoric light of her eyes, the burning imprint of her hand, the agony into which she had thrown me, the sudden change wrought within me when all my piety vanished in a single instant -- these and other things clearly testified to the work of the Evil One, and perhaps that satiny hand was but the glove which concealed his claws. Filled with terror at these fancies, I again picked up the breviary which had slipped from my knees and fallen upon the floor, and once more gave myself up to prayer.

Next morning Sérapion came to take me away. Two mules freighted with our miserable valises awaited us at the gate. He mounted one, and I the other as well as I knew how.

As we passed along the streets of the city, I gazed attentively at all the windows and balconies in the hope of seeing Clarimonde, but it was yet early in the morning, and the city had hardly opened its eyes. Mine sought to penetrate the blinds and window-curtains of all the palaces before which we were passing. Sérapion doubtless attributed this curiosity to my admiration of the architecture, for he slackened the pace of his animal in order to give me time to look around me. At last we passed the city gates and began to mount the hill beyond. When we arrived at its summit I turned to take a last look at the place where Clarimonde dwelt. The shadow of a great cloud hung over all the city; the contrasting colours of its blue and red roofs were lost in the uniform half-tint, through which here and there floated upward, like white flakes of foam, the smoke of freshly kindled fires. By a singular optical effect one edifice, which surpassed in height all the neighbouring buildings that were still dimly veiled by the vapours, towered up, fair and lustrous with the gilding of a solitary beam of sunlight -- although actually more than a league away it seemed quite near. The smallest details of its architecture were plainly distinguishable -- the turrets, the platforms, the window-casements, and even the swallow-tailed weather vanes.

"What is that palace I see over there, all lighted up by the sun?" I asked Sérapion. He shaded his eyes with his hand, and having looked in the direction indicated, replied: "It is the ancient palace which the Prince Concini has given to the courtesan Clarimonde. Awful things are done there!"

At that instant, I know not whether it was a reality or an illusion, I fancied I saw gliding along the terrace a shapely white figure, which gleamed for a moment in passing and as quickly vanished. It was Clarimonde.

Oh, did she know at that very hour, all feverish and restless -- from the height of the rugged road which separated me from her and which, alas! I could never more descend -- I was directing my eyes upon the palace where she dwelt, and which a mocking beam of sunlight seemed to bring nigh to me, as though inviting me to enter therein as its lord? Undoubtedly she must have known it, for her soul was too sympathetically united with mine not to have felt its least emotional thrill, and that subtle sympathy it must have been which prompted her to climb -- although clad only in her nightdress -- to the summit of the terrace, amid the icy dews of the morning.

The shadow gained the palace, and the scene became to the eye only a motionless ocean of roofs and gables, amid which one mountainous undulation was distinctly visible. Sérapion urged his mule forward, my own at once followed at the same gait, and a sharp angle in the road at last hid the city of S_____ for ever from my eyes, as I was destined never to return thither. At the close of a weary three-days' journey through dismal country fields, we caught sight of the cock upon the steeple of the church of which I was to take charge, peeping above the trees, and after having followed some winding roads fringed with thatched cottages and little gardens, we found ourselves in front of the façade, which certainly possessed few features of magnificence. A porch ornamented with some mouldings, and two or three pillars rudely hewn from sandstone; a tiled roof with counterforts of the same sandstone as the pillars, that was all. To the left lay the cemetery, overgrown with high weeds, and having a great iron cross rising up in its centre; to the right stood the presbytery under the shadow of the church. It was a house of the most extreme simplicity and frigid cleanliness. We entered the enclosure. A few chickens were picking up some oats scattered upon the ground; accustomed, seemingly, to the black habit of ecclesiastics, they showed no fear of our presence and scarcely troubled themselves to get out of our way. A hoarse, wheezy barking fell upon our ears, and we saw an aged dog running towards us.

It was my predecessor's dog. He had dull bleared eyes, grizzled hair, and every mark of the greatest age to which a dog can possibly attain. I patted him gently, and he proceeded at once to march alongside me with an air of satisfaction unspeakable. A very old woman, who had been the housekeeper of the former curé, also came to meet us, and after having invited me into a little back parlour, asked whether I intended to retain her. I replied that I would take care of her, and the dog, and the chickens, and all the furniture her master had bequeathed her at his death. At this she became fairly transported with joy, and the Abbé Sérapion at once paid her the price which she asked for her little property.

As soon as my installation was over, the Abbé Sérapion returned to the seminary. I was, therefore, left alone, with no one but myself to look to for aid or counsel. The thought of Clarimonde again began to haunt me, and in spite of all my endeavours to banish it, I always found it present in my meditations. One evening, while promenading in my little garden along the walks bordered with box-plants, I fancied that I saw through the elm-trees the figure of a woman, who followed my every movement, and that I beheld two sea-green eyes gleaming through the foliage; but it was only an illusion, and on going round to the other side of the garden, I could find nothing except a footprint on the sanded walk -- a footprint so small that it seemed to have been made by the foot of a child. The garden was enclosed by very high walls. I searched every nook and corner of it, but could discover no one there. I have never succeeded in fully accounting for this circumstance, which, after all, was nothing compared with the strange things which happened to me afterwards.

For a whole year I lived thus, filling all the duties of my calling with the most scrupulous exactitude, praying and fasting, exhorting and lending aid to the sick, and bestowing alms even to the extent of frequently depriving myself of the very necessaries of life. But I felt a great aridness within me, and the sources of grace seemed closed against me. I never found that happiness which should spring from the fulfilment of a holy mission; my thoughts were far away, and the words of Clarimonde were ever upon my lips like an involuntary refrain. Oh, brother, meditate well on this! Through having but once lifted my eyes to look upon a woman, through one fault apparently so venial, I have for years remained a victim to the most miserable agonies, and the happiness of my life has been destroyed for ever.

I will not longer dwell upon those defeats, or on those inward victories invariably followed by yet more terrible falls, but will at once proceed to the facts of my story. One night my door-bell was long and violently rung. The aged housekeeper arose and opened to the stranger, and the figure of a man, whose complexion was deeply bronzed, and who was richly clad in a foreign costume, with a poniard at his girdle, appeared under the rays of Barbara's lantern. Her first impulse was one of terror, but the stranger reassured her, and stated that he desired to see me at once on matters relating to my holy calling. Barbara invited him upstairs, where I was on the point of retiring. The stranger told me that his mistress, a very noble lady, was lying on the point of death, and desired to see a priest. I replied that I was prepared to follow him, took with me the sacred articles necessary for extreme unction, and descended in all haste. Two horses black as night itself stood without the gate, pawing the ground with impatience, and veiling their chests with long streams of smoky vapour exhaled from their nostrils. He held the stirrup and aided me to mount upon one; then, merely laying his hand upon the pommel of the saddle, he vaulted on the other, pressed the animal's sides with his knees, and loosened rein. The horse bounded forward with the velocity of an arrow. Mine, of which the stranger held the bridle, also started off at a quick gallop, keeping up with his companion. We devoured the road. The ground flowed backward beneath us in a long streaked line of pale grey, and the black silhouettes of the trees seemed fleeing by us on either side like an army in rout. We passed through a forest so profoundly gloomy that I felt my flesh creep in the still darkness with superstitious fear. The showers of bright sparks which flew from the stony ground under the ironshod feet of our horses, remained glowing in our wake like a fiery trail; and had anyone at that hour of the night beheld us both -- my guide and myself -- he must have taken us for two spectres riding upon nightmares. Witch-fires ever and anon flitted across the road before us, and the night-birds shrieked fearsomely in the depth of the woods beyond, where we beheld at intervals the phosphorescent eyes of wild cats. The manes of the horses became ever and more dishevelled, the sweat steamed over their flanks, and their breath came through their nostrils hard and fast. But when he found them slacking pace, the guide reanimated them by uttering a strange, guttural, unearthly cry, and the gallop began again with fury. At last the whirlwind race ceased; a huge black mass pierced through with many bright points of light suddenly rose before us, the hoofs of our horses echoed louder upon a strong wooden drawbridge, and we rode under a great vaulted archway which darkly yawned between two enormous towers. Some great excitement evidently reigned in the castle. Servants with torches were crossing the courtyard in every direction, and, above, lights were ascending and descending from landing to landing. I obtained a confused glimpse of vast masses of architecture -- columns, arcades, flights of steps, stairways -- a royal voluptuousness and elfin magnificence of construction worthy of fairyland. A negro page -- the same who had before brought me the tablet from Clarimonde, and whom I instantly recognized -- approached to aid me in dismounting, and the major-domo, attired in black velvet with a gold chain about his neck, advanced to meet me, supporting himself upon an ivory cane. Tears were falling from his eyes and streaming over his cheeks and white beard. "Too late!" he cried, sorrowfully shaking his venerable head. "Too late, sir priest! But if you have not been able to save the soul, come at least to watch by the poor body."

He took my arm and conducted me to the death-chamber. I wept not less bitterly than he, for I had learned that the dead one was none other than that Clarimonde whom I had so deeply and so wildly loved. A *prie-dieu* stood at the foot of the bed; a bluish flame flickering in a bronze patera filled all the room with a wan, deceptive light, here and there bringing out in the darkness at intervals some projection of furniture or cornice. In a chiselled urn upon the table there was a faded white rose, whose leaves -- excepting one that still held -- had all fallen, like oderous tears, to the foot of the vase. A broken black mask, a fan, and disguises of every variety, which were lying on the arm-chairs, bore witness that death had entered suddenly and unannounced into that sumptuous dwelling. Without daring to cast my eyes upon the bed, I knelt down and began to repeat the Psalms for the Dead, with exceeding fervour, thanking God that he had placed the tomb between me and the memory of this woman, so that I might thereafter be able to utter her name in my prayers as a name for ever sanctified by death. But my fervour gradually weakened, and I fell insensibly into a reverie. That chamber bore no semblance to a chamber of death. In lieu of the odours which I had been accustomed to breathe during such funereal vigils, a languorous vapour of Oriental perfume -- I know not what amorous odour of woman -- softly floated through the tepid air. That pale light seemed rather a twilight gloom contrived for voluptuous pleasure, than a substitute for the yellow-flickering watch-tapers which shine by the side of corpses. I thought upon the strange destiny which enabled me to meet Clarimonde again at the very moment when she was lost to me for ever, and a sigh of regretful anguish escaped from my breast. Then it seemed to me that some one behind me had also sighed, and I turned round to look. It was only an echo. But in that moment my eyes fell upon the bed of death which they had till then avoided. The red damask curtains, decorated with large flowers worked in embroidery, and looped up with gold bullion, permitted me to behold the fair dead, lying at full length, with hands joined upon her bosom. She was covered with a linen wrapping of dazzling whiteness, which formed a strong contrast with the gloomy purple of the hangings, and was of so fine a texture that it concealed nothing of her body's charming form, and allowed the eye to follow those beautiful outlines -- undulating like the neck of a swan -- which even death had not robbed of their supple grace. She seemed an alabaster statue executed by some skilful sculptor to place upon the tomb of a queen, or rather, perhaps, like a slumbering maiden over whom the silent snow had woven a spotless veil.

I could no longer maintain my constrained attitude of prayer. The air of the alcove intoxicated me, that febrile perfume of half-faded roses penetrated my very brain, and I began to pace restlessly up and down the chamber, pausing at each turn before the bier to contemplate the graceful corpse lying beneath the transparency of its shroud. Wild fancies came thronging to my brain. I thought to myself that she might not, perhaps, be really dead; that she might only have feigned death for the purpose of bringing me to her castle, and then declaring her love. At one time I even thought I saw her foot move under the whiteness of the coverings, and slightly dis-arrange the long, straight folds of the winding sheet.

And then I asked myself: "Is this indeed Clarimonde? What proof have I that it is she? Might not that black page have passed into the service of some other lady? Surely, I must be going mad to torture and afflict myself thus!" But my heart answered with a fierce throbbing: "It is she; it is she indeed!" I approached the bed again, and fixed my eyes with redoubled attention upon the object of my incertitude. Ah, must I confess it? That exquisite perfection of bodily form, although purified and made sacred by the shadow of death, affected me more voluptuously than it should have done, and that repose so closely resembled slumber that one might well have mistaken it for such. I forgot that I had come there to perform a funeral ceremony; I fancied myself a young bridegroom entering the chamber of the bride, who all modestly hides her fair face and through coyness seeks to keep herself wholly veiled. Heartbroken with grief, yet wild with hope, shuddering at once with fear and pleasure, I bent over and grasped the corner of the sheet. I lifted it back, holding my breath all the while through fear of waking her. My arteries throbbed with such violence that I felt them hiss through my temples, and the sweat poured from my forehead in streams, as though I had lifted a mighty slab of marble. There, indeed, lay Clarimonde, even as I had seen her at the church on the day of my ordination. She was not less charming than then. With her, death seemed but a last coquetry. The pallor of her cheeks, the less brilliant carnation of her lips, her long eyelashes lowered and relieving their dark fringe against the white skin, lent her an unspeakably seductive aspect of melancholy chastity and mental suffering; her long loose hair, still intertwined with some little blue flowers, made a shining pillow for her head, and veiled the nudity of her shoulders with its thick ringlets; her beautiful hands, purer, more diaphanous than the Host, were crossed on her bosom in an attitude of pious rest and silent prayer, which served to counteract all that might have proved otherwise too alluring -- even after death -- in the exquisite roundness and ivory polish of her bare arms from which the pearl bracelets had not yet been removed. I remained long in mute contemplation, and the more I gazed, the less I could persuade myself that life had really abandoned that beautiful body for ever. I do not know whether it was an illusion or a reflection of the lamplight, but it seemed to me that the blood was again beginning to circulate under that lifeless pallor, although she remained all motionless. I laid my hand lightly on her arm; it was cold, but not colder than her hand on the day when it touched mine at the portals of the church. I resumed my position, bending my face above her, and bathing her cheeks with the warm dew of my tears. Ah, what bitter feelings of despair and helplessness, what agonies unutterable did I endure in that long watch! Vainly did I wish that I could have gathered all my life into one mass that I might give it all to her, and breathe into her chill form the flame which devoured me. The night advanced, and feeling the moment of eternal separation approach, I could not deny myself the last sad sweet pleasure of imprinting a kiss upon the dead lips of her who had been my only love.... Oh, miracle! A faint breath mingled itself with my breath, and the mouth of Clarimonde responded to the passionate pressure of mine. Her eyes unclosed, and lighted up with something of their former brilliancy; she uttered a long sigh, and uncrossing her arms, passed them around my neck with a look of ineffable delight. "Ah, it is thou, Romuald!" she murmured in a voice languishingly sweet as the last vibrations of a harp. "What ailed thee, dearest? I waited so long for thee that I am dead; but we are now betrothed; I can see thee and visit thee. Adieu, Romuald, adieu! I love thee. That is all I wished to tell thee, and I give thee back the life which thy kiss for a moment recalled. We shall soon meet again."

Her head fell back, but her arms yet encircled me, as though to retain me still. A furious whirlwind suddenly burst in the window, and entered the chamber. The last remaining leaf of the white rose for a moment palpitated at the extremity of the stalk like a butterfly's wing, then it detached itself and flew forth through the open casement, bearing with it the soul of Clarimonde. The lamp was extinguished, and I fell insensible upon the bosom of the beautiful dead.

When I came to myself again I was lying on the bed in my little room at the presbytery, and the old dog of the former curé was licking my hand which had been hanging down outside the covers. Barbara, all trembling with age and anxiety, was busying herself about the room, opening and shutting drawers, and emptying powders into glasses. On seeing me open my eyes, the old woman uttered a cry of joy, the dog yelped and wagged his tail, but I was still so weak that I could not speak a single word or make the slightest motion. Afterward I learned that I had lain thus for three days, giving no evidence of life beyond the faintest respiration. Those three days do not reckon in my life, nor could I ever imagine whither my spirit had departed during those three days; I have no recollection of aught relating to them. Barbara told me that the same coppery-complexioned man who came to seek me on the night of my departure from the presbytery, had brought me back the next morning in a closed litter, and departed immediately afterward. When I became able to collect my scattered thoughts, I reviewed within my mind all the circumstances of that fateful night. At first I thought I had been the victim of some magical illusion, but ere long the recollection of other circumstances, real and palpable in themselves, came to forbid that supposition. I could not believe that I had been dreaming, since Barbara as well as myself had seen the strange man with his two black horses, and described with exactness every detail of his figure and apparel. Nevertheless it appeared that none knew of any castle in the neighbourhood answering to the description of that in which I had again found Clarimonde.

One morning I found the Abbé Sérapion in my room. Barbara had advised him that I was ill, and he had come with all speed to see me. Although this haste on his part testified to an affectionate interest in me, yet his visit did not cause me the pleasure which it should have done. The Abbé

Sérapion had something penetrating and inquisitorial in his gaze which made me feel very ill at ease. His presence filled me with embarrassment and a sense of guilt. At the first glance he divined my interior trouble, and I hated him for his clairvoyance.

When he inquired after my health in hypocritically honeyed accents, he constantly kept his two great yellow lion-eyes fixed upon me, and plunged his look into my soul like a sounding lead. Then he asked me how I directed my parish, if I was happy in it, how I passed the leisure hours allowed me in the intervals of pastoral duty, whether I had become acquainted with many of the inhabitants of the place, what was my favourite reading, and a thousand other such questions. I answered these inquiries as briefly as possible, and he, without ever waiting for my answers, passed rapidly from one subject of query to another. That conversation had evidently no connection with what he actually wished to say. At last, without any premonition, but as though repeating a piece of news which he had recalled on the instant, and feared might otherwise be forgotten subsequently, he suddenly said, in a clear vibrant voice, which rang in my ears like the trumpets of the Last Judgement:

"The great courtesan Clarimonde died a few days ago, at the close of an orgy which lasted eight days and eight nights. It was something infernally splendid. The abominations of the banquets of Belshazzar and Cleopatra were re-enacted there. Good God, what age are we living in? The guests were served by swarthy slaves who spoke an unknown tongue, and who seemed to me to be veritable demons. The livery of the very least among them would have served for the gala-dress of an emperor. There have always been very strange stories told of this Clarimonde, and all her lovers came to a violent or miserable end. They used to say that she was a ghoul, a female vampire; but I believe she was none other than Beelzebub himself."

He ceased to speak and began to regard me more attentively than ever, as though to observe the effect of his words on me. I could not refrain from starting when I heard him utter the name of Clarimonde, and this news of her death, in addition to the pain it caused me by reason of its coincidence with the nocturnal scenes I had witnessed, filled me with an agony and terror which my face betrayed, despite my utmost endeavours to appear composed. Sérapion fixed an anxious and severe look upon me, and then observed: "My son, I must warn you that you are standing with foot raised upon the brink of an abyss; take heed lest you fall therein. Satan's claws are long, and tombs are not always true to their trust. The tombstone of Clarimonde should be sealed down with a triple seal, for, if report be true, it is not the first time she has died. May God watch over you, Romuald!"

And with these words the Abbé walked slowly to the door. I did not see him again at that time, for he left for S_____ almost immediately.

I became completely restored to health and resumed my accustomed duties. The memory of Clarimonde and the words of the old Abbé were constantly in my mind; nevertheless no extraordinary event had occurred to verify the funereal predictions of Sérapion, and I had begun to believe that his fears and my own terrors were over-exaggerated, when one night I had a strange dream. I had hardly fallen asleep when I heard my bed-curtains drawn apart, as their rings slid back upon the curtain rod with a sharp sound. I rose up quickly upon my elbow, and beheld the shadow of a woman standing erect before me. I recognized Clarimonde immediately. She bore in her hand a little lamp, shaped like those which are placed in tombs, and its light lent her fingers a rosy transparency, which extended itself by lessening degrees even to the opaque and milky whiteness of her bare arm. Her only garment was the linen winding-sheet which had shrouded her when lying upon the bed of death. She sought to gather its folds over her bosom as though ashamed of being so scantily clad, but her little hand was not equal to the task. She was so white that the colour of the drapery blended with that of her flesh under the pallid rays of the lamp. Enveloped within this subtle tissue which betrayed all the contour of her body, she seemed more like a marble statue than a woman endowed with life. But dead or living, statue or woman, shadow or body, her beauty was still the same, only that the green light of her eyes was less brilliant, and her mouth, once so warmly crimson, was only tinted with a faint tender rosiness, like that of her cheeks. The little blue flowers which I had noticed entwined in her hair were withered and dry, and had lost nearly all their leaves, but this did not prevent her from being charming -- so charming that notwithstanding the strange character of the adventure, and the unexplainable manner in which she had entered my room, I felt not even for a moment the least fear.

She placed the lamp on the table and seated herself at the foot of my bed; then bending towards me, she said, in that voice at once silvery clear and yet velvety in its sweet softness, such as I never heard from any lips save hers:

"I have kept thee long in waiting, dear Romuald, and it must have seemed to thee that I had forgotten thee. But I come from afar off, very far off, and from a land whence no other has yet ever returned. There is neither sun nor moon in that land whence I come: all is but space and shadow; there is neither road nor pathway: no earth for the foot, no air for the wing; and nevertheless behold me here, for Love is stronger than Death and must conquer him in the end. Oh, what sad faces and fearful things I have seen on my way hither! What difficulty my soul, returned to earth through the power of will alone, has had in finding its body and reinstating itself therein! What terrible efforts I had to make ere I could lift the ponderous slab with which they had covered me! See, the palms of my poor hands are all bruised! Kiss them, sweet love, that they may be healed!" She laid the cold palms of her hands upon my mouth, one after the other. I kissed them, indeed, many times, and she the while watched me with a smile of ineffable affection.

I confess to my shame that I had entirely forgotten the advice of the Abbé Sérapion and the sacred office wherewith I had been invested. I had fallen without resistance, and at the first assault. I had not even made the least effort to repel the tempter. The fresh coolness of Clarimonde's skin penetrated my own, and I felt voluptuous tremors pass over my whole body. Poor child! in spite of all I saw afterward, I can hardly yet believe she was a demon; at least she had no appearance of being such, and never did Satan so skilfully conceal his claws and horns. She had drawn her feet up beneath her, and squatted down on the edge of the couch in an attitude full of negligent coquetry. From time to time she passed her little hand through my hair and twisted it into curls, as though trying how a new style of wearing it would become my face. I abandoned myself to her hands with the most guilty pleasure, while she accompanied her gentle play with the prettiest prattle. The most remarkable fact was that I felt no astonishment whatever at so extraordinary an adventure, and as in dreams one finds no difficulty in accepting the most fantastic events as simple facts, so all these circumstances seemed to me perfectly natural in themselves.

"I loved thee long ere I ever saw thee, dear Romuald, and sought thee everywhere. Thou wast my dream, and I first saw thee in the church at the fatal moment. I said at once, *It is he!* I gave thee a look into which I threw all the love I ever had, all the love I now have, all the love I shall ever have for thee -- a look that would have damned a cardinal or brought a king to his knees at my feet in view of all his court. Thou remainedst unmoved, preferring thy God to me!

"Ah, how jealous I am of that God whom thou didst love and still lovest more than me!

"Woe is me, unhappy one that I am! I can never have thy heart all to myself, I whom thou didst recall to life with a kiss -- dead Clarimonde, who for thy sake bursts asunder the gates of the tomb, and comes to consecrate to thee a life which she has resumed only to make thee happy!"

All her words were accompanied with the most impassioned caresses, which bewildered my sense and my reason to such an extent, that I did not fear to utter a frightful blasphemy for the sake of consoling her, and to declare that I loved her as much as God.

Her eyes rekindled and shone like chrysoprases.

"In truth? -- in very truth? -- as much as God!" she cried, flinging her beautiful arms around me. "Since it is so, thou wilt come with me; thou wilt follow me whithersoever I desire. Thou wilt cast away thy ugly black habit. Thou shalt be the proudest and most envied of cavaliers; thou shalt be my lover! To be the acknowledged lover of Clarimonde, who has refused even a Pope, that will be something of which to feel proud! Ah, the fair, unspeakably happy existence, the beautiful golden life we shall live together! And when shall we depart?"

"To-morrow! To-morrow!" I cried in my delirium.

"To-morrow, then, so let it be!" she answered. "In the meanwhile I shall have opportunity to change my toilet, for this is a little too light and in nowise suited for such a journey. I must also forthwith notify all my friends who believe me dead, and mourn for me as deeply as they are capable of doing. The money, the dresses, the carriages -- all will be ready. I shall call for thee at this same hour. Adieu, dear heart!" And she lightly touched my forehead with her lips. The lamp went out, the curtains closed again, and all became dark; a leaden, dreamless sleep feel on me and held me unconscious until the morning following.

I awoke later than usual, and the recollection of this singular adventure troubled me during the whole day. I finally persuaded myself that it was a mere vapour of my heated imagination. Nevertheless its sensations had been so vivid that it was difficult to persuade myself that they were not real, and it was not without some presentiment of what was going to happen that I got into bed at last, after having prayed God to drive far from me all thoughts of evil, and to protect the chastity of my slumber.

I soon fell into a deep sleep, and my dream was continued. The curtains again parted, and I beheld Clarimonde, not as on the former occasion, pale in her pale winding-sheet, with the violets of death upon her cheeks, but gay, sprightly, jaunty, in a superb travelling dress of green velvet, trimmed with gold lace, and looped up on either side to allow a glimpse of satin petticoat. Her blonde hair escaped in thick ringlets from beneath a broad black felt hat, decorated with white feathers whimsically twisted into various shapes. In one hand she held a little riding whip terminated by a gold whistle. She tapped me lightly with it, and exclaimed: "Well, my fine sleeper, is this the way you make your preparations? I thought I should find you up and dressed. Arise quickly, we have no time to lose."

I leaped out of bed at once.

"Come, dress yourself, and let us go," she continued, pointing to a little package she had brought with her. "The horses are becoming impatient of delay and champing their bits at the door. We ought to have been by this time at least ten leagues distant from here."

I dressed myself hurriedly, and she handed me the articles of apparel herself one by one, bursting into laughter from time to time at my awkwardness, as she explained to me the use of a garment when I had made a mistake. She hurriedly arranged my hair, and this done, held up before me a little pocket mirror of Venetian crystal, rimmed with silver filigree-work, and playfully asked: "How dost thou find thyself now? Wilt engage me for thy *valet de chambre?*"

I was no longer the same person, and I could not even recognize myself. I resembled my former self no more than a finished statue resembles a block of stone. My old face seemed but a coarse daub of the one reflected in the mirror. I was handsome, and my vanity was sensibly tickled by the metamorphosis. That elegant apparel, that richly embroidered vest had made

64

of me a totally different personage, and I marvelled at the power of transformation owned by a few yards of cloth cut after a certain pattern. The spirit of my costume penetrated my very skin, and within ten minutes more I had become something of a coxcomb.

In order to feel more at ease in my new attire, I took several turns up and down the room. Clarimonde watched me with an air of maternal pleasure, and appeared well satisfied with her work. "Come, enough of this child's-play! Let us start, Romuald, dear. We have far to go, and we may not get there in time." She took my hand and led me forth. All the doors opened before her at a touch, and we passed by the dog without awaking him.

At the gate we found Margheritone waiting, the same swarthy groom who had once before been my escort. He held the bridles of three horses, all black like those which bore us to the castle -- one for me, one for him, one for Clarimonde. Those horses must have been Spanish genets born of mares fecundated by a zephyr, for they were as fleet as the wind itself, and the moon, which had just risen at our departure to light us on the way, rolled over the sky like a wheel detached from her own chariot. We beheld her on the right leaping from tree to tree, and putting herself out of breath in the effort to keep up with us. Soon we came upon a level plain where, hard by a clump of trees, a carriage with four vigorous horses awaited us. We entered it, and the postilions urged their animals into a mad gallop. I had one arm around Clarimonde's waist, and one of her hands clasped in mine; her head leaned upon my shoulder, and I felt her bosom, half bare, lightly pressing against my arm. I had never known such intense happiness. In that hour I had forgotten everything, and I no more remembered having ever been a priest than I remembered what I had been doing in my mother's womb, so great was the fascination which the evil spirit exerted upon me. From that night my nature seemed in some sort to have become halved, and there were two men within me, neither of whom knew the other. At one moment I believed myself a priest who dreamed nightly that he was a gentleman, at another that I was a gentleman who dreamed he was a priest. I could no longer distinguish the dream from the reality, nor could I discover where the reality began or where ended the dream. The exquisite young lord and libertine railed at the priest, the priest loathed the dissolute habits of the young lord. Two spirals entangled and confounded the one with the other, yet never touching, would afford a fair representation of this bicephalic life which I lived. Despite the strange character of my condition, I do not believe that I ever inclined, even for a moment, to madness. I always retained with extreme vividness all the perceptions of my two lives. Only there was one absurd fact which I could not explain to myself -- namely, that the consciousness of the same individuality existed in two men so opposite in character. It was an anomaly for which I could not account -- whether I believed myself to be the curé of the little village of C_____, or

65

Il Signor Romualdo, the titled lover of Clarimonde.

Be that as it may, I lived, at least I believe that I lived, in Venice. I have never been able to discover rightly how much of illusion and how much of reality there was in this fantastic adventure. We dwelt in a great palace on the Canaleio, filled with frescoes and statues, and containing two Titians in the noblest style of the great master, which were hung in Clarimonde's chamber. It was a palace worthy of a king. We each had our gondola, our *barcarolli* in family livery, our music hall, and our special poet. Clarimonde always lived upon a magnificent scale; there was something of Cleopatra in her nature. As for me, I had the retinue of a prince's son, and I was regarded with as much reverential respect as though I had been of the family of one of the twelve Apostles or the four Evangelists of the Most Serene Republic. I would not have turned aside to allow even the Doge to pass, and I do not believe that since Satan fell from heaven, any creature was ever prouder or more insolent than I. I went to the Ridotto, and played with a luck which seemed absolutely infernal. I received the best of all society -- the sons of ruined families, women of the theatre, shrewd knaves, parasites, hectoring swashbucklers. But notwithstanding the dissipation of such a life, I always remained faithful to Clarimonde. I loved her wildly. She would have excited satiety itself, and chained inconstancy. To have Clarimonde was to have twenty mistresses; aye, to possess all women: so mobile, so varied of aspect, so fresh in new charms was she all in herself -- a very chameleon of a woman, in sooth. She made you commit with her the infidelity you would have committed with another, by donning to perfection the character, the attraction, the style of beauty of the woman who appeared to please you. She returned my love a hundred-fold, and it was in vain that the young patricians and even the Ancients of the Council of Ten made her the most magnificent proposals. A Foscari even went so far as to offer to espouse her. She rejected all his overtures. Of gold she had enough. She wished no longer for anything but love -- a love youthful, pure, evoked by herself, which should be a first and last passion. I would have been perfectly happy but for a cursed nightmare which recurred every night, and in which I believed myself to be a poor village curé, practising mortification and penance for my excesses during the day. Reassured by my constant association with her, I never thought further of the strange manner in which I had become acquainted with Clarimonde. But the words of the Abbé Sérapion concerning her recurred often to my memory, and never ceased to cause me uneasiness.

For some time the health of Clarimonde had not been so good as usual; her complexion grew paler day by day. The physicians who were summoned could not comprehend the nature of her malady and knew not how to treat it. They all prescribed some insignificant remedies, and never called a second time. Her paleness, nevertheless, visibly increased, and she became colder and colder, until she seemed almost as white and dead as upon that memorable night in the unknown castle. I grieved with anguish unspeakable to behold her thus slowly perishing; and she, touched by my agony, smiled upon me sweetly and sadly with the fateful smile of those who feel that they must die.

One morning I was seated at her bedside, and breakfasting from a little table placed close at hand, so that I might not be obliged to leave her for a single instant. In the act of cutting some fruit I accidentally inflicted rather a deep gash on my finger. The blood immediately gushed forth in a little purple jet, and a few drops spurted upon Clarimonde. Her eyes flashed, her face suddenly assumed an expression of savage joy such as I had never before observed in her. She leaped out of her bed with an animal agility -- the agility, as it were, of an ape or a cat -- and sprang upon my wound, which she began to suck with an air of unutterable pleasure. She swallowed the blood in little mouthfuls, slowly and carefully, like a connoisseur tasting a wine from Xeres or Syracuse. Gradually her eyelids half closed, and the pupils of her green eyes became oblong instead of round. From time to time she paused in order to kiss my hand, then she would again press her lips to the wound in order to coax forth a few more drops. When she found that the blood would no longer come, she arose with eyes liquid and brilliant, rosier than a May dawn; her face full and fresh, her hand warm and moist -- in fine, more beautiful than ever, and in the most perfect health.

"I shall not die! I shall not die!" she cried, clinging to my neck, half mad with joy. "I can love thee yet for a long time. My life is thine, and all that is of me comes from thee. A few drops of thy rich and noble blood, more precious and more potent than all the elixirs of the earth, have given me back life."

This scene long haunted my memory, and inspired me with strange doubts in regard to Clarimonde; and the same evening, when slumber had transported me to my presbytery, I beheld the Abbé Sérapion, graver and more anxious of aspect than ever. He gazed attentively at me, and sorrowfully exclaimed: "Not content with losing your soul, you now desire also to lose your body. Wretched young man, into how terrible a plight have you fallen!" The tone in which he uttered these words powerfully affected me, but in spite of its vividness even that impression was soon dissipated, and a thousand other cares erased it from my mind. At last one evening, while looking into a mirror whose traitorous position she had not taken into account, I saw Clarimonde in the act of emptying a powder into the cup of spiced wine which she had long been in the habit of preparing after our repasts. I took the cup, feigned to carry it to my lips, and then placed it on the nearest article of furniture as though intending to finish it at my leisure. Taking advantage of a moment when the fair one's back was turned, I threw the contents under the table, after which I retired to my chamber and went to bed, fully resolved not to sleep, but to watch and discover what should come of all this mystery. I did not have to wait long. Clarimonde entered in her night-dress, and having removed her apparel, crept into bed and lay down beside me. When she felt assured that I was asleep, she bared my arm, and drawing a gold pin from her hair, began to murmur in a low voice:

"One drop, only one drop! One ruby at the end of my needle... Since thou lovest me yet, I must not die!... Ah, poor love! His beautiful blood, so brightly purple, I must drink it. Sleep, my god, my child! I will do thee no harm; I will only take of thy life what I must to keep my own from being for ever extinguished. But that I love thee so much, I could well resolve to have other lovers whose veins I could drain; but since I have known thee all other men have become hateful to me... Ah, the beautiful arm! How round it is! How white it is! How shall I ever dare to prick this pretty blue vein!" And while thus murmuring to herself she wept, and I felt her tears raining on my arm as she clasped it with her hands. At last she took the resolve, slightly punctured me with the pin, and began to suck up the blood which oozed from the place. Although she swallowed only a few drops, the fear of weakening me soon seized her, and she carefully tied a little band around my arm, afterward rubbing the wound with an unguent which immediately cicatrized it.

Further doubts were impossible. The Abbé Sérapion was right. Notwithstanding this positive knowledge, however, I could not cease to love Clarimonde, and I would gladly of my own accord have given her all the blood she required to sustain her factitious life. Moreover, I felt but little fear of her. The woman seemed to plead with me for the vampire, and what I had already heard and seen sufficed to reassure me completely. In those days I had plenteous veins, which would not have been so easily exhaustible as at present; and I would not have thought of bargaining for my blood, drop by drop. I would rather have opened myself the veins of my arm and said to her: "Drink, and may my love infiltrate itself throughout thy body together with my blood!" I carefully avoided ever making the least reference to the narcotic drink she had prepared for me, or to the incident of the pin, and we lived in the most perfect harmony.

Yet my priestly scruples began to torment me more than ever, and I was at a loss to imagine what new penance I could invent in order to mortify and subdue my flesh. Although these visions were involuntary, and though I did not actually participate in anything relating to them, I could not dare to touch the body of Christ with hands so impure and a mind defiled by such debauches whether real or imaginary. In the effort to avoid falling under the influence of these wearisome hallucinations, I strove to prevent myself from being overcome by sleep. I held my eyelids open with my fingers, and stood for hours together leaning upright against the wall, fighting sleep with all my might; but the dust of drowsiness invariably gathered upon my eyes at last, and finding all resistance useless, I would have to let my arms fall in the extremity of despairing weariness, and the current of slumber would again bear me away to the perfidious shores. Sérapion addressed me with the most vehement exhortations, severely reproaching me for my softness and want of fervour. Finally, one day when I was more wretched than usual, he said to me: "There is but one way by which you can obtain relief from this continual torment, and though it is an extreme measure it must be made use of; violent diseases require violent remedies. I know where Clarimonde is buried. It is necessary that we shall disinter her remains, and that you shall behold in how pitiable state the object of your love is. Then you will no longer be tempted to lose your soul for the sake of a corpse ready to crumble into dust. That will assuredly restore you to yourself." For my part, I was so tired of this double life that I at once consented, desiring to ascertain beyond a doubt whether a priest or a gentleman had been the victim of delusion. I had become fully resolved either to kill one of the two men within me for the benefit of the other, or else to kill both, for so terrible an existence could not last long and be endured. The Abbé Sérapion provided himself with a mattock, a lever, and a lantern, and at midnight we made our way to the cemetery of _____, the location and place of which were perfectly familiar to him. After having directed the rays of the dark lantern upon the inscriptions of several tombs, we came at last upon a great slab, half concealed by huge weeds and devoured by mosses and parasitic plants, whereupon we deciphered the opening lines of the epitaph:

Ici gît Clarimonde
Qui fut de son vivant
La plus belle du monde.

"It is here without a doubt," muttered Sérapion, and placing his lantern on the ground, he forced the point of the lever under the edge of the stone and began to raise it. The stone yielded, and he proceeded to work with the mattock. Darker and more silent than the night itself, I stood by and watched him do it, while he, bending over his dismal toil, streamed with sweat, panted, and his hard-coming breath seemed to have the harsh tone of a death rattle. It was a weird scene, and had any persons from without beheld us, they would assuredly have taken us for profane wretches and shroud-stealers than for priests of God. There was something grim and fierce in Sérapion's zeal which lent him the air of a demon rather than of an apostle or an angel, and his great aquiline face, with all its stern features brought out in strong relief by the lantern-light, had something fearsome in it which enhanced the unpleasant fancy. An icy sweat came out upon my forehead in huge beads. Within the depths of my own heart I felt that the act of the austere Sérapion was an abominable sacrilege; and I could have prayed that a triangle of fire would issue from the entrails of the dark clouds, heavily rolling above us, to reduce him to cinders. The owls which had been nestling in the cypress-trees, startled by the gleam of the lantern, flew against it from time to time, striking their dusty wings against its panes, and uttering plaintive cries of lamentation; wild foxes yelped in the far darkness, and a thousand sinister noises detached themselves from the silence. At last Sérapion's mattock struck the coffin itself, making its planks re-echo with a deep sonorous sound, with that terrible sound nothingness utters when stricken. He wrenched apart and tore up the lid, and I beheld Clarimonde, pallid as a figure of marble, with hands joined; her white winding-sheet made but one fold from her head to her feet. A little crimson drop sparkled like a speck of dew at one corner of her colourless mouth. Sérapion, at this spectacle, burst into fury: "Ah, thou art here, demon! Impure courtesan! Drinker of blood and gold!" And he flung holy water upon the corpse and the coffin, over which he traced the sign of the cross with his sprinkler. Poor Clarimonde had no sooner been touched by the blessed spray than her beautiful body crumbled into dust, and became only a shapeless and frightful mass of cinders and half-calcined bones.

"Behold your mistress, my Lord Romuald!" cried the inexorable priest, as he pointed to these sad remains. "Will you be easily tempted after this to promenade on the Lido or at Fusina with your beauty?" I covered my face with my hands; a vast ruin had taken place within me. I returned to my presbytery, and the noble Lord Romuald, the lover of Clarimonde, separated himself from the poor priest with whom he had kept such strange company so long. But once only, the following night, I saw Clarimonde. She said to me, as she had said the first time at the portals of the church: "Unhappy man! Unhappy man! What hast thou done? Wherefore have hearkened to that imbecile priest? And what harm had I ever done thee that thou shouldst violate my poor tomb, and lay bare the miseries of my nothingness? All communication between our souls and our bodies is henceforth for ever broken. Adieu! Thou wilt yet regret me!" She vanished, and I never saw her any more.

Alas! she spoke truly indeed. I have regretted her more than once, and I regret her still. My soul's peace has been very dearly bought. The love of God was not too much to replace such a love as hers. And this, brother, is the story of my youth. Never gaze upon a woman, and walk abroad only with eyes ever fixed upon the ground; for however chaste and watchful one may be, the error of a single moment is enough to make one lose eternity.

Translated by
Lafcadio Hearn

LIGEIA

Edgar Allan Poe

"And the will therein lieth, which dieth not. Who knoweth the mysteries of the will, with its vigour? For God is but a great will pervading all things by nature of its intentness. Man doth not yield himself to the angels, nor unto death utterly, save only through the weakness of his feeble will."   *- Joseph Glanvill.*

I cannot, for my soul, remember how, when, or even precisely where, I first became acquainted with the lady Ligeia. Long years have since elapsed, and my memory is feeble through much suffering. Or, perhaps, I cannot *now* bring these points to mind, because, in truth, the character of my beloved, her rare learning, her singular yet placid caste of beauty, and the thrilling and enthralling eloquence of her low musical language, made their way into my heart by paces so steadily and stealthily progressive, that they have been unnoticed and unknown. Yet I believe that I met her first and most frequently in some large, old, decaying city near the Rhine. Of her family -- I have surely heard her speak. That it is of a remotely ancient date cannot be doubted. Ligeia! Ligeia! Buried in studies of a nature more than all else adapted to deaden impressions of the outward world, it is by that sweet word alone -- by Ligeia -- that I bring before mine eyes in fancy the image of her who is no more. And now, while I write, a recollection flashes upon me that I have *never known* the paternal name of her who was my friend and my betrothed, and who became the partner of my studies, and finally the wife of my bosom. Was it a playful charge on the part of my Ligeia? or was it a test of my strength of affection, that I should institute no inquiries upon this point? or was it rather a caprice of my own -- a wildly romantic offering on the shrine of the most passionate devotion? I but indistinctly recall the fact itself - what wonder that I have utterly forgotten the circumstances which originated or attended? And, indeed, if ever that spirit which is entitled *Romance* -- if ever she, the wan and the misty-winged *Ashtophet* of idolatrous Egypt, presided, as they tell, over marriages ill-omened, then most surely she presided over mine.

There is one dear topic, however, on which my memory fails me not. It is the *person* of Ligeia. In stature she was tall, somewhat slender, and, in her latter days, even emaciated. I would in vain attempt to portray the majesty, the quiet ease, of her demeanour, or the incomprehensible lightness and elasticity of her footfall. She came and departed as a shadow. I was never made aware of her entrance into my closed study, save by the dear music of her low sweet voice, as she placed her marble hand upon my shoulder. In beauty of face no maiden ever equalled her. It was the radiance of an opium-dream -- an airy and spirit-lifting vision more wildly divine than the fantasies which hovered about the slumbering souls of the daughters of Delos. Yet her features were not of that regular mould which we have been falsely taught to worship in the classical labours of the heathen. "There is no exquisite beauty," says Bacon, Lord Verulam, speaking truly of all the forms and *genera* of beauty, "without some *strangeness* in the proportion." Yet, although I saw that the features of Ligeia were not of a classic regularity -- although I perceived that her loveliness was indeed "exquisite", and felt that there was much of "strangeness" pervading it, yet I have tried in vain to detect the irregularity and to trace home my own perception of "the strange". I examined the contour of the lofty and pale forehead -- it was faultless -- how cold indeed that word when applied to a majesty so divine! -- the skin rivalling the purest ivory, the commanding extent and repose, the gentle prominence of the regions above the temples; and then the raven-black, the glossy, the luxuriant and naturally-curling tresses, setting forth the full force of the Homeric epithet, "hyacinthine"! I looked at the delicate outlines of the nose -- and nowhere but in the graceful medallions of the Hebrews had I beheld a similar perfection. There were the same luxurious smoothness of surface, the same scarcely perceptible tendency to the aquiline, the same harmoniously curved nostrils speaking the free spirit. I regarded the sweet mouth. Here was indeed the triumph of all things heavenly -- the magnificent turn of the short upper lip -- the soft, voluptuous slumber of the under -- the dimples which sported, and the colour which spoke -- the teeth glancing back, with a brilliancy almost startling, every ray of the holy light which fell upon them in her serene and placid, yet most exultingly radiant of all smiles. I scrutinized the formation of the chin -- and here, too, I found the gentleness of breadth, the softness and the majesty, the fulness and the spirituality, of the Greek -- the contour which the the god Apollo revealed but in a dream, to Cleomenes, the son of the Athenian. And then I peered into the large eyes of Ligeia.

For eyes we have no models in the remotely antique. It might have been, too, that in these eyes of my beloved lay the secret to which Lord Verulam alludes. They were, I must believe, far larger than the ordinary eyes of our own race. They were even fuller than the fullest of the gazelle eyes of the tribe of the valley of Nourjahad. Yet it was only at intervals -- in moments of intense excitement -- that this peculiarity became more than slightly noticeable in Ligeia. And at such moments was her beauty -- in my heated fancy thus it appeared perhaps -- the beauty of beings either above or apart from the earth -- the beauty of the fabulous Houri of the Turk. The hue of the orbs was the most brilliant of black, and, far over them, hung jetty lashes of great length. The brows, slightly irregular in outline, had the same tint. The "strangeness", however, which I found in the eyes, was of a nature distinct from the formation, or the colour, or the brilliancy of the features, and must, after all, be referred to the *expression*. Ah, word of no meaning! behind whose vast latitude of mere sound we intrench our ignorance of so much of the spiritual. The expression of the eyes of Ligeia! How for long hours have I pondered upon it! How have I, through the whole of a midsummer night, struggled to fathom it! What was it -- that something more profound than the well of Democritus -- which lay far within the pupils of my beloved? what *was* it? I was possessed with a passion to discover. Those eyes, those large, those shining, those divine orbs? they became to me twin stars of Leda, and I to them devoutest of astrologers.

There is no point, among the many incomprehensible anomalies of the science of mind, more thrillingly exciting than the fact -- never, I believe noticed in the schools -- that in our endeavours to recall to memory something long forgotten, we often find ourselves *upon the very verge* of remembrance, without being able, in the end, to remember. And thus how frequently, in my intense scrutiny of Ligeia's eyes, have I felt approaching the full knowledge of their expression -- felt it approaching -- yet not quite be mine -- and so at length entirely depart! And (strange, oh strangest mystery of all!) I found in the commonest objects of the universe, a circle of analogies to that expression. I mean to say that, subsequently to the period when Ligeia's beauty passed into my spirit, there dwelling as in a shrine, I derived, from many existences in the material world, a sentiment such as I felt always around, within me, by her large and luminous orbs. Yet not the more could I define that sentiment, or analyze, or even steadily view it. I recognized it, let me repeat, sometimes in the survey of a rapidly-growing vine -- in the contemplation of a moth, a butterfly, a chrysalis, a stream of running water. I have felt it in the ocean; in the falling of a meteor. I have felt it in the glances of unusually aged people. And there are one or two stars in heaven, (one especially, a star of the sixth magnitude, double and changeable, to be found near the large star in Lyra), in a telescopic scrutiny of which I have been made aware of the feeling. I have been filled with it by certain sounds from stringed instruments, and not infrequently by passages from books. Among innumerable other instances, I well remember something in a volume of Joseph Glanvil, which (perhaps merely from its quaintness -- who shall say?) never failed to inspire me with the sentiment: "And the will therein lieth, which dieth not. Who knoweth the mysteries of the will, with its vigour? For God is but a great will pervading all things by nature of its intentness. Man doth not yield him to the angels, nor unto death utterly, save only through the weakness of his feeble will."

73

Length of years and subsequent reflection have enabled me to trace, indeed, some remote connection between this passage in the English moralist and a portion of the character of Ligeia. An *intensity* in thought, action, or speech, was possibly, in her, a result, or at least an index, of that gigantic volition which, during our long intercourse, failed to give other and more immediate evidence of its existence. Of all the women whom I have ever known, she, the outwardly calm, the ever-placid Ligeia, was the most violently a prey to the tumultuous vultures of stern passion. And of such passion I could form no estimate, save by the miraculous expansion of those eyes which at once so delighted and appalled me -- by the almost magical melody, modulation, distinctness, and placidity of her very low voice -- and by the fierce energy (rendered doubly effective by contrast with her manner of utterance) of the wild words which she habitually uttered.

I have spoken of the learning of Ligeia: it was immense -- such as I have never known in woman. In the classical tongues she was deeply proficient, and as far as my own acquaintances extended in regard to the modern dialects of Europe, I have never known her at fault. Indeed upon any theme of the most admired, because simply the most abstruse of the boasted erudition of the academy, have I *ever* found Ligeia at fault? How singularly -- how thrillingly, this one point in the nature of my wife has forced itself, at this late period only, upon my attention! I said her knowledge was such as I have never known in woman -- but where breathes the man who has traversed, and successfully, *all* the wide areas of moral, physical, and mathematical science? I saw not then what I now clearly perceive, that the acquisitions of Ligeia were gigantic, were astounding; yet I was sufficiently aware of her infinite supremacy to resign myself, with a child-like confidence, to her guidance through the chaotic world of metaphysical investigation at which I was most busily occupied during the earlier years of our marriage. With how vast a triumph -- with how vivid a delight -- with how much of all that is ethereal in hope - did I *feel*, as she bent over me in studies but little sought -- but less known -- that delicious vista by slow degrees expanding before me, down whose long, gorgeous, and all untrodden path, I might at length pass onward to the goal of a wisdom too divinely precious not to be forbidden!

How poignant, then, must have been the grief with which, after some years, I beheld my well-grounded expectations take wings to themselves and fly away! Without Ligeia I was but as a child groping benighted. Her presence, her readings alone, rendered vividly luminous the many mysteries of the transcendentalism in which we were immersed. Wanting the radiant lustre of her eyes, letters, lambent and golden, grew duller than Saturnian lead. And now those eyes shone less and less frequently upon the pages over which I pored. Ligeia grew ill. The wild eyes blazed with a too -- too glorious effulgence; the pale fingers became of the transparent waxen hue of the grave; and the blue veins upon the lofty forehead swelled and sank

74

impetuously with the tides of the most gentle emotion. I saw that she must die -- and I struggled desperately in spirit with the grim Azrael. And the struggles of the passionate wife were, to my astonishment, even more energetic than my own. There had been much in her stern nature to impress me with the belief that, to her, death would have come without its terrors; but not so. Words are impotent to convey any just idea of the fierceness of resistance with which she wrestled with the Shadow. I groaned in anguish at the pitiable spectacle. I would have soothed -- I would have reasoned; but, in the intensity of her wild desire for life -- for life -- *but* for life -- solace and reason were alike the uttermost of folly. Yet not until the last instance, amid the most convulsive writhings of her fierce spirit, was shaken the external placidity of her demeanour. Her voice grew more gentle -- grew more low -- yet I would not wish to dwell upon the wild meaning of the quietly uttered words. My brain reeled as I hearkened, entranced, to a melody more than mortal -- to assumptions and aspirations which mortality had never before known.

That she loved me I should not have doubted; and I might have been easily aware that, in a bosom such as hers, love would have reigned no ordinary passion. But in death only was I fully impressed with the strength of her affection. For long hours, detaining my hand, would she pour out before me the overflowing of a heart whose more than passionate devotion amounted to idolatry. How had I deserved to be so blessed by such confessions? -- how had I deserved to be so cursed with the removal of my beloved in the hour of her making them? But upon this subject I cannot bear to dilate. Let me say only, that in Ligeia's more than womanly abandonment to love, alas! all unmerited, all unworthily bestowed, I at length recognized the principle of her longing, with so wildly earnest a desire, for the life which was now fleeing so rapidly away. It is this wild longing -- it is this eager vehemence of desire for life -- *but* for life -- that I have no power to portray -- no utterance capable of expressing.

At high noon of the night in which she departed, beckoning me, peremptorily, to her side, she bade me repeat certain verses composed by herself not many days before. I obeyed her. They were these:--

Lo! 'tis a gala night
 Within the lonesome latter years!
An angel throng, bewinged, bedight
 In veils, and drowned in tears,
Sit in a theatre, to see
 A play of hopes and fears,
While the orchestra breathes fitfully
 The music of the spheres.

Mimes, in the form of God on high,
  Mutter and mumble low,
And hither and thither fly;
  Mere puppets they, who come and go
At bidding of vast formless things
  That shift the scenery to and fro,
Flapping from out their condor wings
  Invisible Woe!

That motley drama!-- oh, be sure
  It shall not be forgot!
With its Phantom chased for evermore,
  By a crowd that seize it not,
Through a circle that ever returneth in
  To the self-same spot;
And much of Madness, and more of Sin
  And Horror, the soul of the plot!

But see, amid the mimic rout
  A crawling shape intrude!
A blood-red thing that writhes from out
  The scenic solitude!
It writhes!-- it writhes!-- with mortal pangs
  The mimes become its food,
And the seraphs sob at vermin fangs
  In human gore imbued.

Out -- out are the lights -- out all!
  And over each quivering form,
The curtain, a funeral pall,
  Comes down with the rush of a storm --
And the angels, all pallid and wan,
  Uprising, unveiling, affirm
That the play is the tragedy, "Man",
  And its hero, the Conqueror Worm.

"O God!" half-shrieked Ligeia, leaping to her feet and extending her arms aloft with a spasmodic movement, as I made an end of the lines -- "O God! O Divine Father!- shall these things be undeviatingly so?- shall this conqueror be not once conquered? Are we not part and parcel in Thee? Who -- who knoweth the mysteries of the will with its vigour? Man doth not yield him to the angels, *nor unto death utterly*, save only through the weakness of his feeble will."

And now, as if exhausted with emotion, she suffered her white arms to fall, and returned solemnly to her bed of death. And as she breathed her last sighs, there came mingled with them a slow murmur from her lips. I bent them to my ear, and distinguished again, the concluding words of the passage in Glanvil:-- *"Man doth not yield him to the angels, nor unto death utterly, save only through the weakness of his feeble will."*

She died: and I, crushed into the very dust with sorrow, could no longer endure the lonely desolation of my dwelling in the dim and decaying city by the Rhine. I had no lack of what the world calls wealth. Ligeia had brought me far more, very far more than ordinarily falls to the lot of mortals. After a few months, therefore, of weary and aimless wandering, I purchased, and put in some repair, an abbey, which I shall not name, in one of the wildest and least frequented portions of fair England. The gloomy and dreary grandeur of the building, the almost savage aspect of the domain, the many melancholy and time-honoured memories connected with both, had much in unison with with the feelings of utter abandonment which had driven me into that remote and unsocial region of the country. Yet although the external abbey, with its verdant decay hanging about it, suffered but little alteration, I gave way, with child-like perversity, and perchance with a faint hope of alleviating my sorrows, to a display of more than regal magnificence within. For such follies, even in childhood, I had imbibed a taste, and now they came back to me as if in the dotage of grief. Alas, I feel how much even of incipient madness might have been discovered in the gorgeous and fantastic draperies, in the solemn carvings of Egypt, in the wild cornices and furniture, in the Bedlam patterns of the carpets of tufted gold? I had become a bounden slave in the trammels of opium, and my labours and my orders had taken a colouring from my dreams. But these absurdities I must not pause to detail. Let me speak only of that one chamber, whither in a moment of mental alienation, I led from the altar as my bride -- as the successor of the unforgotten Ligeia -- the fair-haired and blue-eyed Lady Rowena Trevanion, of Tremaine.

There is no individual portion of the architecture and decoration of that bridal chamber which is not now visibly before me. Where were the souls of the haughty family of the bride, when, through thirst of gold, they permitted to pass the threshold of an apartment so bedecked, a maiden and a daughter so beloved? I have said, that I minutely remenber the details of the chamber -- yet I am sadly forgetful on topics of deep moment; and here there was no system, no keeping, in the fantastic display, to take hold upon the memory. The room lay in a high turret of the castellated abbey, was pentagonal in shape, and of capacious size. Occupying the whole southern face of the pentagon was the sole window -- an immense sheet of unbroken glass from Venice -- a single pane, and tinted of a leaden hue, so that the rays of either the sun or moon passing through it, fell with a ghastly lustre on the objects within. Over the upper portion of this huge window extended the trellis-work of an aged vine, which clambered up the massy walls of the turret. The ceiling, of gloomy-looking oak, was excessively lofty, vaulted, and elaborately fretted with the wildest and most grotesque specimens of a semi-Gothic, semi-Druidical device. From out the most central recess of this melancholy vaulting, depended, by a single chain of gold with long links, a huge censer of the same metal, Saracenic in pattern, and with many perforations so contrived that there writhed in and out of them, as if endued with a serpent vitality, a continual succession of parti-coloured fires.

Some few ottomans and golden candelabra, of Eastern figure, were in various stations about; and there was the couch, too -- the bridal couch -- of an Indian model, and low, and sculptured of solid ebony, with a pall-like canopy above. In each of the angles of the chamber stood on end a gigantic sarcophagus of black granite, from the tombs of the kings over against Luxor, with their aged lids full of immemorial sculpture. But in the draping of the apartment lay, alas! the chief fantasy of all. The lofty walls, gigantic in height -- even unproportionately so -- were hung from summit to foot, in vast folds, with a heavy and massive-looking tapestry -- tapestry of a material which was found alike as a carpet on the floor, as a covering for the ottomans and the ebony bed, as a canopy for the bed, and as the gorgeous volutes of the curtains which partially shaded the window. The material was the richest cloth of gold. It was spotted all over, at irregular intervals, with arabesque figures, about a foot in diameter, and wrought upon the cloth in patterns of the most jetty black. But these figures partook of the true character of the arabesque only when regarded from a single point of view. By a contrivance now common, and indeed traceable to a very remote period of antiquity, they were made changeable in aspect. To one entering the room, they bore the appearance of simple monstrosities; but upon a farther advance, this appearance gradually departed; and, step by step, as the visitor moved his station in the chamber, he saw himself surrounded by an endless succession of the ghastly forms which belong to the superstition of the Norman, or arise in the guilty slumbers of the monk. The phantasmagoric effect was vastly heightened by the artificial introduction of a strong continual current of wind behind the draperies -- giving a hideous and uneasy animation to the whole.

In halls such as these -- in a bridal chamber such as this -- I passed, with the Lady of Tremaine, the unhallowed hours of the first month of our marriage -- passed them with but little disquietude. That my wife dreaded the fierce moodiness of my temper -- that she shunned me, and loved me but little -- I could not help perceiving; but it gave me rather pleasure than otherwise. I loathed her with a hatred belonging more to demon than to man. My memory flew back (oh, with what intensity of regret!) to Ligeia, the beloved, the august, the beautiful, the entombed. I revelled in recollections of her purity, of her wisdom, of her lofty, her ethereal nature, of her passionate, her idolatrous love. Now, then, did my spirit fully and freely burn with more than all the fires of her own. In the excitement of my opium dreams (for I was habitually fettered in the shackles of the drug), I would call aloud upon her name, during the silence of the night, or among the sheltered recesses of the glens by day, as if, through the wild eagerness, the solemn passion, the consuming ardour of my longing for the departed, I could restore her to the pathway she had abandoned -- ah, *could* it be forever? -- upon the earth.

About the commencement of the second month of the marriage, the Lady Rowena was attacked with a sudden illness, from which her recovery was slow. The fever which consumed her rendered her nights uneasy; and in her perturbed state of half-slumber, she spoke of sounds, and of motions, in and about the chamber of the turret, which I concluded had no origin save in the distemper of her fancy, or perhaps in the phantasmagoric influences of the chamber itself. She became at length convalescent - finally, well. Yet but a brief period elapsed ere a second more violent disorder again threw her upon a bed of suffering; and from this attack her frame, at all times feeble, never altogether recovered. Her illnesses were, after this epoch, of alarming character, and of more alarming recurrence, defying alike the knowledge and the great exertions of her physicians. With the increase of the chronic disease, which had thus, apparently, taken too sure hold upon her constitution to be eradicated by human means, I could not fail to observe a similar increase in the nervous irritation of her temperament, and in her excitability by trivial causes of fear. She spoke again, and now more frequently and pertinaciously, of the sounds -- of the slight sounds -- and of the unusual motions among the tapestries, to which she had formerly alluded.

One night, near the closing in of September, she pressed this distressing subject with more than usual emphasis upon my attention. She had just wakened from an unquiet slumber, and I had been watching, with feelings half of anxiety, half of vague terror, the workings of her emaciated countenance. I sat by the side of her ebony bed, upon one of the ottomans of India. She partly arose, and spoke, in an earnest low whisper, of sounds which she *then* heard, but which I could not hear -- of motions which she *then* saw, but which I could not perceive. The wind was rushing hurriedly behind the tapestries, and I wished to show her (what, let me confess it, I could not *all* believe) that those almost inarticulate breathings, and those very gentle variations of the figures upon the wall, were but the natural effects of that customary rushing of the wind. But a deadly pallor, overspreading her face, had proved to me that my exertions to reassure her would be fruitless. She appeared to be fainting, and no attendants were within call. I remembered where was deposited a decanter of light wine which had been ordered by her physicians, and hastened across the chamber to procure it. But, as I stepped beneath the light of the censer, two circumstances of a startling nature attracted my attention. I had felt that some palpable though invisible object had passed lightly by my person; and I saw that there lay upon the golden carpet, in the very middle of the rich lustre thrown from the censer, a shadow -- a faint, indefinite shadow of angelic aspect -- such as might be fancied for the shadow of a shade. But I was wild with the excitement of an immoderate dose of opium, and heeded these things but little, nor spoke of them to Rowena. Having found the wine,

I recrossed the chamber, and poured out a gobletful, which I held to the lips of the fainting lady. She had now partially recovered, however, and took the vessel herself, while I sank upon an ottoman near me, with my eyes fastened upon her person. It was then that I became distinctly aware of a gentle footfall upon the carpet, and near the couch; and in a second thereafter, as Rowena was in the act of raising the wine to her lips, I saw, or may have dreamed that I saw, fall within the goblet, as if from some invisible spring in the atmosphere of the room, three or four large drops of a brilliant and ruby-coloured fluid. If this I saw -- not so Rowena. She swallowed the wine unhesitatingly, and I forebore to speak to her of a circumstance which must, after all, I considered, have been but the suggestion of a vivid imagination, rendered morbidly active by the terror of the lady, by the opium, and by the hour.

Yet I cannot conceal it from my own perception that, immediately subsequent to the fall of the ruby-drops, a rapid change for the worse took place in the disorder of my wife; so that, on the third subsequent night, the hands of her menials prepared her for the tomb, and on the fourth, I sat alone, with her shrouded body, in that fantastic chamber which had received her as my bride. Wild visions, opium-engendered, flitted, shadow-like, before me. I gazed with unquiet eye upon the sarcophagi in the angles of the room, upon the varying figures of the drapery, and upon the writhing of the parti-coloured fires in the censers overhead. My eyes then fell, as I called to mind the circumstances of a former night, to the spot beneath the glare of the censer where I had seen the faint traces of the shadow. It was there, however, no longer; and breathing with greater freedom, I turned my glances to the pallid and rigid figure upon the bed. Then rushed upon me a thousand memories of Ligeia -- and then came back upon my heart, with the turbulent violence of a flood, the whole of that unutterable woe with which I had regarded *her* thus enshrouded. The night waned; and still, with a bosom full of bitter thoughts of the one only and supremely beloved, I remained gazing upon the body of Rowena.

It might have been midnight, or perhaps earlier, or later, for I had taken no note of time, when a sob, low, gentle, but very distinct, startled me from my revery. I *felt* that it came from the bed of ebony -- the bed of death. I listened in an agony of superstitious terror -- but there was no repetition of the sound. I strained my vision to detect any motion in the corpse -- but there was not the slightest perceptible. Yet I could not have been deceived. I *had* heard the noise, however faint, and my soul was awakened within me. I resolutely and perseveringly kept my attention riveted upon the body. Many minutes elapsed before any circumstance occurred tending to throw light upon the mystery. At length it became evident that a slight, a very feeble, and barely noticeable tinge of colour had flushed up within the cheeks, and along the sunken small veins of the eyelids. Through a species of unutterable horror and awe, for which the language of mortality has no sufficiently energetic expression, I felt my heart cease to beat, my limbs grow rigid where I sat. Yet a sense of duty finally operated to restore my self-possession. I could no longer doubt that we had been precipitate in our preparations -- that Rowena still lived. It was necessary that some immediate exertion be made; yet the turret was altogether apart from the portion of the abbey tenanted by the servants -- there were none within call -- I had no means of summoning them to my aid without leaving the room for many minutes -- and this I could not venture to do. I therefore struggled alone in my endeavours to call back the spirit still hovering. In a short period it was certain, however, that a relapse had taken place; the colour disappeared from both eyelid and cheek, leaving a wanness even more than that of marble; the lips became doubly shrivelled and pinched up in the ghastly expression of death; a repulsive clamminess and coldness overspread rapidly the surface of the body; and all the usual rigorous stiffness immediately supervened. I fell back with a shudder upon the couch from which I had been so startlingly aroused, and again gave myself up to passionate waking visions of Ligeia.

An hour thus elapsed, when (could it be possible?) I was a second time aware of some vague sound issuing from the region of the bed. I listened -- in extremity of horror. The sound came again -- it was a sigh. Rushing to the corpse, I saw -- distinctly saw -- a tremor upon the lips. In a minute afterward they relaxed, disclosing a bright line of the pearly teeth. Amazement now struggled in my bosom with the profound awe which had hitherto reigned there alone. I felt that my vision grew dim, that my reason wandered; and it was only by a violent effort that I at length succeeded in nerving myself to the task which duty thus once more had pointed out. There was now a partial glow upon the forehead and upon the cheek; a perceptible warmth pervaded the whole frame; there was even a slight pulsation at the heart. The lady *lived*; and with a redoubled ardour I betook myself to the task of restoration. I chafed and bathed the temples and the hands, and used every exertion which experience, and no little medical reading, could suggest. But in vain. Suddenly, the colour fled, the pulsation ceased, the lips resumed the expression of the dead, and, in an instant afterward, the whole body took upon itself the icy chilliness, the livid hue, the intense rigidity, the sunken outline, and all the loathesome peculiarities of that which has been, for many days, a tenant of the tomb.

And again I sunk into visions of Ligeia -- and again, (what marvel that I shudder while I write?) *again* there reached my ears a low sob from the region of the ebony bed. But why shall I minutely detail the unspeakable horrors of that night? Why shall I pause to relate how, time after time, until near the period of the grey dawn, this hideous drama of revivification was repeated; how each terrific relapse was only into a sterner and apparently more irredeemable death; how each agony wore the aspect of a struggle with some invisible foe; and how each struggle was succeeded by I know not what of wild change in the personal appearance of the corpse? Let me hurry to a conclusion.

The greater part of the fearful night had worn away, and she who had been dead, once again stirred -- and now more vigorously than hitherto, although arousing from a dissolution more appalling in its utter hopelessness than any. I had long ceased to struggle or to move, and remained sitting rigidly upon the ottoman, a helpless prey to a whirl of violent emotions, of which extreme awe was perhaps the least terrible, the least consuming. The corpse, I repeat, stirred, and now more vigorously than before. The hues of life flushed up with unwonted energy into the countenance -- the limbs relaxed -- and, save that the eyelids were yet pressed heavily together and that the bandages and draperies of the grave still imparted their charnel character to the figure, I might have dreamed that Rowena had indeed shaken off, utterly, the fetters of Death. But if this idea was not, even then, altogether adopted, I could at least doubt no longer, when arising from the bed, tottering, with feeble steps, with closed eyes, and with the manner of one bewildered in a dream, the thing that was enshrouded advanced boldly and palpably into the middle of the apartment.

I trembled not -- I stirred not -- for a crowd of unutterable fancies connected with the air, the stature, the demeanour of the figure, rushing hurriedly through my brain, had paralyzed -- had chilled me into stone. I stirred not -- but gazed upon the apparition. There was a mad disorder in my thoughts -- a tumult unappeasable. Could it, indeed, be the *living* Rowena who confronted me? Could it indeed be Rowena *at all* -- the fair-haired, the blue-eyed Lady Rowena Trevanion of Tremaine? Why, *why* should I doubt it? The bandage lay heavily -- but then might it not be the mouth of the breathing Lady of Tremaine? And the cheeks -- there were the roses as in her noon of life -- yes, these might indeed be the fair cheeks of the living Lady of Tremaine. And the chin, with its dimples, as in health, might it not be hers?- but *had she then grown taller since her malady?* What inexpressible madness seized me with that thought! One bound, and I had reached her feet! Shrinking from my touch, she let fall from her head, unloosened, the ghastly cerements which had confined it, and there streamed forth, into the rushing atmosphere of the chamber, huge masses of long and dishevelled hair; *it was blacker than the raven wings of midnight!* And now slowly opened *the eyes* of the figure which stood before me. "Here then, at least," I shrieked aloud, "can I never -- can I never be mistaken -- these are the full, and the black, and the wild eyes -- of my lost love -- of the Lady -- of the LADY LIGEIA."

THE FEAST OF BLOOD

J.M. Rymer

The solemn tones of an old cathedral clock have announced midnight -- the air is thick and heavy -- a strange, death-like stillness pervades all nature. Like the ominous calm which precedes some more than usually terrific outburst of the elements, they seem to have paused even in their ordinary fluctuations, to gather a terrific strength for the great effort. A faint peal of thunder now comes from far off. Like a signal gun for the battle of the winds to begin, it appeared to awaken them from their lethargy, and one awful, warring hurricane swept over a whole city, producing more devastation in the four or five minutes it lasted, than would a half century of ordinary phenomena.

It was as if some giant had blown upon some toy town, and scattered many of the buildings before the hot blast of his terrific breath; for as suddenly as that blast of wind had come did it cease, and all was as still and calm as before.

Sleepers awakened, and thought that what they had heard must be the chimera of a dream. They trembled and turned to sleep again.

All is still -- still as the very grave. Not a sound breaks the magic of repose. What is that -- a strange, pattering noise, as of a million of fairy feet? It is hail -- yes, a hail-storm has burst over the city. Leaves are dashed from the trees, mingled with the small boughs; windows that lie most opposed to the direct fury of the pelting particles of ice are broken, and the rapt repose that before was so remarkable in its intensity, is exchanged for a noise which, in its accumulation, drowns every cry of surprise or consternation which here and there arose from persons who found their houses invaded by the storm.

Now and then, too, there would come a sudden gust of wind that in its strength, as it blew laterally, would, for a moment, hold millions of the hailstones suspended in mid-air, but it was only to dash them with redoubled force in some new direction, where more mischief was to be done.

Oh, how the storm raged! Hail -- rain -- wind. It was, in very truth, an awful night.

There is an antique chamber in an ancient house. Curious and quaint carvings adorn the walls, and the large chimney-piece is a curiosity of itself. The ceiling is low, and a large bay window, from roof to floor, looks to the west. The window is latticed, and filled with curiously painted glass and rich stained pieces, which send in a strange, yet beautiful light, when sun or moon shines into the apartment. There is but one portrait in that room, although the walls seem panelled for the express purpose of containing a series of pictures. That portrait is of a young man, with a pale face, a stately brow, and a strange expression about the eyes, which no-one cared to look on twice.

There is a stately bed in that chamber, of carved walnutwood is it made, rich in design and elaborate in execution; one of those works of art which owe their existence to the Elizabethan era. It is hung with heavy silken and damask furnishing; nodding feathers are at its corners -- covered in dust are they, and they lend a funereal aspect to the room. The floor is of polished oak.

God! how the hail dashes on the old bay window! Like an occasional discharge of mimic musketry, it comes clashing, beating, and cracking upon the small panes; but they resist it -- their small size saves them; the wind, the hail, the rain, expend their fury in vain.

The bed in that old chamber is occupied. A creature formed in all fashions of loveliness lies in a half sleep upon that ancient couch -- a girl young and beautiful as a Spring morning. Her long hair has escaped from its confinement and streams over the blackened coverings of the bedstead; she has been restless in her sleep, for the clothing of the bed is in much confusion. One arm is over her head, the other hangs nearly off the side of the bed near to which she lies. A neck and bosom that would have formed a study for the rarest sculptor that ever Providence gave genius to, were half disclosed. She moaned slightly in her sleep, and once or twice the lips moved as if in prayer -- at least one might judge so, for the name of Him who suffered for all came once faintly from them.

She has endured much fatigue, and the storm does not awaken her; but it can disturb the slumbers it does not possess the power to destroy completely. The turmoil of the elements wakes the senses, although it cannot entirely break the repose they have lapsed into.

Oh, what a world of witchery was in that mouth, slightly parted, and exhibiting within the pearly teeth that glistened even in the faint light that came from that bay window. How sweetly the long silken eyelashes lay upon the cheek. Now she moves, and one shoulder is entirely visible -- whiter, fairer than the spotless clothing of the bed on which she lies, is the smooth skin of that fair creature, just budding into womanhood, and in that transition state which presents to us all the charms of the girl -- almost of the child, with the more matured beauty and gentleness of advancing years.

Was that lightning? Yes -- an awful, vivid, terrifying flash -- then a roaring peal of thunder, as if a thousand mountains were rolling one over the other in the blue vault of Heaven! Who sleeps now in that ancient city? Not one living soul. The dread trumpet of eternity could not more effectually have awakened anyone.

The hail continues. The wind continues. The uproar of the elements seems at its height. Now she awakens -- that beautiful girl on the antique bed; she opens those eyes of celestial blue, and a faint cry of alarm bursts from her lips. At least it is a cry which, amid the noise and turmoil without, sounds but faint and weak. She sits upon the bed and presses her hands upon her eyes. Heavens! what a wild torrent of wind, and rain, and hail! The thunder likewise seems intent upon awakening sufficient echoes to last until the next flash of forked lightning should again produce the wild concussion of the air. She murmurs a prayer -- a prayer for those she loves best; the names of those dear to her gentle heart come from her lips; she weeps and prays; she thinks then of what devastation the storm must surely produce, and to the great God of Heaven she prays for all living things. Another flash -- a wild, blue, bewildering flash of lightning streams across that bay window, for an instant bringing out every colour in it with terrible distinctness. A shriek bursts from the lips of the young girl, and then, with eyes fixed upon that window, which, in another moment, is all darkness, and with such an expression of terror upon her face as it had never before known, she trembled, and the perspiration of intense fear stood upon her brow.

"What -- what was it?" she gasped; "Real, or delusion? Oh, God, what was it? A figure tall and gaunt, endeavouring from the outside to unclasp the window. I saw it. That flash of lightning revealed it to me. It stood the whole length of the window."

There was a lull of the wind. The hail was not falling so thickly -- moreover, now it fell, what there was of it, straight, and yet a strange clattering sound came upon the glass of that long window. It could not be a delusion -- she is awake, and she hears it. What can produce it? Another flash of lightning -- another shriek -- there could now be no delusion.

A tall figure is standing on the ledge immediately outside the long window. It is its finger-nails upon the glass that produces the sound so like the hail, now that the hail has ceased. Intense fear paralyses the limbs of that beautiful girl. That one shriek is all she can utter -- with hands clasped, a face of marble, a heart beating so wildly in her bosom, that each moment it seems as if it would break its confines, eyes distended and fixed upon the window, she waits, frozen with horror. The pattering and clattering of the nails continue. No word is spoken, and now she fancies she can trace the darker form of that figure against the window, and she can see the long arms moving to and fro, feeling for some mode of entrance. What strange light is

85

that which now gradually creeps up into the air? red and terrible -- brighter and brighter it grows. The lightning has set fire to a mill, and the reflection of the rapidly consuming building falls upon that long window. There can be no mistake. The figure is there, still feeling for an entrance, and clattering against the glass with its long nails, that appear as if the growth of many years had been untouched. She tries to scream again but a choking sensation comes over her, and she cannot. It is too dreadful -- she tries to move -- each limb seems weighed down by tons of lead -- she can but in a hoarse faint whisper:--

"Help -- help -- help -- help!"

And that one word she repeats like a person in a dream. The red glare of the fire continues. It throws up the tall gaunt figure in hideous relief against the long window. It shows, too, upon the one portrait that is in the chamber, and that portrait appears to fix its eyes upon the attempting intruder, while the flickering light from the fire makes it look fearfully life-like. A small pane of glass is broken, and the form from without introduces a long gaunt hand, which seems utterly destitute of flesh. The fastening is removed, and one half of the window, which opens like folding doors, is swung wide open upon its hinges.

And yet now she could not scream -- she could not move. "Help -- help! -- help!" was all she could say. But, oh, that look of terror that sat upon her face, it was dreadful -- a look to haunt the memory for a lifetime -- a look to obtrude itself upon the happiest moments, and turn them to bitterness.

The figure turns half around, and the light falls upon the face. It is perfectly white -- perfectly bloodless. The eyes look like polished tin; the lips are drawn back, and the principal feature next to those dreadful eyes is the teeth -- the fearful-looking teeth -- projecting like those of some wild animal, hideously, glaringly white, and fang-like. It approaches the bed with a strange, gliding movement. It clashes together the long nails that literally appear to hang from the finger ends. No sound comes from its lips. Is she going mad -- that young and beautiful girl exposed to so much terror? she has drawn up all her limbs; she cannot even now say help. The power of articulation is gone, but the power of movement has returned to her; she can draw herself slowly along to the other side of the bed from that towards which the hideous appearance is coming.

But her eyes are fascinated. The glance of a serpent could not have produced a greater effect upon her than did the fixed gaze of those awful, metallic-looking eyes that were bent on her face. Crouching down so that the gigantic height was lost, and the horrible, protruding, white face was the most prominent object, came on the figure. What was it? -- what did it want there? -- what made it look so hideous -- so unlike an inhabitant of the earth, and yet to be on it?

Now she has got to the verge of the bed, and the figure pauses. It seemed as if when it paused she lost the power to proceed. The clothing of the bed was now clutched in her hands with unconscious power. She drew her breath short and thick. Her bosom heaves, and her limbs tremble, yet she cannot withdraw her eyes from that marble-looking face. He holds her with his glittering eye.

The storm has ceased -- all is still. The winds are hushed; the church clock proclaims the hour of one: a hissing sound comes from the throat of the hideous being, and he raises his long, gaunt arms -- the lips move. He advances. The girl places one small foot from the bed on to the floor. She is unconsciously dragging the clothing with her. The door of the room is in that direction -- can she reach it? Has she power to walk? -- can she withdraw her eyes from the face of the intruder, and so break the hideous charm? God of Heaven! is it real, or some dream so like reality as to nearly overturn the judgement for ever?

The figure has paused again, and half on the bed and half out of it that young girl lies trembling. Her long hair streams across the entire width of the bed. As she has slowly moved along she has left it streaming across the pillows. The pause lasted about a minute -- oh, what an age of agony. That minute was, indeed, enough for madness to do its full work in.

With a sudden rush that could not be foreseen -- with a strange howling cry that was enough to awaken terror in every breast, the figure seized the long tresses of her hair, and twining them round his bony hands he held her to the bed. Then she screamed -- Heaven granted her the power to scream. Shriek followed shriek in rapid succession. The bed-clothes fell in a heap by the side of the bed -- she was dragged by her long silken hair completely on to it again. Her beautifully rounded limbs quivered with the agony of her soul. The glassy, horrible eyes of the figure ran over that angelic form with a hideous satisfaction -- horrible profanation. He drags her head to the bed's edge. He forces it back by the long hair still entwined in his grasp. With a hideous plunge he seizes her neck in his fang-like teeth -- a gush of blood, and a hideous sucking noise follows. *The girl has swooned, and the vampyre is at his hideous repast!*

JANE EYRE

Charlotte Brontë

(Chapter XIX)

I had forgotten to draw my curtain, which I usually did, and also to let down my window-blind. The consequence was, that when the moon, which was full and bright (for the night was fine), came in her course to that space in the sky opposite my casement, and looked in at me through the unveiled panes, her glorious gaze roused me. Awakening in the dead of night, I opened my eyes on her disc -- silver-white and crystal clear. It was beautiful, but too solemn: I half rose, and stretched my arm to draw the curtain.

Good God! What a cry!

The night -- its silence -- its rest, was rent in twain by a savage, a sharp, a shrilly sound that ran from end to end of Thornfield Hall.

My pulse stopped: my heart stood still; my stretched arm was paralysed. The cry died, and was not renewed. Indeed, whatever being uttered that fearful shriek could not soon repeat it: not the wildest-winged condor on the Andes could, twice in succession, send out such a yell from the cloud shrouding his eyrie. The thing delivering such utterance must rest ere it could repeat the effort.

It came out of the third storey; for it passed overhead. And overhead -- yes, in the room just above my chamber-ceiling -- I now heard a struggle: a deadly one it seemed from the noise; and a half-smothered voice shouted:--

"Help! help! help!" three times rapidly.

"Will no one come?" it cried; and then, while the staggering and stamping went on wildly, I distinguished through plank and palster:--

"Rochester! Rochester! for God's sake, come!"

A chamber-door opened: some one ran, or rushed, along the gallery. Another step stamped on the flooring above and something fell: and there was silence.

(Chapter XXIV)

... On waking, a gleam dazzled my eyes; I thought oh, it is daylight! But I was mistaken; it was only candlelight. Sophie, I supposed, had come in. There was a light on the dressing-table, and the door of the closet, where, before going to bed, I had hung my wedding-dress and veil, stood open; I heard a rustling there. I asked, "Sophie, what are you doing?" No one answered; but a form emerged from the closet; it took the light, held it aloft, and surveyed the garments pendent from the portmanteau. "Sophie! Sophie!" I again cried: and still it was silent. I had risen up in bed, I bent forward: first surprise, then bewilderment, came over me; and then my blood crept cold through my veins. Mr. Rochester, this was not Sophie, it was not Leah, it was not Mrs. Fairfax: it was not -- no, I was sure of it, and am still -- it was not even that strange woman, Grace Poole."

"It must have been one of them," interrupted my master.

"No, sir, I solemnly assure you to the contrary. The shape standing before me had never crossed my eyes within the precincts of Thornfield Hall before; the height, the contour were new to me."

"Describe it, Jane."

"It seemed, sir, a woman, tall and large, with thick and dark hair hanging long down her back. I know not what dress she had on: it was white and straight; but whether gown, sheet, or shroud, I cannot tell."

"Did you see her face?"

"Not at first. But presently she took my veil from its place: she held it up, gazed at it long, and then, she threw it over her own head, and turned to the mirror. At that moment I saw the reflection of the visage and features quite distinctly in the dark oblong glass."

"And how were they?"

"Fearful and ghastly to me -- oh, sir, I never saw a face like it! It was a discoloured face -- it was a savage face. I wish I could forget the roll of the red eyes and the fearful blackened inflation of the lineaments!"

"Ghosts are usually pale, Jane."

"This, sir, was purple: the lips were swelled and dark; the brow furrowed: the black eyebrows widely raised over the bloodshot eyes. Shall I tell you of what it reminded me?"

"You may."

"Of the foul German spectre - the Vampyre."

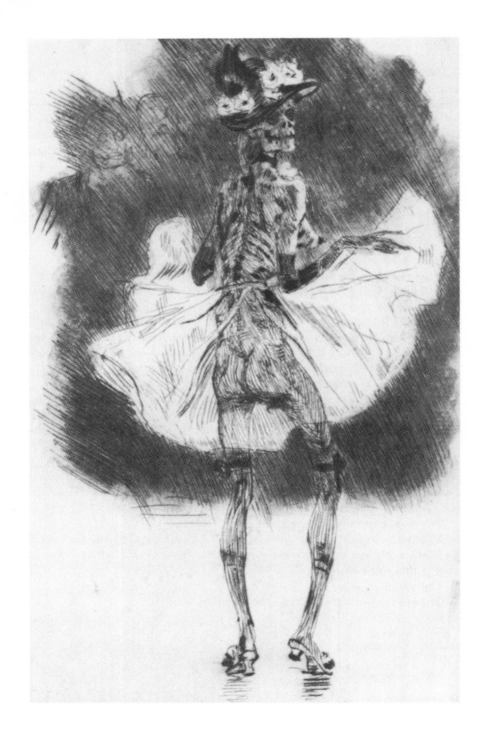

THE VAMPIRE'S METAMORPHOSES

Charles Baudelaire

The woman with the scarlet lipsticked mouth
crackled like a snake spitting on red coals,
popped her melon breasts from a black waspie,
and with her perfumed tongue nibbled these words
into my ear: "My moist red lips convey
the art of extracting a cruel conscience;
couched on my breasts old men revive their youth
and imagine they can make love all day...
Those who see me naked, have seen the stars,
my dexterity in love can entwine
a man with the persistence of a vine;
my arms strangle or crack a back, but they
are so enflamed, so importunately
white-hot on these cushions, they lose all sense
of retribution in my kitten's play."

When she had sucked the pearl beads from my cock,
and I responding to her needling kiss
tried to twist my body on hers, I saw
a leather bottle brimming with impure
toxins from my body; and in her place
occupying the bed's concave hollow,
there shook the remains of a skeleton,
its dry voice creaking like a weathercock
or sign-board that rustily swings
in the wind on a stormy winter's night.

Translated by **Jeremy Reed**

THE HOUSE AND THE BRAIN

Edward Bulwer-Lytton

A friend of mine, who is a man of letters and a philosopher, said to me one day, as if between jest and earnest, -- "Fancy! since we last met, I have discovered a haunted house in the midst of London."

"Really haunted? -- and by what? ghosts?"

"Well, I can't answer that question; all I know is this -- six weeks ago my wife and I were in search of a furnished apartment. Passing a quiet street, we saw on the window of one of the houses a bill, "Apartments Furnished". The situation suited us: we entered the house -- liked the rooms -- engaged them by the week -- and left them the third day. No power on earth could have reconciled my wife to stay longer; and I don't wonder at it."

"What did you see?"

"Excuse me -- I have no desire to be ridiculed as a superstitious dreamer -- nor, on the other hand, could I ask you to accept on my affirmation what you would hold to be incredible without the evidence of your own senses. Let me only say this, it was not so much what we saw or heard (in which you might fairly suppose that we were the dupes of our own excited fancy, or the victims of imposture in others) that drove us away, as it was an undefinable terror which seized both of us whenever we passed by the door of a certain unfurnished room, in which we neither saw nor heard anything. And the strangest marvel of all was, that for once in my life I agreed with my wife, silly woman though she be -- and allowed, after the third night, that it was impossible to stay a fourth in that house. Accordingly, on the fourth morning I summoned the woman who kept the house and attended on us, and told her that the rooms did not quite suit us, and we would not stay out our week. She said, dryly, *I know why; you have stayed longer than any other lodger. Few ever stayed a second night; none before you a third. But I take it they have been very kind to you.*

"*They -- who?* I asked, affecting a smile.

"*Why, they who haunt the house, whoever they are. I don't mind them; I remember them many years ago, when I lived in this house, not as a*

93

*servant; but I know they will be the death of me some day. I don't care --
I'm old, and must die soon anyhow; and then I shall be with them, and in
this house still.* The woman spoke with so dreary a calmness, that really it
was a sort of awe which prevented my conversing with her further. I paid for
my week, and too happy were my wife and I to get off so cheaply."

"You excite my curiosity," said I; "nothing I should like better than to
sleep in a haunted house. Pray give me the address of the one which you left
so ignominiously."

My friend gave me the address; and when we parted, I walked straight
towards the house thus indicated.

It is situated on the north side of Oxford Street, in a dull but respectable
thoroughfare. I found the house shut up -- no bill at the window, and no
response to my knock. As I was turning away, a beer-boy, collecting pewter
pots at the neighbouring areas, said to me, "Do you want any one at that
house, sir?"

"Yes, I heard it was to be let."

"Let! -- why, the woman who kept it is dead -- has been dead these three
weeks, and no one can be found to stay there, though Mr. J_____ offered
ever so much. He offered mother, who chars for him, £1 a week just to open
and shut the windows, and she would not."

"Would not! -- and why?"

"The house is haunted; and the old woman who kept it was found dead
in her bed, with her eyes wide open. They say the devil strangled her."

"Pooh! -- you speak of Mr. J_____. Is he the owner of the house?"

"Yes."

"Where does he live?"

"In G_____ Street, No. _."

"What is he? -- in any business?"

"No, sir -- nothing particular; a single gentleman."

I gave the pot-boy the gratuity earned by his liberal information, and
proceeded to Mr. J_____, in G_____ Street, which was close by the street
which boasted the haunted house. I was lucky enough to find Mr. J_____ at
home -- an elderly man, with intelligent countenance and prepossessing
manners.

I communicated my name and my business frankly. I said I heard the
house was considered to be haunted -- that I had a strong desire to examine
a house with so equivocal a reputation -- that I should be greatly obliged if
he would allow me to hire it, though only for a night. I was willing to pay for
that privilege whatever he might be inclined to ask.

"Sir," said Mr. J_____, with great courtesy, "the house is at your service,
for as short or as long a time as you please. Rent is out of the question -- the
obligation will be on my side should you be able to discover the cause of the
strange phenomena which at present deprive it of all value. I cannot let it,
for I cannot even get a servant to keep it in order or answer the door.

94

Unluckily the house is haunted, if I may use that expression, not only by night, but by day; though at night the disturbances are of a more unpleasant and sometimes of a more alarming character. The poor old woman who died in it three weeks ago was a pauper whom I took out of a workhouse, for in her childhood she had been known to some of my family, and had once been in such good circumstances that she had rented that house of my uncle. She was a woman of superior education and strong mind, and was the only person I could ever induce to remain in the house. Indeed, since her death, which was sudden, and the coroner's inquest, which gave it a notoriety in the neighbourhood, I have so despaired of finding any person to take charge of the house, much more a tenant, that I would willingly let it rent-free for a year to any one who would pay its rates and taxes."

"How long is it since the house acquired this sinister character?"

"That I can scarcely tell you, but very many years since. The old woman I spoke of said it was haunted when she rented it between thirty and forty years ago. The fact is, that my life has been spent in the East Indies, and in the civil service of the Company. I returned to England last year, on inheriting the fortune of an uncle, among whose possessions was the house in question. I found it shut up and uninhabited. I was told that it was haunted, that no one owuld inhabit it. I smiled at what seemed to me so idle a story. I spent some money in repairing it -- added to its old-fashioned furniture a few modern articles -- advertised it, and obtained a lodger for a year. He was a colonel retired on half-pay. He came in with his family, a son and a daughter, and four or five servants: they all left the house the next day; and, although each of them declared that he had seen something different from that which had scared the others, a something still was equally terrible to all. I really could not in conscience sue, nor even blame, the colonel for breach of agreement. Then I put in the old woman I have spoken of, and she was empowered to let the house in apartments. I never had one lodger who stayed more than three days. I do not tell you their stories -- to no two lodgers have there been exactly the same phenomena repeated. It is better that you should judge for yourself, than enter the house with an imagination influenced by previous narratives; only be prepared to see and to hear something or other, and take whatever precautions you yourself please."

"Have you never had a curiosity yourself to pass a night in that house?"

"Yes. I passed not a night, but three hours in broad daylight alone in that house. My curiosity is not satisfied, but it is quenched. I have no desire to renew the experiment. You cannot complain, you see, sir, that I am not sufficiently candid; and unless your interest be exceedingly eager and your nerves unusually strong, I honestly add, that I advise you *not* to pass a night in that house."

"My interest *is* exceedingly keen," said I, "and though only a coward will boast of his nerves in situations wholly unfamiliar to him, yet my nerves

95

have been seasoned in such variety of danger that I have the right to rely on them -- even in a haunted house."

Mr. J_____ said very little more; he took the keys of the house out of his bureau, gave them to me, -- and, thanking him cordially for his frankness, and his urbane concession to my wish, I carried off my prize.

Impatient for the experiment, as soon as I reached home, I summoned my confidential servant -- a young man of gay spirits, fearless temper, and as free from superstitious prejudice as any one I could think of.

"F_____," said I, "you remember in Germany how disappointed we were at not finding a ghost in that old castle, which was said to be haunted by a headless apparition? Well, I have heard of a house in London which, I have reason to hope, is decidedly haunted. I mean to sleep there to-night. From what I hear, there is no doubt that something will allow itself to be seen or to be heard -- something, perhaps, excessively horrible. Do you think if I take you with me, I may rely on your presence of mind, whatever may happen?"

"Oh, sir! pray trust me," answered F_____, grinning with delight.

"Very well; then here are the keys of the house -- this is the address. Go now, -- select for me any bedroom you please; and since the house has not been inhabited for weeks, make up a good fire -- air the bed well -- see, of course, that there are candles as well as fuel. Take with you my revolver and my dagger -- so much for my weapons -- arm yourself equally well; and if we are not a match for a dozen ghosts, we shall be but a sorry couple of Englishmen."

I was engaged for the rest of the day on business so urgent that I had not leisure to think much on the nocturnal adventure to which I had plighted my honour. I dined alone, and very late, and while dining, read, as is my habit. I selected one of the volumes of Macaulay's Essays. I thought to myself that I would take the book with me; there was so much of healthfulness in the style, and practical life in the subjects, that it would serve as an antidote against the influences of superstitious fancy.

Accordingly, about half-past nine, I put the book into my pocket, and strolled leisurely towards the haunted house. I took with me a favourite dog, -- an exceedingly sharp, bold, and vigilant bull-terrier, -- a dog fond of prowling about strange ghostly corners and passages at night in search of rats -- a dog of dogs for a ghost.

It was a summer night, but chilly, the sky somewhat gloomy and overcast. Still, there was a moon -- faint and sickly, but still a moon -- and if the clouds permitted, after midnight it would be brighter.

I reached the house, knocked, and my servant opened with a cheerful smile.

"All right, sir, and very comfortable."

"Oh!" said I, rather disappointed; "have you not seen nor heard anything remarkable?"

"Well, sir, I must own I have heard something queer."

"What? -- what?"

"The sound of feet pattering behind me; and once or twice small noises like whispers close at my ear -- nothing more."

"You are not at all frightened?"

"I! not a bit of it, sir;" and the man's bold look reassured me on one point -- viz. that happen what might, he would not desert me.

We were in the hall, the street-door closed, and my attention was now drawn to my dog. He had at first run in eagerly enough, but had sneaked back to the door, and was scratching and whining to get out. After patting him on the head, and encouraging him gently, the dog seemed to reconcile himself to the situation, and followed me and F_____ through the house, but keeping close at my heels instead of hurrying inquisitively in advance, which was his usual and normal habit in all strange places. We first visited the subterranean apartments, the kitchen and other offices, and especially the cellars, in which last there were two or three bottles of wine still left in a bin, covered with cobwebs, and evidently, by their appearance, undisturbed for many years. It was clear that the ghosts were not winebibbers. For the rest we discovered nothing of interest. There was a gloomy little backyard, with very high walls. The stones of this yard were very damp; and what with the damp, and what with the dust and smoke-grime on the pavement, our feet left a slight impression where we passed. And now appeared the first strange phenomenon witnessed by myself in this strange abode. I saw, just before me, the print of a foot suddenly form itself, as it were. I stopped, caught hold of my servant, and pointed to it. In advance of that footprint as suddenly dropped another. We both saw it. I advanced quickly to the place; the footprint kept advancing before me, a small footprint -- the foot of a child: the impression was too faint thoroughly to distinguish the shape, but it seemed to us both that it was the print of a naked foot. This phenomenon ceased when we arrived at the opposite wall, nor did it repeat itself on returning. We remounted the stairs, and entered the rooms on the ground floor, a dining parlour, a small back-parlour, and a still smaller third room that had been probably appropriated to a footman -- all still as death. We then visited the drawing-rooms, which seemed fresh and new. In the front room I seated myself in an armchair. F_____ placed on the table the candlestick with which he had lighted us. I told him to shut the door. As he turned to do so, a chair opposite to me moved from the wall quickly and noiselessly, and dropped itself about a yard from my own chair, immediately fronting it.

"Why, this is better than the turning-tables," said I, with a half-laugh; and as I laughed, my dog put back his head and howled.

F_____, coming back, had not observed the movement of the chair. He employed himself now in stilling the dog. I continued to gaze on the chair, and fancied I saw on it a pale blue misty outline of a human figure, but an outline so indistinct that I could only distrust my own vision. The dog now was quiet.

"Put back that chair opposite to me," said I to F_____; "put it back to the wall."

F_____ obeyed. "Was that you, sir?" said he, turning abruptly.

"I! -- what?"

"Why, something struck me. I felt it sharply on the shoulder -- just here."

"No," said I. "But we have jugglers present, and though we may not discover their tricks, we shall catch *them* before they frighten *us*."

We did not stay long in the drawing-rooms -- in fact, they felt so damp and chilly that I was glad to get to the fire upstairs. We locked the doors of the drawing-rooms -- a precaution which, I should observe, we had taken with all the rooms we had searched below. The bedroom my servant had selected for me was the best on the floor -- a large one, with two windows fronting the street. The four-posted bed, which took up no inconsiderable space, was opposite to the fire, which burnt clear and bright; a door in the wall to the left, between the bed and the window, communicated with the room which my servant appropriated to himself. This last was a small roon with a sofa-bed, and had no communication with the landing-place -- no other door but that which conducted to the bedroom I was to occupy. On either side of my fire-place was a cupboard, without locks, flush with the wall, and covered with the same dull-brown paper. We examined these cupboards -- only hooks to suspend female dresses -- nothing else; we sounded the walls -- evidently solid -- the outer walls of the building. Having finished the survey of these apartments, warmed myself a few moments, and lighted my cigar, I then, still accompanied by F_____, went forth to complete my reconnoitre. In the landing-place there was another door; it was closed firmly. "Sir," said my servant, in surprise, "I unlocked this door with all the others when I first came; it cannot have got locked from the inside, for _____"

Before he had finished his sentence, the door, which neither of us then was touching, opened quietly of itself. We looked at each other a single instant. The same thought seized both -- some human agency might be detected here. I rushed in first, my servant followed. A small blank dreary room without furniture -- a few empty boxes and hampers in a corner -- a small window -- the shutters closed -- not even a fire-place -- no other door but that by which we had entered -- no carpet on the floor, and the floor seemed very old, uneven, worm-eaten, mended here and there, as was shown by the whiter patches on the wood; but no living being, and no visible place in which a living being could have hidden. As we stood gazing round, the door by which we had entered closed as quietly as it had before opened: we were imprisoned.

For the first time I felt a creep of undefinable horror. Not so my servant. "Why, they don't think to trap us, sir; I could break that trumpery door with a kick of my foot."

"Try first if it will open to your hand," said I, shaking off the vague apprehension that had seized me, "while I unclose the shutters and see what is without."

I unbarred the shutters -- the window looked on the little back yard I have before described; there was no ledge without -- nothing to break the sheer descent of the wall. No man getting out of that window would have found any footing till he had fallen on the stones below.

F_____, meanwhile, was vainly attempting to open the door. He now turned round to me and asked my permission to use force. And I should here state, in justice to the servant, that, far from evincing any superstitious terrors, his nerve, composure, and even gaiety amidst circumstances so extraordinary, compelled my admiration, and made me congratulate myself on having secured a companion in every way fitted to the occasion. I willingly gave him the permission he required. But though he was a remarkably strong man, his force was as idle as his milder efforts; the door did not even shake to his stoutest kick. Breathless and panting, he desisted. I then tried the door myself, equally in vain. As I ceased from the effort, again that creep of horror came over me; but this time it was more cold and stubborn. I felt as if some strange and ghastly exhalation were rising up from the chinks of that rugged floor, and filling the atmosphere with a venomous influence hostile to human life. The door now very slowly and quietly opened as of its own accord. We precipitated ourselves into the landing-place. We both saw a large pale light -- as large as the human figure, but shapeless and unsubstantial -- move before us, and ascend the stairs that led from the landing into the attics. I followed the light, and my servant followed me. It entered, to the right of the landing, a small garret, of which the door stood open. I entered in the same instant. The light then collapsed into a small globule, exceedingly brilliant and vivid; rested a moment on a bed in the corner, quivered, and vanished. We approached the bed and examined it -- a half-tester, such as is commonly found in attics devoted to servants. On the drawers that stood near it we perceived an old faded silk kerchief, with the needle still left in a rent half repaired. The kerchief was covered with dust; probably it had belonged to the old woman who had last died in that house, and this might have been her sleeping room. I had sufficient curiosity to open the drawers: there were a few odds and ends of female dress, and two letters tied round with a narrow ribbon of faded yellow. I took the liberty to possess myself of the letters. We found nothing else in the room worth noticing -- nor did the light reappear; but we distinctly heard, as we turned to go, a pattering footfall on the floor -- just before us. We went through the other attics (in all four), the footfall still preceding us. Nothing to be seen -- nothing but the footfall heard. I had the letters in my hand: just as I was descending the stairs I distinctly felt my wrist seized, and a faint soft effort

99

made to draw the letters from my clasp. I only held them the more tightly, and the effort ceased.

We regained the bedchamber appropriated to myself, and I then remarked that my dog had not followed us when we had left it. He was thrusting himself close to the fire, and trembling. I was impatient to examine the letters; and while I read them, my servant opened a little box in which he had deposited the weapons I had ordered him to bring; took them out, placed them on a table close at my bed-head, and then occupied himself in soothing the dog, who, however, seemed to heed him very little.

The letters were short -- they were dated; the dates exactly thirty-five years ago. They were evidently from a lover to his mistress, or a husband to some young wife. Not only the terms of expression, but a distinct reference to a former voyage, indicated the writer to have been a seafarer. The spelling and handwriting were those of a man imperfectly educated, but still the language itself was forcible. In the expressions of endearment there was a kind of rough wild love; but here and there were dark unintelligible hints at some secret not of love -- some secret that seemed of crime. "We ought to love each other," was one of the sentences I remember, "for how every one else would execrate us if all was known." Again: "Don't let any one be in the same room with you at night -- you talk in your sleep." And again: "What's done can't be undone; and I tell you there's nothing against us unless the dead could come to life." Here there was underlined in a better handwriting (a female's), "They do!" At the end of the letter latest in date the same female hand had written these words: "Lost at sea the 4th of June, the same day as _____."

I put down the letters, and began to muse over their contents.

Fearing, however, that the train of thought into which I fell might unsteady my nerves, I fully determined to keep my mind in a fit state to cope with whatever of marvellous the advancing night might bring forth. I roused myself -- laid the letters on the table -- stirred up the fire, which was still bright and cheering -- and opened my volume of Macaulay. I read quietly enough till about half-past eleven. I then threw myself dressed upon the bed, and told my servant he might retire to his own room, but must keep himself awake. I bade him leave open the door between the two rooms. Thus alone, I kept two candles burning on the table by my bed-head. I placed my watch beside the weapons, and calmly resumed my Macaulay. Opposite to me the fire burned clear; and on the hearthrug, seemingly asleep, lay the dog. In about twenty minutes I felt an exceedingly cold air pass by my cheek, like a sudden draught. I fancied the door to my right, communicating with the landing-place, must have got open; but no -- it was closed. I then turned my glance to my left, and saw the flame of the candles violently swayed as by a wind. At the same moment the watch beside the revolver softly slid from the table -- softly, softly -- no visible hand -- it was gone. I sprang up, seizing the revolver with the one hand, the dagger with the other: I was not willing that my weapons should share the fate of the watch. Thus armed, I looked round the floor -- no sign of the watch. Three slow, loud, distinct knocks were now heard at the bed-head; my servant called out, "Is that you, sir?"

"No; be on your guard."

The dog now roused himself and sat on his haunches, his ears moving quickly backwards and forwards. He kept his eyes fixed on me with a look so strange that he concentred all my attention on himself. Slowly he rose up, all his hair bristling, and stood perfectly rigid, and with the same wild stare. I had no time, however, to examine the dog. Presently my servant emerged from his room; and if ever I saw horror in the human face, it was then. I should not have recognised him had we met in the street, so altered was every lineament. He passed by me quickly, saying in a whisper that seemed scarcely to come from his lips, "Run -- run! it is after me!" He gained the door to the landing, pulled it open, and rushed forth. I followed him into the landing involuntarily, calling him to stop; but, without heeding me, he bounded down the stairs, clinging to the balusters, and taking several steps at a time. I heard, where I stood, the street-door open -- heard it again clap to. I was left alone in the haunted house.

It was but for a moment that I remained undecided whether or not to follow my servant; pride and curiosity alike forbade so dastardly a flight. I re-entered my room, closing the door after me, and proceeded cautiously into the interior chamber. I encountered nothing to justify my servant's terror. I again carefully examined the walls, to see if there were any concealed door. I could find no trace of one -- not even a seam in the dull-brown paper with which the room was hung. How, then, had the THING, whatever it was, which had so scared him, obtained ingress except through my own chamber?

I returned to my room, shut and locked the door that opened upon the interior one, and stood on the hearth, expectant and prepared. I now perceived that the dog had slunk into an angle of the wall, and was pressing himself close against it, as if literally striving to force his way into it. I approached the animal and spoke to it; the poor brute was evidently beside itself with terror. It showed all its teeth, the slaver dropping from its jaws, and would certainly have bitten me if I had touched it. It did not seem to recognise me. Whoever has seen at the Zoological Gardens a rabbit fascinated by a serpent, cowering in a corner, may form some idea of the anguish which the dog exhibited. Finding all efforts to soothe the animal in vain, and fearing that his bite might be as venomous in that state as in the madness of hydrophobia, I left him alone, placed my weapons on the table beside the fire, seated myself, and recommenced my Macaulay.

Perhaps, in order not to appear seeking credit for a courage, or rather a coolness, which the reader may conceive I exaggerate, I may be pardoned if I pause to indulge in one or two egotistical remarks.

As I hold presence of mind, or what is called courage, to be precisely proportioned to familiarity with the circumstances that lead to it, so I should say that I had been long sufficiently familiar with all experiments that appertain to the Marvellous. I had witnessed many very extraordinary phenomena in various parts of the world -- phenomena that would be either totally disbelieved if I stated them, or ascribed to supernatural agencies. Now, my theory is that the Supernatural is the Impossible, and that what is called supernatural is only a something in the laws of nature of which we have been hitherto ignorant. Therefore, if a ghost rise before me, I have not the right to say, "So, then, the supernatural is possible," but rather, "So, then, the apparition of a ghost is, contrary to received opinion, within the laws of nature -- *ie*, not supernatural."

Now, in all that I had hitherto witnessed, and indeed in all the wonders which the amateurs of mystery in our age record as facts, a material living agency is always required. On the Continent you will find still magicians who assert that they can raise spirits. Assume for the moment that they assert truly, still the living material form of the magician is present; and he is the material agency by which, from some constitutional peculiarities, certain strange phenomena, are represented to your natural senses.

Accept, again, as truthful, the tales of Spirit Manifestation in America -- musical or other sounds -- writings on paper, produced by no discernible hand -- articles of furniture moved without apparent human agency -- or the actual sight and touch of hands, to which no bodies seem to belong -- still there must be found the MEDIUM or living being, with constitutional peculiarities capable of obtaining these signs. In fine, in all such marvels, supposing even that there is no imposture, there must be a human being like ourselves by whom, or through whom, the effects presented to human beings are produced. It is so with the now familiar phenomena of mesmerism or electro-biology; the mind of the person operated on is affected through a material living agent. Nor, supposing it true that a mesmerised patient can respond to the will or passes of a mesmeriser a hundred miles distant, is the response less occasioned by a material being; it may be through a material fluid -- call it Electric, call it Odic, call it what you will -- which has the power of traversing space and passing obstacles, that the material effect is communicated from one to the other. Hence all that I had hitherto witnessed, or expected to witness, in this strange house, I believed to be occasioned through some agency or medium as mortal as myself; and this idea necessarily prevented the awe with which those who regard as supernatural, things that are not within the ordinary operations of nature, might have been impressed by the adventures of that memorable night.

As, then, it was my conjecture that all that was presented, or would be presented to my senses, must originate in some human being gifted by constitution with the power so to present them, and having some motive so to do, I felt an interest in my theory which, in its way, was rather philosophical than superstitious. And I can sincerely say that I was in as tranqil a temper for observation as any practical experimentalist could be in awaiting the effects of some rare, though perhaps perilous, chemical combination. Of course, the more I kept my mind detached from fancy, the more the temper fitted for observation would be obtained; and I therefore riveted eye and thought on the strong daylight sense in the page of my Macaulay.

I now became aware that something interposed between the page and the light -- the page was overshadowed: I looked up, and I saw what I shall find it very difficult, perhaps impossible, to describe.

It was a Darkness shaping itself forth from the air in very undefined outline. I cannot say it was of a human form, and yet it had more resemblance to a human form, or rather shadow, than to anything else. As it stood, wholly apart and distinct from the air and the light around it, its dimensions seemed gigantic, the summit nearly touching the ceiling. While I gazed, a feeling of intense cold seized me. An iceberg before me could not more have chilled me; nor could the cold of an iceberg have been more purely physical. I feel convinced that it was not the cold caused by fear. As I continued to gaze, I thought -- but this I cannot say with precision -- that I distinguished two eyes looking down on me from the height. One moment I fancied that I distinguished them clearly, the next they seemed gone; but still two rays of a pale-blue light frequently shot through the darkness, as from the height on which I half believed, half doubted, that I had encountered the eyes.

I strove to speak -- my voice utterly failed me; I could only think to myself, "Is this fear? it is *not* fear!" I strove to rise -- in vain; I felt as if weighed down by an irresistible force. Indeed, my impression was that of an immense and overwhelming Power opposed to my volition; -- that sense of utter inadequacy to cope with a force beyond man's, which one may feel *physically* in a storm at sea, in a conflagration, or when confronting some terrible wild beast, or rather, perhaps, the shark of the ocean, I felt *morally*. Opposed to my will was another will, as far superior to its strength as storm, fire, and shark are superior in material force to the force of man.

And now, as this impression grew on me -- now came, at last, horror -- horror to a degree that no words can convey. Still I retained pride, if not courage; and in my own mind I said, "This is horror, but it is not fear; unless I fear I cannot be harmed; my reason rejects this thing; it is an illusion -- I do not fear." With a violent effort I succeeded at last in stretching out my hand towards the weapon on the table: as I did so, on the arm and shoulder I received a strange shock, and my arm fell to my side powerless. And now, to add to my horror, the light began slowly to wane from the candles -- they were not, as it were, extinguished, but their flame seemed very gradually withdrawn: it was the same with the fire -- the light was extracted from the fuel; in a few minutes the room was in utter darkness. The dread that came over me, to be thus in the dark with that dark Thing, whose power was so intensely felt, brought a reaction of nerve. In fact, terror had reached that climax, that either my senses must have deserted me, or I must have burst through the spell. I did burst through it. I found voice, though the voice was a shriek. I remember that I broke forth with words like these -- "I do not fear; my soul does not fear;" and at the same time I found the strength to rise. Still in that profound gloom I rushed to one of the windows -- tore aside the curtains -- flung open the shutters; my first thought was -- LIGHT. And when I saw the moon high, clear, and calm, I felt a joy that almost compensated for the previous terror. There, was the moon, there, was also the light from the gas-lamps in the deserted slumberous street. I turned to look back into the room; the moon penetrated its shadow very palely and partially -- but still there was light. The dark Thing, whatever it might be, was gone -- except that I could yet see a dim shadow, which seemed the shadow of that shade, against the opposite wall.

My eye now rested on the table, and from under the table (which was without cloth or cover -- an old mahogany round table) there rose a hand, visible as far as the wrist. It was a hand, seemingly, as much of flesh and blood as my own, but the hand of an aged person -- lean, wrinkled, small too -- a woman's hand. That hand very softly closed on the two letters that lay on the table: hand and letters both vanished. There then came the same three loud measured knocks I had heard at the bed-head before this extraordinary drama had commenced.

As those sounds slowly ceased, I felt the whole room vibrate sensibly; and at the far end there rose, as from the floor, sparks or globules like bubbles of light, many-coloured -- green, yellow, fire-red, azure. Up and down, to and fro, hither, thither, as tiny Will-o'-the-Wisps, the sparks moved, slow or swift, each at its own caprice. A chair (as in the drawing-room below) was now advanced from the wall without apparent agency, and placed at the opposite side of the table. Suddenly, as forth from the chair, there grew a shape -- a woman's shape. It was distinct as a shape of life -- ghastly as a shape of death. The face was that of youth, with a strange mournful beauty; the throat and shoulders were bare, the rest of the form in a loose robe of cloudy white. It began sleeking its long yellow hair, which fell over its shoulders; its eyes were not turned towards me, but to the door; it seemed listening, watching, waiting. The shadow of the shade in the background grew darker; and again I thought I beheld the eyes gleaming out from the summit of the shadow -- eyes fixed upon that shape.

As if from the door, though it did not open, there grew out another shape, equally distinct, equally ghastly -- a man's shape -- a young man's. It was in the dress of the last century, or rather in a likeness of such dress (for both the male shape and the female, though defined, were evidently unsubstantial, impalpable -- simulacra -- phantasms); and there was something incongruous, grotesque, yet fearful, in the contrast between the elaborate finery, the courtly precision of that old-fashioned garb, with its ruffles and lace and buckles, and the corpse-like aspect and ghost-like stillness of the flitting wearer. Just as the male shape approached the female, the dark Shadow started from the wall, all three for a moment wrapped in darkness. When the pale light returned, the two phantoms were as if in the grasp of the Shadow that towered between them; and there was a blood-stain on the breast of the female; and the phantom male was leaning on its phantom sword, and blood seemed trickling fast from the ruffles, from the lace; and the darkness of the intermediate Shadow swallowed them up -- they were gone. And again the bubbles of light shot, and sailed, and undulated, growing thicker and thicker and more wildly confused in their movements.

The closet door to the right of the fireplace now opened, and from the aperture there came the form of an aged woman. In her hand she held letters -- the very letters over which I had seen *the* Hand close; and behind her I heard a footstep. She turned round as if to listen, and then she opened the letters and seemed to read; and over her shoulder I saw a livid face, the face of a man long drowned -- bloated, bleached, seaweed tangled in its dripping hair; and at her feet lay a form as of a corpse, and beside the corpse there cowered a child, a miserable squalid child, with famine in its cheeks and fear in its eyes. And as I looked in the old woman's face, the wrinkles and lines vanished, and it became a face of youth -- hard-eyed, stony, but still youth; and the Shadow darted forth, and darkened over these phantoms as it had darkened over the last.

Nothing now was left but the Shadow, and on that my eyes were intently fixed, till again eyes grew out of the Shadow -- malignant, serpent eyes. And the bubbles of light again rose and fell, and in their disordered, irregular, turbulent maze, mingled with the wan moonlight. And now from these globules themselves, as from the shell of an egg, monstrous things burst out; the air grew filled with them; larvæ so bloodless and so hideous that I can in no way describe them except to remind the reader of the swarming life which the solar microscope brings before his eyes in a drop of water -- things transparent, supple, agile, chasing each other, devouring each other -- forms like nought ever beheld by the naked eye. As the shapes were without symmetry, so their movements were without order. In their very vagrancies there was no sport; they came round me and round, thicker and faster and swifter, swarming over my head, crawling over my right arm, which was outstretched in involuntary command against all evil beings. Sometimes I felt myself touched, but not by them; invisible hands touched me. Once I felt the clutch as of cold fingers at my throat. I was still equally conscious that if I gave way to fear I should be in bodily peril; and I concentrated all my faculties in the single focus of resisting, stubborn will. And I turned my sight from the Shadow -- above all, from those strange serpent eyes -- eyes that had now become distinctly visible. For there, though in nought else around me, I was aware that was a WILL, and a will of intense, creative, working evil, which might crush down my own.

The pale atmosphere in the room began now to redden as if in the air of some near conflagration. The larvæ grew lurid as things that live in fire. Again the room vibrated; again were heard the three measured knocks; and again all things were swallowed up in the darkness of the dark Shadow; as if out of that darkness all had come, into that darkness all returned.

As the gloom receded, the Shadow was wholly gone. Slowly as it had been withdrawn, the flame grew again into the candles on the table, again into the fuel in the grate. The whole room came once more calmly, healthfully into sight.

The two doors were still closed, the door communicating with the servant's room still locked. In the corner of the wall, into which he had so convulsively niched himself, lay the dog. I called to him -- no movement; I approached -- the animal was dead; his eyes protruded; his tongue out of his mouth; the froth gathered round his jaws. I took him in my arms; I brought him to the fire; I felt acute grief for the loss of my poor favourite -- acute self-reproach; I accused myself of his death; I imagined he had died of fright. But what was my surprise on finding that his neck was actually broken. Had this been done in the dark? -- must it not have been by a hand human as mine? -- must there not have been a human agency all the while in that room? Good cause to suspect it. I cannot tell. I cannot do more than state the fact fairly; the reader may draw his own inference.

Another surprising circumstance -- my watch was restored to the table from which it had been so mysteriously withdrawn; nor, despite all the skill of the watchmaker, has it ever gone since -- that is, it will go in a strange erratic way for a few hours, and then come to a dead stop -- it is worthless.

Nothing more chanced for the rest of the night. Nor, indeed, had I long to wait before the dawn broke. Nor till it was broad daylight did I quit the haunted house. Before I did so, I revisited the little blind room in which my servant and myself had been for a time imprisoned. I had a strong impression -- for which I could not account -- that from that room had originated the mechanism of the phenomena -- if I may use the term -- which had been experienced in my chamber. And though I entered it now in the clear day, with the sun peering through the filmy window, I still felt, as I stood on its floor, the creep of the horror which I had first there experienced the night before, and which had been so aggravated by what had passed in my own chamber. I could not, indeed, bear to stay more than half a minute within those walls. I descended the stairs, and again I heard the footfall before me; and when I opened the street door, I thought I could distinguish a very low laugh. I gained my own home, expecting to find my runaway servant there. But he had not presented himself; nor did I hear more of him for three days, when I received a letter from him, dated from Liverpool, to this effect:

"HONOURED SIR, -- I humbly entreat your pardon, though I can scarcely hope that you will think I deserve it, unless -- which Heaven forbid! -- you saw what I did. I feel that it will be years before I can recover myself; and as to being fit for service, it is out of the question. I am therefore going to my brother-in-law at Melbourne. The ship sails to-morrow. Perhaps the long voyage may set me up. I do nothing now but start and tremble, and fancy it is behind me. I humbly beg you, honoured sir, to order my clothes, and whatever wages are due to me, to be sent to my mother's, at Walworth -- John knows her address."

The letter ended with additional apologies, somewhat incoherent, and explanatory details as to effects that had been under the writer's charge.

This flight may perhaps warrant a suspicion that the man wished to go to Australia, and had been somehow or other fraudulently mixed up with the events of the night. I say nothing in refutation of that conjecture; rather, I suggest it as one that would seem to many persons the most probable solution of improbable occurrences. My belief in my own theory remained unshaken. I returned in the evening to the house, to bring away in a hack cab the things I had left there, with my poor dog's body. In this task I was not disturbed, nor did any incident worth note befall me, except that still, on ascending and descending the stairs, I heard the same footfall in advance. On leaving the house, I went to Mr. J____'s. He was at home. I returned him the keys, told him that my curiosity was sufficiently gratified, and was about to relate quickly what had passed, when he stopped me, and said, though with much politeness, that he had no longer any interest in a mystery which none had ever solved.

I determined to tell him of the two letters I had read, as well as of the extraordinary manner in which they had disappeared, and then I inquired if he thought they had been addressed to the woman who had died in the house, and if there were anything in her early history which could possibly confirm the dark suspicions to which the letters gave rise. Mr. J____ seemed startled, and, after musing a few moments, answered, "I am but little acquainted with the woman's earlier history, except, as I before told you, that her family were known to mine. But you revive some vague reminiscences to her prejudice. I will make inquiries, and inform you of their result. Still, even if we could admit the popular superstition that a person who had been either the perpetrator or the victim of dark crimes in life could revisit, as a restless spirit, the scene in which those crimes had been committed, I should observe that the house was infested by strange sights and sounds before the old woman died -- you smile -- what would you say?"

"I would say this, that I am convinced, if we could get to the bottom of these mysteries, we should find a living human agency."

"What! you believe it is all an imposture? for what object?"

"Not an imposture in the ordinary sense of the word. If suddenly I were to sink into a deep sleep, from which you could not awake me, but in that sleep could answer questions with an accuracy which I could not pretend to when awake -- tell you what money you had in your pocket -- nay, describe your very thoughts -- it is not necessarily an imposture, any more than it is necessarily supernatural. I should be, unconsciously to myself, under a mesmeric influence, conveyed to me from a distance by a human being who had acquired power over me by previous *rapport*."

"But if a mesmeriser could so affect another living being, can you suppose that a mesmeriser could also affect inanimate objects: move chairs -- open and shut doors?"

"Or impress our senses with the belief in such effects -- we never having been *en rapport* with the person acting on us? No. What is commonly called mesmerism could not do this; but there may be a power akin to mesmerism, and superior to it -- the power that in the old days was called Magic. That such a power may extend to all inanimate objects of matter, I do not say; but if so, it would not be against nature -- it would only be a rare power in nature which might be given to constitutions with certain peculiarities, and cultivated by practice to an extraordinary degree. That such a power might extend over the dead -- that is, over certain thoughts and memories that the dead may still retain -- and compel, not that which ought properly to be called the SOUL, and which is far beyond human reach, but rather a phantom of what has been most earth-stained on earth, to make itself apparent to our senses -- is a very ancient though obsolete theory, upon which I will hazard no opinion. But I do not conceive the power would be supernatural. Let me illustrate what I mean from an experiment which Paracelsus describes as not difficult, and which the author of the *Curiosities of Literature* cites as credible:-- A flower perishes; you burn it. Whatever were the elements of that flower while it lived are gone, dispersed, you know not whither; you can never discover nor re-collect them. But you can, by chemistry, out of the burnt dust of that flower, raise a spectrum of the flower, just as it seemed in life. It may be the same with the human being. The soul has as much escaped you as the essence or elements of the flower. Still you may make a spectrum of it. And this phantom, though in the popular superstition it is held to be the soul of the departed, must not be confounded with the true soul; it is but an eidolon of the dead form. Hence, like the best-attested stories of ghosts or spirits, the thing that most strikes us is the absence of what we hold to be the soul; that is, of superior emancipated intelligence. These apparitions come for little or no object -- they seldom speak when they do come; if they speak, they utter no ideas above those of an ordinary person on earth. American spirit-seers have published volumes of communications in prose and verse, which they assert to be given in the names of the most illustrious dead -- Shakespeare, Bacon -- heaven knows whom. Those communications, taking the best, are certainly not of a whit of higher order than would be communications from living persons of fair talent and education; they are wondrously inferior to what Bacon, Shakespeare, and Plato said and wrote when on earth. Nor, what is more noticeable, do they ever contain an idea that was not on the earth before. Wonderful, therefore, as such phenomena may be (granting them to be truthful), I see much that philosophy may question, nothing that it is incumbent on philosophy to deny -- viz., nothing supernatural. They are but ideas conveyed somehow or other (we have not yet discovered the means) from one mortal brain to another. Whether, in so doing, tables walk of their own accord, or fiend-like shapes appear in a magic circle, or bodyless hands rise and remove material objects, or a Thing of Darkness, such as presented itself to me, freeze our blood -- still I am persuaded that these are but agencies conveyed, as by electric wires, to my own brain from the brain of another. In some constitutions there is a natural chemistry, and these constitutions may produce chemical wonders -- in others a natural fluid, call it electricity, and these may produce electric wonders. But the wonders differ from Normal Science in this -- they are alike objectless, purposeless, puerile, frivolous. They lead on to no grand results; and therefore the world does not heed, and true sages have not cultivated them. But sure I am, that of all I saw or heard, a man, human as myself, was the remote originator; and I believe unconsciously to himself as to the exact effects produced, for this reason: no two persons, you say, have ever told you that they experienced exactly the same thing. Well, observe, no two persons ever experience exactly the same dream. If this were an ordinary imposture, the machinery would be arranged for results that would but little vary; if it were a supernatural agency permitted by the Almighty, it would surely be for some definite end. These phenomena belong to neither class; my persuasion is, that they originate in some brain now far distant; that that brain had no distinct volition in anything that occurred; that what does occur reflects but its devious, motley, ever-shifting, half-formed thoughts; in short, that it has been but the dreams of such a brain put into action and invested with a semi-substance. That this brain is of immense power, that it can set matter into movement, that it is malignant and destructive, I believe; some material force must have killed my dog; the same force might, for aught I know, have sufficed to kill myself, had I been as subjugated by terror as the dog -- had my intellect or my spirit given me no countervailing resistance in my will."

"It killed your dog! that is fearful! indeed it is strange that no animal can be induced to stay in that house; not even a cat. Rats and mice are never found in it."

"The instincts of the brute creation detect influences deadly to their existence. Man's reason has a sense less subtle, because it has a resisting power more supreme. But enough; do you comprehend any theory?"

"Yes, though imperfectly -- and I accept any crotchet (pardon the word), however odd, rather than embrace at once the notion of ghosts and hobgoblins we imbibed in our nurseries. Still, to my unfortunate house the evil is the same. What on earth can I do with the house?"

"I will tell you what I would do. I am convinced from my own internal feelings that the small unfurnished room at right angles to the door of the bedroom which I occupied, forms a starting-point or receptacle for the influences which haunt the house; and I strongly advise you to have the walls opened, the floor removed -- nay, the whole room pulled down. I observe that it is detached from the body of the house, built over the small back-yard, and could be removed without injury to the rest of the building."

"And you think, if I did that --"

"You would cut off the telegraph wires. Try it. I am so persuaded that I am right, that I will pay half the expense if you will allow me to direct the operations."

"Nay, I am well able to afford the cost; for the rest, allow me to write to you."

About ten days afterwards I received a letter from Mr. J_____, telling me that he had visited the house since I had seen him; that he found the two letters I had described, replaced in the drawer from which I had taken them; that he had read them with misgivings like my own; that he had instituted a cautious inquiry about the woman to whom I rightly conjectured they had been written. It seemed that thirty-six years ago (a year before the date of the letters) she had married, against the wish of her relations, an American of very suspicious character; in fact, he was generally believed to have been a pirate. She herself was the daughter of very respectable tradespeople, and had served in the capacity of a nursery governess before her marriage. She had a brother, a widower, who was considered wealthy, and who had one child of about six years old. A month after the marriage, the body of this brother was found in the Thames, near London Bridge; there seemed some marks of violence about his throat, but they were not deemed sufficient to warrant any other verdict than that of "found drowned".

The American and his wife took charge of the little boy, the deceased brother having by his will left his sister the guardian of his only child -- and in event of the child's death, the sister inherited. The child died about six months afterwards -- it was supposed to have been neglected and ill-treated. The neighbours deposed to have heard it shriek at night. The surgeon who had examined it after death, said that it was emaciated as if from want of nourishment, and the body was covered with livid bruises. It seemed that one winter night the child had sought to escape -- crept out into the back-yard -- tried to scale the wall -- fallen back exhausted, and been found at morning on the stones in a dying state. But though there was some evidence of cruelty, there was none of murder; and the aunt and her husband had sought to palliate cruelty by alleging the exceeding stubborness and perversity of the child, who was declared to be half-witted. Be that as it may, at the orphan's death the aunt inherited her brother's fortune. Before the first wedding year was out, the American quitted England abruptly, and never returned to it. He obtained a cruising vessel, which was lost in the Atlantic two years afterwards. The widow was left in affluence: but reverses of various kinds had befallen her: a bank broke -- an investment failed -- she went into a small business and became insolvent -- then she entered into service, sinking lower and lower, from housekeeper down to maid-of-all-work -- never long retaining a place, though nothing decided against her character was ever alleged. She was considered sober, honest, and peculiarly quiet in her ways; still nothing prospered with her. And so she had dropped into the workhouse, from which Mr. J_____ had taken her, to be placed in charge of the very house which she had rented as mistress in the first year of her wedded life.

Mr. J_____ added that he had passed an hour alone in the unfurnished room which I had urged him to destroy, and that his impressions of dread while there were so great, though he had neither heard nor seen anything, that he was eager to have the walls bared and the floors removed as I had suggested. He had engaged persons for the work, and would commence any day I would name.

The day was accordingly fixed. I repaired to the haunted house -- we went into the blind dreary room, took up the skirting, and then the floors. Under the rafters, covered with rubbish, was found a trapdoor, quite large enough to admit a man. It was closely nailed down, with clamps and rivets of iron. On removing these we descended into a room below, the existence of which had never been suspected. In this room there had been a window and a flue, but they had been bricked over, evidently for many years. By the help of candles we examined this place; it still retained some mouldering furniture -- three chairs, an oak settle, a table -- all of the fashion of about eighty years ago. There was a chest of drawers against the wall, in which we found, half-rotted away, old-fashioned articles of a man's dress, such as might have been worn eighty or a hundred years ago by a gentleman of some rank -- costly steel buckles and buttons, like those yet worn in court-dresses, a handsome court sword -- in a waistcoat which had once been rich with gold-lace, but which was now blackened and foul with damp, we found five guineas, a few silver coins, and an ivory ticket, probably for some place of entertainment long since passed away. But our main discovery was in a kind of iron safe fixed to the wall, the lock of which it cost us much trouble to get picked.

In this safe were three shelves, and two small drawers. Ranged on the shelves were several small bottles of crystal, hermetically stopped. They contained colourless volatile essences, of the nature of which I shall only say that they were not poisons -- phosphor and ammonia entered into some of them. There were also some very curious glass tubes, and a small pointed rod of iron, with a large lump of rock-crystal, and another of amber -- also a loadstone of great power.

In one of the drawers we found a miniature portrait set in gold, and

111

retaining the freshness of its colours most remarkably, considering the length of time it had probably been there. The portrait was that of a man who might be somewhat advanced in middle life, perhaps forty-seven or forty-eight.

It was a remarkable face -- a most impressive face. If you could fancy some mighty serpent transformed into man, preserving in the human lineaments the old serpent type, you would have a better idea of that countenance than long descriptions can convey: the width and flatness of frontal -- the tapering elegance of contour disguising the strength of the deadly jaw -- the long, large, terrible eye, glittering and green as the emerald -- and withal a certain ruthless calm, as if from the consciousness of an immense power.

Mechanically I turned round the miniature to examine the back of it, and on the back was engraved a pentacle; in the middle of the pentacle a ladder, and the third step of the ladder was formed by the date 1765. Examining still more minutely, I detected a spring; this, on being pressed, opened the back of the miniature as a lid. Within-side the lid were engraved, "Marianna to thee -- Be faithful in life and in death to --." Here follows a name that I will not mention, but it was not unfamiliar to me. I had heard it spoken of by old men in my childhood as the name borne by a dazzling charlatan who had made a great sensation in London for a year or so, and had fled the country on the charge of a double murder within his own house -- that of his mistress and his rival. I said nothing of this to Mr. J_____, to whom reluctantly I resigned the miniature.

We had no difficulty in opening the first drawer within the iron safe; we found great difficulty in opening the second: it was not locked, but it resisted all efforts, till we inserted in the chinks the edge of a chisel. When we had thus drawn it forth, we found a very singular apparatus in the nicest order. Upon a small thin book, or rather tablet, was placed a saucer of crystal; this saucer was filled with a clear liquid -- on that liquid floated a kind of compass, with a needle shifting rapidly round; but instead of the usual points of a compass were seven strange characters, not very unlike those used by astrologers to denote the planets. A peculiar, but not strong nor displeasing odour, came from this drawer, which was lined with a wood that we afterwards discovered to be hazel. Whatever the cause of this odour, it produced a material effect on the nerves. We all felt it, even the two workmen who were in the room -- a creeping tingling sensation from the tips of the fingers to the roots of the hair. Impatient to examine the tablet, I removed the saucer. As I did so the needle of the compass went round and round with exceeding swiftness, and I felt a shock that ran through my whole frame, so that I dropped the saucer on the floor. The liquid was spilt -- the saucer was broken -- the compass rolled to the end of the room -- and at that instant the walls shook to and fro, as if a giant had swayed and rocked them.

112

The two workmen were so frightened that they ran up the ladder by which we had descended from the trap-door; but seeing that nothing more happened, they were easily induced to return.

Meanwhile I had opened the tablet; it was bound in plain red leather, with a silver clasp; it contained but one sheet of thick vellum, and on that sheet were inscribed, within a double pentacle, words in old monkish Latin, which are literally to be translated thus: "On all that it can reach within these walls -- sentient or inanimate, living or dead -- as moves the needle, so work my will! Accursed be the house, and restless be the dwellers therein."

We found no more. Mr. J_____ burnt the tablet and its anathema. He razed to the foundations the part of the building containing the secret room with the chamber over it. He had then the courage to inhabit the house himself for a month, and a quieter, better-conditioned house could not be found in all London. Subsequently he let it to his advantage, and his tenant has made no complaints.

PHANTOMS

Ivan Turgenev

"One instant...and the fairy tale is over,
And once again the actual fills the soul..."
- *A. FET*

I

For a long time I could not get to sleep, and kept turning from side to side. "Confound this foolishness about table-turning!" I thought. "It simply upsets one's nerves."...Drowsiness began to overtake me at last...

Suddenly it seemed to me as though there were the faint and plaintive sound of a harp-string in the room.

I raised my head. The moon was low in the sky, and looked me straight in the face. White as chalk lay its light upon the floor...The strange sound was distinctly repeated.

I leaned on my elbow. A faint feeling of awe plucked at my heart. A minute passed, another...Somewhere, far away, a cock crowed; another answered still more remote.

I let my head sink back on the pillow. "See what one can work oneself up to," I thought again,..."there's a singing in my ears."

After a little while I fell asleep -- or I thought I fell asleep. I had an extraordinary dream. I fancied I was lying in my room, in my bed -- and was not asleep, could not even close my eyes. And again I heard the sound...I turned over...The moonlight on the floor began softly to lift, to rise up, to round off slightly above...Before me, impalpable as mist, a white woman was standing motionless.

"Who are you?" I asked with an effort.

A voice made answer, like the rustle of leaves: "it is I...I...I...I have come for you."

"For me? But who are you?"

"Come by night to the edge of the wood where there stands an old

115

oak-tree. I will be there."

I tried to look closely into the face of the mysterious woman -- and suddenly I gave an involuntary shudder: there was a chilly breath upon me. And then I was not lying down, but sitting up in my bed; and where, as I fancied, the phantom had stood, the moonlight lay in a long streak of white upon the floor.

II

The day passed somehow. I tried, I remember, to read, to work...everything was a failure. The night came. My heart was throbbing within me, as though it expected something. I lay down, and turned with my face to the wall.

"Why did you not come?" sounded a distinct whisper in the room.

I looked round quickly.

Again she...again the mysterious phantom. Motionless eyes in a motionless face, and a gaze full of sadness.

"Come!" I heard the whisper again.

"I will come," I replied with instinctive horror. The phantom bent slowly forward, and undulating faintly like smoke, melted away altogether. And again the moon shone white and untroubled on the smooth floor.

III

I passed the day in unrest. At supper I drank almost a whole bottle of wine, and all but went out on to the steps; but I turned back and flung myself into my bed. My blood was pulsing painfully.

Again the sound was heard...I started, but did not look round. All at once I felt that some one had tight hold of me from behind, and was whispering in my very ear: "Come, come, come."...Trembling with terror, I moaned out: "I will come!" and sat up.

A woman stood stooping close to my very pillow. She smiled dimly and vanished. I had time, though, to make out her face. It seemed to me I had seen her before -- but where, when? I got up late, and spent the whole day wandering about the country. I went to the old oak at the edge of the forest, and looked carefully all around.

Towards evening I sat at the open window in my study. My old housekeeper set a cup of tea before me, but I did not touch it...I kept asking myself in bewilderment: "Am not I going out of my mind?" The sun had just set: and not the sky alone was flushed with red; the whole atmosphere was suddenly filled with an almost unnatural purple. The leaves and grass never stirred, stiff as though freshly coated with varnish. In their stony rigidity, in the vivid sharpness of their outlines, in this combination of intense

116

brightness and death-like stillness, there was something weird and mysterious. A rather large grey bird suddenly flew up without a sound and settled on the very window sill...I looked at it, and it looked at me sideways with its round, dark eye. "Were you sent to remind me, then?" I wondered.

At once the bird fluttered its soft wings, and without a sound -- as before -- flew away. I sat a long time still at the window, but I was no longer a prey to uncertainty. I had, as it were, come within the enchanted circle, and I was borne along by an irresistible though gentle force, as a boat is borne along by the current long before it reaches the waterfall. I started up at last. The purple had long vanished from the air, the colours were darkened, and the enchanted silence was broken. There was the flutter of a gust of wind, the moon came out brighter and brighter in the sky that was glowing bluer, and soon the leaves of the trees were weaving patterns of black and silver in her cold beams. My old housekeeper came into the study with a lighted candle, but there was a draught from the window and the flame went out. I could restrain myself no longer. I jumped up, clapped on my cap, and set off to the corner of the forest, to the old oak-tree.

IV

This oak had, many years before, been struck by lightning; the top of the tree had been shattered, and was withered up, but there was still life left in it for centuries to come. As I was coming up to it, a cloud passed over the moon: it was very dark under its thick branches. At first I noticed nothing special; but I glanced on one side, and my heart fairly failed me -- a white figure was standing motionless beside a tall bush between the oak and the forest. My hair stood upright on my head, but I plucked up my courage and went towards the forest.

Yes, it was she, my visitor of the night. As I approached her, the moon shone out again. She seemed all, as it were, spun out of half-transparent, milky mist -- through her face I could see a branch faintly stirring in the wind; only the hair and eyes were a little dark, and on one of the fingers of her clasped hands a slender ring shone with a gleam of pale gold. I stood still before her, and tried to speak; but the voice died away in my throat, though it was no longer fear exactly I felt. Her eyes were turned upon me; their gaze expressed neither distress nor delight, but a sort of lifeless attention. I waited to see whether she would utter a word, but she remained motionless and speechless, and still gazed at me with her deathly intent eyes. Dread came over me again.

"I have come!" I cried at last with an effort. My voice sounded muffled and strange to me.

"I love you," I heard her whisper.

"You love me!" I repeated in amazement.

117

"Give yourself up to me," was whispered me again in reply.

"Give myself up to you! But you are a phantom; you have no body even." A strange animation came upon me. "What are you -- smoke, air, vapour? Give myself up to you! Answer me first, Who are you? Have you lived upon the earth? Whence have you come?"

"Give yourself up to me. I will do you no harm. Only say two words: *Take me.*"

I looked at her. *What is she saying?* I thought. *What does it all mean? And how can she take me? Shall I try?*

"Very well," I said, and unexpectedly loudly, as though some one had given me a push from behind; "take me!"

I had hardly uttered these words when the mysterious figure, with a sort of inward laugh, which set her face quivering for an instant, bent forward, and stretched out her arms wide apart...I tried to dart away, but I was already in her power. She seized me, my body rose a foot from the ground, and we both floated smoothly over the wet, still grass.

V

At first I felt giddy, and instinctively opened my eyes...A minute later I opened them again. We were floating as before; but the forest was now nowhere to be seen. Under us stretched a plain, spotted here and there with dark patches. With horror I felt that we had risen to a fearful height.

"I am lost; I am in the power of Satan," flashed through me like lightning. Till that instant the idea of a temptation of the evil one, of the possibility of perdition, had never entered my head. We whirled still on, and seemed to be mounting higher and higher.

"Where will you take me?" I moaned at last.

"Where you like," my companion answered. She clung close to me; her face was almost resting upon my face. But I was scarcely conscious of her touch.

"Let me sink down to the earth, I am giddy at this height."

."Very well; only shut your eyes and hold your breath."

I obeyed, and at once felt that I was falling like a stone flung from the hand...the air whistled in my ears. When I could think again, we were floating smoothly once more just above the earth, so that we caught our feet in the tops of the tall grass.

"Put me on my feet," I began. "What pleasure is there in flying? I'm not a bird."

"I thought you would like it. We have no other pastime."

"You? Then what are you?"

There was no answer.

"You don't dare tell me that?"

The plaintive sound which had awakened me the first night quivered in my ears. Meanwhile we were still, scarcely perceptibly, moving in the damp night air.

"Let me go!" I said. My companion moved slowly away, and I found myself on my feet. She stopped before me and again folded her hands. I grew more composed and looked into her face; as before it expressed submissive sadness.

"Where are we?" I asked. I did not recognize the country about me.

"Far from your home, but you can be there in an instant."

"How can that be done? by trusting myself to you again?"

"I have done you no harm and will do you none. Let us fly till dawn, that is all. I can bear you away wherever you fancy -- to the ends of the earth. Give yourself up to me! Say only: *Take me!*"

She again pressed close to me, again my feet left the earth -- and we were flying.

VI

"Which way?" she asked me.

"Straight on, keep straight on."

"But here is a forest."

"Lift us over the forest, only slower."

We darted upwards like a wild snipe flying up into a birch-tree, and again flew on in a straight line. Instead of grass, we caught glimpses of tree-tops just under our feet. It was strange to see the forest from above, its bristling back lighted up by the moon. It looked like some huge slumbering wild beast, and accompanied us with a vast unceasing murmur, like some inarticulate roar. In one place we crossed a small glade; intensely black was the jagged streak of shadow along one side of it. Now and then there was the plaintive cry of a hare below us; above us the owl hooted, plaintively too; there was a scent in the air of mushrooms, buds, and dawn-flowers; the moon fairly flooded everything on all sides with its cold, hard light; the Pleiades gleamed just over our heads. And now the forest was left behind; a streak of fog stretched out across the open country; it was the river. We flew along one of its banks, above the bushes, still and weighted down with moisture. The river's waters at one moment glimmered with a flash of blue, at another flowed on in darkness, as it were, in wrath. Here and there a delicate mist moved strangely over the water, and the water-lilies' cups shone white in maiden pomp with every petal open to its full, as though they knew their safety out of reach. I longed to pick one of them, and behold, I found myself at once on the river's surface...the damp air struck me an angry blow in the face, just as I broke the thick stalk of a great flower. We began to fly across from bank to bank, like the water-fowl we were continually waking up and chasing before us. More than once we chanced to swoop down on a family of wild ducks, settled in a circle on an open spot among the reeds, but they did not stir; at most one of them would thrust out its neck from under its wing, stare at us, and anxiously poke its beak away again in its fluffy feathers, and another faintly quacked, while its body twitched a little all over. We startled one heron; it flew up out of a willow bush, brandishing its legs and fluttering its wings with clumsy eagerness: it struck me as remarkably like a German. There was not the splash of a fish to be heard, they too were asleep. I began to get used to the sensation of flying, and even to find a pleasure in it; any one will understand me, who has experienced flying in dreams. I proceeded to scrutinise with close attention the strange being, by whose good offices such unlikely adventures had befallen me.

VII

She was a woman with a small un-Russian face. Greyish-white, half-transparent, with scarcely marked shades, she reminded one of the alabaster figures on a vase lighted up within, and again her face seemed familiar to me.

"Can I speak with you?" I asked.

"Speak."

"I see a ring on your finger; you have lived then on the earth, you have been married?"

I waited...There was no answer.

"What is your name, or, at least, what was it?"

"Call me Alice."

"Alice! That's an English name! Are you an Englishwoman? Did you know me in former days?"

"No."

"Why is it then you have come to me?"

"I love you."

"And are you content?"

"Yes; we float, we whirl together in the fresh air."

"Alice!" I said all at once, "you are perhaps a sinful, condemned soul?"

. My companion's head bent towards me. "I don't understand you," she murmured.

"I adjure you in God's name..." I was beginning.

"What are you saying?" she put in perplexity. "I don't understand."

I fancied that the arm that lay like a chilly girdle about my waist softly trembled...

"Don't be afraid," said Alice, "don't be afraid, my dear one!" Her face turned and moved towards my face...I felt on my lips a strange sensation, like the faintest prick of a soft and delicate sting...Leeches might prick so in

120

mild and drowsy mood.

VIII

I glanced downwards. We had now risen again to a considerable height. We were flying over some provincial town I did not know, situated on the side of a wide slope. Churches rose up high among the dark mass of wooden roofs and orchards; a long bridge stood out black at the bend of a river; everything was hushed, buried in slumber. The very crosses and cupolas seemed to gleam with a silent brilliance; silently stood the tall posts of the wells beside the round tops of the willows; silently the straight whitish road darted arrow-like into one end of the town, and silently it ran out again at the opposite end on to the dark waste of monotonous fields.

"What town is this?" I asked.

"X..."

"X...in Y...province?"

"Yes."

"I'm a long distance indeed from home!"

"Distance is not for us."

"Really?" I was fired by a sudden recklessness. "Then take me to South America!"

"To America I cannot. It's daylight there by now."

"And we are night-birds. Well, anywhere, where you can, only far, far away."

"Shut your eyes and hold your breath," answered Alice, and we flew along with the speed of a whirlwind. With a deafening noise the air rushed into my ears. We stopped, but the noise did not cease. On the contrary, it changed into a sort of menacing roar, the roll of thunder...

"Now you can open your eyes," said Alice.

IX

I obeyed...Good God, where was I?

Overhead, ponderous, smoke-like storm-clouds; they huddled, they moved on like a herd of furious monsters...and there below, another monster; a raging, yes, raging sea...The white foam gleamed with spasmodic fury, and surged up in hillocks upon it, and hurling up shaggy billows, it beat with a sullen roar against a huge cliff, black as pitch. The howling of the tempest, the chilling gasp of the storm-rocked abyss, the weighty splash of the breakers, in which from time to time one fancied something like a wail, like distant cannon-shots, like a bell ringing -- the tearing crunch and grind of the shingle on the beach, the sudden shriek of an unseen gull, on the murky horizon the disabled hulk of a ship -- on every side death, death and horror...Giddiness overcame me, and I shut my eyes again with a sinking heart...

"What is this? Where are we?"

"On the south coast of the Isle of Wight opposite the Blackgang cliff where ships are so often wrecked," said Alice, speaking this time with peculiar distinctness, and as it seemed to me with a certain malignant pleasure...

"Take me away, away from here...home! home!" I shrank up, hid my face in my hands...I felt that we were moving faster than before; the wind now was not roaring or moaning, it whistled in my hair, in my clothes...I caught my breath...

"Stand on your feet now," I heard Alice's voice saying. I tried to master myself, to regain consciousness...I felt the earth under the soles of my feet, and I heard nothing, as though everything had swooned away about me...only in my temples the blood throbbed irregularly, and my head was still giddy with a faint ringing in my ears. I drew myself up and opened my eyes.

X

We were on the bank of my pond. Straight before me there were glimpses through the pointed leaves of the willows of its broad surface with threads of fluffy mist clinging here and there upon it. To the right a field of rye shone dimly; on the left stood up my orchard trees, tall, rigid, drenched it seemed in dew...The breath of the morning was already upon them. Across the pure grey sky stretched like streaks of smoke, two or three slanting clouds; they had a yellowish tinge, the first faint glow of dawn fell on them; one could not say whence it came; the eye could not detect on the horizon, which was gradually growing lighter, the spot where the sun was to rise. The stars had disappeared; nothing was astir yet, though everything was already on the point of awakening in the enchanted stillness of the morning twilight.

"Morning! see, it is morning!" cried Alice in my ear. "Farewell till to-morrow."

I turned round...Lightly rising from the earth, she floated by, and suddenly she raised both hands above her head. The head and hands and shoulders glowed for an instant with warm, corporeal light; living sparks gleamed in the dark eyes; a smile of mysterious tenderness stirred the reddening lips...A lovely woman had suddenly arisen before me...But as though dropping into a swoon, she fell back instantly and melted away like vapour.

I remained passive.

When I recovered myself and looked round me, it seemed to me that the corporeal, pale-rosy colour that had flitted over the figure of my phantom had not yet vanished, and was enfolding me, diffused in the air...It was the flush of dawn. All at once I was conscious of extreme fatigue and turned homewards. As I passed the poultry-yard, I heard the first morning cackling of the geese (no birds wake earlier than they do); along the roof at the end of each beam sat a rook, and they were all busily and silently pluming themselves, standing out in sharp outline against the milky sky. From time to time they all rose at once, and after a short flight, settled again in a row, without uttering a caw...From the wood close by came twice repeated the drowsy, fresh chuck-chuck of the black-cock, beginning to fly into the dewy grass, overgrown by brambles...With a faint tremor all over me I made my way to my bed, and soon fell into a sound sleep.

XI

The next night, as I was approaching the old oak, Alice moved to meet me, as if I were an old friend. I was not afraid of her as I had been the day before, I was almost rejoiced at seeing her; I did not even attempt to comprehend what was happening to me; I was simply longing to fly farther to interesting places.

Alice's arm again twined about me, and we took flight again.

"Let us go to Italy," I whispered in her ear.

"Wherever you wish, my dear one," she answered solemnly and slowly, and slowly and solemnly she turned her face toward me. It struck me as less transparent than on the eve; more womanlike and more imposing; it recalled to me the being I had had a glimpse of in the early dawn at parting.

"This night is a great night," Alice went on. "It comes rarely -- when seven times thirteen..."

At this point I could not catch a few words.

"To-night we can see what is hidden at other times."

"Alice!" I implored, "but who are you, tell me at last?"

Silently she lifted her long white hand. In the dark sky, where her finger was pointing, a comet flashed, a reddish streak among the tiny stars.

"How am I to understand you?" I began, "Or, as that comet floats between the planets and the sun, do you float among men or what?"

But Alice's hand was suddenly passed before my eyes...It was as though a white mist from the damp valley had fallen on me...

"To Italy! to Italy!" I heard her whisper. "This night is a great night!"

XII

The mist cleared away from before my eyes, and I saw below me an immense plain. But already, by the mere breath of the warm air upon my cheeks, I could tell I was not in Russia; and the plain, too, was not like our Russian plains. It was a vast dark expanse, apparently desert and not overgrown with grass; here and there over its whole extent gleamed pools of water, like broken pieces of looking-glass; in the distance could be dimly described a noiseless motionless sea. Great stars shone bright in the spaces between the big beautiful clouds; the murmur of thousands, subdued but never-ceasing, rose on all sides, and very strange was this shrill but drowsy chorus, this voice of the darkness and the desert...

"The Pontine marshes," said Alice. "Do you hear the frogs? do you smell the sulphur?"

"The Pontine marshes..." I repeated, and a sense of grandeur and of desolation came upon me. "But why have you brought me here, to this gloomy forsaken place? Let us fly to Rome instead."

"Rome is near," answered Alice..."Prepare yourself!"

We sank lower, and flew along an ancient Roman road. A bullock slowly lifted from the slimy mud its shaggy monstrous head, with short tufts of bristles between its crooked backward-bent horns. It turned the whites of its dull malignant eyes askance, and sniffed a heavy snorting breath into its wet nostrils, as though scenting us.

"Rome, Rome is near..." whispered Alice. "Look, look in front..."

I raised my eyes.

What was the blur of black on the edge of the night sky? Were these the lofty arches of an immense bridge? What river did it span? Why was it broken down in parts? No, it was not a bridge, it was an ancient aqueduct. All around was the holy ground of the Campagna, and there, in the distance, the Albanian hills, and their peaks and the grey ridge of the old aqueduct gleamed dimly in the beams of the rising moon...

We suddenly darted upwards, and floated in the air before a deserted ruin. No one could have said what it had been: sepulchre, palace, or castle...Dark ivy encircled it all over in its deadly clasp, and below gaped yawning a half-ruined vault. A heavy underground smell rose in my face from this heap of tiny closely-fitted stones, whence the granite facing of the wall had long crumbled away.

"Here," Alice pronounced, and she raised her hand: "Here! call aloud three times running the name of the mighty Roman!"

"What will happen?"

"You will see."

I wondered. "*Divus Caius Julius Caesar!*" I cried suddenly; "*Divus Caius Julius Caesar!*" I repeated deliberately; "*Caesar!*"

XIII

The last echoes of my voice had hardly died away, when I heard...

It is difficult to say what I did hear. At first there reached me a confused din the ear could scarcely catch, the endlessly-repeated clamour of the blare of trumpets, and the clapping of hands. It seemed that somewhere, immensely far away, at some fathomless depth, a multitude innumerable was suddenly astir, and was rising up, rising up in agitation, calling to one another, faintly, as if muffled in sleep, the suffocating sleep of ages. Then the air began moving in dark currents over the ruin...Shades began flitting before me, myriads of shades, millions of outlines, the rounded curves of helmets, the long straight lines of lances; the moonbeams were broken into momentary gleams of blue upon these helmets and lances, and all this army, this multitude, came closer and closer, and grew, in more and more rapid movement...An indescribable force, a force fit to set the whole world moving, could be felt in it; but not one figure stood out clearly...And suddenly I fancied a sort of tremor ran all round, as if it were the rush and rolling apart of some huge waves..."*Caesar, Caesar venit!*" sounded voices, like the leaves of a forest when a storm has suddenly broken upon it...a muffled shout thundered through the multitude, and a pale stern head, in a wreath of laurel, with downcast eyelids, the head of the emperor, began slowly to rise out of the ruin...

There is no word in the tongue of man to express the horror which clutched at my heart...I felt that were that head to raise its eyes, to part its lips, I must perish on the spot! "Alice!" I moaned, "I won't, I can't, I don't want Rome, coarse, terrible Rome...Away, away from here!"

"Coward!" she whispered, and away we flew. I just had time to hear behind me the iron voice of the legions, like a peal of thunder...then all was darkness.

XIV

"Look round," Alice said to me, "and don't fear."

I obeyed -- and, I remember, my first impression was so sweet that I could only sigh. A sort of smoky-grey, silvery-soft, half-light, half-mist, enveloped me on all sides. At first I made out nothing: I was dazzled by this azure brilliance; but little by little began to emerge the outlines of beautiful mountains and forests; a lake lay at my feet, with stars quivering in its depths, and the musical plash of waves. The fragrance of orange flowers met me with a rush, and with it -- and also as it were with a rush -- came floating the pure powerful notes of a woman's young voice. This fragrance, this music, fairly drew me downwards, and I began to sink...to sink down towards a magnificent marble palace, which stood, invitingly white, in the midst of a wood of cypress. The music flowed out from its wide open windows, the waves of the lake, flecked with the pollen of flowers, splashed upon its walls, and just opposite, all clothed in the dark green of orange flowers and laurels, enveloped in shining mist, and studded with statues, slender columns, and the porticoes of temples, a lofty round island rose out of the water...

"Isola Bella!" said Alice..."Lago Maggiore..."

I murmured only "Ah!" and continued to drop. The woman's voice sounded louder and clearer in the palace; I was irresistibly drawn towards it...I wanted to look at the face of the singer, who, in such music, gave voice to such a night. We stood still before the window.

In the centre of a room, furnished in the style of Pompeii, and more like an ancient temple than a modern drawing-room, surrounded by Greek statues, Etruscan vases, rare plants, and precious stuffs, lighted up by the soft radiance of two lamps enclosed in crystal globes, a young woman was sitting at the piano. Her head slightly bowed and her eyes half-closed, she sang an Italian melody; she sang and smiled, and at the same time her face wore an expression of gravity, almost sterness...a token of perfect rapture! She smiled...and Praxiteles' Faun, indolent, youthful as she, effeminate, and voluptuous, seemed to smile back at her from a corner, under the branches of an oleander, across the delicate smoke that curled upwards from a bronze censer on an antique tripod. The beautiful singer was alone. Spell-bound by the music, her beauty, the splendour and sweet fragrance of the night, moved to the heart by the picture of this youthful, serene, and untroubled happiness, I utterly forgot my companion, I forgot the strange way in which I had become a witness of this life, and I was on the point of tapping at the window, of speaking...

I was set trembling all over by a violent shock -- just as though I had touched a galvanic battery. I looked round...The face of Alice was -- for all its transparency -- dark and menacing; there was a dull glow of anger in her eyes, which were suddenly wide and round...

"Away!" she murmured wrathfully, and again whirling and darkness and giddiness...Only this time not the shout of legions, but the voice of the singer, breaking on a high note, lingered in my ears...

We stopped. The high note, the same note was still ringing and did not cease to ring in my ears, though I was breathing quite a different air, a different scent...a breeze was blowing upon me, fresh and invigorating, as though from a great river, and there was a smell of hay, smoke and hemp. The long-drawn-out note was followed by a second, and a third, but with an expression so unmistakable, a trill so familiar, so peculiarly our own, that I said to myself at once: "That's a Russian singing a Russian song!" and at that very instant everything grew clear about me.

126

XV

We found ourselves on a flat riverside plain. To the left, newly-mown meadows, with rows of huge hayricks, stretched endlessly till they were lost in the distance; to the right extended the smooth surface of a vast mighty river, till it too was lost in the distance. Not far from the bank, big dark barges slowly rocked at anchor, slightly tilting their slender masts, like pointing fingers. From one of these barges came floating up to me the sounds of a liquid voice, and a fire was burning in it, throwing a long red light that danced and quivered on the water. Here and there, both on the river and in the fields, other lights were glimmering, whether close at hand or far away, the eye could not distinguish; they shrank together, then suddenly lengthened out into great blurs of light; grass-hoppers innumerable kept up an unceasing churr, persistent as the frogs of the Pontine marshes; and across the cloudless, but dark lowering sky floated from time to time the cries of unseen birds.

"Are we in Russia?" I asked of Alice.

"It is the Volga," she answered.

We flew along the river-bank. "Why did you tear me away from there, from that lovely country?" I began. "Were you envious, or was it jealousy in you?"

The lips of Alice faintly stirred, and again there was a menacing light in her eyes...But her whole face grew stony again at once.

"I want to go home," I said.

"Wait a little, wait a little," answered Alice. "To-night is a great night. It will not soon return. You may be a spectator...Wait a little."

And we suddenly flew across the Volga in a slanting direction, keeping close to the water's surface, with the low impetuous flight of swallows before a storm. The broad waves murmured heavily below us, the sharp river breeze beat upon us with its strong cold wing...the high right bank began soon to rise up before us in the half-darkness. Steep mountains appeared with great ravines between. We came near to them.

"Shout: *Lads, to the barges!*" Alice whispered to me. I remembered the terror I had suffered at the apparition of the Roman phantoms. I felt strangely weary and strangely heavy, as though my heart were ebbing away within me. I wished not to utter the fatal words; I knew beforehand that in response to them there would appear, as in the wolves' valley of the Freischütz, some monstrous thing; but my lips parted against my will, and in a weak forced voice I shouted, also against my will: "Lads, to the barges!"

XVI

At first all was silence, even as it was at the Roman ruins, but suddenly I heard close to my very ear a coarse bargeman's laugh, and with a moan something dropped into the water and a gurgling sound followed...I looked round: no one was anywhere to be seen, but from the bank the echo came bounding back, and at once from all sides rose a deafening din. There was a medley of everything in this chaos of sound: shouting and whining, furious abuse and laughter, laughter above everything; the plash of oars and the cleaving of hatchets, a crash as of the smashing of doors and chests, the grating of rigging and wheels, and the neighing of horses, and the clang of the alarm bell and the clink of chains, the roar and cackle of fire, drunken songs and quick, gnashing chatter, weeping inconsolable, plaintive despairing prayers, and shouts of command, the dying gasp and the reckless whistle, the guffaw and the thud of the dance..."Kill them! Hang them! Drown them! rip them up! bravo! bravo! don't spare them!" could be heard distinctly; I could even hear the hurried breathing of men panting. And meanwhile all around, as far as the eye could reach, nothing could be seen, nothing was changed; the river rolled by mysteriously, almost sullenly, the very bank seemed more deserted and desolate -- and that was all.

I turned to Alice, but she put her finger to her lips...

"Stepan Timofeitch! Stepan Timofeitch is coming!" was shouted noisily all round; "he is coming, our father, our ataman, our bread-giver!" As before I saw nothing but it seemed to me as though a huge body were moving straight at me..."Frolka! where art thou, dog?" thundered an awful voice. "Set fire to every corner at once -- and to the hatchet with them, the white-handed scoundrels!"

I felt the hot breath of the flame close by, and tasted the bitter savour of the smoke; and at the same instant something warm like blood spurted over my face and hands...A savage roar of laughter broke out all round...

I lost consciousness, and when I came to myself, Alice and I were gliding along beside the familiar bushes that bordered my wood, straight towards the old oak...

"Do you see the little path?" Alice said to me, "where the moon shines dimly and where are two birch-trees overhanging? Will you go there?"

But I felt so shattered and exhausted that I could only say in reply: "Home! home!"

"You are at home," replied Alice.

I was in fact standing at the very door of my house -- alone. Alice had vanished. The yard-dog was about to approach, he scanned me suspiciously -- and with a bark ran away.

With difficulty I dragged myself up to my bed and fell asleep without undressing.

XVII

All the following morning my head ached, and I could scarcely move my legs; but I cared little for my bodily discomfort; I was devoured by regret, overwhelmed with vexation.

I was excessively annoyed with myself. "Coward!" I repeated incessantly; "yes -- Alice was right. What was I frightened of? how could I miss such an opportunity?...I might have seen Cæsar himself -- and I was senseless with terror, I whimpered and turned away, like a child at the sight of the rod. Razin, now -- that's another matter. As a nobleman and landowner...though, indeed, even then what had I really to fear? Coward! coward!"...

"But wasn't it all a dream?" I asked myself at last. I called my housekeeper.

"Marfa, what o'clock did I go to bed yesterday -- do you remember?"

"Why, who can tell, master?...Late enough, surely. Before it was quite dark you went out of the house; and you were tramping about in your bedroom when the night was more than half over. Just on morning -- yes. And this is the third day it's been the same. You've something on your mind, it's easy to see."

"Aha-ha!" I thought. "Then there's no doubt about the flying. Well, and how do I look to-day?" I added aloud.

"How do you look? Let me have a look at you. You've got thinner a bit. Yes, and you're pale, master; to be sure, there's not a drop of blood in your face."

I felt a slight twinge of uneasiness...I dismissed Marfa.

"Why, going on like this, you'll die, or go out of your mind, perhaps," I reasoned with myself, as I sat deep in thought at the window. "I must give it all up. It's dangerous. And now my heart beats so strangely. And when I fly, I keep feeling as though some one were sucking at it, or as it were drawing something out of it -- as the spring sap is drawn out of the birch-tree, if you stick an axe into it. I'm sorry, though. And Alice too...She is playing cat and mouse with me...still she can hardly wish me harm. I will give myself up to her for the last time -- and then...But if she is drinking my blood? That's awful. Besides, such rapid locomotion cannot fail to be injurious; even in England, I'm told, on the railways, it's against the law to go more than one hundred miles an hour..."

So I reasoned with myself -- but at ten o'clock in the evening, I was already at my post before the old oak-tree.

XVIII

The night was cold, dull, grey; there was a feeling of rain in the air. To my amazement, I found no one under the oak; I walked several times round it, went up to the edge of the wood, turned back again, peered anxiously into the darkness...All was emptiness. I waited a little, then several times I uttered the name, Alice, each time a little louder,...but she did not appear. I felt sad, almost sick at heart; my previous apprehensions vanished; I could not resign myself to the idea that my companion would not come back to me again.

"Alice! Alice! come! Can it be you will not come?" I shouted, for the last time.

A crow, who had been waked by my voice, suddenly darted upwards into a tree-top close by, and catching in the twigs, fluttered his wings...But Alice did not appear.

With downcast head, I turned homewards. Already I could discern the black outlines of the willows on the pond's edge, and the light in my window peeped out at me through the apple-trees in the orchard -- peeped at me, and hid again, like the eye of some man keeping watch on me -- when suddenly I heard behind me the faint swish of the rapidly parted air, and something at once embraced and snatched me upward, as a buzzard pounces on and snatches up a quail...It was Alice sweeping down upon me. I felt her cheek against my cheek, her enfolding arm about my body, and like a cutting cold her whisper pierced to my ear, "Here I am." I was frightened and delighted both at once...We flew at no great height above the ground.

"You did not mean to come to-day?" I said.

"And you were dull without me? You love me? Oh, you are mine!"

The last words of Alice confused me...I did not know what to say.

"I was kept," she went on; "I was watched."

"Who could keep you?"

"Where would you like to go?" inquired Alice, as usual not answering my question.

"Take me to Italy -- to that lake, you remember."

Alice turned a little away, and shook her head in refusal. At that point I noticed for the first time that she had ceased to be transparent. And her face seemed tinged with colour; there was a faint glow of red over its misty whiteness. I glanced at her eyes...and felt a pang of dread; in those eyes something was astir -- with the slow, continuous, malignant movement of the benumbed snake, twisting and turning as the sun begins to thaw it.

"Alice," I cried, "who are you? Tell me who you are."

Alice simply shrugged her shoulders.

I felt angry...I longed to punish her; and suddenly the idea occurred to me to tell her to fly with me to Paris. "That's the place for you to be jealous," I thought. "Alice," I said aloud, "you are not afraid of big towns -- Paris, for instance?"

"No."

"Not even those parts where it is as light as in the boulevards?"

"It is not the light of day."

"Good; then take me at once to the Boulevard des Italiens."

Alice wrapped the end of her long hanging sleeve about my head. I was at once enfolded in a sort of white vapour full of the drowsy fragrance of the poppy. Everything disappeared at once; every light, every sound, and almost consciousness itself. Only the sense of being alive remained, and that was not unpleasant.

Suddenly the vapour vanished; Alice took her sleeve from my head, and I saw at my feet a huge mass of closely-packed buildings, brilliant light, movement, noisy traffic...I saw Paris.

XIX

I had been in Paris before, and so I recognised at once the place to which Alice had directed her course. It was the Garden of the Tuileries with its old chestnut-trees, its iron railings, its fortress moat, and its brutal-looking Zouave sentinels. Passing the palace, passing the Church of St. Roche, on the steps of which the first Napoleon for the first time shed French blood, we came to a halt high over the Boulevard des Italiens, where the third Napoleon did the same thing and with the same success. Crowds of people, dandies young and old, workmen in blouses, women in gaudy dresses, were thronging on the pavements; the gilded restaurants and cafés were flaring with lights; omnibuses, carriages of all sorts and shapes, moved to and fro along the boulevard; everything was bustle, everything was brightness, wherever one chanced to look...But, strange to say, I had no inclination to get nearer to this human ant-hill. It seemed as though a hot, heavy, reddish vapour rose from it, half-fragrance, half-stench; so many lives were flung struggling in one heap together there. I was hesitating...But suddenly, sharp as the clang of iron bars, the voice of a harlot of the streets floated up to me; like an insolent tongue, it was thrust out, this voice; it stung me like the sting of a viper. At once I saw in imagination the strong, heavy-jawed, greedy, flat Parisian face, the mercenary eyes, the paint and powder, the frizzed hair, and the nosegay of gaudy artificial flowers under the high-pointed hat, the polished nails like talons, the hideous crinoline...I could fancy too one of our sons of the steppes running with pitiful eagerness after the doll put up for sale...I could fancy him with clumsy coarseness and violent stammering, trying to imitate the manners of the waiters at Véfour's, mincing, flattering, wheedling...and a feeling of loathing gained possession of me..."No," I thought, "here Alice has no need to be jealous..."

Meanwhile I perceived that we had gradually begun to descend...Paris was rising to meet us with all its din and odour...

"Stop," I said to Alice. "Are you not stifled and oppressed here?"

"You asked me to bring you here yourself."

"I am to blame, I take back my word. Take me away, Alice, I beseech

131

you. To be sure, here is Prince Kulmametov hobbling along the boulevard; and his friend Serge Varaksin, waves his hand to him, shouting: "Ivan Stepanitch, *allons souper*, make haste, zhay angazha Rigol-bouche itself!" Take me away from these furnished apartments and *maisons dorées*, from the Jockey Club and the Figaro, from close-shaven military heads and varnished barracks, from sergents-de-ville with Napoleonic beards, and from glasses of muddy absinthe, from gamblers playing dominoes at the cafes, and gamblers on the Bourse, from red ribbons in button-holes, from M. de Four, inventor of "matrimonial specialities", and the gratuitous consultations of Dr. Charles Albert, from liberal lectures and government pamphlets, from Parisian comedies and Parisian operas, from Parisian wit and Parisian ignorance...Away! away! away!"

"Look down," Alice answered; "you are not now in Paris."

I lowered my eyes...It was true. A dark plain, intersected here and there by the whitish lines of roads, was rushing rapidly by below us, and only behind us on the horizon, like the reflection of an immense conflagration, rose the great glow of the innumerable lights of the capital of the world.

XX

Again a veil fell over my eyes...Again I lost consciousness. The veil was withdrawn at last. What was it down there below? What was this park, with avenues of lopped lime-trees, with isolated fir-trees of the shape of parasols, with porticoes and temples in the Pompadour style, with statues of satyrs and nymphs of the Bernini school, with rococo tritons in the midst of meandering lakes, closed in by low parapets of blackened marble? Wasn't it Versailles? No, it was not Versailles. A small palace, also rococo, peeped out behind a clump of bushy oaks. The moon shone dimly, shrouded in mist, and over the earth there was, as it were spread out, a delicate smoke. The eye could not decide what it was, whether moonlight or fog. On one of the lakes a swan was asleep; its long back was white as the snow of the frost-bound steppes, while glow-worms gleamed like diamonds in the bluish shadow at the base of a statue.

"We are near Mannheim," said Alice; "this is the Schwetzingen garden."

"We are in Germany," I thought, and I fell to listening. All was silence, except somewhere, secluded and unseen, the splash and babble of falling water. It seemed continually to repeat the same words: "Aye, aye, aye, for aye, aye." And all at once I fancied that in the very centre of one of the avenues, between clipped walls of green, a cavalier came tripping along in red-heeled boots, a gold-braided coat, with lace ruffs at his wrists, a light steel rapier at his thigh, smilingly offering his arm to a lady in a powdered wig and a gay chintz...Strange, pale faces...I tried to look into them...But already everything had vanished, and as before there was nothing but the babbling water.

"Those are dreams wandering," whispered Alice; "yesterday there was so much -- oh, much -- to see; to-day, even the dreams avoid man's eye. Forward! forward!"

We soared higher and flew farther on. So smooth and easy was our flight that it seemed that we moved not, but everything moved to meet us. Mountains came into view, dark, undulating, covered with forest; they rose up and swam towards us...And now they were slipping by beneath us, with all their windings, hollows, and narrow glades, with gleams of light from rapid brooks among the slumbering trees at the bottom of the dales; and in front of us more mountains sprung up again and floated towards us...We were in the heart of the Black Forest.

Mountains, still mountains...and forest, magnificent, ancient, stately forest. The night sky was clear; I could recognise some kinds of trees, especially the splendid firs, with their straight white trunks. Here and there on the edge of the forest, wild goats could be seen; graceful and alert, they stood on their slender legs and listened, turning their heads prettily and pricking up their great funnel-shaped ears. A ruined tower, sightless and gloomy, on the crest of a bare cliff, laid bare its crumbling turrets; above the old forgotten stones, a little golden star was shining peacefully. From a small almost black lake rose, like a mysterious wail, the plaintive croak of tiny frogs. I fancied other notes, long-drawn-out, languid like the strains of an Æolian harp...Here we were in the home of legend! The same delicate moonlight mist, which had struck me in Schwetzingen, was shed here on every side, and farther away the mountains, the thicker was this mist. I counted up five, six, ten different tones of shadow at different heights on the mountain slopes, and over all this realm of varied silence the moon queened it pensively. The air blew in soft, light currents. I felt myself a lightness at heart, and, as it were, a lofty calm and melancholy...

"Alice, you must love this country!"

"I love nothing."

"How so? Not me?"

"Yes...you!" she answered indifferently.

It seemed to me that her arm clasped my waist more tightly than before.

"Forward! forward!" said Alice, with a sort of cold fervour.

"Forward!" I repeated.

XXI

A loud, thrilling cry rang out suddenly over our heads, and was at once repeated a little in front.

"Those are belated cranes flying to you, to the north," said Alice; "would you like to join them?"

"Yes, yes! raise me up to them."

We darted upwards and in one instant found ourselves beside the flying flock.

The big handsome birds (there were thirteen of them) were flying in a triangle, with slow sharp flaps of their hollow wings; with their heads and legs stretched rigidly out, and their breasts stiffly pressed forward, they pushed on persistently and so swiftly that the air whistled about them. It was marvellous at such a height, so remote from all things living, to see such passionate, strenuous life, such unflinching will, untiringly cleaving their triumphant way through space. The cranes now and then called to one another, the foremost to the hindmost; and there was a certain pride, dignity, and invincible faith in these loud cries, this converse in the clouds. "We shall get there, be sure, hard though it be," they seemed to say, cheering one another on. And then the thought came to me that men, such as these birds -- in Russia -- nay, in the whole world, are few.

"We are flying towards Russia now," observed Alice. I noticed now, not for the first time, that she almost always knew what I was thinking of. "Would you like to go back?"

"Let us go back...or no! I have been in Paris; take me to Petersburg."

"Now?"

"At once...Only wrap my head in your veil, or it will go ill with me."

Alice raised her hand...but before the mist enfolded me, I had time to feel on my lips the contact of that soft, dull sting...

XXII

"Li-i-isten!" sounded in my ears a long drawn out cry. "Li-i-isten!" was echoed back with a sort of desperation in the distance. "Li-i-isten!" died away somewhere far, far away. I started. A tall golden spire flashed on my eyes; I recognised the fortress of St. Peter and St. Paul.

A northern, pale night! But was it night at all? Was it not rather a pallid, sickly daylight? I never liked Petersburg nights; but this time the night seemed even fearful to me; the face of Alice had vanished completely, melted away like the mist of morning in the July sun, and I saw her whole body clearly, as it hung, heavy and solitary on a level with the Alexander column. So here was Petersburg! Yes, it was Petersburg, no doubt. The wide empty grey streets; the greyish-white, and yellowish-grey and greyish-lilac houses, covered with stucco, which was peeling off, with their sunken windows, gaudy sign-boards, iron canopies over steps, and wretched little green-grocer's shops; the facades, inscriptions, sentry-boxes, troughs; the golden cap of St. Isaac's; the senseless motley Bourse; the granite walls of the fortress, and the broken wooden pavement; the barges loaded with hay and timber; the smell of dust, cabbage, matting, and hemp; the stony-faced dvorniks in sheep-skin coats, with high collars; the cab-drivers, huddled up dead asleep on their decrepit cabs -- yes, this was Petersburg, our northern Palmyra. Everything was visible; everything was clear -- cruelly clear and distinct -- and everything was mournfully sleeping, standing out in strange huddled masses in the dull clear air. The flush of sunset -- a hectic flush -- had not yet gone, and would not be gone till morning from the white starless sky; it was reflected on the silken surface of the Neva, while faintly gurgling and faintly moving, the cold blue waves hurried on...

"Let us fly away," Alice implored.

And without waiting for my reply, she bore me away across the Neva, over the palace square to Liteiny Street. Steps and voices were audible beneath us; a group of young men, with worn faces, came along the street talking about dancing-classes. "Sub-lieutenant Stolpakov's seventh!" shouted suddenly a soldier, standing half-asleep on guard at a pyramid of rusty bullets; and a little farther on, at an open window in a tall house, I saw a girl in a creased silk dress, without cuffs, with a pearl net on her hair, and a cigarette in her mouth. She was reading a book with reverent attention; it was a volume of the works of one of our modern Juvenals.

"Let us fly away!" I said to Alice.

One instant more, and there were glimpses below us of the rotting pine copses and mossy bogs surrounding Petersburg. We bent our course straight to the south; sky, earth, all grew gradually darker and darker. The sick night; the sick daylight; the sick town -- all were left behind us.

XXIII

We flew more slowly than usual, and I was able to follow with my eyes the immense expanse of my native land gradually unfolding before me, like the unrolling of an endless panorama. Forests, copses, fields, ravines, rivers -- here and there villages and churches -- and again fields and forests and copses and ravines...Sadness came over me, and a kind of indifferent dreariness. And I was not sad and dreary simply because it was Russia I was flying over. No. The earth itself, this flat surface which lay spread out beneath me; the whole earthly globe, with its populations, multitudinous, feeble, crushed by want, grief and diseases, bound to a clod of pitiful dust; this brittle, rough crust, this shell over the fiery sands of our planet, overspread with the mildew we call the organic, vegetable kingdom; these human flies; a thousand times paltrier than flies; their dwellings glued together with filth, the pitiful traces of their tiny, monotonous bustle, of their comic struggle with the unchanging and inevitable, how revolting it all suddenly was to me. My heart turned slowly sick, and I could not bear to gaze longer on these trivial pictures, on this vulgar show...Yes, I felt dreary, worse than dreary. Even pity I felt nothing of for my brother men: all feelings in me were merged in one which I scarcely dare to name: a feeling of loathing, and stronger than all and more than all within me was the loathing -- for myself.

"Cease," whispered Alice, "cease, or I cannot carry you. You have grown heavy."

"Home," I answered her in the very tone in which I used to say the word to my coachman, when I came out at four o'clock at night from some Moscow friends', where I had been talking since dinner-time of the future of Russia and the significance of the commune. "Home," I repeated, and closed my eyes.

XXIV

But I soon opened them again. Alice seemed huddling strangely up to me; she was almost pushing against me. I looked at her and my blood froze at the sight. One who has chanced to behold on the face of another a sudden look of intense terror, the cause of which he does not suspect, will understand me. By terror, overmastering terror, the pale features of Alice were drawn and contorted, almost effaced. I had never seen anything like it even on a living human face. A lifeless, misty phantom, a shade...and this deadly horror...

"Alice, what is it?" I said at last.

"She...she..." she answered with an effort. "She."

"She? Who is she?"

"Do not utter her name, not her name," Alice faltered hurriedly. "We must escape, or there will be an end to everything, and for ever... Look, over there!"

I turned my head in the direction in which her trembling hand was pointing, and discerned something...something horrible indeed.

This something was the more horrible that it had no definite shape. Something bulky, dark, yellowish-black, spotted like a lizard's belly, not a storm-cloud, and not smoke, was crawling with a snake-like motion over the earth. A wide rhythmic undulating movement from above downwards, and from below upwards, an undulation recalling the malignant sweep of the wings of a vulture seeking its prey; at times an indescribably revolting grovelling on the earth, as of a spider stooping over its captured fly...Who are you, what are you, menacing mass? Under her influence, I saw it, I felt it -- all sank into nothingness, all was dumb...A putrefying, pestilential chill came from it. At this chill breath the heart turned sick, and the eyes grew dim, and the hair stood up on the head. It was a power moving; that power which there is no resisting, to which all is subject, which, sightless, shapeless, senseless, sees all, knows all, and like a bird of prey picks out its victims, like a snake, stifles them and stabs them with its frozen sting...

"Alice! Alice!" I shrieked like one in frenzy. "It is death! death itself!"

The wailing sound I had heard before broke from Alice's lips; this time it was more like a human wail of despair, and we flew. But our flight was strangely and alarmingly unsteady; Alice turned over in the air, fell, rushed from side to side like a partridge mortally wounded, or trying to attract a dog away from her young. And meanwhile in pursuit of us, parting from the indescribable mass of horror, rushed sort of long undulating tentacles, like outstretched arms, like talons...Suddenly a huge shape, a muffled figure on a pale horse, sprang up and flew upwards into the very heavens...Still more fearfully, still more desperately Alice struggled. "She has seen! All is over! I am lost!" I heard her broken whisper. "Oh, I am miserable! I might have profited, have won life,...and now...Nothingness, nothingness!" It was too unbearable...I lost consciousness.

XXV

When I came to myself, I was lying on my back in the grass, feeling a dull ache all over me, as from a bad bruise. The dawn was beginning in the sky: I could clearly distinguish things. Not far off, alongside a birch copse, ran a road planted with willows: the country seemed familiar to me. I began to recollect what had happened to me, and shuddered all over directly my mind recalled the last, hideous apparition...

"But what was Alice afraid of?" I thought. "Can she too be subject to that power? Is she not immortal? Can she too be in danger of annihilation, dissolution? How is it possible?"

A soft moan sounded close by me. I turned my head. Two paces from me lay stretched out motionless a young woman in a white gown, with thick disordered tresses, with bare shoulders. One arm was thrown behind her head, the other had fallen on her bosom. Her eyes were closed, and on her tightly shut lips stood a fleck of crimson stain. Could it be Alice? But Alice was a phantom, and I was looking upon a living woman. I crept up to her, bent down...

"Alice, is it you?" I cried. Suddenly, slowly quivering, the wide eyelids rose; dark piercing eyes were fastened upon me, and at the same instant lips too fastened upon me, warm, moist, smelling of blood...soft arms twined tightly round my neck, a burning, full heart pressed convulsively to mine. "Farewell, farewell for ever!" the dying voice uttered distinctly, and everything vanished.

I got up, staggering like a drunken man, and passing my hands several times over my face, looked carefully about me. I found myself near the high road, a mile and a half from my own place. The sun had just risen when I got home.

All the following nights I awaited -- and I confess not without alarm --

the appearance of my phantom; but it did not visit me again. I even set off one day, in the dusk, to the old oak, but nothing took place there out of the common. I did not, however, overmuch regret the discontinuance of this strange acquaintance. I reflected much and long over this inexplicable, almost unintelligible phenomenon; and I am convinced that not only science cannot explain it, but that even in fairy tales and legends nothing like it is to be met with. What was Alice, after all? An apparition, a restless soul, an evil spirit, a sylphide, a vampire, or what? Sometimes it struck me again that Alice was a woman I had known at some time or other, and I made tremendous efforts to recall where I had seen her...Yes, yes, I thought sometimes, directly, this minute, I shall remember...In a flash everything had melted away again like a dream. Yes, I thought a great deal, and, as is always the way, came to no conclusion. The advice or opinion of others I could not bring myself to invite; fearing to be taken for a madman. I gave up all reflection upon it at last; to tell the truth, I had no time for it. For one thing, the emancipation had come along with the redistribution of property, etc; and for another, my own health failed; I suffered from my chest, with sleeplessness, and a cough. I got thin all over. My face was yellow as a dead man's. The doctor declares I have too little blood, calls my illness by the Greek name, "anæmia", and is sending me to Gastein. The arbitrator swears that without me there's no coming to an understanding with the peasants. Well, what's one to do?

But what is the meaning of the piercingly-pure, shrill notes, the notes of an harmonica, which I hear directly any one's death is spoken of before me? They keep growing louder, more penetrating...And why do I shudder in such anguish at the mere thought of annihilation?

Translated by
Constance Garnett

MALDOROR

Isidore Ducasse

THE FIRST SONG

May it please Heaven that the reader, emboldened, and become momentarily as fierce as what he reads, find without loss of bearing a wild and sudden way across the desolate swamps of these sombre, poison-filled pages. For unless he bring to his reading a rigorous logic and mental application at least tough enough to balance his distrust, the deadly issues of this book will lap up his soul as water does sugar.

No good for everyone to read the pages which follow; only the few may relish this bitter fruit without danger. So, timid soul, before further penetration of such uncharted steppes, retrace your steps, do not advance. Hear my words well: retrace your steps, do not advance, resemble the eyes of a son who respectfully looks away when faced with an august maternal gaze; or, rather, a horizon of chilly cranes which in winter with much meditation fly powerfully through the silence, full sail, toward a specific spot on the skyline, whence springs a strange strong wind -- sudden herald of the storm. The oldest crane, forming by herself the spearhead's tip, sees this, and shakes her head like a rational person, causing her beak to click, uneasy (as I would be in her place), while her old neck, denuded of feathers and contemporaneous with three generations of cranes, cranes in peevish waves which give warning of the ever-approaching tempest. Calmly, after surveying all sides several times with her experienced eyes, cautiously, the leader (for it's she who has the privilege of displaying her tail-plumage to her less intelligent companions), with the vigilant cry of a doleful sentry, to repel the common enemy, deftly swerves the apex of the geometric figure (perhaps a triangle, but impossible to see the third side traced in space by these curious birds of passage), now port, now starboard, like a clever captain: and manoeuvring with wings apparently no larger than a sparrow's, she takes then, being no booby, another -- safer and more philosophic -- course.

Perhaps, reader, you would have me invoke hatred at the opening of this work! How do you know you won't sniff it up, paddling in innumerable pleasures, as much of it as you wish, with your wide, thin, haughty nostrils, your belly uppermost like a shark in the dark fine air, as if you understood the importance of this action no less than the importance of your legitimate appetite, slow and majestic, for the ruby flux? I assure you that the latter will delight those twin hideous holes in your unspeakable snout, O monster, if first you set yourself to inhale three thousand times the accursed awareness of The Eternal! Your nostrils, vastly dilated with sublime content, with static ecstasy, will ask nothing better of space -- now become embalmed as if in perfumes and incense -- for they shall be sated with a perfect happiness, like angels living in the magnificence and peace of the pleasant heavens.

I shall set down in a few lines how upright Maldoror was during his early years, when he lived happy. There: done.

He later perceived he was born wicked: strange mischance! For a great many years he concealed his character as best he could; but in the end, because this effort was not natural to him, each day the blood would rush to his head until, unable any longer to bear such a life, he hurled himself resolutely into a career of evil... sweet atmosphere! Who could guess whenever he hugged a rosycheeked young child, that he was longing to hack off those cheeks with a razor and would have done so had not the idea of Justice and her long cortège of punishments restrained him on every occasion. No liar, he confessed the truth, admitting he was cruel. Mankind, did you hear? He dares repeat it with this quivering quill! A force, then, stronger than the will... Curse it! Would a stone want to elude the law of gravity? Impossible. Impossible for evil to form alliance with good. As I was saying above.

There are some who write seeking the commendation of their fellows by means of noble sentiments which their imaginations invent or they possibly may possess. But *I* set my genius to portray the pleasures of cruelty! These are no fickle, artificial delights, they began with man and with him they will die. Cannot genius be cruelty's ally in the secret resolutions of Providence? Or, if cruel, can't one possess genius? My words will provide the proof: all you need do is listen to them, if you like...

Excuse me: I seemed to feel my hair stand on end, but it's nothing, for with my hand I easily manage to restore it to rest.

He who sings here does not claim any novelty in his cavatinas. On the

contrary, he congratulates himself that the elevated and evil thoughts of his
hero are in every man.

Throughout my life I have seen, without one exception, narrow-shouldered
men performing innumerable idiotic acts, brutalising their fellows, and
corrupting souls by every means. The motive for their actions they call
Glory. Seeing these exhibitions I've longed to laugh, with the rest, but that
strange imitation was impossible. Taking a penknife with a sharp-edged
blade, I slit the flesh at the points joining the lips. For an instant I believed
my aim was achieved. I saw in a mirror the mouth ruined at my own will!
An error! Besides, the blood gushing freely from the two wounds prevented
my distinguishing whether this really was the grin of others. But after some
moments of comparison I saw quite clearly that my smile did not resemble
that of humans: the fact is, I was not laughing.

I have seen men, hideous men with eyes sunk deep in their sockets,
outmatch the hardness of rock, the rigidity of cast steel, the shark's cruelty,
the insolence of youth, the insane fury of criminals, the hypocrite's
treachery, the most extraordinary play-actors, priests' strength of character,
and the most secretive, coldest creatures of heaven and earth. I have seen
moralists weary of laying bare their hearts and bringing down on themselves
the implacable wrath from on high. I have seen them all together -- the most
powerful fist levelled at heaven like that of a child already wilful towards its
mother -- probably stimulated by some denizen of hell, their eyes brimful of
remorse and yet smarting with hatred, in glacial silence, not daring to spill
out the unfruitful and mighty meditations harboured in their hearts,
meditations so crammed with injustice and horror, enough to sadden the God
of mercy with compassion. Or I've seen them at every moment of the day
from the start of infancy to the end of dotage, while disgorging incredible
curses, insensate curses against all that breathes, against themselves and
Providence, prostitute women and children and thus dishonour those parts
of the body consecrated to modesty. Then the seas swell their waters,
swallow ships in their abysses; earth tremors and hurricanes topple houses;
plagues and divers epidemics decimate praying families. Yet men are
unaware of all this. I have seen them also blushing and blenching with shame
at their behaviour on earth -- but rarely. Tempests, sisters of cyclones;
bluish firmament whose beauty I do not admit; hypocrite sea, image of my
heart; earth with mysterious womb; inhabitants of the spheres; the whole
universe; God who grandly created it, you I invoke: Show me one honest
man!... May your grace multiply my natural strength tenfold, for at the sight
of such a monster I might die of astonishment. One dies at less.

One should let one's fingernails grow for a fortnight. Oh! how sweet to snatch brutally from his bed a boy who as yet has nothing upon his upper lip, and, with eyes wide open, to feign to stroke his forehead softly, brushing back his beautiful locks! And all of a sudden, just when he least expects it, to sink your long nails into his tender breast, but not so that he dies, for if he died you would miss the sight of his subsequent sufferings. Then you drink his blood, sucking the wounds, and during this time, which should last an eternity, the child weeps. Nothing is as good as his blood, still warm, and extracted in the manner mentioned -- except it be his tears, bitter as salt. O Man, have you ever tasted your blood, when you've inadvertently cut a finger? Good, isn't it, for it has no taste. Besides, don't you recall how one day in your dismal reflections you raised a hand, palm cupped, to your sickly face moistened by the tears falling from your eyes? And then how the hand inevitably found its way to the mouth, and the mouth drained the tears in long draughts from this cup which faltered like the teeth of a schoolboy who glances sidelong at his born oppressor? How good they are: they taste of vinegar. The tears, one might say, of her who loves most of all; but the child's please the palate more. The latter, not yet knowing evil, does not deceive, while the most loving of women will, sooner or later, betray... This I surmise by analogy though I do not know what friendship and love are (it's unlikely that I shall ever accept them, and not, at any rate, from the human race). Feed then, since your blood and tears do not disgust you, feed confidently upon the adolescent's tears and blood. Blindfold his eyes while you rip his quivering flesh, and having listened for long hours to his sublime screams akin to the piercing death-rattles forced from the throats of the mortally injured in a battle, rush off like an avalanche, race back from the nextdoor room, and pretend to be coming to his aid. You'll untie his hands with their swollen nerves and veins, restore sight to his distraught eyes as you resume sucking his tears, his blood. Then how real repentance is! The divine spark within us, which so rarely appears, manifests itself -- too late! How the heart overflows at being able to console the innocent whom one has harmed!

"Child, you who have just suffered cruel pains: who could have perpetrated upon you a crime I do not know how to name! Unfortunate youth, how you must suffer! And even if your mother knew this she would be no nearer death (so abhorrent to the guilty) than I am now. Alas, what is good and what is evil? Are they both one single thing with which we furiously attest our impotence and passion to attain the infinite by even the maddest means? Or are they two different things? Yes...they had sooner be one and the same...for if not, what will become of me on Judgement Day? Forgive me, child: he who confronts your noble and holy countenance -- he it is who broke your bones and tore the flesh that hangs from various parts of your body. Was it my sick mind's delirium? Was it a hidden instinct distinct from reason, like that of an eagle tearing at its prey, that drove me to commit this crime? And yet I suffered as much as my victim! Forgive me,

142

child. I want us -- once freed from this fleeting life -- to be entwined throughout eternity, to form one being only, my mouth gummed to yours. Even in this way my punishment will not be complete, for you will rend me incessantly with both teeth and nails. I shall deck my body with scented garlands for this expiatory holocaust, and together we shall suffer, you through tearing me, I through being torn...my mouth gummed to yours. O blond, soft-eyed child, will you now do what I counsel you? I want you to do it despite yourself, and you will gladden my conscience."

This said, you will simultaneously wrong a human being and have that same human being love you: the greatest happiness one can conceive. Later, you could place him in hospital, since the cripple couldn't earn a living. They'll call you a good man: laurel wreaths and gold medals shall hide your bare feet, and be strewn over the great tomb with its ancient slab.

O You whose name I do not wish to inscribe upon this page consecrated to the sanctity of crime: I know your forgiveness was as immense as the universe. But *I* still exist!

I have made a pact with prostitution so as to sow chaos among families. I remember the night preceding this dangerous liaison. Before me I saw a tomb. I heard a glowworm huge as a house say to me: "I shall enlighten you. Read the inscription. This supreme command comes not from me."

A vast blood-red light -- at the sight of which my jaws chattered and my arms fell limp -- spread throughout the air to the horizon. Feeling I would fall, I leaned against a ruined wall, and read: "Here lies a youth who died of consumption. You know why. Do not pray for him."

Many men would not, perhaps, have had as much courage as I. Meanwhile a beautiful woman, naked, came and lay down at my feet.

I (sad-faced, to her): "You may rise." I held out to her that hand with which the fratricide slits his sister's throat.

The glowworm (to me): "You, take a stone and kill her."

"Why?" I asked him.

He (to me): "Beware, you are the weaker, for I am the stronger. This woman's name is *Prostitution*."

Tears in my eyes, rage in my heart, I felt an unknown strength born within me. I grasped a great rock, and after many attempts raised it, with difficulty, chest-high. My arms got it on to one shoulder. I clambered to the top of a mountain, and from there I crushed the glowworm. Its head sank underground to the depth of a man; the boulder rebounded as high as six churches and toppled back, into a lake whose waters subsided a moment, swirling, hollowing out an immense inverted cone. Calm returned to the surface. The sanguine glow shone no more.

"Alas!" screamed the beautiful nude: "Alas, what have you done?"

I (to her): "I prefer you to him because I pity the unfortunate. No fault

143

of yours if eternal justice created you."

She (to me): "One day men will do me justice. I'll tell you nothing more. Let me leave, so I can go and conceal my infinite sorrow at the bottom of the sea. Only you, and the loathesome monsters seething in those black abysses, do not despise me. You are good. Farewell, you who have loved me!"

I (to her): "Farewell, again farewell! I shall always love you!...From today I abandon virtue."

That is why, O earth-people, when you hear the winter wind howl on the sea and near its shores, or over great towns which have long worn mourning for me, or across cold polar regions -- you must say: "It is not the spirit of God passing, only the piercing sigh of Prostitution united with the heavy groans of the Montevidean."

Children, it is I who tell you this. So kneel down, filled with pity; and may men, more numerous than lice, say lengthy prayers.

By moonlight near the sea, in isolated country places, one sees (when sunk in bitter reflection) all things assume yellowish shapes, imprecise and fantastic. Tree shadows -- now swift, now slow -- race, chase, return in diverse forms, flattening themselves and sticking close to the ground.

In days gone by, borne on the wings of youth, this made me dream, seemed strange to me: now I'm used to it. The wind groans its languorous tones through the leaves, and the owl intones his deep lament which makes the hair of those who hear stand on end. Then dogs, driven wild, snap their chains and escape from far-off farms. They run hither and thither through the countryside, in the throes of madness. Suddenly they stop, stare in every direction with a fierce unease, their eyes ablaze, and, as elephants in the desert look up one last time at the sky before dying, desperately lifting their trunks, leaving their ears laid back, so the dogs lay back their ears, lift their heads, puff out their awful necks, and begin to bark in turn, sometimes like a child crying in hunger, or like a cat with wounded belly atop a roof, or a woman in labour, or a plague victim dying in hospital, or a young girl singing a sublime refrain... They howl -- at the northern stars, the southern stars, and the stars in the west.

At the moon.

At mountains that resemble at a distance gigantic rocks looming from the darkness.

At the cold air they inhale in deep lungfuls, that inflames and reddens the insides of their nostrils.

At the silence of the night.

At owls bearing rat or frog in their beaks (sweet, live food for fledgelings) -- whose oblique flight grazes the dogs' muzzles.

At hares that vanish at the wink of an eye.

At the highwayman who gallops off on his horse after committing a crime.

At snakes rustling in the heather, making the dogs' flesh creep and their teeth grind together.

At their own barking, by which they scare themselves.

At toads which they crunch with a single crack of the jaw (why have the toads strayed far from the swamp?).

At trees whose leaves, softly swayed, are so many mysteries they do not understand and want to seek out with their steady, intelligent eyes.

At spiders suspended between their own long legs, who scuttle up trees to escape.

At crows, that have found nothing to eat all day and return to the perch with weary wings.

At the rocks on the shore.

At the navigation lights to be seen on the masts of invisible vessels.

At the dull sound of the waves.

At the great fish, which while swimming show their black backs then sink into the depths.

And at Man, who makes them slaves!

-- After which they resume their racing across the countryside, bounding with bleeding paws over ditches, paths, fields, grasses and steep rocks.

One would think them rabid, seeking some vast pond in which to slake their thirst. Their continuing howls terrify nature. Beware, the tardy traveller! The frequenters of cemeteries will hurl themselves upon him, ripping, devouring him with bloddy, dripping jaws -- the dogs' teeth are not carious. Wild animals, not daring draw near to partake of this feast of flesh, flee out of sight, quaking.

After several hours the dogs, worn out rushing to and fro, half-dead, tongues lolling from their mouths, spring at each other not knowing what they do, and with incredible rapidity rip themselves into a thousand shreds. They do not act thus out of cruelty.

One day my mother, glassy-eyed, said to me: "Whenever you are in bed and hear the dogs' howling in the fields, hide under the bedclothes, don't deride what they do: they thirst insatiably for the infinite, like you, like me, and the rest of us humans with our long, pale faces. I even allow you to stand at the window and gaze upon this quite exalted spectacle."

Since that time I have respected the dead woman's wish. Like the dogs, I too feel the longing for the infinite...I cannot, can not satisfy this need! I am son of man and woman, so they tell me. That astounds me...I thought myself more! Moreover, what does it matter whence I came? If it had been up to *me,* I'd far rather have been the son of a female shark, whose hunger is the friend of tempests, and of the tiger, whose cruelty is well-known: I would not be so wicked. You who look on me, keep your distance, for my breath exhales poisoned air. No one has yet seen the green fissures on my

145

forehead; nor the bones protruding from my spare features, akin to the spiky fins of some huge fish, or to rocks that cover the seashore, or to the steep Alpine mountains I often scaled when I had hair of a different hue on my head.

And while through thundery nights I rove about the dwellings of men, fiery-eyed, hair whipped by storm-winds, alone, like a stone in the middle of the road -- I cover my branded face with a scrap of velvet black as the soot that clogs chimney flues. No eyes must witness the ugliness which the Supreme Being, with a smile of mighty spite, has set upon me.

Each morning when the sun rises for others, spreading joy and wholesome warmth throughout all nature, none of my features stirs as I stare fixedly at space (full of shadows): I am crouched near the back of my beloved cave, in a despair as intoxicant as wine, and with my strong hands tear my breast to tatters. Yet I do not feel rage-stricken! Nor do I feel that I alone suffer! But I do feel I am breathing! As a condemned man soon to mount the scaffold flexes his muscles, reflecting on their fate, so, upright upon my straw pallet, my eyes shut, I turn my neck slowly, right to left, left to right, for whole hours on end. I do not fall stone dead. From time to time when my neck can no longer continue to turn in one direction, and stops so as to resume its turning the opposite way, I glance suddenly at the horizon, through the few chinks left in the thick brushwood that covers the cave's entrance: I see nothing! Nothing...except for the fields in a whirling dance with the trees and long trails of birds traversing the air. That disturbs my blood and brain...So who deals those blows on my head with an iron bar, like a hammer hitting an anvil?

I propose, without my being upset, to declaim in loud tones the cold and sober stanza you are about to hear. Pay heed to what it contains, and beware of the painful impact it will not fail to leave like a blight on your disordered imaginations. Do not believe I am on the verge of death, for I am not yet a skeleton, and old age cleaves not to my brow. Let us consequently wave aside any idea of comparison with the swan at that moment when its life flies off, and before you, behold merely a monster whose face I am glad you cannot see: but the face is less horrible than the soul. I am not, however a criminal... Enough of this topic.

Not long ago I saw the sea again and trod the decks of ships, and my memories are as green as if I'd left the sea only yesterday. Nevertheless, if you can, on reading what I already regret offering you, be as calm as I, and do not blush at the thought of what the human heart is.

O octopus of the silken glance! you whose soul is inseparable from mine; you the most handsome inhabitant of the terrestrial globe, who govern a seragloi of four hundred suction-cups; you in whom are nobly enthroned as

146

in their natural habitat, by common consent and an indestructible bond, the sweet virtue of communication and the divine graces -- why are you not with me, your quicksilver belly against my breast of aluminium, both of us seated on some rock by the shore, to meditate upon this spectacle I adore!

Old ocean, with your crystal waves you resemble (by analogy) the parallel azure lines one sees upon the bruised backs of cabin-boys; you are an immense blue bruise slapped on the body of earth -- I like this comparison. So, at first sight of you, a long-drawnout sigh of sadness that one might believe to be the murmur of your bland breeze passes over the deeply disturbed soul, leaving ineradicable scars, and you remind your lovers (though they don't always bear it in mind) of man's crude origins, when he became acquainted with the sorrow that is never to desert him. I hail you, old ocean!

Old ocean, your harmoniously spherical form that rejoices the grave face of geometry reminds me overmuch of man's tiny eyes -- akin to the peccary's in minuteness and to those of the nightbirds in their circular perfection of contour. Yet down the ages man has deemed himself beautiful. As for me, I prefer to assume that man believes in his own beauty only out of *amour-propre*, but is not really goodlooking, and guesses as much; why else does he gaze on the face of his fellow with so great a contempt? I hail you, old ocean!

Old ocean, you are the symbol of identity: always equal unto yourself. In essence, you never change, and if somewhere your waves are enraged, farther off in some other zone they are in the most complete calm. You are not like man -- who stops in the street to see two bulldogs seize each other by the scruff of the neck, but does not stop when a funeral passes. Man who in the morning is affable and in the evening ill-humoured. Who laughs today and weeps tomorrow. I hail you, old ocean!

Old ocean, it might well be possible that you conceal in your breast future utilities for man. You have already given him the whale. You do not easily let the avid eyes of natural science divine the thousand secrets of your inmost oeconomy: you are modest. Man boasts incessantly -- over trifles. I hail you, old ocean!

Old ocean, the different species of fish that you nurture have not sworn brotherhood among themselves. The varying temperaments and conformations of each one satisfactorily explain what at first appears an anomaly. So it is with man, who has not the same motives as excuse. If a piece of land be occupied by thirty million human beings, *they* consider they have no obligation to concern themselves with the existence of their neighbours who are settled like roots in the adjacent patch of land. And descending from the general to the particular, each man lives like a savage in his den and rarely leaves it to visit his fellow -- crouching alike in another lair. The great universal human family is a utopia worthy of the most paltry logic. Besides, from the spectacle of your fecund breasts emerges the notion of ingratitude, for one thinks immediately of those innumerable parents

147

ungrateful enough towards the Creator to abandon the fruit of their sorry unions. I hail you, old ocean!

Old ocean, your physical magnitude is only discernable if one can imagine the energy to beget your entire mass. A glance cannot encompass you. To envision you, the sight must turn its telescope in one continuous movement towards the four points of the horizon, the same way that a mathematician, in order to resolve an algebraic equation, has to examine the various possible solutions before settling the problem. Man consumes nutritious substances and makes other attempts -- worthy of a better fate -- to appear fat. Let this adorable frog puff itself up as much as it pleases. Be calm: it will never equal you in volume. At least I suppose not. I hail you, old ocean!

Old ocean, your waters are bitter. They have the same taste as the bile which criticism secretes upon the fine arts, the sciences, on everything. If someone has genius, one makes him out an idiot. If another has a handsome body, he becomes a hideous hunchback. Man must certainly feel his imperfections strongly indeed -- threequarters of them, moreover, are his own fault -- to criticise them thus! I hail you, old ocean!

Old ocean, men, despite the excellence of their methods, and being aided by scientific means of investigation, have still not managed to measure your dizzying unfathomed depths. You have some that the longest, heaviest plummets have recognised to be inaccessible. Fish have permission, but not man. I've often wondered which was the easier to acknowledge: the depth of the ocean or the depths of the human heart! Often, standing aboard ship, my hands to my brow, while the moon balanced askew between the masts, I've astonished myself, disregarding all save the goal I pursued, striving to solve this difficult problem! Yes, which is the deeper, the more impenetrable of the two: the ocean or the human heart? If thirty years' experience of life can tilt the scale toward one or the other of these solutions, I may be permitted to state that, despite the depth of the ocean, it cannot, within the context of such a comparison, match the depth of the human heart. I have had dealings with men who were virtuous. They would die at sixty, and everyone never failed to exclaim: "They did good on earth -- that's to say they were charitable -- that's all, not difficult, anyone could do as much." Who can understand why two lovers who idolised one another the night before, because of one word misinterpreted, split up, eastward one, west the other, goaded by hate, revenge, love and remorse, and never to see each other again, both cloaked in lonely pride. This is a miracle renewed every day and is none the less miraculous for that. Who can understand why we relish not only the general misfortunes of our fellow men but also the particular ones of our dearest friends, while at the same time grieved by them? One indisputable example to conclude the series: Man hypocritically says Yes and thinks No. That is why the wild boars of humanity trust each other so much and are not egoists. Psychology still has a great deal of progress to make. I hail you, old ocean!

Old ocean, you are so powerful that men have learned this to their own cost. Well may they employ all the resources of their genius...incapable of ruling you. They have found their master. I say they have found something stronger than themselves. This something has a name. This name is: the ocean! The fear you inspire in them is such that they respect you. In spite of that, you make their heaviest machines waltz with grace, elegance and ease. You make them leap gymnastically into the sky, and dive marvellously down into the depths of your domain: a circus tumbler would be jealous. Happy are they whom you do not ultimately envelop in your foaming folds, so they can enter your aqueous entrails, railwayless, and see how the fish fare, and above all, how they themselves do. Man says: "I am more intelligent than the ocean." It's possible, even quite true; but the ocean is more formidable to him, than he to the ocean. No proof of this is necessary.

That patriarchal observer, contemporary of the first epochs of our suspended globe, smiles with pity when present at the naval encounters of nations. Here are a hundred leviathans sprung from human hands. The officers' bombastic orders, the shrieks of the wounded, the cannon blasts -- all noise purposely made to annihilate a few seconds. The drama appears to be over, and the ocean has drawn everything into its belly. A formidable maw. It must be vast towards the bottom, in the direction of the unknown! Finally, to crown the foolish farce, which is not even interesting, one sees right there in the air some tired, straggling stork that, without its wingspan faltering, cries: "Look, that's not funny! There were black spots below. I shut my eyes and they'd gone." I hail you, old ocean!

Old ocean, great celibate -- when you survey the solemn solitude of your stolid kingdoms, you rightly pride yourself on your innate magnificence and on the true eulogies that I hasten to attribute to you. Voluptuously swayed by the soft effluvia of your majestic deliberation -- the grandest among those characteristics which the sovereign power has conferred upon you -- in the midst of a sombre mystery, with the calm sense of your eternal strength, you unfurl all along your sublime surface your incomparable waves. Parallel, they follow each other, separated by short intervals. Hardly has one abated than another goes, growing, to meet it. They are accompanied by the melancholy sound of foam dissolving, to warn us that all is foam. (Thus humans, those living waves, die in a dreary way one after the other: but leave no frothy noise.) The bird of passage rests confidently on the waves, lets itself be borne by their motion, full of proud grace, until its wing-bones have regained customary vigour to continue the aerial pilgrimage. I wish that human majesty were but the embodiment of the reflection of your own. I ask much, and this sincere wish casts glory on you. Your moral magnitude, image of the infinite, is vast as the philosopher's meditation, woman's love, the heavenly beauty of a bird, or the musings of the poet. You are more beautiful than the night.

Answer me ocean, do you want to be my brother? Stir yourself, impetuously...more...still more if you want me to compare you to the vengeance of God. Extend your livid claws, tearing out a pathway in your own breast...that's it. Unroll your frightful breakers, hideous ocean -- understood by me alone -- before whom, at whose knees, I fall prostrate.

Man's majesty is borrowed; it shall not awe me: you, yes. Oh! when you advance, crest high and fearsome, surrounded by tortuous coils as by a royal court, mesmeric and savage, rolling your waves one on the other, conscious of what you are, while you force from the depths of your bosom as if overwhelmed by an intense remorse I cannot fathom, this perpetual muffled booming which men so much dread even when they contemplate you in safety, trembling on the shore: then I see that I do not possess the notable right of declaring myself your equal.

That is why in the presence of your superiority I would give you all my love (and no one knows how much love my aspirations towards the beautiful contain) if you did not make me dwell sadly upon my fellow men who, in highly ironic contrast to you, form the most buffoonish antithesis ever seen in creation. I cannot love you, I loathe you. Why do I return to you for the thousandth time, to your friendly arms that open to caress my burning brow -- which sees fever flee upon their contact! Your secret destiny I know not: all that concerns you interests me.

Tell me whether you are the abode of the Prince of Darkness... Tell me, ocean (me alone, so as not to sadden those who have as yet known only illusions); tell me if Satan's breath creates the storms that hurl your salty waters up to the clouds. This you must tell me because I would rejoice at knowing hell so close to man.

I want this to be the last stanza of my invocation. Consequently, just once more I would hail you and bid you farewell! Old ocean, with waves of crystal... My eyes well with copious tears, and I have not strength to proceed, for I feel that the moment has come to return among men, with their brutal demeanour. But...take heart! Let us make a great effort, and with a sense of duty fulfil our destiny upon this earth. I hail you, old ocean!

I will not be seen, in my last hour -- I write this on my deathbed -- surrounded by priests. I want to die cradled on the waves of the stormy sea or standing on a mountain...my eyes aloft -- no; I know my annihilation will be total. Besides, I would have no remission to hope for.

Who is opening the door of my funeral chamber? I had said that none should enter. Whoever you are, keep away. But if you do discern some mark of sorrow on my hyena's face (I use this metaphor although the hyena is handsomer than I, and more pleasant to look upon) -- be undeceived. Approach, then.

A winter night it is, with the elements clashing on all sides: man is afraid, and the adolescent contemplates some crime against one of his friends, if he is as I was during my youth. May the wind -- whose whinings have saddened humanity since wind and humanity existed -- bear me (a few moments before my death-throes) on the bones of his wings, across the world, eager for my death. Once again I shall secretly gloat over the numerous examples of human wickedness (a brother loves to watch unseen the deeds of his brothers). Eagle, crow, the immortal pelican, the wild duck, the wandering crane, waking, shaking with cold, will see me pass in the glow of lightning, a horrid and happy apparition. They won't know what it means. On earth, the viper, the toad's vast eye, tiger, elephant; in the sea, whale, shark, hammer-head shark, shapeless ray, the tooth of the polar seal -- all will wonder at this deviation from the law of nature. Man, trembling, groaning, will glue his forehead to the ground.

"Yes, I outdo you all in my innate cruelty -- cruelty whose suppression does not lie with me. Is this the reason for your prostrating yourselves before me thus? Or else because you see me, new phenomenon, race like an appalling comet across blood-stained space?"

(A rain of blood falls from my vast body, akin to the blackish cloud that the hurricane thrusts ahead.)

"Fear naught, my children, I do not wish to curse you. The evil you have done me, the wrong I have done you, is too great, too great to be spontaneous. You have gone your way, I mine, both alike, both perverse. Therefore through this character resemblance we must needs have met: the resultant shock has been mutually fatal."

Then men, regaining courage, will lift their heads little by little, stretching out their necks like snails, to see who thus addresses them. Suddenly, their blazing distraught faces displaying the most frightful passions grimace fit for wolves to feel fear. All at once they rise upright like an immense spring. What curses! what rending voices! They have recognised me. Now the beasts of earth join together with men -- make their weird hubbub heard. No more mutual hatred: the two hates are turned against the common foe, myself. Reconciliation by universal assent.

Supporting winds, raise me higher: I fear perfidy. Yes, let's gradually disappear from their sight -- once again completely satisfied witness to the consequences of passion.

I thank you, O Rhinolophus, you whose snout is topped by a horseshoe-shaped crest, for having woken me with the motion of your wings. Indeed, I perceive it was unfortunately but a fleeting sickness, and with disgust I feel myself restored to life. Some say you approached me to suck what little blood is to be found in my body: why is this hypothesis not reality!

A family, seated round a lamp set on the table.

151

-- My son, hand me the scissors there on that chair.

-- They are not there, mother.

-- Then go and look for them in the other room. Do you recall the time, my dear master, when we prayed to have a child in whom we would be born again and who would be our support in old age?

-- I remember, and God answered our prayers. We need not complain of our lot on Earth. Each day we bless Providence for her gifts. Our Edward possesses all his mother's graces.

-- And his father's masculine qualities.

-- Here are the scissors, mother. I found them at last.

He resumes his homework....

But someone has appeared at the front door and for a few moments observes the tableau before his eyes:

-- What does this scene mean? There are many people less happy than these. What argument do they themselves advance for loving life? Be off, Maldoror, leave this peaceful hearth: you have no place here.

He has withdrawn!

-- I don't know why it is, but I feel human faculties start warring within my heart. My soul is uneasy without knowing why. It's so close.

-- Wife, I feel the same as you do. I dread to think that some misfortune might befall us. Let's trust in God; in Him is the supreme hope.

-- Mother, I can hardly breathe: my head aches.

-- You too, son! I shall moisten your brow and temples with vinegar.

-- No, mother dear...

See, he slumps against the back of the chair, exhausted.

-- Something makes me queasy, I can't explain it. The merest trifle vexes me now.

-- How pale you are! This evening will not end before some fatal incident plunges the three of us into the lake of despair!

I hear in the distance prolonged screams of the most poignant anguish.

-- My son!

-- Oh mother, I'm scared!

-- Tell me quickly if you are in pain.

-- No, mother, I'm not...I'm not telling the truth.

The father cannot overcome his astonishment:

-- Those cries are sometimes to be heard in the silence of starless nights. Although we can hear the cries, he who utters them is not nearby, since the groans can be heard three leagues off, borne on the wind from one city to another. I have often heard tell of this phenomenon but I've never had the chance myself to judge its truth. Wife, you mentioned misfortune. If truer misfortune existed within the long spiral of time, it is his misfortune who now disturbs the sleep of his fellow men.

I hear in the distance prolonged screams of the most poignant anguish.

-- Heaven grant that his birth be not a calamity for his country, which

152

has driven him from her breast. From land to land he goes, hated everywhere. Some say he has been stricken since childhood by a type of inherited madness. Others hold that he is of an extreme and instinctive cruelty of which he himself is ashamed, and that his parents died of grief because of it. There are those who maintain that he was branded with a nickname in his youth and that he has for the rest of his existence remained inconsolable, because his wounded pride saw in this a flagrant proof of men's wickedness, which shows itself from earliest years and increases thereafter. This nickname was *The Vampire!*

I hear in the distance prolonged screams of the most poignant anguish.

-- They add that night and day without respite or rest, horrible nightmares have him bleeding from ears and mouth, and that spectres squat at the head of his bed, and, impelled despite themselves by an unknown force, fling in his face, now softly, now with voices like warcries, and with implacable persistence, this ever enduring, always hideous epithet which will perish only with the universe itself. Some have even asserted that love reduced him to this state, or that his cries show remorse for some crime shrouded in the night of his mysterious past. But the majority think an immeasurable pride tortures him, as it once did Satan, and that he would like to be God's equal...

I hear in the distance prolonged screams of the most poignant anguish.

-- My son, these are exceptional confidences: I pity your hearing them at your age, and I hope you will never imitate the man.

-- Speak, Edward, say you will never imitate that man.

-- Beloved mother, to whom I owe the light of day, I promise, if a child's hallowed promise has any meaning, never to imitate that man.

-- That's fine, my son. One's mother must be obeyed in everything.

The screams are heard no more.

-- Wife, have you finished your work?

-- A few stitches left to put in this shirt, although we have stayed up rather late.

-- And *I've* not finished a chapter I began. Let us take advantage of the last glimmers of lamplight -- for there is hardly any more oil -- and each complete our work...

The child cries out:

-- If God lets us live!

-- Radiant angel, come to me. You shall stroll in the meadow, morning till night. You shall not work at all. My magnificent palace is built of silver walls, golden columns and diamond doors. You shall go to bed when you will, to the strains of celestial music, without having to say your prayers. When in the morning the sun displays his resplendent rays and the joyous lark transports its song out of sight in the skies, you may still stay in bed -- until that wearies you. You shall tread the most precious carpets; you shall be constantly embalmed in an atmosphere composed of the perfumed

153

essences of the most fragrant flowers.

-- It is time to rest body and soul. Arise, mother of my family, on your strong ankles. It is fitting that your stiffened fingers abandon the needle of needless toil. One shouldn't go to extremes.

-- Oh! how sweet your existence will be! I shall give you an enchanted ring. When you twist its ruby you'll be invisible like the princes in fairy tales.

-- Put away your day-to-day utensils in the safety of the cupboard, while I for my part clear away my things.

-- When you turn it back to its original position, you will reappear as nature fashioned you, O young magician. This is because I love you and strive for your happiness.

-- Whoever you are, go away - don't grip my shoulders.

-- My son, don't fall asleep, cradled on childhood's dreams: our evening prayers have not begun and your clothes are not yet set tidily on a chair... Kneel down! "Eternal Creator of the Universe, Thou showest Thine inexhaustible goodness even in the smallest things."

-- Then do you not love limpid streams where thousands of little fish -- red, blue, and silvery -- are gliding? You shall catch them with a net so beautiful that it will of itself attract them until filled. From the surface you shall see shiny pebbles, more polished than marble.

-- Mother, look at those claws: I distrust him. But my conscience is clear, for I've nothing with which to reproach myself.

-- "Thou seest us prostrate at Thy feet, overwhelmed by the sense of Thy greatness. If any proud thought insinuate itself into our imagination, we reject it immediately with the spittle of disdain and surrender it irremissibly unto Thee."

-- There you will bathe with little girls who will entwine you in their arms. Once out of the bath, they will deck you with wreaths of roses and carnations. They will have transparent butterfly wings, and long wavy hair that floats about the sweetness of their brows.

-- Even though your palace were more beautiful than crystal, I would not leave this house to follow you. I think you only an impostor, since you talk to me so softly for fear of being overheard. Abandoning one's parents is an evil act. I shan't play the ungrateful son. As for your little girls, they are not so beautiful as my mother's eyes.

-- "All our life is spent in praises of Thy glory. Such as we have been heretofore, so shall we be until that time when we receive from Thee the command to depart this earth."

-- They will obey you at the slightest nod and have only your pleasure in mind. If you desire for the bird that never rests, they will bring it you. If you desire the coach of snow that in the twinkling of an eye bears one to the sun, they will bring it you. What will they not bring you! They will even bring you the kite, tall as a tower, that's hidden on the moon, and from whose tail birds of every species are suspended by silken threads. Heed yourself...take my advice.

-- Do what you will. I don't want to interrupt prayers by calling for help. Although your body vanishes when I would ward it off, know that I do not fear you.

-- "Before Thee nothing is great unless it be the flame issuing forth from a pure heart."

-- Think over what I have told you. If not, you will regret it.

-- "Heavenly Father, exorcise, avert the misfortunes that can swoop down upon our family."

-- You will not be off then, evil phantom?

-- "Preserve this beloved wife who has consoled me in my despondency..."

-- Since you reject me I shall make you weep and gnash your teeth like a hanged man.

-- "And this loving son, whose chaste lips have scarcely opened to the kisses of life's dawn."

-- Mother, he's choking me...Father, help me!...I can no longer breathe!... Your blessing!

A cry of boundless irony rises up into the skies. See how eagles fall stunned from the topmost clouds, tumbling over one another, literally struck down by the column of air.

-- His heart beats no more...And she too has died, at the same instant as the fruit of her womb -- fruit I no longer recognise, so greatly is he disfigured...My wife! My son! I recall a distant time when I was husband and father.

He told himself, faced with the scene presenting itself to his eyes, that he would not endure this injustice. If the power the infernal demons have granted him (or rather that he summons from within himself) be effective, then before the night slips by this child should be no more.

He who knows not how to weep (for he has always suppressed the suffering within) noted that he found himself in Norway. On the Faroe Isles he participated in the search for seabirds' nests along sheer crevasses, and was amazed that the three-hundred metre rope which supports the explorer above the precipice was selected for its strength. Whatever one says, he saw in this a striking example of human kindness, and could not believe his eyes. If *he* had had to prepare the rope, he would have slashed it at several spots so it would snap and plunge the hunter into the sea!

One evening he headed for a cemetery, and those youths who find pleasure in raping the corpses of beautiful women recently dead could, had they wished, have overheard the following conversation frittered away within the context of a plot that is to unfold simultaneously.

-- Sexton, do you not wish to converse with me? A spermwhale rises

155

gradually from the seabed and shows its head above the waters so as to see the ship that passes by these solitary latitudes. Curiosity was born with the universe.

-- Friend, it is impossible for me to exchange ideas with you. Long have the moonbeams made the tombs' marble gleam. It is the silent hour when more than one human being dreams he sees chained women appear, dragging their shrouds covered with bloodstains -- as a black sky is with stars. The sleeper utters groans like those of one condemned to death, until he wakes and realises that reality is thrice worse than dream. I must finish digging this grave with my tireless spade so it be ready tomorrow morning. To perform serious work one must not do two things at once.

-- He thinks digging a grave is serious work! You think grave digging is serious work!

-- When the brutal pelican brings itself to offer its breast for its brood to devour -- having as witness only He who knew how to create such a love as would shame men -- although the sacrifice be great, the act is quite natural. When a young man sees a woman whom he worshipped in the arms of his friend, he takes to smoking a cigar; doesn't leave the house, and clings with indissoluble friendship to sorrow: again, quite natural. When a boarder at a *lycée* is ruled for years (which are centuries), from morning till night and night till morning, by an outcast of civilisation whose eyes are constantly upon him, he feels tumultuous torrents of an undying hatred mount like heavy fumes to his head that seems about to burst. From the moment he was hurled into prison, until that time near to hand when he will leave it, a high fever yellows his face, knits his brows, and hollows his eyes. At night he muses, because he does not want to sleep. By day his thoughts vault over the walls of the abode of degradation, toward the moment when he escapes this perpetual cloister or they expel him from it like one stricken by plague. Quite natural too. Digging a grave is often beyond the forces of nature. Stranger, how would you like my pick to turn up this earth which first feeds us then gives us a comfortable bed sheltered from the winter wind furiously blowing about these freezing regions, when he who wields the pick with trembling hands, having all day long convulsively fingered the cheeks of those once living who return to his kingdom, sees before him in the evening, written in letters of flame on every wooden cross the terms of the fearful problem that mankind has not yet solved: the mortality or immortality of the soul. I have always preserved my love for the Creator of the universe, but were we to exist no more after death why, most nights, do I see each coffin open and its occupant softly lift the leaden lid so as to emerge and breathe the fresh air?

-- Cease your work. Emotion saps your strength. To me you seem feeble as a reed. It would be sheer madness to continue. I am strong, I'm going to take your place. You, stand aside. You shall advise me if I don't do well.

-- How muscular his arms are, and what pleasure to watch him dig the soil with such ease!

-- You must not let a useless doubt torment your thoughts. All these tombs that are scattered about the cemetery like flowers in a meadow (a simile lacking truth) are worthy of being measured by the serene orientation of the philosopher. Dangerous hallucinations may appear by day, but they come mainly at night. Do not, therefore, be amazed by fantastic visions your eyes seem to see. During the daytime when the mind is at rest, question your conscience: it will assuredly tell you that God who created man with a particle of His own intelligence is possessed of limitless benevolence and will, after its earthly death, receive this masterpiece into His bosom. Why do you weep, gravedigger? Why these womanish tears? Remember this well: we are aboard this dismasted vessel in order to suffer. It is a credit to man that God has judged him capable of overcoming his deepest sufferings. Speak, if your tongue is made like other men's, and since, according to your most cherished wishes, there should be no suffering, tell me then what virtue is, that ideal each one of us strives to achieve.

-- Where am I? Have I not changed character? I feel a strong breath of consolation brush my unruffled brow, like the spring breeze reviving hope in old men. What kind of man is this, whose sublime speech has said things not everybody would have uttered? What beauty -- as of music -- in the incomparable melody of his voice! I had rather hear him talk than others sing. Yet the more I observe him, the less candid his face. The general cast of his features contrasts queerly with these words which the love of God alone could have inspired. Puckered by wrinkles, his brow is branded with an indelible stigma. Is this stigma, which has aged him before his time, honourable or infamous? Should his wrinkles be regarded with veneration? I do not know, and dread knowing. Though he says what he does not believe, I think nonetheless he has reasons for acting as he has done, roused by the tattered remnants of a charity destroyed within him. He is absorbed in meditations unknown to me, and redoubles his activity in difficult work he's not used to undertaking. Sweat moistens his skin, he does not notice it. He is sadder than feelings which the sight of a child in its cradle inspires... Oh! how gloomy he is!...Whence do you come? Stranger, let me touch you, and let my hands, which seldom grasp those of the living, venture upon the nobility of your body. Come what may, I'd know where I stand. This hair is the finest I've ever touched in my life. Who would be bold enough to claim I could not judge the quality of hair?

-- What do you want of me while I'm digging a grave? The lion does not wish to be provoked as he gorges his fill. If you don't know this, I shall teach you it. Come, hurry: perform what it is you yearn for.

-- What shudders at my touch, making me shudder myself, is flesh and blood beyond doubt. It's true...I am not dreaming! Who are you then, you who stoop there digging a grave while I, like a sluggard who eats the bread of others, do nothing? It's the time for sleep, or for sacrificing rest to

157

learning. In any case, no one strays from home, and men guard against leaving doors open, so as not to let in burglars. They lock themselves up in their rooms as best they can, while the embers in the old fireplace still manage to warm the chamber with a remnant of heat. *You* do not behave like other men. Your clothes suggest you are an inhabitant of some distant country.

-- Although I am not tired, it's useless to dig any more. Undress me now, then place me inside it.

-- Our conversation together these last few moments has been so odd I do not know how to answer you...(I think he's joking.)

-- Yes, yes, that's right, I was joking. Take no notice of what I said.

He collapsed and the gravedigger was quick to support him.

-- What's the matter?

-- Yes, yes, it's true, I lied...I was exhausted when I laid down the pick...It's the first time I've tackled such work...Take no notice of what I said.

-- My opinion steadily gains ground: here is someone with appalling sorrows. Heaven forfend that I question him. I would rather remain in doubt, such is the pity he inspires in me. Besides, he would not want to reply, that's certain. To open one's heart when in such an abnormal state is to suffer doubly.

-- Let me leave this cemetery. I shall continue on my way.

-- Your legs would not carry you. You would lose the way as you trudged on. I'm duty bound to offer you a homely bed: I have no other. Trust me, for hospitality will not demand infringing your secrets.

-- O venerable louse, whose body is bereft of elytra, one day you bitterly reproached me for not caring sufficiently for your sublime understanding, which is no open book. Perhaps you were right, since I do not even feel gratitude towards this man. Lantern of Maldoror, whither do you guide his footsteps?

-- To my home. Whether you be a criminal who has not taken the precaution of scrubbing his right hand with soap after committing his crime and is easily recognised upon inspection of this hand; or a brother who has lost his sister; or some dethroned monarch fleeing his kingdom, my truly awe-inspiring palace is worthy to receive you. It was not constructed of diamonds and precious stones; it's only a poor hut, poorly built, but this famous hut has an historic past that the present renews and incessantly continues. If it could speak it would astound you, you who seem to be astounded by nothing. How often have that hut and I seen funeral biers wind before us, hearses containing bones soon to be more worm-eaten than the back of my door against which I leant. My innumerable subjects increase daily. I need no census on set dates to realise that. Here, it is as with the living: each one pays a tax proportionate to the richness of the residence chosen; and should some miser refuse to hand over his quota I am authorised in such instances to act as bailiffs do: there's no lack of jackals and vultures longing to have a good meal. I have seen arrayed in death's ranks those who had been handsome; those whom death had not disfigured; men, women, beggars and kings' sons; the illusions of youth, the skeletons of the aged; genius and madness; sloth and its opposite; those who were false, those who were true; the mask of the haughty, the modesty of the humble; vice crowned with flowers and innocence betrayed.

-- No, I certainly shan't refuse your bed - which is worthy of me -- until daybreak, which will not be long. Thank you for your kindness... Gravedigger, it is fine to contemplate the ruins of cities, but finer far to contemplate the ruins of men!

The brother to the leech paced slowly through the forest. Again and again he would stop and open his mouth to speak. But each time his throat would contract and choke back the abortive attempt. At last he cried out:

"Man, when you came across a dog lying dead on its back, wedged against a sluicegate that prevents its being swept off, do not (like others) go and grasp a handful of maggots crawling from its bloated belly and gaze at them in astonishment, then open a claspknife and cut a large number of them, telling yourself that you too will be no more than this dog. What mystery do you seek? Neither I nor the four flippers of the sea-bear of the Boreal ocean have been able to solve the riddle of life. Take care, night draws nigh and you have been there since morning...What will your family, your little sister, say when they see you turn up so late? Wash your hands, take the road that leads to sleep...

"Who is that being, there on the horizon, who dares approach me fearlessly with tormented, oblique leaps? And what majesty, mingled with serene mildness! His look, though soft, is profound. His enormous eyelids frolic in the breeze, and seem alive. He is beyond my ken.

"Meeting his monstrous eyes, my body quakes -- for the first time since I sucked the dry dugs of what one calls a mother. There is a sort of halo of dazzling light about this being. When he spoke, all nature was stilled, and shared in a huge shudder. Since it pleases you to come to me, as if drawn by a magnet, I've no objection to that. How handsome he is! It pains me to say so. You must be strong, for you have a superhuman countenance, sad as the universe, beautiful as suicide. I abhor you to the utmost, and would rather see a serpent coiled round my neck from time immemorial than miss your eyes...

"What!...It's you, toad!...Fat toad!...Ill fated toad!...Forgive me!... Forgive me!...Why are you on this earth where the accursed are? But what have you done to your viscous, foetid pustules that you should have so sweet a look? When, by a higher command, you came down from above on a mission to comfort the various breeds of existing creatures, you swooped upon earth with the speed of a kite, wings unwearied by this long, splendid errand. I saw you! Poor toad! How I mused then on the infinite, as well as on my frailty. "One more being," I told myself, "who is superior to those on earth; and that by divine will. Why not I too? What place has injustice in the supreme decrees? Is the Creator mad? He is, though, the strongest, and his wrath terrible!" Since you appeared to me, monarch of marshes and ponds, clad in a glory that belongs only to God, you have, in some measure, consoled me. But my wavering wits are engulfed by such majesty! Who are you? Stay...Oh! stay longer on this earth! Fold your white wings, and do not look upward with anxious eyes...If you leave, let us leave together!"

The toad sat down on his haunches (so like man's!) and while slugs, woodlice, and snails fled at the sight of their deadly enemy, thus uttered:

"Hear me, Maldoror. Note my face, calm as a mirror. And I believe I have an intelligence equal to yours. One day you called me the mainstay of your life. Since then I have not belied the trust you placed in me. True, I'm only a common inhabitant of the reeds, but thanks to your own contact, and taking after only what was beautiful in you, my mind has grown and I can talk to you. I came to snatch you from the abyss. Those who call themselves your friends, smitten with consternation, stare at you whenever they meet your pale and stooping figure at the theatre, in public places, in churches, or squeezing between your two sinewy thighs that horse who gallops only by night, bearing his phantom master swathed in a long black cloak. Abandon these thoughts which make your heart empty as a desert: they are more scorching than fire. Your mind is so sick that you do not realise it, and think yourself normal every time crazy words (though filled with an infernal grandeur) gush from your mouth. Wretch! What have you said since the day of your birth? O sad relic of an immortal intellect, created by God with such love! You have begotten only maledictions more frightful than the sight of famished panthers! *I* would sooner have my eyelids stuck together, my body armless and legless -- or have murdered a man, than be *you*! Because I hate you. Why have this character which puzzles me? By what right do you come on earth to hold its inhabitants to ridicule, you rotting wreck buffeted by scepticism? If you don't like it here, you should go back to the spheres whence you came. A city-dweller ought not to live like a stranger in villages. We know that in space exist globes more spacious than ours, and whose creatures have an intelligence we cannot even begin to understand. Very well, be off then!...Leave this fleeting earth!...At last display your divine nature, hitherto hidden. And as soon as possible steer your ascending flight towards your own globe, which we do not covet at all, proud one that you are! -- I have not yet succeeded in identifying you as man or more-than-man! Farewell, then. Hope no longer to encounter the toad on your journey. You have been the cause of my death. *I* set out for eternity, that I may beg your forgiveness!"

If it is sometimes logical to put one's faith in the appearance of phenomena, this first canto ends here. Be not too harsh with one who still only tunes his lyre: it makes so strange a sound! If, however, you would be impartial, you will already discern a strong hand in the midst of the imperfections. As for me, I shall resume work to produce a second canto in not too long a time. The end of the nineteenth century shall see its poet (though at the outset he should not begin with a masterpiece, but follow the law of nature).

He was born on South American shores, at the mouth of the River Plate, where two peoples once enemies now struggle to outdo each other in material and moral progress. Buenos Aires, queen of the south, and Montevideo, the coquette, extend friendly hands across the argentine waters of the great estuary. But everlasting war has imposed his destructive rule upon the fields, and joyfully reaps his countless victims.

Greybeard, farewell, and if you have read this, think of me. You, young man, do not despair, for despite your opinion to the contrary, you have a friend in the vampire. Counting the *acarus sarcoptes* that causes crabs, you have two!

Translated by
Alexis Lykiard

161

CARMILLA

J. Sheridan Le Fanu

I
An Early Fright

In Styria, we, though by no means magnificent people, inhabit a castle, or schloss. A small income, in that part of the world, goes a great way. Eight or nine hundred a year does wonders. Scantily enough ours would have answered among wealthy people at home. My father is English, and I bear an English name, although I never saw England. But here, in this lonely and primitive place, where everything is so marvelously cheap, I don't really see how ever so much more money would at all materially add to our comforts, or even luxuries.

My father was in the Austrian service, and retired upon a pension and his patrimony, and purchased this feudal residence, and the small estate on which it stands, a bargain.

Nothing can be more picturesque or solitary. It stands on a slight eminence in a forest. The road, very old and narrow, passes in front of its drawbridge, never raised in my time, and its moat, stocked with perch, and sailed over by many swans, and floating on its surface white fleets of water-lilies.

Over all this the schloss shows its many-windowed front, its towers, and its Gothic chapel.

The forest opens in an irregular and very picturesque glade before its gate, and at the right a steep Gothic bridge carries the road over a stream that winds in deep shadow through the wood.

I have said that this is a very lonely place. Judge whether I say truth. Looking from the hall door towards the road, the forest in which our castle stands extends fifteen miles to the right, and twelve to the left. The nearest inhabited village is about seven of your English miles to the left. The nearest inhabited schloss of any historic associations, is that of old General Spielsdorf, nearly twenty miles away to the right.

I have said *the nearest inhabited village*, because there is, only three miles westward, that is to say in the direction of General Spielsdorf's schloss, a ruined village, with its quaint little church, now roofless, in the aisle of which are the mouldering tombs of the proud family of Karnstein, now extinct, who once owned the equally-desolate château which, in the thick of the forest, overlooks the silent ruins of the town.

Respecting the cause of the desertion of this striking and melancholy spot, there is a legend which I shall relate to you another time.

I must tell you now, how very small is the party who constitute the inhabitants of our castle. I don't include servants, or those dependents who occupy rooms in the buildings attached to the schloss. Listen, and wonder! My father, who is the kindest man on earth, but growing old; and I, at the date of my story, only nineteen. Eight years have passed since then. I and my father constituted the family at the schloss. My mother, a Styrian lady, died in my infancy, but I had a good-natured governess, who had been with me from, I might almost say, my infancy. I could not remember the time when her fat, benignant face was not a familiar picture in my memory. This was Madame Perrodon, a native of Berne, whose care and good nature in part supplied to me the loss of my mother, whom I do not even remember, so early I lost her. She made a third at our little dinner party. There was a fourth, Mademoiselle De Lafontaine, a lady such as you term, I believe, a "finishing governess." She spoke French and German, Madame Perrodon French and broken English, to which my father and I added English, which, partly to prevent its becoming a lost language among us, and partly from patriotic motives, we spoke every day. The consequence was a Babel, at which strangers used to laugh, and which I shall make no attempt to reproduce in this narrative. And there were two or three young lady friends besides, pretty nearly of my own age, who were occasional visitors, for longer or shorter terms; and these visits I sometimes returned.

These were our regular social resources; but of course there were chance visits from "neighbours" of only five or six leagues' distance. My life was, notwithstanding, rather a solitary one, I can assure you.

My gouvernantes had just so much control over me as you might conjecture such sage persons would have in this case of a rather spoiled girl, whose only parent allowed her pretty nearly her own way in everything.

The first occurence in my existence, which produced a terrible impression upon my mind, which, in fact, never has been effaced, was one of the very earliest incidents of my life which I can recollect. Some people will think it so trifling that it should not be recorded here. You will see, however, by-and-by, why I mention it. The nursery, as it was called, though I had it all to myself, was a large room in the upper story of the castle, with a steep oak roof. I can't have been more than six years old, when one night I awoke, and looking round the room from my bed, failed to see the nursery-maid. Neither was my nurse there; and I thought myself alone. I was not frightened, for I was one of those happy children who are studiously kept in ignorance of ghost stories, of fairy tales, and of all such lore that makes us cover up our heads when the door creaks suddenly, or the flicker of an expiring candle makes the shadow of a bed-post dance upon the wall, nearer to our faces. I was vexed and insulted at finding myself, as I conceived, neglected, and I began to whimper, preparatory to a hearty bout of roaring; when to my surprise, I saw a solemn, but very pretty face looking at me from the side of the bed. It was that of a young lady who was kneeling, with her hands under the coverlet. I looked at her with a kind of pleased wonder, and ceased whimpering. She caressed me with her hands, and lay down beside me on the bed, and drew me towards her, smiling; I felt immediately delightfully soothed, and fell asleep again. I was wakened by a sensation as if two needles ran into my breast very deep at the same moment, and I cried loudly. The lady started back, with her eyes fixed on me, and then slipped down upon the floor, and, as I thought, hid herself under the bed.

I was now for the first time frightened, and I yelled with all my might and main. Nurse, nursery-maid, housekeeper, all came running in, and hearing my story, they made light of it, soothing me all they could meanwhile. But, child as I was, I could perceive that their faces were pale with an unwonted look of anxiety, and I saw them look under the bed, and about the room, and peep under the tables and pluck open cupboards; and the housekeeper whispered to the nurse, "Lay your hand along that hollow in the bed; some one *did* lie there, so sure as you did not; the place is still warm."

I remember the nursery-maid petting me, and all three examining my chest, where I told them I felt the puncture, and pronouncing that there was no sign visible that any such thing had happened to me.

The housekeeper and the two other servants who were in charge of the nursery, remained sitting up all night; and from that time a servant always sat up in the nursery until I was about fourteen.

I was very nervous for a long time after this. A doctor was called in, he was pallid and elderly. How well I remember his long saturnine face, pitted with small-pox, and his chestnut wig. For a good while, every second day, he came and gave me medicine, which of course I hated.

The morning after I saw this apparition I was in a state of terror, and could not bear to be left alone, daylight though it was, for a moment.

I remember my father coming up and standing by the bedside, and talking cheerfully, and asking the nurse a number of questions, and laughing very heartily at one of the answers; and patting me on the shoulder, and kissing me, and telling me not to be frightened, that it was nothing but a dream and could not hurt me.

But I was not comforted, for I knew the visit of the strange woman was *not* a dream; and I was *awfully* frightened.

I was a little consoled by the nursery-maid's assuring me that it was she

165

who had come and looked at me, and lain down beside me in the bed, and that I must have been half-dreaming not to have known her face. But this, though supported by the nurse, did not quite satisfy me.

I remember, in the course of that day, a venerable old man, in a black cassock, coming into the room with the nurse and housekeeper, and talking a little to them, and very kindly to me; his face was very sweet and gentle, and he told me they were going to pray, and joined my hands together, and desired me to say, softly, while they were praying, "Lord, hear all good prayers for us, for Jesus' sake." I think these were the very words, for I often repeated them to myself, and my nurse used for years to make me say them in my prayers.

I remember so well the thoughtful sweet face of that white-haired old man, in his black cassock, as he stood in that rude, lofty, brown room, with the clumsy furniture of a fashion three hundred years old, about him, and the scanty light entering its shadowy atmosphere through the small lattice. He kneeled, and the three women with him, and prayed aloud with an earnest quavering voice for, what appeared to me, a long time. I forget all my life preceding that event, and for some time after it is all obscure also; but the scenes I have just described stand out vivid as the isolated pictures of the phantasmagoria surrounded by darkness.

II
A Guest

I am now going to tell you something so strange that it will require all your faith in my veracity to believe my story. It is not only true, nevertheless, but truth of which I have been an eyewitness.

It was a sweet summer evening, and my father asked me, as he sometimes did, to take a little ramble with him along that beautiful forest vista which I have mentioned as lying in front of the scloss.

"General Spielsdorf cannot come to us so soon as I had hoped," said my father, as we pursued our walk.

He was to have paid us a visit of some weeks, and we had expected his arrival next day. He was to have brought with him a young lady, his niece and ward, Mademoiselle Rheinfeldt, whom I had never seen, but whom I had heard described as a very charming girl, and in whose society I had promised myself many happy days. I was more disappointed than a young lady living in a town, or a bustling neighbourhood can possibly imagine. This visit, and the new acquaintance it promised, had furnished my day dream for many weeks.

"And how soon does he come?" I asked.

"Not till autumn. Not for two months, I dare say," he answered. "And I am very glad now, dear, that you never knew Mademoiselle Rheinfeldt."

"And why?" I asked, both mortified and curious.

"Because the poor young lady is dead," he replied. "I quite forgot I had not told you, but you were not in the room when I received the General's letter this evening."

I was very much shocked. General Spielsdorf had mentioned in his first letter, six or seven weeks before, that she was not so well as he would wish her, but there was nothing to suggest the remotest suspicion of danger.

"Here is the General's letter," he said, handing it to me. "I am afraid he is in great affliction; the letter appears to me to have been written very nearly in distraction."

We sat down on a rude bench, under a group of magnificent lime trees. The sun was setting with all its melancholy splendour behind the sylvan horizon, and the stream that flows beside our home, and passes under the steep old bridge I have mentioned, wound through many a group of noble trees, almost at our feet, reflecting in its current the fading crimson of the sky. General Spielsdorf's letter was extraordinary, so vehement, and in some places so self-contradictory, that I read it twice over -- the second time aloud to my father -- and was still unable to account for it, except by supposing that grief had unsettled his mind.

It said, "I have lost my darling daughter, for as such I loved her. During the last days of dear Bertha's illness I was not able to write to you. Before then I had no idea of her danger. I have lost her, and now learn *all*, too late. She died in the peace of innocence and in the glorious hope of a blessed futurity. The fiend who betrayed our infatuated hospitality has done it all. I thought I was receiving into my house innocence, gaiety, a charming companion for my lost Bertha. Heavens! what a fool I have been! I thank God my child died without a suspicion of the cause of her sufferings. She is gone without so much as conjecturing the nature of her illness, and the accursed passion of the agent of all this misery. I devote my remaining days to tracking and extinguishing a monster. I am told I may hope to accomplish my righteous and merciful purpose. At present there is scarely a gleam of light to guide me. I curse my conceited incredulity, my despicable affectation of superiority, my blindness, my obstinacy -- all -- too late. I cannot write or talk collectedly now. I am distracted. So soon as I shall have a little recovered, I mean to devote myself for a time to inquiry, which may possibly lead me as far as Vienna. Some time in the autumn, two months hence, or earlier if I live, I will see you -- that is, if you permit me; I will then tell you all that I scarce dare put upon paper now. Farewell. Pray for me, dear friend."

In these terms ended this strange letter. Though I had never seen Bertha Rheinfeldt, my eyes filled with tears at the sudden intelligence; I was startled, as well as profoundly disappointed.

The sun had now set, and it was twilight by the time I had returned the General's letter to my father.

It was a soft clear evening, and we loitered, speculating upon the possible meanings of the violent and incoherent sentences which I had just been reading. We had nearly a mile to walk before reaching the road that passes the scloss in front, and by that time the moon was shining brilliantly. At the drawbridge we met Madame Perrodon and Mademoiselle De Lafontaine, who had come out, without their bonnets, to enjoy the exquisite moonlight.

We heard their voices gabbling in animated dialogue as we approached. We joined them at the drawbridge, and turned about to admire with them the beautiful scene.

The glade through which we had just walked lay before us. At our left the narrow road wound away under clumps of lordly trees, and was lost to sight amid the thickening forest. At the right the same road crosses the steep and picturesque bridge, near which stands a ruined tower, which once guarded that pass; and beyond the bridge an abrupt eminence rises, covered with trees, and showing in the shadow some grey ivy-clustered rocks.

Over the sward and low grounds, a thin film of mist was stealing, like smoke, marking the distances with a transparent veil; and here and there we could see the river faintly flashing in the moonlight.

No softer, sweeter scene could be imagined. The news I had just heard made it melancholy; but nothing could disturb its character of profound serenity, and the enchanted glory and vagueness of prospect.

My father, who enjoyed the picturesque, and I, stood looking in silence over the expanse beneath us. The two good governesses, standing a little way behind us, discoursed upon the scene, and were eloquent upon the moon.

Madame Perrodon was fat, middle-aged and romantic, and talked and sighed poetically. Mademoiselle De Lafontaine -- in right of her father, who was a German, assumed to be psychological, metaphysical and something of a mystic -- now declared that when the moon shone with a light so intense it was well known that it indicated a special spiritual activity. The effect of the full moon in such a state of brilliancy was manifold. It acted on dreams, it acted on lunacy, it acted on nervous people; it had marvellous physical influences connected with life. Mademoiselle related that her cousin, who was mate of a merchant ship, having taken a nap on deck on such a night, lying on his back, with his face full in the light of the moon, had wakened, after a dream of an old woman clawing him by the cheek, with his features horribly drawn to one side; and his countenance had never quite recovered its equilibrium.

"The moon, this night," she said, "is full of odylic and magnetic influence -- and see, when you look behind you at the front of the schloss, how all its windows flash and twinkle with that silvery splendour, as if unseen hands had lighted up the rooms to receive fairy guests."

There are indolent states of the spirits in which, indisposed to talk ourselves, the talk of others is pleasant to our listless ears; and I gazed on, pleased with the tinkle of the ladies' conversation.

"I have got into one of my moping moods tonight," said my father, after a silence, and quoting Shakespeare, whom, by way of keeping up our English, he used to read aloud, he said:--

"In truth I know not why I am so sad:
It wearies me; you say it wearies you;
But how I got it - came by it.

"I forget the rest. But I feel as if some great misfortune were hanging over us. I suppose the poor general's afflicted letter has had something to do with it."

At this moment the unwonted sound of carriage wheels and many hoofs upon the road, arrested our attention.

They seemed to be approaching from the high ground overlooking the bridge, and very soon the equipage emerged from that point. Two horsemen first crossed the bridge, then came a carriage drawn by four horses, and two men rode behind.

It seemed to be the travelling carriage of a person of rank; and we were all immediately absorbed in watching that very unusual spectacle. It became, in a few moments, greatly more interesting, for just as the carriage had passed the summit of the steep bridge, one of the leaders, taking fright, communicated his panic to the rest, and, after a plunge or two, the whole team broke into a wild gallop together, and dashing between the horsemen who rode in front, came thundering along the road towards us with the speed of a hurricane.

The excitement of the scene was made more painful by the clear, long-drawn screams of a female voice from the carriage window.

We all advanced in curiosity and horror; my father in silence, the rest with various ejaculations of terror.

Our suspense did not last long. Just before you reach the castle drawbridge, on the route they were coming, there stands by the roadside a magnificent lime tree, on the other side stands an ancient stone cross, at sight of which the horses, now going at a pace that was perfectly frightful, swerved so as to bring the wheel over the projecting roots of the tree.

I knew what was coming. I covered my eyes, unable to see it out, and turned my head away; at the same moment I heard a cry from my lady-friends, who had gone on a little.

Curiosity opened my eyes, and I saw a scene of utter confusion. Two of the horses were on the ground, the carriage lay upon its side, with two wheels in the air; the men were busy removing the traces, and a lady, with a commanding air and figure had got out, and stood with clasped hands, raising the handkerchief that was in them every now and then to her eyes. Through the carriage door was now lifted a young lady, who appeared to be lifeless. My dear old father was already beside the elder lady, with his hat

169

in his hand, evidently tendering his aid and the resources of his schloss. The lady did not appear to hear him, or to have eyes for anything but the slender girl who was being placed against the slope of the bank.

I approached; the young lady was apparently stunned, but she was certainly not dead. My father, who piqued himself on being something of a physician, had just had his fingers to her wrist and assured the lady, who declared herself her mother, that her pulse, though faint and irregular, was undoubtedly still distinguishable. The lady clasped her hands and looked upward, as if in a momentary transport of gratitude; but immediately she broke out again in that threatrical way which is, I believe, natural to some people.

She was what is called a fine-looking woman for her time of life, and must have been handsome; she was tall, but not thin, and dressed in black velvet, and looked rather pale, but with a proud and commanding countenance, though now agitated strangely.

"Was ever being so born to calamity?" I heard her say, with clasped hands, as I came up. "Here am I, on a journey of life and death, in prosecuting which to lose an hour is possibly to lose all. My child will not have recovered sufficiently to resume her route for who can say how long. I must leave her; I cannot, dare not, delay. How far on, sir, can you tell, is the nearest village? I must leave her there; and shall not see my darling, or even hear of her till my return, three months hence."

I plucked my father by the coat, and whispered earnestly in his ear, "Oh! papa, pray ask her to let her stay with us -- it would be so delightful. Do, pray."

"If Madame will entrust her child to the care of my daughter, and of her good gouvernante, Madame Perrodon, and permit her to remain as our guest, under my charge, until her return, it will confer a distinction and an obligation upon us, and we shall treat her with all the care and devotion which so sacred a trust deserves."

"I cannot do that, sir, it would be to task your kindness and chivalry too cruelly," said the lady, distractedly.

"It would, on the contrary, be to confer on us a very great kindness at the moment when we most need it. My daughter has just been diasppointed by a cruel misfortune, in a visit from which she had long anticipated a great deal of happiness. If you confide this young lady to our care it will be her best consolation. The nearest village on your route is distant, and affords no such inn as you could think of placing your daughter at; you cannot allow her to continue her journey for any considerable distance without danger. If, as you say, you cannot suspend your journey, you must part with her to-night, and nowhere could you do so with more honest assurances of care and tenderness than here."

There was something in this lady's air and appearance so distinguished, and even imposing, and in her manner so engaging, as to impress one, quite apart from the dignity of her equipage, with a conviction that she was a person of consequence.

By this time the carriage was replaced in its upright position, and the horses, quite tractable, in the traces again.

The lady threw on her daughter a glance which I fancied was not quite so affectionate as one might have anticipated from the beginning of the scene; then beckoned slightly to my father, and withdrew two or three steps with him out of hearing; and talked to him with a fixed and stern countenance, not at all like that with which she had hitherto spoken.

I was filled with wonder that my father did not seem to perceive the change, and also unspeakably curious to learn what it could be that she was speaking, almost in his ear, with so much earnestness and rapidity.

Two or three minutes at most, I think, she remained thus employed, then she turned, and a few steps brought her to where her daughter lay, supported by Madame Perrodon. She kneeled beside her for a moment and whispered, as Madame supposed, a little benediction in her ear; then hastily kissing her, she stepped into her carriage, the door was closed, the footmen in stately liveries jumped up behind, the outriders spurred on, the postilions cracked their whips, the horses plunged and broke suddenly into a furious canter that threatened soon again to become a gallop, and the carriage whirled away, followed at the same rapid pace by the two horsemen in the rear.

III
We Compare Notes

We followed the *cortège* with our eyes until it was swiftly lost to sight in the misty wood; and the very sound of the hoofs and wheels died away in the silent night air.

Nothing remained to assure us that the adventure had not been an illusion of a moment but the young lady, who just at that moment opened her eyes. I could not see, for her face was turned from me, but she raised her head, evidently looking about her, and I heard a very sweet voice ask complainingly, "Where is mamma?"

Our good Madame Perrodon answered tenderly, and added some comfortable assurances.

I then heard her ask:

"Where am I? What is this place?" and after that she said, "I don't see the carriage; and Matska, where is she?"

Madame answered all her questions in so far as she understood them; and gradually the young lady remembered how the misadventure came about, and was glad that no one in, or in attendance on, the carriage was hurt; and on learning that her mamma had left her here, till her return in about three months, she wept.

I was going to add my consolations to those of Madame Perrodon when Mademoiselle De Lafontaine placed her hand upon my arm, saying:

"Don't approach, one at a time is as much as she can at present converse with; a very little excitement would possibly overpower her now."

As soon as she is comfortably in bed, I thought, I will run up to her room and see her.

My father in the meantime had sent a servant on horseback for the physician, who lived about two leagues away; and a bedroom was being prepared for the young lady's reception.

The stranger now rose, and leaning on Madame's arm, walked slowly over the drawbridge and into the castle gate.

In the hall, servants waited to receive her, and she was conducted forthwith to her room.

The room we usually sat in as our drawing-room is long, having four windows, that looked over the moat and drawbridge, upon the forest scene I have just described.

It is furnished in old carved oak, with large carved cabinets, and the chairs are cushioned with crimson Utrecht velvet. The walls are covered with tapestry, and surrounded with great gold frames, the figures being as large as life, in ancient and very curious costume, and the subjects represented are hunting, hawking, and generally festive. It is not too stately to be extremely comfortable; and here we had our tea, for with his usual patriotic leanings he insisted that the national beverage should make its appearance regularly with our coffee and chocolate.

We sat here this night, and with candles lighted, were talking over the adventure of the evening.

Madame Perrodon and Mademoiselle De Lafontaine were both of our party. The young stranger had hardly lain down in her bed when she sank into a deep sleep; and those ladies had left her in the care of a servant.

"How do you like our guest?" I asked, as soon as Madame entered. "Tell me all about her?"

"I like her extremely," answered Madame, "she is, I almost think, the prettiest creature I ever saw; about your age, and so gentle and nice."

"She is absolutely beautiful," threw in Mademoiselle, who had peeped for a moment into the stranger's room.

"And such a sweet voice!" added Madame Perrodon.

"Did you remark a woman in the carriage, after it was set up again, who did not get out," inquired Mademoiselle, "but only looked from the window?"

No, we had not seen her.

Then she described a hideous black woman, with a sort of coloured turban on her head, who was gazing all the time from the carriage window, nodding and grinning derisively towards the ladies, with gleaming eyes and large white eye-balls, and her teeth set as if in fury.

"Did you remark what an ill-looking pack of men the servants were?" asked Madame.

"Yes," said my father, who had just come in, "ugly, hang-dog looking fellows, as ever I beheld in my life. I hope they mayn't rob the poor lady in the forest. They are clever rogues, however; they got everything to rights in a minute."

"I dare say they are worn out with too long travelling," said Madame. "Besides looking wicked, their faces were so strangely lean, and dark, and sullen. I am very curious, I own; but I dare say the young lady will tell us all about it to-morrow, if she is sufficiently recovered."

"I don't think she will," said my father, with a mysterious smile, and a little nod of his head, as if he knew more about it than he cared to tell us.

This made me all the more inquisitive as to what had passed between him and the lady in the black velvet, in the brief but earnest interview that had immediately preceded her departure.

We were scarcely alone, when I entreated him to tell me. He did not need much pressing.

"There is no particular reason why I should not tell you. She expressed a reluctance to trouble us with the care of her daughter, saying she was in delicate health, and nervous, but not subject to any kind of seizure -- she volunteered that -- nor to any illusion; being, in fact, perfectly sane."

"How very odd to say all that!" I interpolated. "It was so unnecessary."

"At all events it *was* said," he laughed, "and as you wish to know all that passed, which was indeed very little, I tell you. She then said, *I am making a long journey of vital importance* -- she emphasized the word -- *rapid and secret; I shall return for my child in three months; in the meantime, she will be silent as to who we are, whence we come, and whither we are travelling.* That is all she said. She spoke very pure French. When she said the word 'secret', she paused for a few seconds, looking sternly, her eyes fixed on mine. I fancy she makes a great point of that. You saw how quickly she was gone. I hope I have not done a foolish thing, in taking charge of the young lady."

For my part, I was delighted. I was longing to see and talk to her; and only waiting till the doctor should give me leave. You, who live in towns, can have no idea how great an event the introduction of a new friend is, in such a solitude as surrounded us.

The doctor did not arrive till nearly one o'clock; but I could no more have gone to my bed and slept, than I could have overtaken, on foot, the carriage in which the princess in black velvet had driven away.

When the physician came down to the drawing-room, it was to report very favourably upon his patient. She was now sitting up, her pulse quite regular, apparently perfectly well. She had sustained no injury, and the little shock to her nerves had passed away quite harmlessly. There could be no harm certainly in my seeing her, if we both wished it; and with this permission, I sent, forthwith, to know whether she would allow me to visit her for a few minutes in her room.

The servant returned immediately to say that she desired nothing more.

You may be sure I was not long in availing myself of this permission.

Our visitor lay in one of the handsomest rooms in the schloss. It was, perhaps, a little stately. There was a sombre piece of tapestry opposite the foot of the bed, representing Cleopatra with the asps to her bosom; and other solemn classic scenes were displayed, a little faded, upon the other walls. But there was gold carving, and rich and varied colour enough in the other decorations of the room, to more than redeem the gloom of the old tapestry.

There were candles at the bed side. She was sitting up; her slender pretty figure enveloped in the soft silk dressing-gown, embroidered with flowers, and lined with thick quilted silk, which her mother had thrown over her feet as she lay upon the ground.

What was it that, as I reached the bed side and had just begun my little greeting, struck me dumb in a moment, and made me recoil a step or two from before her? I will tell you.

I saw the very face which had visited me in my childhood at night, which remained so fixed in my memory, and on which I had for so many years so often ruminated with horror, when no one suspected of what I was thinking.

It was pretty, even beautiful; and when I first beheld it, wore the same melancholy expression.

But this almost instantly lighted into a strange fixed smile of recognition.

There was a silence of fully a minute, and then at length *she* spoke; *I* could not.

"How wonderful!" she exclaimed. "Twelve years ago, I saw your face in a dream, and it has haunted me ever since."

"Wonderful indeed!" I repeated, overcoming with an effort the horror that had for a time suspended my utterances. "Twelve years ago, in vision or reality, *I* certainly saw you. I could not forget your face. It has remained before my eyes ever since."

Her smile had softened. Whatever I had fancied strange in it, was gone, and it and her dimpling cheeks were now delightfully pretty and intelligent.

I felt reassured, and continued more in the vein which hospitality indicated, to bid her welcome, and to tell her how much pleasure her accidental arrival had given us all, and especially what a happiness it was to me.

I took her hand as I spoke. I was a little shy, as lonely people are, but the situation made me eloquent, and even bold. She pressed my hand, she laid hers upon it, and her eyes glowed, as, looking hastily into mine, she smiled again, and blushed.

She answered my welcome very prettily. I sat down beside her, still wondering; and she said:

"I must tell you my vision about you; it is so very strange that you and I should have had, each of the other, so vivid a dream, that each should have seen, I you and you me, looking as we do now, when of course we both were mere children. I was a child, about six years old, and I awoke from a confused and troubled dream, and found myself in a room, unlike my nursery, wainscoted clumsily in some dark wood, and with cupboards and bedsteads, and chairs and benches placed about it. The beds were, I thought, all empty, and the room itself without any one but myself in it; and I, after looking about me for some time, and admiring especially an iron candlestick, with two branches, which I should certainly know again, crept under one of the beds to reach the window; but as I got under the bed, I heard some one crying; and looking up, while I was still upon my knees, I saw *you* -- most assuredly you -- as I see you now; a beautiful young lady, with golden hair and large blue eyes, and lips -- your lips -- you, as you are here. Your looks won me; I climbed on the bed and put my arms about you, and I think we both fell asleep. I was aroused by a scream; you were sitting up screaming. I was frightened, and slipped down upon the ground, and, it seemed to me, lost consciousness for a moment; and when I came to myself, I was again in my nursery at home. Your face I have never forgotten since. I could not be misled by mere resemblance. You *are* the lady whom I then saw."

It was now my turn to relate my corresponding vision, which I did, to the undisguised wonder of my new acquaintance.

"I don't know which should be most afraid of the other," she said, again smiling. "If you were less pretty I think I should be very much afraid of you, but being as you are, and you and I both so young, I feel only that I have made your acquaintance twelve years ago, and have already a right to your intimacy; at all events, it does seem as if we were destined, from our earliest childhood, to be friends. I wonder whether you feel as strangely drawn towards me as I do to you; I have never had a friend -- shall I find one now?" She sighed, and her fine dark eyes gazed passionately on me.

Now the truth is, I felt rather unaccountably towards the beautiful stranger. I did feel, as she said, "drawn towards her," but there was also something of repulsion. In this ambiguous feeling, however, the sense of attraction immensely prevailed. She interested and won me; she was so beautiful and so indescribably engaging.

I perceived now something of languor and exhaustion stealing over her, and hastened to bid her good night.

"The doctor thinks," I added, "that you ought to have a maid to sit up with you to-night; one of ours is waiting, and you will find her a useful and quiet creature."

"How kind of you, but I could not sleep, I never could with an attendant in the room. I shan't require any assistance -- and, shall I confess my weakness, I am haunted with a terror of robbers. Our house was robbed

175

once, and two servants murdered, so I always lock my door. It has become a habit -- and you look so kind I know you will forgive me. I see there is a key in the lock."

She held me close in her pretty arms for a moment and whispered in my ear, "Good-night, darling, it is very hard to part with you, but good-night; to-morrow, but not early, I shall see you again."

She sank back on the pillow with a sigh, and her fine eyes followed me with a fond and melancholy gaze, and she murmured again, "Good-night, dear friend."

Young people like, and even love, on impulse. I was flattered by the evident, though as yet undeserved, fondness she showed me. I liked the confidence with which she at once received me. She was determined that we should be very dear friends.

Next day came and we met again. I was delighted with my companion; that is to say, in many respects.

Her looks lost nothing in daylight -- she was certainly the most beautiful creature I had ever seen, and the unpleasant remembrance of the face presented in my early dream, had lost the effect of the first unexpected recognition.

She confessed that she had experienced a similar shock on seeing me, and precisely the same faint antipathy that had mingled with my admiration of her. We now laughed together over our momentary horrors.

IV

Her Habits - A Saunter

I told you that I was charmed with her in most particulars.

There were some that did not please me so well.

She was above the middle height of women. I shall begin by describing her. She was slender, and wonderfully graceful. Except that her movements were languid -- *very* languid -- indeed, there was nothing in her appearance to indicate an invalid. Her complexion was rich and brilliant; her features were small and beautifully formed; her eyes large, dark, and lustrous; her hair quite wonderful, I never saw hair so magnificently thick and long when it was down about her shoulders; I have often placed my hands under it, and laughed with wonder at its weight. It was exquisitely fine and soft, and in colour a rich very dark brown, with something of gold. I loved to let it down, tumbling with its own weight, as, in her room, she lay back in her chair talking in her sweet low voice, I used to fold and braid it, and spread it out and play with it. Heavens! If I had but known all!

I said there were particulars which did not please me. I have told you that her confidence won me the first night I saw her; but I found that she exercised with respect to herself, her mother, her history, everything in fact connected with her life, plans, and people, an ever-wakeful reserve. I dare say I was unreasonable, perhaps I was wrong; I dare say I ought to have respected the solemn injunction laid upon my father by the stately lady in black velvet. But curiosity is a restless and unscrupulous passion, and no one girl can endure, with patience, that hers should be baffled by another. What harm could it do anyone to tell me what I so ardently desired to know? Had she no trust in my good sense or honour? Why would she not believe me when I assured her, so solemnly, that I would not divulge one syllable of what she told me to any mortal breathing?

There was a coldness, it seemed to me, beyond her years, in her smiling melancholy persistent refusal to afford me the least ray of light.

I cannot say we quarrelled upon this point, for she would not quarrel upon any. It was, of course, very unfair of me to press her, very ill-bred, but I really could not help it; and I might just as well have let it alone.

What she did tell me amounted, in my unconscionable estimation -- to nothing.

It was all summed up in three very vague disclosures:

First:-- Her name was Carmilla.

Second:-- Her family was very ancient and noble.

Third:-- Her home lay in the direction of the west.

She would not tell me the name of her family, nor their armorial bearings, nor the name of their estate, nor even that of the country they lived in.

You are not to suppose that I worried her incessantly on these subjects. I watched opportunity, and rather insinuated than urged my inquiries. Once or twice, indeed, I did attack her more directly. But no matter what my tactics, utter failure was invariably the result. Reproaches and caresses were all lost upon her. But I must add this, that her evasion was conducted with so pretty a melancholy and deprecation, with so many, and even passionate declarations of her liking for me, and trust in my honour, and with so many promises that I should at last know all, that I could not find it in my heart long to be offended with her.

She used to place her pretty arms about my neck, draw me to her, and laying her cheek to mine, murmur with her lips near my ear, "Dearest, your little heart is wounded; think me not cruel because I obey the irresistible law of my strength and weakness; if your heart is wounded, my wild heart bleeds with yours. In the rapture of my enormous humiliation I live in your warm life, and you shall die -- die, sweetly die -- into mine. I cannot help it; as I draw near to you, you, in your turn, will draw near to others, and learn the rapture of that cruelty, which yet is love; so, for a while, seek to know no more of me and mine, but trust me with all your loving spirit."

And when she had spoken such a rhapsody, she would press me more closely in her trembling embrace, and her lips in soft kisses gently glow upon my cheek.

Her agitations and her language were unintelligible to me.

From these foolish embraces, which were not of very frequent occurrence, I must allow, I used to wish to extricate myself; but my energies seemed to fail me. Her murmured words sounded like a lullaby in my ear, and soothed my resistance into a trance, from which I only seemed to recover myself when she withdrew her arms.

In these mysterious moods I did not like her. I experienced a strange tumultuous excitement that was pleasurable, ever and anon, mingled with a vague sense of fear and disgust. I had no distinct thoughts about her while such scenes lasted, but I was conscious of a love growing into adoration, and also of abhorrence. This I know is paradox, but I can make no other attempt to explain the feeling.

I now write, after an interval of more than ten years, with a trembling hand, with a confused and horrible recollection of certain occurrences and situations, in the ordeal through which I was unconsciously passing; though with a vivid and very sharp remembrance of the main current of my story. But, I suspect, in all lives there are certain emotional scenes, those in which our passions have been most wildly and terribly roused, that are of all others the most vaguely and dimly remembered.

Sometimes after an hour of apathy, my strange and beautiful companion would take my hand and hold it with a fond pressure, renewed again and again; blushing softly, gazing in my face with languid and burning eyes, and breathing so fast that her dress rose and fell with the tumultuous respiration. It was like the ardour of a lover; it embarrassed me; it was hateful and yet overpowering; and with gloating eys she drew me to her, and her hot lips travelled along my cheek in kisses; and she would whisper, almost in sobs, "You are mine, you *shall* be mine, and you and I are one for ever." Then she has thrown herself back in her chair, with her small hands over her eyes, leaving me trembling.

"Are we related," I used to ask; "what can you mean by all this? I remind you perhaps of some one whom you love; but you must not, I hate it; I don't know you -- I don't know myself when you look so and talk so."

She used to sigh at my vehemence, then turn away and drop my hand.

Respecting these very extraordinary manifestations I strove in vain to form any satisfactory theory -- I could not refer them to affectation or trick. It was unmistakably the momentary breaking out of suppressed instinct and emotion. Was she, notwithstanding her mother's volunteered denial, subject to brief visitations of insanity; or was there here a disguise and a romance? I had read in old story books of such things. What if a boyish lover had found his way into the house, and sought to prosecute his suit in masquerade, with the assistance of a clever old adventuress? But there were many things against this hypothesis, highly interesting as it was to my vanity.

I could boast of no little attentions such as masculine gallantry delights to offer. Between these passionate moments there were long intervals of common-place, of gaiety, of brooding melancholy, during which, except that I detected her eyes so full of melancholy fire, following me, at times I might have been as nothing to her. Except in these brief periods of mysterious excitement her ways were girlish; and there was always a languor about her, quite incompatible with a masculine state of health.

In some respects her habits were odd. Perhaps not so singular in the opinion of a town lady like you, as they appeared to us rustic people. She used to come down very late, generally not till one o'clock, she would then take a cup of chocolate, but eat nothing; we then went out for a walk, which was a mere saunter, and she seemed, almost immediately, exhausted, and either returned to the schloss or sat on one of the benches that were placed, here and there, among the trees. This was a bodily languor in which her mind did not sympathise. She was always an animated talker, and very intelligent.

She sometimes alluded for a moment to her own home, or mentioned an adventure or situation, or an early recollection, which indicated a people of strange manners, and described customs of which we knew nothing. I gathered from these chance hints that her native country was much more remote than I had at first fancied.

As we sat thus one afternoon under the trees a funeral passed us by. It was that of a pretty young girl, whom I had often seen, the daughter of one of the rangers of the forest. The poor man was walking behind the coffin of his darling; she was his only child, and he looked quite heartbroken. Peasants walking two-and-two came behind, they were singing a funeral hymn.

I rose to mark my respect as they passed, and joined in the hymn they were very sweetly singing.

My companion shook me a little roughly, and I turned surprised.

She said brusquely, "Don't you perceive how discordant that is?"

"I think it very sweet, on the contrary," I answered, vexed at the interruption, and very uncomfortable, lest the people who composed the little procession should observe and resent what was passing.

I resumed, therefore, instantly, and was again interrupted. "You pierce my ears," said Carmilla, almost angrily, and stopping her ears with her tiny fingers. "Besides, how can you tell that your religion and mine are the same; your forms wound me, and I hate funerals. What a fuss! Why, *you* must die -- *everyone* must die; and all are happier when they do. Come home."

"My father has gone on with the clergyman to the churchyard. I thought you knew she was to be buried to-day."

"*She?* I don't trouble my head about peasants. I don't know who she is," answered Carmilla, with a flash from her fine eyes.

"She is the poor girl who fancied she saw a ghost a fortnight ago, and has been dying ever since, till yesterday, when she expired."

179

"Tell me nothing about ghosts. I shan't sleep to-night if you do."

"I hope there is no plague or fever coming; all this looks very like it," I continued. "The swineherd's young wife died only a week ago, and she thought something seized her by the throat as she lay in her bed, and nearly strangled her. Papa says such horrible fancies do accompany some forms of fever. She was quite well the day before. She sank afterwards, and died before a week."

"Well, *her* funeral is over, I hope, and *her* hymn sung; and our ears shan't be tortured with that discord and jargon. It has made me nervous. Sit down here, beside me; sit close; hold my hand; press it hard -- hard -- harder."

We had moved a little back, and had come to another seat.

She sat down. Her face underwent a change that alarmed and even terrified me for a moment. It darkened, and became horribly livid; her teeth and hands were clenched, and she frowned and compressed her lips, while she stared down upon the ground at her feet, and trembled all over with a continued shudder as irrepressible as ague. All her energies seemed strained to suppress a fit, with which she was then breathlessly tugging; and at length a low convulsive cry of suffering broke from her, and gradually the hysteria subsided. "There! That comes of strangling people with hymns!" she said at last. "Hold me, hold me still. It is passing away."

And so gradually it did; and perhaps to dissipate the sombre impression which the spectacle had left upon me, she became unusually animated and chatty; and so we got home.

This was the first time I had seen her exhibit any definable symptoms of that delicacy of health which her mother had spoken of. It was the first time, also, I had seen her exhibit anything like temper.

Both passed away like a summer cloud; and never but once afterwards did I witness on her part a momentary sign of anger. I will tell you how it happened.

She and I were looking out of one of the long drawing-room windows, when there entered the court-yard, over the drawbridge, a figure of a wanderer whom I knew very well. He used to visit the schloss generally twice a year.

It was the figure of a hunchback, with the sharp lean features that generally accompany deformity. He wore a pointed black beard, and he was smiling from ear to ear, showing his white fangs. He was dressed in buff, black, and scarlet, and crossed with more straps and belts than I could count, from which hung all manner of things. Behind, he carried a magic-lantern, and two boxes, which I well knew, in one of which was a salamander, and in the other a mandrake. These monsters used to make my father laugh. They were compounded of parts of monkeys, parrots, squirrels, fish, and hedgehogs, dried and stitched together with great neatness and startling effect. He had a fiddle, a box of conjuring apparatus, a pair of foils and masks attached to his belt, several other mysterious cases dangling about him, and a black staff with copper ferrules in his hand. His companion was a rough spare dog, that followed at his heels, but stopped short, suspiciously at the drawbridge, and in a little while began to howl dismally.

In the meantime, the mountebank, standing in the midst of the courtyard, raised his grotesque hat, and made us a very ceremonious bow, paying his compliments very volubly in execrable French, and German not much better. Then, disengaging his fiddle, he began to scrape a lively air, to which he sang with a merry discord, dancing with ludicrous airs and activity, that made me laugh, in spite of the dog's howling.

Then he advanced to the window with many smiles and salutations, and his hat in his left hand, his fiddle under his arm, and with a fluency that never took breath, he gabbled a long advertisement of all his accomplishments, and the resources of the various arts which he placed at our service, and the curiosities and entertainments which it was in his power, at our bidding to display.

"Will your ladyships be pleased to buy an amulet against the oupire, which is going like the wolf, I hear, through these woods," he said, dropping his hat on the pavement. "They are dying of it right and left, and here is a charm that never fails; only pinned to the pillow, and you may laugh in his face."

These charms consisted of oblong slips of vellum, with cabalistic ciphers and diagrams upon them.

Carmilla instantly purchased one, and so did I.

He was looking up, and we were smiling down upon him, amused; at least, I could answer for myself. His piercing black eye, as he looked up in our faces, seemed to detect something that fixed for a moment his curiosity.

In an instant he unrolled a leather case, full of all manner of odd little steel instruments.

"See here, my lady," he said, displaying it, and addressing me, "I profess, among other things less useful, the art of dentistry. Plague take the dog!" he interpolated. "Silence, beast! He howls so that your ladyships can scarcely hear a word. Your noble friend, the young lady at your right, has the sharpest tooth -- long, thin, pointed, like an awl, like a needle; ha, ha! With my sharp and long sight, as I look up, I have seen it distinctly; now if it happens to hurt the young lady, and I think it must, here am I, here are my file, my punch, my nippers; I will make it round and blunt, if her ladyship pleases; no longer the tooth of a fish, but of a beautiful young lady as she is. Hey? Is the young lady displeased? Have I been too bold? Have I offended her?"

The young lady, indeed, looked very angry as she drew back from the window.

"How dare that mountebank insult us so? Where is your father? I shall

181

demand redress from him. My father would have had the wretch tied up to the pump, and flogged with a cart-whip, and burnt to the bones with the castle brand!"

She retired from the window a step or two, and sat down, and had hardly lost sight of the offender, when her wrath subsided as suddenly as it had risen, and she gradually recovered her usual tone, and seemed to forget the little hunchback and his follies.

My father was out of spirits that evening. On coming in he told us that there had been another case very similar to the two fatal ones which had lately occurred. The sister of a young peasant on his estate, only a mile away, was very ill, had been, as she described it, attacked very nearly in the same way, and was now slowly but steadily sinking.

"All this," said my father, "is strictly referable to natural causes. These poor people infect one another with their superstitions, and so repeat in imagination the images of terror that have infested their neighbours."

"But that very circumstance frightens one horribly," said Carmilla.

"How so?" inquired my father.

"I am so afraid of fancying I see such things; I think it would be as bad as reality."

"We are in God's hands; nothing can happen without His permission, and all will end well for those who love Him. He is our faithful creator; He has made us all, and will take care of us."

"Creator! *Nature!*" said the young lady in answer to my gentle father. "And this disease that invades the country is natural. Nature. All things proceed from Nature -- don't they? All things in the heaven, in the earth, and under the earth, act and live as Nature ordains? I think so."

"The doctor said he would come here to-day," said my father, after a silence. "I want to know what he thinks about it, and what he thinks we had better do."

"Doctors never did me any good," said Carmilla.

"Then you have been ill?" I asked.

"More ill than ever you were," she answered.

"Long ago?"

"Yes, a long time. I suffered from this very illness; but I forget all but my pain and weakness, and they were not so bad as are suffered in other diseases."

"You were very young then?"

"I dare say; let us talk no more of it. You would not wound a friend?" She looked languidly in my eyes, and passed her arm round my waist lovingly, and let me out of the room. My father was busy over some papers near the window.

"Why does your papa like to frighten us?" said the pretty girl, with a sigh and a little shudder.

"He doesn't, dear Carmilla, it is the very furthest thing from his mind.

"Are you afraid, dearest?"

"I should be very much if I fancied there was any real danger of my being attacked as those poor people were."

"You are afraid to die?"

"Yes, everyone is."

"But to die as lovers may -- to die together, so that they may live together. Girls are caterpillars while they live in the world, to be finally butterflies when the summer comes; but in the meantime there are grubs and larvae, don't you see -- each with their peculiar propensities, necessities and structure. So says Monsieur Buffon, in his big book, in the next room."

Later in the day the doctor came, and was closeted with papa for some time. He was a skilful man, of sixty and upwards, he wore powder, and shaved his pale face smooth as a pumpkin. He and papa emerged from the room together, and I heard papa laugh, and say as they came out:

"Well, I do wonder at a wise man like you. What do you say to hippogriffs and dragons?"

The doctor was smiling, and made answer, shaking his head:--

"Nevertheless, life and death are mysterious states, and we know little of the resources of either."

And so they walked on, and I heard no more. I did not then know what the doctor had been broaching, but I think I guess it now.

V

A Wonderful Likeness

This evening there arrived from Gratz the grave, dark-faced son of the picture-cleaner, with a horse and cart laden with two large packing-cases, having many pictures in each. It was a journey of ten leagues, and whenever a messenger arrived at the schloss from our little capital of Gratz, we used to crowd about him in the hall, to hear the news.

This arrival created in our secluded quarters quite a sensation. The cases remained in the hall, and the messenger was taken charge of by the servants till he had eaten his supper. Then with assistants, and armed with hammer, ripping chisel, and turnscrew, he met us in the hall, where we had assembled to witness the unpacking of the cases.

Carmilla sat looking listlessly on, while one after the other the old pictures, nearly all portraits, which had undergone the process of renovation, were brought to light. My mother was of an old Hungarian family, and most of these pictures, which were about to be restored to their places, had come to us through her.

My father had a list in his hand, from which he read, as the artist rummaged out the corresponding numbers. I don't know that the pictures were very good, but they were, undoubtably, very old, and some of them very curious also. They had, for the most part, the merit of being now seen by me, I may say, for the first time; for the smoke and dust of time had all but obliterated them.

"There is a picture that I have not seen yet," said my father. "In one corner, at the top of it, is the name, as well as I could read, *Marcia Karnstein*, and the date *1698*; and I am curious to see how it has turned out."

I remembered it; it was a small picture, about a foot and a half high, and nearly square, without a frame; but it was so blackened by age that I could not make it out.

The artist now produced it, with evident pride. It was quite beautiful; it was startling; it seemed to live. It was the effigy of Carmilla!

"Carmilla, dear, here is an absolute miracle. Here you are, living, smiling, ready to speak, in this picture. Isn't it beautiful, papa? And see, even the mole on her throat."

My father laughed, and said, "Certainly it is a wonderful likeness," but he looked away, and to my surprise seemed but little struck by it, and went on talking to the picture-cleaner, who was also something of an artist, and discoursed with intelligence about the portraits or other works, which his art had just brought into light and colour, while *I* was more and more lost in wonder the more I looked at the picture.

"Will you let me hang this picture in my room, papa?" I asked.

"Certainly, dear," said he, smiling, "I'm very glad you think it so like. It must be prettier even than I thought it, if it is."

The young lady did not acknowledge this pretty speech, did not seem to hear it. She was leaning back in her seat, her fine eyes under their long lashes gazing on me in contemplation, and she smiled in a kind of rapture.

"And now you can read quite plainly the name that is written in the corner. It is not Marcia; it looks as if it was done in gold. The name is *Mircalla, Countess Karnstein*, and this is a little coronet over it, and underneath *A.D. 1698*. I am descended from the Karnsteins; that is, mamma was."

"Ah!" said the lady, languidly, "so am I, I think, a very long descent, very ancient. Are there any Karnsteins living now?"

"None who bear the name, I believe. The family were ruined, I believe, in some civil wars, long ago but the ruins of the castle are only about three miles away."

"How interesting!" she said, languidly. "But see what beautiful moonlight!" She glanced through the hall door, which stood a little open. "Suppose you take a little ramble round the court, and look down at the road and river."

"It is so like the night you came to us," I said.

She sighed, smiling.

She rose, and each with her arm about the other's waist, we walked out

184

upon the pavement.

In silence, slowly we walked down to the drawbridge, where the beautiful landscape opened before us.

"And so you were thinking of the night I came here?" she almost whispered. "Are you glad I came?"

"Delighted, dear Carmilla," I answered.

"And you ask for a picture you think like me, to hang in your room," she murmured with a sigh, as she drew her arm closer about my waist, and let her pretty head sink upon my shoulder.

"How romantic you are, Carmilla," I said. "Whenever you tell me your story, it will be made up chiefly of some one great romance."

She kissed me silently.

"I am sure, Carmilla, you have been in love; that there is, at this moment, an affair of the heart going on."

"I have been in love with no one, and never shall," she whispered, "unless it should be you."

How beautiful she looked in the moonlight!

Shy and strange was the look with which she quickly hid her face in my neck and hair, with tumultuous sighs, that seemed almost to sob, and pressed in mine a hand that trembled.

Her soft cheek was glowing against mine. "Darling, darling," she murmured, "I live in you; and you would die for me, I love you so."

I started from her.

She was gazing on me with eyes from which all fire, all meaning had flown, and a face colourless and apathetic.

"Is there a chill in the air, dear?" she said drowsily. "I almost shiver; have I been dreaming? Let us come in. Come, come; come in."

"You look ill, Carmilla; a little faint. You certainly must take some wine," I said.

"Yes, I will. I'm better now. I shall be quite well in a few minutes. Yes, do give me a little wine," answered Carmilla, as we approached the door. "Let us look again for a moment; it is the last time, perhaps, I shall see the moonlight with you."

"How do you feel now, dear Carmilla? Are you really better?" I asked.

I was beginning to take alarm, lest she should have been stricken with the strange epidemic that they said had invaded the country about us.

"Papa would be grieved beyond measure," I added, "if he thought you were ever so little ill, without immediately letting us know. We have a very skilful doctor near this, the physician who was with papa to-day."

"I'm sure he is. I know how kind you all are: but, dear child, I am quite well again. There is nothing ever wrong with me, but a little weakness. People say I am languid; I am incapable of exertion; I can scarcely walk as far as a child of three years old; and every now and then the little strength I have falters, and I become as you have just seen me. But after all I am very easily set up again; in a moment I am perfectly myself. See how I have recovered."

So, indeed, she had; and she and I talked a great deal, and very animated she was; and the remainder of that evening passed without any recurrence of what I called her infatuations. I mean her crazy talk and looks, which embarrassed, and even frightened me.

But there occurred that night an event which gave my thoughts quite a new turn, and seemed to startle even Carmilla's languid nature into momentary energy.

VI

A Very Strange Agony

When we got into the drawing-room, and had sat down to our coffee and chocolate, although Carmilla did not take any, she seemed quite herself again, and Madame, and Mademoiselle De Lafontaine, joined us, and made a little card party, in the course of which papa came in for what he called his "dish of tea".

When the game was over he sat down beside Carmilla on the sofa, and asked her, a little anxiously, whether she had heard from her mother since her arrival.

She answered "No."

He then asked her whether she knew where a letter would reach her at present.

"I cannot tell," she answered, ambiguously, "but I have been thinking of leaving you; you have been already too hospitable and too kind to me. I have given you an infinity of trouble, and I should wish to take a carriage to-morrow, and post in pursuit of her; I know where I shall ultimately find her, although I dare not yet tell you."

"But you must not dream of such a thing," exclaimed my father, to my great relief. "We can't afford to lose you so, and I won't consent to your leaving us, except under the care of your mother, who was so good as to consent to your remaining with us till she should herself return. I should be quite happy if I knew that you heard from her; but this evening the accounts of the progress of the mysterious disease that has invaded our neighbourhood, grow even more alarming; and my beautiful guest, I do feel the responsibility, unaided by advice from your mother, very much. But I shall do my best; and one thing is certain, that you must not think of leaving us without her distinct direction to that effect. We should suffer too much in parting from you to consent to it easily."

"Thank you, sir, a thousand times for your hospitality," she answered, smiling bashfully. "You have all been too kind to me; I have seldom been so happy in all my life before, as in your beautiful château, under your care, and in the society of your dear daughter."

So he gallantly, in his old-fashioned way, kissed her hand, smiling, and pleased at her little speech.

I accompanied Carmilla as usual to her room, and sat and chatted with her while she prepared for bed.

"Do you think," I said, at length, "that you will ever confide fully in me?"

She turned around smiling, but made no answer, only continued to smile on me.

"You won't answer that?" I said. "You can't answer pleasantly; I ought not to have asked you."

"You were quite right to ask me that, or anything. You do not know how dear you are to me, or you could not think any confidence too great to look for. But I am under vows, no nun half so awfully, and I dare not tell my story yet, even to you. The time is very near when you shall know everything. You will think me cruel, very selfish, but love is always selfish; the more ardent the more selfish. How jealous I am you cannot know. You must come with me, loving me, to death; or else hate me, and still come with me, and *hating* me through death and after. There is no such word as indifference in my apathetic nature."

"Now, Carmilla, you are going to talk your wild nonsense again," I said hastily.

"Not I, silly little fool as I am, and full of whims and fancies; for your sake I'll talk like a sage. Were you ever at a ball?"

"No; how you do run on. What is it like? How charming it must be."

"I almost forget, it is years ago."

I laughed.

"You are not so old. Your first ball can hardly be forgotten yet."

"I remember everything about it -- with an effort. I see it all, as divers see what is going on above them, through a medium, dense, rippling, but transparent. There occurred that night what has confused the picture, and made its colours faint. I was all but assassinated in my bed, wounded *here*," she touched her breast, "and never was the same since."

"Were you near dying?"

"Yes, a very -- cruel love -- strange love, that would have taken my life. Love will have its sacrifices. No sacrifice without blood. Let us go to sleep now; I feel lazy. How can I get up just now and lock my door?"

She was lying with her tiny hands buried in her rich wavy hair, under her cheek, her little head upon the pillow, and her glittering eyes followed me wherever I moved, with a kind of shy smile that I could not decipher.

I bid her good-night, and crept from the room with an uncomfortable sensation.

I often wondered whether our pretty guest ever said her prayers. I certainly had never seen her upon her knees. In the morning she never came down until long after our family prayers were over, and at night she never

187

left the drawing room to attend our brief evening prayers in the hall.

If it had not been that it had casually come out in one of our careless talks that she had been baptised, I should have doubted her being a Christian. Religion was a subject on which I had never heard her speak a word. If I had known of the world better, this particular neglect or antipathy would not have so much surprised me.

The precautions of nervous people are infectious, and persons of a temperament are pretty sure, after a time, to imitate them. I had adopted Carmilla's habit of locking her bed-room door, having taken into my head all her whimsical alarms about midnight invaders, and prowling assassins. I had also adopted her precaution of making a brief search through her room, to satisfy herself that no lurking assassin or robber was "ensconced".

These wise measures taken, I got into my bed and fell asleep. A light was burning in my room. This was an old habit, of a very early date, and which nothing could have tempted me to dispense with.

Thus fortified I might take my rest in peace. But dreams come through stone walls, light up dark rooms, or darken light ones, and their persons make their exits and their entrances as they please, and laugh at locksmiths.

I had a dream that night that was the beginning of a very strange agony.

I cannot call it a nightmare, for I was quite conscious of being asleep. But I was equally conscious of being in my room, and lying in bed, precisely as I actually was. I saw, or fancied I saw, the room and its furniture just as I had seen it last, except that it was very dark, and I saw something moving round the foot of the bed, which at first I could not accurately distinguish. But I soon saw that it was a sooty-black animal that resembled a monstrous cat. It appeared to me about four or five feet long, for it measured fully the length of the hearth-rug as it passed over it; and it continued to-ing and fro-ing with the lithe sinister restlessness of a beast in a cage. I could not cry out, although as you may suppose, I was terrified. Its pace was growing faster, and the room rapidly darker and darker, and at length so dark that I could no longer see anything of it but its eyes. I felt it spring lightly on the bed. The two broad eyes approached my face, and suddenly I felt a stinging pain as if two large needles darted, an inch or two apart, deep into my breast. I waked with a scream. The room was lighted by the candle that burnt there all through the night, and I saw a female figure standing at the foot of the bed, a little at the right side. It was in a dark loose dress, and its hair was down and covered its shoulders. A block of stone could not have been more still. There was not the slightest stir of respiration. As I stared at it, the figure appeared to have changed its place, and was now nearer the door; then, close to it, the door opened, and it passed out.

I was now relieved, and able to breathe and move. My first thought was that Carmilla had been playing me a trick, and that I had forgotten to secure my door. I hastened to it, and found it locked as usual on the inside. I was afraid to open it -- I was horrified. I sprang into my bed and covered my head up in the bedclothes, and lay there more dead than alive till morning.

VII
Descending

It would be vain my attempting to tell you the horror with which, even now, I recall the occurrence of that night. It was no such transitory terror as a dream leaves behind it. It seemed to deepen by time, and communicated itself to the room and the very furniture that had encompassed the apparition.

I could not bear the next day to be alone for a moment. I should have told papa, but for two opposite reasons. At one time I thought he would laugh at my story, and I could not bear its being treated as a jest; and at another, I thought he might fancy that I had been attcked by the mysterious complaint which had invaded our neighbourhood. I had myself no misgivings of the kind, and as he had been rather an invalid for some time, I was afraid of alarming him.

I was comfortable enough with my good-natured companions, Madame Perrodon, and the vivacious Mademoiselle Lafontaine. They both perceived that I was out of spirits and nervous, and at length I told them what lay so heavy at my heart.

Mademoiselle laughed, but I fancied that Madame Perrodon looked anxious.

"By-the-by," said Mademoiselle, laughing, "the long lime tree walk, behind Carmilla's bedroom window, is haunted!"

"Nonsense!" exclaimed Madame, who probably thought the theme rather inopportune, "and who tells that story, my dear?"

"Martin says that he came up twice, when the old yard-gate was being repaired before sunrise, and twice saw the same female figure walking down the lime tree avenue."

"So he well might, as long as they have cows to milk in the river fields," said Madame.

"I daresay; but Martin chooses to be frightened, and never did I see fool *more* frightened."

"You must not say a word about it to Carmilla, because she can see down that walk from her room window," I interposed, "and she is, if possible, a greater coward than I."

Carmilla came down rather later than usual that day.

"I was so frightened last night," she said, so soon as we were together, "and I am sure I should have seen something dreadful if it had not been for that charm I bought from the poor little hunchback whom I called such hard names. I had a dream of something black coming round my bed, and I awoke in a perfect horror, and I really thought, for some seconds, I saw a dark figure near the chimney piece, but I felt under my pillow for my charm, and the moment my fingers touched it, the figure disappeared, and I felt quite certain, only that I had it by me, that something frightful would have made its appearance, and, perhaps, throttled me, as it did those poor people we heard of."

"Well, listen to me," I began, and recounted my adventure, at the recital of which she appeared horrified.

"And had you the charm near you?" she asked, earnestly.

"No, I had dropped it into a china vase in the drawing-room, but I shall certainly take it with me to-night, as you have so much faith in it."

At this distance of time I cannot tell you, or even understand, how I overcame my horror so effectually as to lie alone in my room that night. I remember distinctly that I pinned the charm to my pillow. I fell asleep almost immediately, and slept even more soundly than usual all night.

Next night I passed as well. My sleep was delightfully deep and dreamless. But I wakened with a sense of lassitude and melancholy, which, however, did not exceed a degree that was almost luxurious.

"Well, I told you so," said Carmilla, when I described my quiet sleep, "I had such delightful sleep myself last night; I pinned the charm to the breast of my nightdress. It was too far away the night before. I am quite sure it was all fancy, except the dreams. I used to think that evil spirits made dreams, but our doctor told me it is no such thing. Only a fever passing by, or some other malady, as they often do, he said, knocks at the door, and not being able to get in, passes on, with that alarm."

"And what do you think the charm is?" said I.

"It has been fumigated or immersed in some drug, and is an antidote against the malaria," she answered.

"Then it acts only on the body?"

"Certainly; you don't suppose that evil spirits are frightened by bits of ribbon, or the perfumes of a druggist's shop? No, these complaints, wandering in the air, begin by trying the nerves, and so infect the brain; but before they can seize upon you, the antidote repels them. That I am sure is what the charm has done for us. It is nothing magical, it is simply natural."

I should have been happier if I could quite have agreed with Carmilla, but I did my best, and the impression was losing its force.

For some nights I slept profoundly; but still every morning I felt the same lassitude, and a languor weighed upon me all day. I felt myself a changed girl. A strange melancholy was stealing over me, a melancholy that I would not have interrupted. Dim thoughts of death began to open, and an idea that I was slowly sinking took gentle, and, somehow, not unwelcome possession of me. If it was sad, the tone of mind which this induced was also sweet. Whatever it might be, my soul acquiesced in it.

I would not admit that I was ill, I would not consent to tell papa, or to have the doctor sent for.

Carmilla became more devoted to me than ever, and her strange paroxysms of languid adoration more frequent. She used to gloat on me with increasing ardour the more my strength and spirits waned. This always shocked me like a momentary glare of insanity.

Without knowing it, I was now in a pretty advanced stage of the strangest illness under which mortal ever suffered. There was an unaccountable fascination in its earlier symptoms that more than reconciled me to the incapacitating effect of that stage of the malady. This fascination increased for a time, until it reached a certain point, when gradually a sense of the horrible mingled itself with it, deepening, as you shall hear, until it discoloured and perverted the whole state of my life.

The first change I experienced was rather agreeable. It was very near the turning point from which began the descent of Avernus.

Certain vague and strange sensations visited me in my sleep. The prevailing one was of that pleasant, peculiar cold thrill which we feel in bathing, when we move against the current of a river. This was soon accompanied by dreams that seemed interminable, and were so vague that I could never recollect their scenery and persons, or any one connected portion of their action. But they left an awful impression, and a sense of exhaustion, as if I had passed through a long period of great mental exertion and danger. After all these dreams there remained on waking a remembrance of having been in a place very nearly dark, and of having spoken to people whom I could not see; and especially of one clear voice, of a female's, very deep, that spoke as if at a distance, slowly, and producing always the same sensation of indescribable solemnity and fear. Sometimes there came a sensation as if a hand was drawn softly along my cheek and neck. Sometimes it was as if warm lips kissed me, and longer and more lovingly as they reached my throat, but there the caress fixed itself. My heart beat faster, my breathing rose and fell rapidly and full drawn; a sobbing, that rose into a sense of strangulation, supervened, and turned into a dreadful convulsion, in which my senses left me, and I became unconscious.

It was now three weeks since the commencement of this unaccountable state. My sufferings had, during the last week, told upon my appearance. I had grown pale, my eyes were dilated and darkened underneath, and the languor which I had long felt began to display itself in my countenance.

My father asked me often whether I was ill; but, with an obstinacy which now seems unaccountable, I persisted in assuring him that I was quite well.

In a sense this was true. I had no pain, I could complain of no bodily derangement. My complaint seemed to be one of the imagination, or the nerves, and, horrible as my sufferings were, I kept them, with a morbid reserve, very nearly to myself.

It could not be that terrible complaint which the peasants call the oupire, for I had now been suffering for three weeks, and they were seldom ill for much more than three days, when death put an end to their miseries.

191

Carmilla complained of dreams and feverish sensations, but by no means of so alarming a kind as mine. I say that mine were extremely alarming. Had I been capable of comprehending my condition, I would have invoked aid and advice on my knees. The narcotic of an unsuspected influence was acting upon me, and my perceptions were benumbed.

I am going to tell you now of a dream that led immediately to an odd discovery.

One night, instead of the voice I was accustomed to hear in the dark, I heard one, sweet and tender, and at the same time terrible, which said, "Your mother warns you to beware of the assassin." At the same time a light unexpectedly sprang up, and I saw Carmilla, standing, near the foot of my bed, in her white nightdress, bathed, from her chin to her feet, in one great stain of blood.

I wakened with a shriek, possessed with the one idea that Carmilla was being murdered. I remember springing from my bed, and my next recollection is that of standing on the lobby, crying for help.

Madame and Mademoiselle came scurrying out of their rooms in alarm; a lamp burned always on the lobby, and seeing me, they soon learned the cause of my terror.

I insisted on our knocking at Carmilla's door. Our knocking was unanswered. It soon became a pounding and an uproar. We shrieked her name, but all was vain.

We all grew frightened, for the door was locked. We hurried back, in panic, to my room. There we rang the bell long and furiously. If my father's room had been at that side of the house, we would have called him up at once to our aid. But, alas! he was quite out of hearing, and to reach him involved an excursion for which we none of us had courage.

Servants, however, soon came running up the stairs; I had got on my dressing-gown and slippers meanwhile, and my companions were already similarly furnished. Recognizing the voices of the servants on the lobby, we sallied out together; and having renewed, as fruitlessly, our summons at Carmilla's door, I ordered the men to force the lock. They did so, and we stood, holding our lights aloft, in the doorway, and so stared into the room.

We called her by name; but there was still no reply. We looked around the room. Everything was undisturbed. It was exactly in the state in which I left it on bidding her good night. But Carmilla was gone.

VIII
Search

At sight of the room, perfectly undisturbed except for our violent entrance, we began to cool a little, and soon recovered our senses sufficiently to dismiss the men. It had struck Mademoiselle that possibly Carmilla had been wakened by the uproar at her door, and in her first panic had jumped from her bed, and hid herself in a press, or behind a curtain, from which she could not, of course, emerge until the major-domo and his myrmidons had withdrawn. We now recommenced our search, and began to call her by name again.

It was all to no purpose. Our perplexity and agitation increased. We examined the windows, but they were secured. I implored of Carmilla, if she had concealed herself, to play this cruel trick no longer -- to come out, and to end our anxieties. It was all useless. I was by this time convinced that she was not in the room, nor in the dressing-room, the door of which was still locked on this side. She could not have passed it. I was utterly puzzled. Had Carmilla discovered one of those secret passages which the old housekeeper said were known to exist in the schloss, although the tradition of their exact situation had been lost? A little time would, no doubt, explain all -- utterly perplexed as, for the present, we were.

It was past four o'clock, and I preferred passing the remaining hours of darkness in Madame's room. Daylight brought no solution of the difficulty.

The whole household, with my father at its head, was in a state of agitation next morning. Every part of the château was searched. The grounds were explored. Not a trace of the missing lady could be discovered. The stream was about to be dragged; my father was in distraction; what a tale to have to tell the poor girl's mother on her return. I, too, was almost beside myself, though my grief was quite of a different kind.

The morning was passed in alarm and excitement. It was now one o'clock, and still no tidings. I ran up to Carmilla's room, and found her standing at her dressing-table. I was astounded. I could not believe my eyes. She beckoned me to her with her pretty finger, in silence. Her face expressed extreme fear.

I ran to her in an ecstasy of joy; I kissed and embraced her again and again. I ran to the bell and rang it vehemently, to bring others to the spot, who might at once relieve my father's anxiety.

"Dear Carmilla, what has become of you all this time? We have been in agonies of anxiety about you," I exclaimed. "Where have you been? How did you come back?"

"Last night has been a night of wonders," she said.

"For mercy's sake, explain all you can."

"It was past two last night," she said, "when I went to sleep as usual in my bed, with my doors locked, that of the dressing-room, and that opening upon the gallery. My sleep was uninterrupted, and, so far as I know, dreamless; but I awoke just now on the sofa in the dressing-room there, and I found the door between the rooms open, and the other door forced. How could all this have happened without my being wakened? It must have been accompanied with a great deal of noise, and I am particularly easily wakened; and how could I have been carried out of my bed without my sleep having been interrupted, I whom the slightest stir startles?"

By this time, Madame, Mademoiselle, my father, and a number of the servants were in the room. Carmilla, was, of course, overwhelmed with inquiries, congratulations, and welcomes. She had but one story to tell, and seemed the least able of all the party to suggest any way of accounting for what had happened.

My father took a turn up and down the room, thinking. I saw Carmilla's eye follow him for a moment with a sly, dark glance.

When my father had sent the servants away, Mademoiselle having gone in search of a little bottle of valerian and sal-volatile, and there being no one in the room with Carmilla except my father, Madame, and myself, he came to her thoughtfully, took her hand very kindly, led her to the sofa, and sat down beside her.

"Will you forgive me, my dear, if I risk a conjecture, and ask a question?"

"Who can have a better right?" she said. "Ask what you please, and I will tell you everything. But my story is simply one of bewilderment and darkness. I know absolutely nothing. Put any question you please. But you know, of course, the limitations mamma has placed me under."

"Perfectly, my dear child. I need not approach the topics on which she desires our silence. Now, the marvel of last night consists in your having been removed from your bed and your room without being wakened, and this removal having occurred apparently while the windows were still secured, and the two doors locked upon the inside. I will tell you my theory, and first ask you a question."

Carmilla was leaning on her hand dejectedly; Madame and I were listening breathlessly.

"Now, my question is this. Have you ever been suspected of walking in your sleep?"

"Never since I was very young indeed."

"But you did walk in your sleep when you were very young?"

"Yes; I know I did. I have been told so often by my old nurse."

My father smiled and nodded.

"Well, what has happened is this. You got up in your sleep, unlocked the door, not leaving the key, as usual, in the lock, but taking it out and locking it on the outside; you again took the key out, and carried it away with you to some one of the five-and-twenty rooms on this floor, or perhaps upstairs or downstairs. There are so many rooms and closets, so much heavy furniture, and such accumulations of lumber, that it would require a week to search this old house thoroughly. Do you see, now, what I mean?"

"I do, but not all," she answered.

"And how, papa, do you account for her finding herself on the sofa in the dressing-room, which we had searched so carefully?"

"She came there after you had searched it, still in her sleep, and at last

194

awoke spontaneously, and was as much surprised to find herself where she was as any one else. I wish all mysteries were as easily and innocently explained as yours, Carmilla," he said, laughing. "And so we may congratulate ourselves on the certainty that the most natural explanation of the occurrence is one that involves no drugging, no tampering with locks, no burglars, or poisoners, or witches -- nothing that need alarm Carmilla, or any one else, for our safety."

Carmilla was looking charmingly. Nothing could be more beautiful than her tints. Her beauty was, I think, enhanced by that graceful languor that was peculiar to her. I think my father was silently contrasting her looks with mine, for he said:--

"I wish my poor Laura was looking more like herself;" and he sighed.

So our alarms were happily ended, and Carmilla restored to her friends.

IX

The Doctor

As Carmilla would not hear of an attendant sleeping in her room, my father arranged that a servant should sleep outside her door, so that she could not attempt to make another such excursion without being arrested at her own door.

That night passed quickly; and next morning early, the doctor, whom my father had sent for without telling me a word about it, arrived to see me.

Madame accompanied me to the library; and there the grave little doctor, with white hair and spectacles, whom I mentioned before, was waiting to receive me.

I told him my story, and as I proceeded he grew graver and graver.

We were standing, he and I, in the recess of one of the windows, facing one another. When my statement was over, he leaned with his shoulders against the wall, and with his eyes fixed on me earnestly, with an interest in which was a dash of horror.

After a minute's reflection, he asked Madame if he could see my father.

He was sent for accordingly, and as he entered, smiling, he said:

"I dare say, doctor, you are going to tell me that I am an old fool for having brought you here; I hope I am."

But his smile faded into shadow as the doctor, with a very grave face, beckoned him to him.

He and the doctor talked for some time in the same recess where I had just conferred with the physician. It seemed an earnest and argumentative conversation. The room is very large, and I and Madame stood together, burning with curiosity, at the further end. Not a word could we hear, however, for they spoke in a very low tone, and the deep recess of the window quite concealed the doctor from view, and very nearly my father,

195

whose foot, arm, and shoulder only could we see: and the voices were, I suppose, all the less audible for the sort of closet which the thick wall and window formed.

After a time my father's face looked into the room; it was pale, thoughtful, and, I fancied, agitated.

"Laura, dear, come here for a moment. Madame, we shan't trouble you, the doctor says, at present."

Accordingly I approached, for the first time a little alarmed; for, although I felt very weak, I did not feel ill; and strength, one always fancies, is a thing that may be picked up when we please.

My father held out his hand to me as I drew near, but he was looking at the doctor, and he said:

"It certainly *is* very odd; I don't understand it quite. Laura, come here, dear; now attend to Doctor Spielsberg, and recollect yourself."

"You mentioned a sensation like that of two needles piercing the skin, somewhere about your neck, on the night when you experienced your first horrible dream. Is there still any soreness?"

"None at all," I answered.

"Can you indicate with your finger about the point at which you think this occurred?"

"Very little below my throat -- *here*," I answered.

I wore a morning dress, which covered the place I pointed to.

"Now you can satisfy yourself," said the doctor. "You won't mind your papa's lowering your dress a very little. It is necessary, to detect a symptom of the complaint under which you have been suffering."

I acquiesced. It was only an inch or two below the edge of my collar.

"God bless me! - so it is," exclaimed my father, growing pale.

"You see it now with your own eyes," said the doctor, with a gloomy triumph.

"What is it?" I exclaimed, beginning to be frightened.

"Nothing, my dear young lady, but a small blue spot, about the size of the tip of your little finger; and now," he continued, turning to papa, "the question is what is the best to be done?"

"Is there any danger?" I urged, in great trepidation.

"I trust not, my dear," answered the doctor. "I don't see why you should not recover. I don't see why you should not begin *immediately* to get better. That is the point at which the sense of strangulation begins?"

"Yes," I answered.

"And -- recollect as well as you can -- the same point was a kind of centre of that thrill which you described just now like the current of a cold stream running against you?"

"It may have been; I think it was."

"Ay, you see?" he added, turning to my father. "Shall I say a word to Madame?"

196

"Certainly," said my father.

He called Madame to him, and said:

"I find my young friend here far from well. It won't be of any great consequence, I hope; but it will be necessary that some steps be taken, which I will explain by-and-by; but in the meantime, Madame, you will be so good as not to let Miss Laura be alone for one moment. That is the only direction I need give for the present. It is indispensable."

"We may rely upon your kindness, Madame, I know," added my father.

Madame satisfied him eagerly.

"And you, dear Laura, I know you will observe the doctor's direction."

"I shall have to ask your opinion upon another patient, whose symptoms slightly resemble those of my daughter, that have just been detailed to you -- very much milder in degree, but I believe quite of the same sort. She is a young lady -- our guest; but as you say you will be passing this way again this evening, you can't do better than take your supper here, and you can then see her. She does not come down till the afternoon."

"I thank you," said the doctor. "I shall be with you, then, at about seven this evening."

And then they repeated their directions to me and to Madame, and with this parting charge my father left us, and walked out with the doctor; and I saw them pacing together up and down between the road and the moat, on the grassy platform in front of the castle, evidently absorbed in earnest conversation.

The doctor did not return. I saw him mount his horse there, take his leave, and ride away eastward through the forest. Nearly at the same time I saw the man arrive from Dranfeld with the letters, and dismount and hand the bag to my father.

In the meantime, Madame and I were both busy, lost in conjecture as to the reasons of the singular and earnest direction which the doctor and my father had concurred in imposing. Madame, as she afterwards told me, was afraid the doctor apprehended a sudden seizure, and that, without prompt assistance, I might either lose my life, or at least be seriously hurt.

This interpretation did not strike me; and I fancied, perhaps luckily for my nerves, that the arrangement was prescribed simply to secure a companion, who would prevent my taking too much exercise, or eating unripe fruit, or doing any of the fifty foolish things to which young people are supposed to be prone.

About half-an-hour after my father came in -- he had a letter in his hand -- and said:

"This letter has been delayed; it is from General Spielsdorf. He might have been here yesterday, he may not come till to-morrow, or he may be here to-day."

He put the open letter into my hand; but he did not look pleased, as he used to when a guest, especially one so much loved as the General, was coming. On the contrary, he looked as if he wished him at the bottom of the Red Sea. There was plainly something on his mind which he did not choose to divulge.

"Papa, darling, will you tell me this?" said I, suddenly laying my hand on his arm, and looking, I am sure, imploringly in his face.

"Perhaps," he answered, smoothing my hair caressingly over my eyes.

"Does the doctor think me very ill?"

"No, dear; he thinks, if right steps are taken, you will be quite well again, at least on the high road to a complete recovery, in a day or two," he answered, a little drily. "I wish our good friend, the General, had chosen any other time; that is, I wish you had been perfectly well to receive him."

"But do tell me papa," I insisted, "*what* does he think is the matter with me?"

"Nothing; you must not plague me with questions," he answered, with more irritation than I ever remember him to have displayed before; and seeing that I looked wounded, I suppose, he kissed me, and added, "You shall know all about it in a day or two; that is, all that *I* know. In the meantime, you are not to trouble your head about it."

He turned and left the room, but came back before I had done wondering and puzzling over the oddity of all this; it was merely to say that he was going to Karnstein, and had ordered the carriage to be ready at twelve, and that I and Madame should accompany him; he was going to see the priest who lived near those picturesque grounds, upon business, and as Carmilla had never seen them, she could follow, when she came down, with Mademoiselle, who would bring materials for what you call a pic-nic, which might be laid for us in the ruined castle.

At twelve o'clock, accordingly, I was ready, and not long after, my father, Madame and I set out upon our projected drive. Passing the drawbridge we turn to the right, and follow the road over the steep Gothic bridge, westward, to reach the deserted village and ruined castle of Karnstein.

No sylvan drive can be fancied prettier. The ground breaks into gentle hills and hollows, all clothed with beautiful wood, totally destitute of the comparative formality which artificial planting and early culture and pruning impart.

The irregularities of the ground often lead the road out of its course, and cause it to wind beautifully round the sides of broken hollows and steeper sides of the hills, among varieties of ground almost inexhaustible.

Turning one of these points, we suddenly encountered our old friend, the General, riding towards us, attended by a mounted servant. His portmanteaus were following in a hired waggon, such as we term a cart.

The General dismounted as we pulled up, and, after the usual greetings, was easily persuaded to accept the vacant seat in the carriage, and send his horse on with his servant to the schloss.

X
Bereaved

It was about ten months since we had last seen him; but that time had sufficed to make an alteration of years in his appearance. He had grown thinner; something of gloom and anxiety had taken the place of that cordial serenity which used to characterise his features. His dark blue eyes, always penetrating, now gleamed with a sterner light from under his shaggy grey eyebrows. It was not such a change as grief alone usually induces, and angrier passions seemed to have had their share in bringing it about.

We had not long resumed our drive, when the General began to talk, with his usual soldierly directness, of the bereavement, as he termed it, which he had sustained in the death of his beloved niece and ward; and he then broke out in a tone of intense bitterness and fury, inveighing against the "hellish arts" to which she had fallen a victim, and expressing with more exasperation than piety, his wonder that Heaven should tolerate so monstrous an indulgence of the lusts and malignity of hell.

My father, who saw at once that something very extraordinary had befallen, asked him, if not too painful to him, to detail the circumstances which he thought justified the strong terms in which he expressed himself.

"I should tell you all with pleasure," said the General, "but you would not believe me."

"Why should I not?" he asked.

"Because," he answered testily, "you believe in nothing but what consists with your own prejudices and illusions. I remember when I was like you, but I have learned better."

"Try me," said my father, "I am not such a dogmatist as you suppose. Besides which, I very well know that you generally require proof for what you believe and am, therefore, very strongly predisposed to respect your conclusions."

"You are right in supposing that I have not been led lightly into a belief in the marvellous -- for what I have experienced *is* marvellous -- and I have been forced by extraordinary evidence to credit that which ran counter, diametrically, to all my theories. I have been made the dupe of a preternatural conspiracy."

Notwithstanding his profession of confidence in the General's penetration, I saw my father, at this point, glance at the General, with, as I thought, a marked suspicion of his sanity.

The General did not see it, luckily. He was looking gloomily and curiously into the glades and vistas of the woods that were opening before us.

"You are going to the Ruins of Karnstein?" he said. "Yes, it is a lucky coincidence; do you know I was going to ask you to bring me there to inspect them. I have a special object in exploring. There is a ruined chapel, ain't there, with a great many tombs of that extinct family?"

"So there are -- highly interesting," said my father, "I hope you are thinking of claiming the title and estates?"

My father said this gaily, but the General did not recollect the laugh, or even smile, which courtesy exacts for a friend's joke; on the contrary, he looked grave and even fierce, ruminating on a matter that stirred his anger and horror.

"Something very different," he said, gruffly. "I mean to unearth some of those fine people. I hope by God's blessing, to accomplish a pious sacrilege here, which will relieve our earth of certain monsters, and enable honest people to sleep in their beds without being assailed by murderers. I have strange things to tell you, my dear friend, such as I myself would have scouted as incredible a few months since."

My father looked at him again, but this time not with a glance of suspicion -- with an eye, rather, of keen intelligence and alarm.

"The house of Karnstein," he said, "has been long extinct: a hundred years at least. My dear wife was maternally descended from the Karnsteins. But the name and title have long ceased to exist. The castle is a ruin; the very village is deserted; it is fifty years since the smoke of a chimney was seen there; not a roof left."

"Quite true. I have heard a great deal about that since I last saw you; a great deal that will astonish you. But I had better relate everything in the order in which it occurred," said the General. "You saw my dear ward -- my child, I may call her. No creature could have been more beautiful, and only three months ago none more blooming."

"Yes, poor thing! when I saw her last she certainly was quite lovely," said my father. "I was grieved and shocked more than I can tell you, my dear friend; I knew what a blow it was to you."

He took the General's hand, and they exchanged a kind pressure. Tears gathered in the old soldier's eyes. He did not seek to conceal them. He said:

"We have been very old friends; I knew you would feel for me, childless as I am. She had become an object of very dear interest to me, and repaid my care by an affection that cheered my home and made my life happy. This is all gone. The years that remain to me on earth may not be very long; but by God's mercy I hope to accomplish a service to mankind before I die, and to subserve the vengeance of Heaven upon the fiends who have murdered my poor child in the spring of her hopes and beauty!"

"You said, just now, that you intended relating everything as it occurred," said my father. "Pray do; I assure you that it is not mere curiosity that prompts me."

By this time we had reached the point at which the Drunstall road, by which the General had come, diverges from the road which we were travelling to Karnstein.

"How far is it to the ruins?" inquired the General, looking anxiously forward.

"About half a league," answered my father. "Pray let us hear the story you were so good as to promise."

XI

The Story

"With all my heart," said the General, with an effort; and after a pause in which to arrange his subject, he commenced one of the strangest narratives I ever heard.

"My dear child was looking forward with great pleasure to the visit you had been so good as to arrange for her to your charming daughter." Here he made me a gallant but melancholy bow. "In the meantime we had an invitation to my old friend the Count Carlsfeld, whose schloss is about six leagues to the other side of Karnstein. It was to attend the series of fêtes which, you remember, were given by him in honor of his illustrious visitor, the Grand Duke Charles."

"Yes; and very splendid, I believe they were," said my father.

"Princely! But then his hospitalities are quite regal. He has Aladdin's lamp. The night from which my sorrow dates was devoted to a magnificent masquerade. The grounds were thrown open, the trees hung with coloured lamps. There was such a display of fireworks as Paris itself had never witnessed. And such music -- music, you know, is my weakness -- such ravishing music! The finest instrumental band, perhaps, in the world, and the finest singers who could be collected from all the great operas in Europe. As you wandered through those fantastically illuminated grounds, the moon-lighted château throwing a rosy light from its long row of windows, you would suddenly hear these ravishing voices stealing from the silence of some grove, or rising from boats upon the lake. I felt myself, as I looked and listened, carried back into the romance and poetry of my early youth.

"When the fireworks were ended, and the ball beginning, we returned to the noble suite of rooms that were thrown open to the dancers. A masked ball, you know, is a beautiful sight; but so brilliant a spectacle of the kind I never saw before.

"It was a very aristocratic assembly. I saw myself almost the only 'nobody' present.

"My dear child was looking quite beautiful. She wore no mask. Her excitement and delight added an unspeakable charm to her features, always lovely. I remarked a young lady, dressed magnificently, but wearing a mask, who appeared to me to be observing my ward with extraordinary interest. I had seen her, earlier in the evening, in the great hall, and again, for a few minutes, walking near us, on the terrace under the castle windows, similarly employed. A lady, also masked, richly and gravely dressed, and with stately

201

air, like a person of rank, accompanied her as a chaperon. Had the young lady not worn a mask, I could of course, have been much more certain upon the question whether she was really watching my poor darling. I am now well assured that she was.

"We were in one of the *salons*. My poor dear child had been dancing, and was resting a little in one of the chairs near the door; I was standing near. The two ladies I have mentioned had approached, and the younger took the chair next my ward; while her companion stood beside me, and for a little time addressed herself, in a low tone, to her charge.

"Availing herself of the privilege of her mask, she turned to me, and in the tone of an old friend, and calling me by my name, opened a conversation with me, which piqued my curiosity a good deal. She referred to many scenes where she had met me -- at Court, and at distinguished houses. She alluded to little incidents which I had long ceased to think of, but which, I found, had only lain in abeyance in my memory, for they instantly started into life at her touch.

"I became more and more curious to ascertain who she was, every moment. She parried my attempts to discover very adroitly and pleasantly. The knowledge she showed of many passages in my life seemed to me all but unaccountable; and she appeared to take a not unnatural pleasure in foiling my curiosity, and in seeing me flounder, in my eager perlexity, from one conjecture to another.

"In the meantime the young lady, whom her mother called by the odd name of Millarca, when she once or twice addressed her, had, with the same ease and grace, got into conversation with my ward.

"She introduced herself by saying that her mother was a very old acquaintance of mine. She spoke of the agreeable audacity which a mask rendered practicable; she talked like a friend; she admired her dress, and insinuated very prettily her admiration of her beauty. She amused her with laughing criticisms upon the people who crowded the ballroom, and laughed at my poor child's fun. She was very witty and lively when she pleased, and after a time they had grown very good friends, and the young stranger lowered her mask, displaying a remarkably beautiful face. I had never seen it before, neither had my dear child. But though it was new to us, the features were so engaging, as well as lovely, that it was impossible not to feel the attraction powerfully. My poor girl did so. I never saw anyone more taken with another at first sight, unless, indeed, it was the stranger herself, who seemed quite to have lost her heart to her.

"In the meantime, availing myself of the licence of a masquerade, I put not a few questions to the elder lady.

"*You have puzzled me utterly*, I said, laughing. *Is that not enough? won't you, now, consent to stand on equal terms, and do me the kindness to remove your mask?*

"*Can any request be more unreasonable?* she replied. *Ask a lady to yield*

202

an advantage! Beside, how do you know you should recognize me? Years make changes.

"*As you see,* I said, with a bow, and, I suppose, a rather melancholy little laugh.

"*As philosophers tell us,* she said; *and how do you know that a sight of my face would help you?*

"*I should take chance for that,* I answered. *It is vain trying to make yourself out an old woman; your figure betrays you.*

"*Years, nevertheless, have passed since I saw you, rather since you saw me, for that is what I am considering. Millarca, there, is my daughter; I cannot then be young, even in the opinion of people whom time has taught to be indulgent, and I may not like to be compared with what you remember me. You have no mask to remove. You can offer me nothing in exchange.*

"*My petition is to your pity, to remove it.*

"*And mine to yours, to let it stay where it is,* she replied.

"*Well, then, at least you will tell me whether you are French or German; you speak both languages so perfectly.*

"*I don't think I shall tell you that, General; you intend a surprise, and are meditating the particular point of attack.*

"*At all events, you won't deny this,* I said, *that being honoured by your permission to converse, I ought to know how to address you. Shall I say Madame la Comtesse?*

"She laughed, and she would, no doubt, have met me with another evasion -- if, indeed, I can treat any occurrence in an interview every circumstance of which was pre-arranged, as I now believe, with the profoundest cunning, as liable to be modified by accident.

"*As to that,* she began; but she was interrupted, almost as she opened her lips, by a gentleman, dressed in black, who looked particularly elegant and distinguished, with this drawback, that his face was the most deadly pale I ever saw, except in death. He was in no masquerade -- in the plain evening dress of a gentleman; and he said, without a smile, but with a courtly and unusually low bow:-

"*Will Madame la Comtesse permit me to say a very few words which may interest her?*

"The lady turned quickly to him, and touched her lip in a token of silence; she then said to me, *Keep my place for me, General; I shall return when I have said a few words.*

"And with this injunction, playfully given, she walked a little aside with the gentleman in black, and talked for some minutes, apparently very earnestly. They then walked away slowly together in the crowd, and I lost them for some minutes.

"I spent the interval in cudgelling my brains for conjecture as to the identity of the lady who seemed to remember me so kindly, and I was thinking of turning about and joining in the conversation between my pretty

203

ward and the Countess's daughter, and trying whether, by the time she returned, I might not have a surprise in store for her, by having her name, title, château, and estates at my fingers' ends. But at this moment she returned, accompanied by the pale man in black, who said:

"*I shall return and inform Madame la Comtesse when her carriage is at the door.*

"He withdrew with a bow.

XII
A Petition

"*Then we are to lose Madame la Comtesse, but I hope only for a few hours,* I said, with a low bow.

"*It may be that only, or it may be a few weeks. It was very unlucky his speaking to me just now as he did. Do you now know me?*

"I assured her I did not.

"*You shall know me,* she said, *but not at present. We are older and better friends than, perhaps, you suspect. I cannot yet declare myself. I shall in three weeks pass your beautiful schloss about which I have been making enquiries. I shall then look in upon you for an hour or two, and renew a friendship which I never think of without a thousand pleasant recollections. This moment a piece of news has reached me like a thunderbolt. I must set out now, and travel by a devious route, nearly a hundred miles, with all the dispatch I can possibly make. My perplexities multiply. I am only deterred by the compulsory reserve I practise as to my name from making a very singular request of you. My poor child has not quite recovered her strength. Her horse fell with her, at a hunt which she had ridden out to witness, her nerves have not yet recovered the shock, and our physician says that she must on no account exert herself for some time to come. We came here, in consequence, by very easy stages -- hardly six leagues a day. I must now travel day and night, on a mission of life and death -- a mission the critical and momentous nature of which I shall be able to explain to you when we meet, as I hope we shall, in a few weeks, without the necessity of any concealment.*

"She went on to make her petition, and it was in the tone of a person from whom such a request amounted to conferring, rather than seeking a favour. This was only in manner, and, as it seemed, quite unconsciously. Then the terms in which it was expressed, nothing could be more deprecatory. It was simply that I would consent to take charge of her daughter during her absence.

"This was, all things considered, a strange, not to say, an audacious request. She in some sort disarmed me, by stating and admitting everything that could be urged against it, and throwing herself entirely upon my chivalry. At the same moment, by a fatality that seems to have predetermined all that happened, my poor child came to my side, and, in an undertone, besought me to invite her new friend, Millarca, to pay us a visit. She had just been sounding her, and thought, if her mamma would allow her, she would like it extremely.

"At another time I should have told her to wait a little, until, at least, we knew who they were. But I had not a moment to think in. The two ladies assailed me together; and I must confess the refined and beautiful face of the young lady, about which there was something extremely engaging, as well as the elegance and fire of high birth, determined me; and quite overpowered, I submitted, and undertook, too easily, the care of the young lady, whom her mother called Millarca.

"The Countess beckoned to her daughter, who listened with grave attention while she told her, in general terms, how suddenly and peremptorily she had been summoned, and also of the arrangement she had made for her under my care, adding that I was one of her earliest and most valued friends.

"I made, of course, such speeches as the case seemed to call for, and found myself, on reflection, in a position which I did not half like.

"The gentleman in black returned, and very ceremoniously conducted the lady from the room.

"The demeanour of this gentleman was such as to impress me with the conviction that the Countess was a lady of very much more importance than her modest title alone might have led me to assume.

"Her last charge to me was that no attempt was to be made to learn more about her than I might have already guessed, until her return. Our distinguished host, whose guest she was, knew her reasons.

"*But here*, she said, *neither I nor my daughter could safely remain more than a day. I removed my mask imprudently for a moment, about an hour ago, and, too late, I fancied you saw me. So I have resolved to seek an opportunity of talking a little to you. Had I found that you had seen me, I should have thrown myself on your high sense of honour to keep my secret for some weeks. As it is, I am satisfied that you did not see me; but if you now suspect, or, on reflection, should suspect, who I am, I commit myself, in like manner, entirely to your honour. My daughter will observe the same secrecy, and I well know that you will, from time to time, remind her, lest she should thoughtlessly disclose it.*

"She whispered a few words to her daughter, kissed her hurriedly twice, and went away, accompanied by the pale gentleman in black, and disappeared in the crowd.

"*In the next room*, said Millarca, *there is a window that looks upon the hall door. I should like to see the last of mamma, and to kiss my hand to her.*

"We assented, of course, and accompanied her to the window. We looked out, and saw a handsome old-fashioned carriage, with a troop of couriers and footmen. We saw the slim figure of the pale gentleman in black, as he held a thick velvet cloak, and placed it about her shoulders and threw the hood over her head. She nodded to him, and just touched his hand with hers. He bowed low repeatedly as the door closed, and the carriage began to move.

"*She is gone*, said Millarca with a sigh.

"*She is gone*, I repeated to myself, for the first time -- in the hurried moments that had elapsed since my consent -- reflecting upon the folly of my act.

"*She did not look up*, said the young lady, plaintively.

"*The Countess had taken off her mask, perhaps, and did not care to show her face*, I said; *and she could not know that you were in the window*.

"She sighed and looked in my face. She was so beautiful that I relented. I was sorry I had for a moment repented of my hospitality, and I determined to make her amends for the unavowed churlishness of my reception.

"The young lady, replacing her mask, joined my ward in persuading me to return to the grounds, where the concert was soon to be renewed. We did so, and walked up and down the terrace that lies under the castle windows. Millarca became very intimate with us, and amused us with lively descriptions and stories of most of the great people whom we saw upon the terrace. I liked her more and more every minute. Her gossip, without being ill-natured, was extremely diverting to me, who had been so long out of the great world. I thought what life she would give to our sometimes lonely evenings at home.

"This ball was not over until the morning sun had almost reached the horizon. It pleased the Grand Duke to dance till then, so loyal people could not go away, or think of bed.

"We had just got through a crowded saloon, when my ward asked me what had become of Millarca. I thought she had been by her side, and she fancied she was by mine. The fact was, we had lost her.

"All my efforts to find her were in vain. I feared that she had mistaken, in the confusion of the momentary separation from us, other people for her new friends, and had, possibly, pursued and lost them in the extensive grounds which were thrown open to us.

"Now, in its full force, I recognized a new folly in my having undertaken the charge of a young lady without so much as knowing her name; and fettered as I was by promises, of the reasons for imposing which I knew nothing, I could not even point my inquiries by saying that the missing young lady was the daughter of the Countess who had taken her departure a few hours before.

"Morning broke. It was clear daylight before I gave up my search. It was not till near two o'clock next day that we heard anything of my missing charge.

"At about that time a servant knocked at my niece's door, to say that he had been earnestly requested by a young lady, who appeared to be in great distress, to make out where she could find the General Baron Spielsdorf and the young lady, his daughter, in whose charge she had been left by her mother.

"There could be no doubt, notwithstanding the slight inaccuracy, that our young friend had turned up; and so she had. Would to Heaven we had lost her!

"She told my poor child a story to account for her having failed to recover us for so long. Very late, she said, she had got into the housekeeper's bedroom in despair of finding us, and had then fallen into a deep sleep which, long as it was, had hardly sufficed to recruit her strength after the fatigues of the ball.

"That day Millarca came home with us. I was only too happy, after all, to have secured so charming a companion for my dear girl.

XIII

The Wood-Man

"There soon, however, appeared some drawbacks. In the first place, Millarca complained of extreme languor -- the weakness that remained after her late illness -- and she never emerged from her room till the afternoon was pretty far advanced. In the next place, it was accidentally discovered, although she always locked her door on the inside, and never disturbed the key from its place, till she admitted the maid to assist at her toilet, that she was undoubtably sometimes absent from her room in the very early morning, and at various times later in the day, before she wished it to be understood that she was stirring. She was repeatedly seen from the windows of the schloss, in the first faint grey of the morning, walking through the trees, in an easterly direction, and looking like a person in a trance. This convinced me that she walked in her sleep. But this hypothesis did not solve the puzzle. How did she pass out from her room, leaving the door locked on the inside? How did she escape from the house without unbarring door or window?

"In the midst of my perplexities, an anxiety of a far more urgent kind presented itself.

"My dear child began to lose her looks and health, and that in a manner so mysterious, and even horrible, that I became thoroughly frightened.

"She was at first visited by appalling dreams; then, as she fancied, by a spectre, sometimes resembling Millarca, sometimes in the shape of a beast, indistinctly seen, walking round the foot of her bed, from side to side. Lastly came sensations. One, not unpleasant, but very peculiar, she said, resembled the flow of an icy stream against her breast. At a later time, she felt something like a pair of large needles pierce her, a little below the throat,

207

with a very sharp pain. A few nights after, followed a gradual and convulsive sense of strangulation; then came unconsciousness."

I could hear distinctly every word the kind old General was saying, because by this time we were driving upon the short grass that spreads on either side of the road as you approach the roofless village which had not shown the smoke of a chimney for more than half a century.

You may guess how strangely I felt as I heard my own symptoms so exactly described in those which had been experienced by the poor girl who, but for the catastrophe which followed, would have been at that moment a visitor at my father's château. You may suppose, also, how I felt as I heard him detail habits and mysterious peculiarities which were, in fact, those of our beautiful guest, Carmilla!

A vista opened in the forest; we were of a sudden under the chimneys and gables of the ruined village, and the towers and battlements of the dismantled castle, round which gigantic trees are grouped, overhung us from a slight eminence.

In a frightened dream I got down from the carriage, and in silence, for we had each abundant matter for thinking; we soon mounted the ascent, and were among spacious chambers, winding stairs, and dark corridors of the castle.

"And this was once the palatial residence of the Karnsteins!" said the old General at length, as from a great window he looked out across the village, and saw the wide, undulating expanse of forest. "It was a bad family, and here its blood-stained annals were written," he continued. "It is hard that they should, after death, continue to plague the human race with their atrocious lusts. That is the chapel of the Karnsteins, down there."

He pointed down to the grey walls of the Gothic building, partly visible through the foliage, a little way down the steep. "And I hear the axe of a woodman," he added, "busy among the trees that surround it; he possibly may give us the information of which I am in search, and point out the grave of Mircalla, Countess of Karnstein. These rustics preserve the local traditions of great families, whose stories die out among the rich and titled so soon as the families themselves become extinct."

"We have a portrait, at home, of Mircalla, the Countess Karnstein; should you like to see it?" asked my father.

"Time enough, dear friend," replied the General. "I believe that I have seen the original; and one motive which has led me to you earlier than I at first intended, was to explore the chapel which we are now approaching."

"What! see the Countess Mircalla," exclaimed my father; "why, she has been dead more than a century!"

"Not so dead as you fancy, I am told," answered the General.

"I confess, General, you puzzle me utterly," replied my father, looking at him, I fancied, for a moment with a return of the suspicion I detected before. But although there was anger and detestation, at times, in the old

General's manner, there was nothing flighty.

"There remains to me," he said, as we passed under the heavy arch of the Gothic church -- for its dimensions would have justified its being so styled -- "but one object which can interest me during the few years that remain to me on earth, and that is to wreak on her the vengeance which, I thank God, may still be accomplished by a mortal arm."

"What vengeance can you mean?" asked my father, in increasing amazement.

"I mean, to decapitate the monster," he answered, with a fierce flush, and a stamp that echoed mournfully through the hollow ruin, and his clenched hand was at the same moment raised, as if it grasped the handle of an axe, while he shook it ferociously in the air.

"What!" exclaimed my father, more than ever bewildered.

"To strike her head off."

"Cut her head off!"

"Aye, with a hatchet, with a spade, or with anything that can cleave through her murderous throat. You shall hear," he answered, trembling with rage. And hurrying forward he said:

"That beam will answer for a seat; your dear child is fatigued; let her be seated, and I will, in a few sentences, close my dreadful story."

The squared block of wood, which lay on the grass-grown pavement of the chapel, formed a bench on which I was very glad to seat myself, and in the meantime the General called to the woodman, who had been removing some boughs which leaned upon the old walls; and, axe in hand, the hardy old fellow stood before us.

He could not tell us anything of these monuments; but there was an old man, he said, a ranger of this forest, at present sojourning in the house of the priest, about two miles away, who could point out every monument of the old Karnstein family; and, for a trifle, he undertook to bring back with him, if we would lend him one of our horses, in little more than half-an-hour.

"Have you been long employed about this forest?" asked my father of the old man.

"I have been a woodman here," he answered in his *patois*, "under the forester, all my days; so has my father before me, and so on, as many generations as I can count up. I could show you the very house in the village here, in which my ancestors lived."

"How came the village to be deserted?" asked the General.

"It was troubled by *revenants*, sir; several were tracked to their graves, there detected by the usual tests, and extinguished in the usual way, by decapitation, by the stake, and by burning; but not until many of the villagers were killed.

"But after all these proceedings according to law," he continued -- "so many graves opened, and so many vampires deprived of their horrible animation -- the village was not relieved. But a Moravian nobleman, who happened to be travelling this way, heard how matters were, and being skilled -- as many people are in his country -- in such affairs, he offered to deliver the village from its tormentor. He did so thus: There being a bright moon that night, he ascended, shortly after sunset, the tower of the chapel here, from whence he could distinctly see the churchyard beneath him; you can see it from that window. From this point he watched until he saw the vampire come out of his grave, and place near it the linen clothes in which he had been folded, and glide away towards the village to plague its inhabitants.

"The stranger, having seen all this, came down from the steeple, took the linen wrappings of the vampire, and carried them up to the top of the tower, which he again mounted. When the vampire returned from his prowlings and missed his clothes, he cried furiously to the Moravian, whom he saw at the summit of the tower, and who, in reply, beckoned him to ascend and take them. Whereupon the vampire, accepting his invitation, began to climb the steeple, and so soon as he had reached the battlements, the Moravian, with a stroke of his sword, clove his skull in twain, hurling him down to the churchyard, whither, descending by the winding stairs, the stranger followed and cut his head off, and next day delivered it and the body to the villagers, who duly impaled and burnt them.

"This Moravian nobleman had the authority from the then head of the family to remove the tomb of Mircalla, Countess Karnstein, which he did effectually, so that in a little while its site was quite forgotten."

"Can you point out where it stood?" asked the General, eagerly.

The forester shook his head and smiled.

"Not a living soul could tell you that now," he said; "besides, they say her body was removed; but no one is sure of that either."

Having thus spoken, as time pressed, he dropped his axe and departed, leaving us to hear the remainder of the General's strange story.

XIV
The Meeting

"My beloved child," he resumed, "was now growing rapidly worse. The physician who attended her had failed to produce the slightest impression upon her disease, for such I then supposed it to be. He saw my alarm, and suggested a consultation. I called in an abler physician, from Gratz. Several days elapsed before he arrived. He was a good and pious, as well as a learned man. Having seen my poor ward together, they withdrew to my library to confer and discuss. I, from the adjoining room, where I awaited their summons, heard these two gentlemen's voices raised in something sharper than a strictly philosophical discussion. I knocked at the door and entered. I found the old physician from Gratz maintaining his theory. His

210

rival was combating it with undisguised ridicule, accompanied with bursts of laughter. This unseemly manifestation subsided and the altercation ended on my entrance.

"*Sir,* said my first physician, *my learned brother seems to think that you want a conjuror, and not a doctor.*

"*Pardon me,* said the old physician from Gratz, looking displeased, *I shall state my own view of the case in my own way another time. I grieve, Monsieur le Général, that by my skill and science I can be of no use. Before I go I shall do myself the honour to suggest something to you.*

"He seemed thoughtful, and sat down at a table, and began to write. Profoundly disappointed, I made my bow, and as I turned to go, the other doctor pointed over his shoulder to his companion who was writing, and then, with a shrug, significantly touched his forehead.

"This consultation, then, left me precisely where I was. I walked out into the grounds, all but distracted. The doctor from Gratz, in ten or fifteen minutes, overtook me. He apologised for having followed me, but said that he could not conscientiously take his leave without a few words more. He told me that he could not be mistaken; no natural disease exhibited the same symptoms; and that death was already very near. There remained, however, a day, or possibly two, of life. If the fatal seizure were at once arrested, with great care and skill her strength might possibly return. But all hung now upon the confines of the irrevocable. One more assault might extinguish the last spark of vitality which is, every moment, ready to die.

"*And what is the nature of the seizure you speak of?* I entreated.

"*I have stated all fully in this note, which I place in your hands, upon the distinct condition that you send for the nearest clergyman, and open my letter in his presence, and on no account read it till he is with you; you would despise it else, and it is a matter of life and death. Should the priest fail you, then, indeed, you may read it.*

"He asked me, before taking his leave finally, whether I would wish to see a man curiously learned upon the very subject, which, after I had read his letter, would probably interest me above all others, and he urged me earnestly to invite him to visit him there; and so took his leave.

"The ecclesiastic was absent, and I read the letter by myself. At another time, or in another case, it might have excited my ridicule. But into what quackeries will not people rush for a last chance, where all accustomed means have failed, and the life of a beloved object is at stake?

"Nothing, you will say, could be more absurd than the learned man's letter. It was monstrous enough to have consigned him to a madhouse. He said that the patient was suffering from the visits of a vampire! The punctures which she described as having occurred near the throat, were, he insisted, the insertion of those two long, thin, and sharp teeth which, it is well known, are peculiar to vampires; and there could be no doubt, he added, as to the well defined presence of the small livid mark which all

211

concurred in describing as that induced by the demon's lips, and every symptom described by the sufferer was in exact conformity with those recorded in every case of a similar visitation.

"Being myself wholly sceptical as to the existence of any such portent as the vampire, the supernatural theory of the good doctor furnished, in my opinion, but another instance of learning and intelligence oddly associated with some one hallucination. I was so miserable, however, that, rather than try nothing, I acted upon the instructions of the letter.

"I concealed myself in the dark dressing-room, that opened upon the poor patient's room, in which a candle was burning, and watched there until she was fast asleep. I stood at the door, peeping through the small crevice, my sword laid on the table beside me, as my directions prescribed, until, a little after one, I saw a large black object, very ill-defined, crawl, as it seemed to me, over the foot of the bed, and swiftly spread itself up to the poor girl's throat, where it swelled, in a moment, into a great, palpitating mass.

"For a few moments I had stood petrified. I now sprang forward, with my sword in my hand. The black creature suddenly contracted toward the foot of the bed, glided over it, and, standing on the floor about a yard below the foot of the bed, with a glare of skulking ferocity and horror fixed on me, I saw Millarca. Speculating I know not what, I struck at her instantly with my sword; but I saw her standing near the door, unscathed. Horrified, I pursued, and struck again. She was gone! and my sword flew to shivers against the door.

"I can't describe to you all that passed on that horrible night. The whole house was up and stirring. The spectre Millarca was gone. But her victim was sinking fast, and before the morning dawned, she died."

The old General was agitated. We did not speak to him. My father walked to some little distance, and began reading the inscriptions on the tombstones; and thus occupied, he strolled into the door of a side chapel to prosecute his researches. The General leaned against the wall, dried his eyes, and sighed heavily. I was relieved on hearing the voices of Carmilla and Madame, who were at that moment approaching. The voices died away.

In this solitude, having just listened to so strange a story, connected, as it was, with the great and titled dead, whose monuments were moulding among the dust and ivy round us, and every incident of which bore so awfully upon my own mysterious case -- in this haunted spot, darkened by the towering foliage that rose on every side, dense and high above its noiseless walls -- a horror began to steal over me, and my heart sank as I thought that my friends were, after all, now about to enter and disturb this triste and ominous scene.

The old General's eyes were fixed on the ground, as he leaned with his hand upon the basement of a shattered monument.

Under a narrow, arched doorway, surmounted by one of those

demoniacal grotesques in which the cynical and ghastly fancy of old Gothic carving delights, I saw very gladly the beautiful face and figure of Carmilla enter the shadowy chapel.

I was just about to rise and speak, and nodded smiling, in answer to her peculiarly engaging smile; when with a cry, the old man by my side caught up the woodman's hatchet, and started forward. On seeing him a brutalised change came over her features. It was an instantaneous and horrible transformation, as she made a crouching step backwards. Before I could utter a scream, he struck at her with all his force, but she dived under his blow, and unscathed, caught him in her tiny grasp by the wrist. He struggled for a moment to release his arm, but his hand opened, the axe fell to the ground, and the girl was gone.

He staggered against the wall. His grey hair stood upon his head, and a moisture shone over his face, as if he were at the point of death.

The frightful scene had passed in a moment. The first thing I recollect after, is Madame standing before me, and impatiently repeating again and again, the question, "Where is Mademoiselle Carmilla?"

I answered at length, "I don't know -- I can't tell -- she went there," and I pointed to the door through which Madame had just entered; "only a minute or two since."

"But I have been standing there, in the passage, ever since Mademoiselle Carmilla entered; and she did not return."

She then began to call "Carmilla" through every door and passage and from the windows, but no answer came.

"She called herself Carmilla?" asked the General, still agitated.

"Carmilla, yes," I answered.

"Aye," he said, "that is Millarca. That is the same person who long ago was called Mircalla, Countess Karnstein. Depart from this accursed ground, my poor child, as quickly as you can. Drive to the clergyman's house, and stay there till we come. Begone! May you never behold Carmilla more; you will not find her here."

XV
Ordeal and Execution

As he spoke one of the strangest-looking men I ever beheld, entered the chapel at the door through which Carmilla had made her entrance and her exit. He was tall, narrow-chested, stooping, with high shoulders, and dressed in black. His face was brown and dried in deep furrows; he wore an oddly-shaped hat with a broad leaf. His hair, long and grizzled, hung on his shoulders. He wore a pair of gold spectacles, and walked slowly, with an odd shambling gait, with his face sometimes turned up to the sky, and sometimes bowed down toward the ground, seemed to wear a perpetual smile; his long thin arms were swinging, and his lank hands, in old black gloves ever so much too wide for them, waving and gesticulating in utter abstraction.

"The very man!" exclaimed the General, advancing with manifest delight. "My dear Baron, how happy I am to see you, I had no hope of meeting you so soon." He signed to my father, who had by this time returned, and leading the fantastic old gentleman, whom he called the Baron, to meet him. He introduced him formally, and they at once entered into earnest conversation. The stranger took a roll of paper from his pocket, and spread it on the worn surface of a tomb that stood by. He had a pencil case in his fingers, with which he traced imaginary lines from point to point on the paper, which from their often glancing from it, together, at certain points of the building, I concluded to be a plan of the chapel. He accompanied, what I may term his lecture, with occasional readings from a dirty little book, whose yellow leaves were closely written over.

They sauntered together down the side aisle, opposite to the spot where I was standing, conversing as they went; then they begun measuring distances by paces, and finally they all stood together, facing a piece of the side-wall, which they began to examine with great minuteness; pulling off the ivy that clung over it, and rapping the plaster with the ends of their sticks, scraping here, and knocking there. At length they ascertained the existence of a broad marble tablet, with letters carved in relief upon it.

With the assistance of the woodman, who soon returned, a monumental inscription, and carved escutcheon, were disclosed. They proved to be of those of the long lost monument of Mircalla, Countess Karnstein.

The old General, though not I fear given to the praying mood, raised his hands and eyes to heaven, in mute thanksgiving for some moments.

"To-morrow," I heard him say; "the commissioner will be here, and the Inquisition will be held according to law."

Then turning to the old man with the gold spectacles, whom I have described, he shook him warmly by both hands and said:

"Baron, how can I thank you? How can we all thank you? You will have delivered this region from a plague that has scourged its inhabitants for more than a century. The horrible enemy, thank God, is at last tracked."

My father led the stranger aside, and the General followed. I knew that he had led them out of hearing, that he might relate my case, and I saw them glance often quickly at me, as the discussion proceeded.

My father came to me, kissed me again and again, and leading me from the chapel said:

"It is time to return, but before we go home, we must add to our party the good priest, who lives but a little way from this; and persuade him to accompany us to the schloss."

In this quest we were successful: and I was glad, being unspeakably fatigued when we reached home. But my satisfaction was changed to dismay, on discovering that there were no tidings of Carmilla. Of the scene that had occurred in the ruined chapel, no explanation was offered to me, and it was clear that it was a secret which my father for the present determined to keep from me.

The sinister absence of Carmilla made the remembrance of the scene more horrible to me. The arrangements for that night were singular. Two servants and Madame were to sit up in my room that night; and the ecclesiastic with my father kept watch in the adjoining dressing-room.

The priest had performed certain solemn rites that night, the purport of which I did not understand any more than I comprehended the reason of this extraordinary precaution taken for my safety during sleep.

I saw all clearly a few days later.

The disappearance of Carmilla was followed by the discontinuance of my nightly sufferings.

You have heard, no doubt, of the appalling superstition that prevails in Upper and Lower Styria, in Moravia, Silesia, in Turkish Servia, in Poland, even in Russia; the superstition, so we must call it, of the vampire.

If human testimony, taken with every care and solemnity, judicially, before commissions innumerable, each consisting of many members, all chosen for integrity and intelligence, and constituting reports more voluminous perhaps that exist upon any other class of cases, is worth anything, it is difficult to deny, or even doubt the existence of such a phenomenon as the vampire.

For my part I have heard no theory by which to explain what I myself have witnessed and experienced, other than that supplied by the ancient and well-attested belief of the country.

The next day the formal proceedings took place in the Chapel of Karnstein. The grave of the Countess Mircalla was opened; and the General and my father recognized each his perfidious and beautiful guest, in the face now disclosed to view. The features, though a hundred and fifty years had passed since her funeral, were tinted with the warmth of life. Her eyes were open; no cadaverous smell exhaled from the coffin. The two medical men, one officially present, the other on the part of the promoter of the inquiry, attested the marvellous fact, that there was a faint, but appreciable respiration, and a corresponding action of the heart. The limbs were perfectly flexible, the flesh elastic; and the leaden coffin floated with blood, in which to a depth of seven inches, the body lay immersed. Here then, were all the admitted signs and proofs of vampirism. The body, therefore, in accordance with the ancient practice, was raised, and a sharp stake driven through the heart of the vampire, who uttered a piercing shriek at the moment, in all respects such as might escape from a living person in the last agony. Then the head was struck off, and a torrent of blood flowed from the severed neck. The body and head were next placed on a pile of wood, and reduced to ashes, which were thrown upon the river and borne away, and that territory has never since been plagued by the visits of a vampire.

215

My father has a copy of the report of the Imperial Commission, with the signatures of all who were present at these proceedings, attached in verification of the statement. It is from this official paper that I have summarized my account of this last shocking scene.

XVI
Conclusion

I write all this you suppose with composure. But far from it; I cannot think of it without agitation. Nothing but your earnest desire so repeatedly expressed, could have induced me to sit down to a task that has unstrung my nerves for months to come, and reinduced a shadow of the unspeakable horror which years after my deliverance continued to make my days and nights dreadful, and solitude insupportably terrific.

Let me add a word or two about that quaint Baron Vordenburg, to whose curious lore we were indebted for the discovery of the Countess Mircalla's grave.

He had taken up his abode in Gratz, where, living upon a mere pittance, which was all that remained to him of the once princely estates of his family, in Upper Styria, he devoted himself to the minute and laborious investigation of the marvellously authenticated tradition of vampirism. He had at his fingers' ends all the great and little works upon the subject. *Magia Posthuma, Phlegon de Mirabilibus, Augustinus de curâ pro Mortuis, Philosophicae et Christianae Cogitationes de Vampiris*, by John Christofer Harenberg; and a thousand others, among which I remember only a few of those which he lent to my father. He had a voluminous digest of all the judicial cases, from which he had extracted a system of principles that appear to govern -- some always, others occasionally only -- the condition of the vampire. I may mention, in passing, that the deadly pallor attributed to that sort of *revenants*, is a mere melodramatic fiction. They present, in the grave, and when they show themselves in human society, the appearance of healthy life. When disclosed to light in their coffins, they exhibit all the symptoms that are enumerated as those which proved the vampire life of the long-dead Countess Karnstein.

How they escape from their graves and return to them for certain hours every day, without displacing the clay or leaving any trace of disturbance in the state of the coffin or the cerements, has always been admitted to be utterly inexplicable. The amphibious existence of the vampire is sustained by daily renewed slumber in the grave. Its horrible lust for living blood supplies the vigour of its waking existence. The vampire is prone to be fascinated with an engrossing vehemence, resembling the passion of love, by particular persons. In pursuit of these it will exercise inexhaustible patience and stratagem, for access to a particular object may be obstructed in a hundred ways. It will never desist until it has satiated its passion, and drained the very life of its coveted victim. But it will, in these cases, husband and protract its murderous enjoyment with the refinement of an epicure, and heighten it by the gradual approaches of an artful courtship. In these cases it seems to yearn for something like sympathy and consent. In ordinary ones it goes direct to its object, overpowers with violence, and strangles and exhausts often at a single feast.

The vampire is, apparently, subject, in certain situations, to special conditions. In the particular instance of which I have given you a relation, Mircalla seemed to be limited to a name which, if not her real one, should at least reproduce, without the omission or addition of a single letter, those, as we say, anagrammatically, which compose it. *Carmilla* did this; so did *Millarca*.

My father related to the Baron Vordenburg, who remained with us for two or three weeks after the expulsion of Carmilla, the story about the Moravian nobleman and the vampire at Karnstein churchyard, and then he asked the Baron how he had discovered the exact position of the long-concealed tomb of the Countess Millarca? The Baron's grotesque features puckered up into a mysterious smile; he looked down, still smiling, on his worn spectacle-case and fumbled with it. Then looking up, he said:

"I have many journals, and other papers, written by that remarkable man; the most curious among them is one treating of the visit of which you speak, to Karnstein. The tradition, of course, discolours and distorts a little. He might have been termed a Moravian nobleman, for he had changed his abode to that territory, and was, beside, a noble. But he was, in truth, a native of Upper Styria. It is enough to say that in very early youth he had been a passionate and favoured lover of the beautiful Mircalla, Countess Karnstein. Her early death plunged him into inconsolable grief. It is the nature of vampires to increase and multiply, but according to an ascertained and ghostly law.

"Assume, at starting, a territory perfectly free from that pest. How does it begin, and how does it multiply itself? I will tell you. A person, more or less wicked, puts an end to himself. A suicide, under certain circumstances, becomes a vampire. That spectre visits living people in their slumbers; *they* die, and almost invariably, in the grave, develop into vampires. This happened in the case of the beautiful Mircalla, who was haunted by one of those demons. My ancestor, Vordenburg, whose title I still bear, soon discovered this, and in the course of the studies to which he devoted himself, learned a great deal more.

"Among other things, he concluded that suspicion of vampirism would probably fall, sooner or later, upon the dead Countess, who in life had been his idol. He conceived a horror, be she what she might, of her remains being profaned by the outrage of a posthumous execution. He has left a curious paper to prove that the vampire, on its expulsion from its amphibious existence, is projected into a far more horrible life; and resolved to save his once beloved Mircalla from this.

"He adopted the stratagem of a journey here, a pretended removal of her remains, and a real obliteration of her monument. When age had stolen upon him, and from the vale of years he looked back on the scenes he was leaving, he considered, in a different spirit, what he had done; and a horror took possession of him. He made the tracings and notes which have guided me to the very spot, and drew up a confession of the deception that he had practised. If he had intended any further action in this matter, death prevented him; and the hand of a remote descendant has, too late for many, directed the pursuit to the lair of the beast."

We talked a little more, and among other things he said was this:

"One sign of the vampire is the power of the hand. The slender hand of Mircalla closed like a vice of steel on the General's wrist when he raised the hatchet to strike. But its power is not confined to its grasp; it leaves a numbness in the limb it seizes, which is slowly, if ever, recovered from."

The following Spring my father took me on a tour through Italy. We remained away for more than a year. It was long before the terror of recent events subsided; and to this hour the image of Carmilla returns to memory with ambiguous alternations -- sometimes the playful, languid, beautiful girl; sometimes the writhing fiend I saw in the ruined church; and often from a reverie I have started, fancying I heard the light step of Carmilla at the drawing-room door.

THE HORLA

Guy de Maupassant

8th May

What a glorious day! I have spent the whole morning lying on the lawn in front of my house, under the spreading plane tree which shelters and shades it entirely. I love this country-side, where I have my roots, those deep-reaching, delicate fibres, which attach a man to the land where his ancestors were born and died, which link him to the local ways of thought, local diet, local idioms, to the intonations of the country-folk, to the odours of the soil, the village, the very atmosphere.

I love this house of mine, in which my childhood was passed. From end to end, my garden skirts the river Seine. I have only to look from my windows across the road to see that great and noble river, covered with the shipping which passes up and down between Rouen and Le Havre.

Yonder on my left lies Rouen, the great slate-roofed city. From it rises a spiky forest of Gothic belfries, too numerous to count. Some are slender, some are massive, and over them towers the iron spire of the Cathedral. Their bells ring out in the misty blue of exquisite mornings. The distant music of clanging iron or sonorous bronze is borne to my ears, varying in volume as the breeze rises or falls.

What a beautiful morning it is!

About eleven o'clock a long convoy of ships moves upstream, towed by a tug-boat no larger than a fly, which pants and groans under the strain, and vomits out dense clouds of smoke. Next come two English schooners, with their red ensigns fluttering in the breeze, and after them a superb Brazilian three-masted ship, painted white all over and beautiful spick and span. The sight of her gave me so much pleasure that for some reason or other I saluted her.

I have been feverish for the last few days. I am feeling unwell, or, to be more precise, out of spirits. What is the source of these mysterious influences which convert our happiness into depression and our confidence into anxiety? It would seem as if the air, the invisible atmosphere, were charged with forces which we can never know, and as if we were subjected to strange effects from their proximity. I sometimes wake in the morning so full of gaiety that I can hardly repress my desire to sing. What is the cause of this access of cheerfulness? Then perhaps I take a walk along the river bank, and in a moment my high spirits have vanished. I turn homewards in a woebegone frame of mind, as though I expected to hear of some misfortune, as soon as I set foot in my house. Why should I feel like this? Is it merely because a cold current of air has breathed upon me, affecting my nerves and throwing a dark shadow over my soul? Have my thoughts been perturbed by the shape of the clouds, the aspect of the day, the ever-varying colours of the objects that pass before my eyes? Who can explain it? Although the mind is unaware, our whole environment, everything we see, everything we brush past without realizing, everything we touch subconsciously, in short all that our senses encounter without discernment, has on ourselves and on our organs and, through the latter, on our ideas and on our soul itself, rapid, astonishing and inexplicable effects.

How profound is the mystery of the invisible! To sound its depth we use in vain our contemptible equipment of senses; our eyes fail to perceive a thing because it is too small or too large, too near or too far. The dwellers in a star are as invisible to our eyes, as the bacteria in a drop of water. Our ears are ever deceptive, because they convert mere atmospheric vibrations into musical tones; they are wizards, who perform this miracle of transmitting mere oscillatory movement into sound, and by this metamorphosis give birth to music, which changes nature's silent vibrations into audible notes. Our sense of smell is feebler than that of a hound. Our sense of taste hardly serves us to decide the age of a wine. Ah! if only we were endowed with other senses, which would perform other wonders for us, how much more widely could we appreciate our surroundings!

16th May

I am not well. There is no doubt about it. And last month I was in such splendid health. I am dreadfully feverish, or rather, I am suffering from a febrile languor, which affects mind no less than body. I am continually obsessed by a terrifying sensation of menacing danger, of impending disaster or approaching death. These presentiments are doubtless the herald of some evil yet undeclared, which is germinating in my frame.

18th May

I have just returned from a consultation with my doctor, whom I went to see, because I was suffering from sleeplessness. His examination revealed an unduly quick pulse, dilated pupils, and disordered nerves, but there was no indication of anything serious. I am to have a course of shower-baths and take bromide of potassium.

25th May

No change. My condition is certainly curious. As evening approaches, I am possessed by an incomprehensible restlessness, just as if the coming darkness held for me some terrible menace. I hurry through my dinner, after which I try to read a book, but I cannot understand the words, indeed I can hardly distinguish the letters. I pace my drawing-room in all directions; I am under the malign influence of some vague, irresistible fear, which makes me dread not only sleep itself, but even my bed.

I go up to my bedroom at about two in the morning. The moment I enter I double-lock the door, and shoot the bolts. I am afraid...but of what?..I have never been a timid man...but now I open my wardrobe, I look under the bed, I listen...listen...for what? How strange it is, that a mere indisposition, a defect of the circulation, the irritation of some fibre, a slight congestion, some minute disturbance in the imperfect and delicate mechanism of the body, can afflict the most cheerful of men with melancholy, and convert a brave man into a coward. And, later, when I actually go to bed, I await the coming of sleep, as one would await the arrival of one's executioner. I anticipate its approach with horror. My heart beats faster, my limbs tremble, my whole frame shivers even under the warm blankets, and this lasts, until the moment when I suddenly succumb to sleep. I am plunged into it, as a man is plunged into a pit of stagnant water and drowned. I do not feel myself dozing off as I used to do. The sleep that comes upon me is a perfidious thing. It lurks near me; it watches me like a spy; it is like someone, who is waiting to seize me by the head, to close my eyes, and thrust me into oblivion.

I sleep for an appreciable time, some two or three hours. Then a dream ...no, a nightmare, strangles me. I am fully aware that I am lying asleep in bed. I not only feel it, but see it. And I feel, too, that there is someone creeping towards me -- someone who looks at me, passes his hands over me, climbs up on to the bed, kneels on my chest, grasps my throat with both hands, and squeezes. .squeezes...with all his might, in an effort to strangle me. I struggle and struggle. It is all that I can do. I am bound hand and foot by that horrible impotence, which paralyses us in our dreams. I try to cry out but I cannot make a sound. I endeavour to move, but in vain. I make the most fearful efforts; I strive to turn over and hurl off this being, that is crushing and smothering me. But my struggles are of no avail. Then suddenly I awake, with my mind distraught and my body bathed in perspiration. I light a candle. But there is nobody there.

This nightly crisis past, I fall into peaceful slumber, which lasts till dawn.

2nd June

I am getting worse and worse. What can be wrong with me? The bromide has done me no good; the shower-baths have no effect. One day, in order to induce physical fatigue, though I was weary enough already, I went for a walk in the forest of Roumare. At first I believed that the cool woodland air, so pure and balmy with the perfume of the leaves and grass, would renew the blood in my veins and imbue my heart with fresh energy. Entering the forest by a great riding avenue, I turned off towards La Bouille, down a narrow path which lay between two ranks of giant trees. Their arching branches formed a green roof, dense and sombre, shutting out the sky. I was suddenly afflicted with a shivering fit, which was not the result of a chill, but an inexplicable shudder of apprehension. I felt ill at ease, all alone in the wood, and I hastened my steps. The profound solitude begot in me blind, unreasoning terror. Then all of a sudden the conviction came over me that I was being followed. Someone was treading on my heels, so closely as almost to touch me. I turned sharply. But there was no one there. The wide, straight avenue of towering trees was empty, with an emptiness that daunted me. Behind me, before me, in either direction, it ran on and on, monotonous and terrifying, until it was lost in the distance.

I closed my eyes, I know not why. And I began to spin round on one heel, very quickly, like a teetotum till I nearly fell. When I opened my eyes again, the trees were swaying, the solid ground was undulating. I had to sit down. I could not remember the way I had come. I positively had no idea. An absurd situation! Haphazard, I set off to the right, and presently found myself again in the main avenue, by which I had reached the heart of the forest.

3rd June

A dreadful night. I am going away for a few weeks. A little travelling will doubtless put me right.

2nd July

Home again, and fully restored to health, besides which, I have had a delightful trip. I went to Mont Saint-Michel, a place I had never yet visited.

If you arrive at Avranches about sunset, as I did, a vision of beauty rewards you. The town of Avranches is situated on a hill. I was shown the way to the public gardens, which are at one end of the little city, and the view from this point provoked from me a cry of amazement. A prodigiously wide arm of the sea lay before me. On either side of the coast line stretched out until lost to view in the haze. In the midst of this immense expanse of water, tawny under a cloudless, saffron sky, a weird and sombre hill soared upwards from the sandy shallows. The sun was setting. The silhouette of this fantastic rock, bearing upon its summit a structure not less unearthly, stood out sharply against the flaming sky.

At dawn on the following day I set out for the Mount. The tide was low, as on the previous evening. The nearer I drew, the more impressively did this astonishing Abbey stand out. After a walk of several hours, I reached the enormous congeries of rock with its group of houses and the great church towering above it. I climbed the steep and narrow street and entered the Abbey, the most perfect masterpiece of Gothic architecture ever created for the dwelling-place of God on earth. Great as a city, it has a series of low-pitched halls with massive, vaulted roofs, and lofty galleries supported on slender columns. It is a gigantic jewel, hewn out of granite; yet delicate as a wisp of lace. There are towers everywhere; and winding staircases which lead upwards into slender belfries. Into the azure sky of day, or into the dark firmament of night these belfries soar. Their grotesque roof-lines bristle with chimæras, devils, fantastic beasts, prodigious flowers; and each belfry is linked to its neighbour by a graceful arch of wrought stonework.

When I reached the summit, I said to the monk who was acting as my guide:

"Father, you ought surely to be happy here."

"It is a windy spot, sir," he replied.

We entered into a conversation, while we watched the rising tide course across the sand, covering it with a breastplate of steely blue. The monk told me legend after legend, all old stories of the Mount. One of them specially impressed me. The natives of the place assert that human speech is often heard on the sands at night, and the bleating of two goats, one with a strong voice and the other with a weak one. The incredulous maintain that the sounds are the cries of sea-birds which sometimes resemble the bleating of goats and at other times plaintive human cries. But fishermen, coming home late at night, vow that they have met an old shepherd roaming over the sands at low water and prowling round the little settlement, which has been planted so far away from the world. This ancient shepherd wears his cloak over his head, so that no one has ever seen his face. He walks on ahead, leading his goats, one of which has the face of a man and the other that of a woman. Both animals have long white hair, and they never cease from talking and wrangling in an unknown tongue, except when they break off to bleat with all their might.

"Do you believe it?" I asked the monk.

"I cannot tell," he replied.

To this I rejoined:

"If there were really such strange beings on earth, how is it how is it that we have not found out all about them long ago? Wouldn't you and I have seen them?"

"Do you imagine," he replied, "that we see the hundred-thousandth part of what exists? Consider for example the wind, which is the greatest of the forces of nature. It knocks men down, demolishes houses, uproots trees, stirs up the sea into mountainous waves, breaks away the cliffs, and drives great ships on to the breakers. The wind whistles, groans, bellows, sometimes it even kills. Have you seen it? Will you ever see it? It exists nevertheless."

I made no reply to this ingenious logic. The man might be a sage, or, on the other hand, a fool. Far be it from me to decide. In any case, he succeeded in silencing me, for his remarks agreed closely with certain reflections of my own.

3rd July

I slept badly. I am sure there is a morbid influence at work here. My coachman has had the same symptoms as myself. On my return home I noticed his singular pallor and I asked him:

"What is the matter with you, Jean?"

"Somehow, sir, I can't get to sleep. I have had something hanging over me like a spell ever since you went away."

The other servants, however, seem in good health. What I am afraid of is a return of the same symptoms in myself.

4th July

There is no doubt about it. It has seized upon me again. My former nightmares have come back. Last night I felt that there was something squatting on my chest. His mouth was on my mouth and he was drinking my life from between my lips. He was draining my vitality like a leech. Then, when he had had his fill, he rose and left me, and I awoke. I was too prostrate, too crushed and exhausted to move. If this continues I shall go away again.

5th July

Have I lost my reason? The events of last night are so strange that my head reels when I think of them. I had locked my bedroom door, as is now nightly practice. Being thirsty, I drank half a tumbler of water, and in doing so I happened to notice that my water-bottle had been filled right up to the crystal stopper. When I went to bed, I fell into one of my frightful dreams. Two hours later I was roused by a horror that was even more terrible than the nightmare itself. Imagine the condition of a man, who is being murdered while he sleeps. He awakes with a knife through his lungs, with the death rattle in his throat. He is bathed in blood. He struggles in vain for breath; he is in the very article of death; and yet he understands nothing of what is happening. That was my case. My reasoning powers at last returned to me. Feeling thirsty again, I lit my candle and went towards the table, on which I had put my water-bottle. I lifted it and tilted it over my tumbler. Not a drop came out. It was empty. Absolutely empty. For the moment I was utterly bewildered; but very soon I was conscious of such poignant emotion that I sank, or rather, collapsed into a chair. Then I leapt to my feet and cast a look around me. Aghast with amazement and terror. I sat down in front of the crystal decanter, and gazed at it intently, trying to solve its mystery. My hands were shaking. Someone must have drunk the water. But who? I myself? Yes, surely it must have been I. In that case I was a somnambulist. Unconsciously I was living that mysterious double life which makes us wonder whether there are two selves within us, or whether some alien personality, elusive and invisible, seizes the moment when the soul is heavy with sleep, takes possession of the body, and exacts from it an obedience equal to, or greater than, that which it yields to the rightful owner when awake.

Ah, who can realize my unspeakable anguish? Who can understand the consternation on the part of a man, sane, fully awake, and with all his mental powers about him, gazing at a glass carafe and searching terror-stricken for the water it should contain. I did not dare to go back to bed, but remained sitting where I was until daybreak.

6th July

I must be going mad. Again the contents of my water-bottle had been drunk by someone during the night. Was it I myself? Was it I? Who else could it be? Who indeed? Oh my God! I am going mad. Who will deliver me?

10th July

I carried out some tests, with surprising results. The conclusion that I have come to is that I must be insane. And yet? On the 6th July, before going to bed, I placed on my table the following things: wine, milk, water, bread and strawberries. Somebody, possibly I myself, drank up all the water and a little of the milk. The wine and the strawberries were not touched. On the 7th July I repeated the experiment with the same result. On the 8th July, I omitted the water and the milk. Nothing was touched. And finally on the 9th July I put only water and milk on the table, but I took the precaution of wrapping up both carafes in pieces of white muslin, and tying the stoppers on with string. Then I rubbed my lips, my moustache and my hands with black lead. After this I went to bed. The usual heavy sleep fell upon me, followed presently by the customary, horrible awakening. I had not moved at all. Even the sheets had no trace of the black lead. I untied the string. I was palpitating with terror. All the water had been drunk! And all the milk too! Ah! my God!... I am leaving immediately for Paris.

12th July

Paris. Seemingly I was out of my mind those last few days. I must have been the plaything of my sick fancies, unless I am really a somnambulist, or have been subjected to one of those influences, which we know to exist, but cannot yet explain and which we call suggestions. In any case, although my mental disorder was verging on dementia, twenty-four hours of Paris have sufficed to restore my balance. Yesterday I did some shopping and paid a few calls, and found my mind greatly vivified and refreshed thereby. In the evening I went to the Théâtre-Français, and saw a play by Alexandre Dumas the younger. My cure was completed by that vivid and commanding genius. Undoubtedly solitude is dangerous for the overwrought intellect. One needs the companionship of men and women, who can both think and express their thoughts. If we are left too long alone, we people the void with phantoms. In excellent spirits, I strolled back by the boulevards to my hotel. Amidst the elbowings of the crowd I could smile ironically at my terrors and fancies of the preceding week, when I had believed, actually believed, that there was an invisible being who shared my house with me. How feeble is our self-control, how quickly we are scared and bewildered when we are brought up against the tiniest manifestation of the unknown! Instead of coming to the obvious conclusion that if one does not understand, it is merely because the cause is hidden, one forthwith imagines terrifying mysteries and the workings of supernatural powers.

14th July

The National Festival. I walked abroad through the streets, and took a childish delight in the fireworks and decorations. Still, it is a silly business, being joyful to order, on a date fixed by Government decree. The public are an imbecile herd, oscillating between patient stupidity and revolutionary ferocity. They are ordered to amuse themselves and they proceed to amuse themselves; to wage war with an adjoining country, and they wage war accordingly; to vote for an Emperor, and forthwith they vote for an Emperor; to vote for a Republic, and, behold, they vote for a Republic.

The leaders of the people are equally besotted, only instead of obeying men, they obey principles, which are *ipso facto* childish, barren and ill-grounded, because, generally speaking, these so-called principles are supposed to be invariable, and this is in a world where one can be sure of nothing, where even light is an illusion, and sound itself a fictitious thing.

16th July

Today I witnessed some phenomena which disturbed me greatly. I dined at the house of my cousin Madame Sablé, whose husband commands the 76th Chasseurs at Limoges. The other two guests were two ladies and a Doctor Parent, the husband of one of them. Doctor Parent devotes himself to maladies of the nerves and the extraordinary manifestations to which the modern experiments in hypnotism and suggestion gives rise. He recounted to us at some length the marvellous results which have been obtained by English investigators and the Nancy Medical School. The incidents he mentioned seemed to me so preposterous that I flatly declared myself incredulous.

"We are," he proclaimed, "on the verge of discovering one of the most important of nature's secrets, that is to say, of nature's terrestrial secrets, for there are undoubtedly other mysteries of the stellar universe, which are of the utmost importance. Ever since mankind has learnt to think and to express his thoughts in speech and writing, he has felt the hovering presence of a mystery, which his senses are too gross and imperfect to enable him to divine. He is now endeavouring, through the medium of his intelligence, to make up this deficiency, which is due to the inadequacy of the organs of the senses. As long as man's intelligence remained on its rudimentary stage, these intimations of the invisible manifested themselves in terrifying phenomena of the crudest description. Hence arose the popular belief in the supernatural, the legends of prowling spirits, of fairies, gnomes and ghosts; even I may add, the legend of God, for our conceptions of the unknown Creator, from whatever religions they are derived, are undeniably the most commonplace, the most stupid, the most unconvincing product of the panic-stricken brains of created beings. There was never a truer word than that saying of Voltaire's: "God made man after His own image and man returned the compliment". It is a little more than a century since mankind obtained a first inkling of these new developments. Mesmer and several others have opened out to us an unexpected pathway and we have achieved astonishing results, especially during the past four or five years."

My cousin, who was as incredulous as myself, smiled sceptically; whereupon Doctor Parent said:

"Would you like me to try to put you to sleep?"

"Yes, certainly."

She seated herself in an arm-chair, and the doctor proceeded to direct upon her a concentrated and mesmeric gaze. The sight of this induced in me a sudden uneasiness. My heart beat faster, and I felt a constriction of the throat. I saw Madame Sablé's eyes grow heavy; her lips contracted, and her bosom rose and sank. In ten minutes she was asleep.

"Go behind her chair," said the doctor.

I took a seat behind her. He put into her hands a visiting card.

"This," he said, "is a looking-glass. What do you see in it?"

"I see my cousin," she answered.

"What is your cousin doing?"

"He is twisting his moustache."

"And now what is he doing?"

"He is taking a photograph out of his pocket."

"Whose photograph?"

"It is a photograph of himself."

It was true, and that photograph had been delivered to me only that evening at my hotel.

"Describe the photograph."

"He is standing up. He is holding his hat in his hand."

Apparently she saw in this blank card the reflection she would have seen in a mirror.

The other women present were frightened and exclaimed:

"That's enough. That's enough."

The doctor however continued:

"Tomorrow," he ordered, "you will get up at eight o'clock. You will call on your cousin at his hotel, and you will beg him to lend you five thousand francs. Your husband has asked you for his sum and you are to produce it when he returns to Paris."

Then he awakened her.

On my return to the hotel, my mind was busy with this curious séance. I had no doubt of the absolute and unimpeachable good faith of my cousin, whom I had known like my own sister from childhood. What I did suspect was some trickery on part of the doctor. Had he held, concealed in the palm of his hand, a mirror and shown it to the sleeping woman simultaneously with the visiting card? Professional conjurers perform feats which are, after their own fashion, quite as extraordinary. I went to bed, and to sleep, and was awakened on the following morning, that is to say, early today, by my valet, who announced that Madame Sablé wanted to see me immediately. I hurriedly dressed myself to receive her.

She seemed in great distress, and did not raise her eyes to mine. Taking a chair, and without lifting her veil, she said:

"My dear cousin, I have a great favour to ask you."

"What is it?"

"I hate telling you and yet I must. I want five thousand francs. I simply must have them."

"Surely not for yourself."

"Yes. It is for myself, or rather for my husband, who has ordered me to get this money for him."

I was so taken aback that I could hardly speak. I was wondering whether she were in league with Doctor Parent to make fun of me, whether the whole thing was not a hoax, which they had rehearsed beforehand and were now very cleverly acting. But when I looked more closely at my cousin, my doubts vanished. The proceeding was evidently most distasteful to her and was causing her great distress. I could see that she could hardly restrain her tears.

Knowing her to be wealthy, I said:

"It's odd that your husband can't lay hands on five thousand francs. Think again. Are you sure he ordered you to get the money from me?"

She hesitated a few moments as though making a strenuous effort to search her memory. Then she replied:

"Yes. Yes. I'm quite sure."

"Did he write to you about it?"

Again she hesitated, and tried to remember. I could divine the painful struggle that was going on in her mind. She could not answer my question. All that she knew was that she had to borrow five thousand francs from me on behalf of her husband. She took refuge in a falsehood.

"Yes. He wrote to me."

"When was that? You didn't mention it yesterday."

"I got his letter only this morning."

"Could you let me see it?"

"No, no. There were things in it private, personal things. I... I burnt it.'

"I gather that your husband has got into debt."

"I don't know," she replied, after some hesitation.

On this I declared abruptly:

"My dear cousin, the fact is that for the moment I haven't five thousand francs available."

She uttered a cry of anguish.

"Oh, oh, I implore you. Try to get them for me."

Her agitation was increasing. She clasped her hands as though in prayer. I could hear her voice break. She wept and stammered, tormented and overwhelmed by the irresistible command which had been laid upon her.

"I implore you," she repeated. "If you only knew the agony I am suffering. I positively must have the money today."

I took pity on her.

"I'll let you have it immediately. I give you my word."

"Oh how can I thank you?" she cried. "How kind you are."

"Do you remember," I asked her, "what happened yesterday in your house?"

"Yes."

"Do you remember that Doctor Parent put you to sleep?"

"Yes."

"Well, Doctor Parent ordered you to come to me this morning and borrow five thousand francs. At this moment you are only obeying his suggestion."

She considered this for a few moments. Then she replied:

"But don't you understand that it is my husband who wants the money?"

For a good hour I endeavoured to convince her, but my efforts were of no avail. After she had left me, I went at once to see Doctor Parent. He was just going out. He listened to me with a smile.

"Now do you believe?" he asked.

"As if I could help it!"

"Let us go and see Madame Sablé."

We found my cousin dozing in a *chaise-longue*. She was utterly worn out. The doctor felt her pulse, and looked at her for some time. He held his hand before her eyes, which gradually closed under the irresistible influence of his magnetic power. As soon as she was asleep, he spoke to her:

"Your husband no longer requires the five thousand francs. You may therefore forget that you asked your cousin to lend you the money. If he says anything about it to you, you won't understand."

Then he awakened her.

I took out my pocket-book.

"Here is the money you asked me for this morning."

She was so surprised that I could not press the point. I made an effort to recall to her memory what had passed between us, but she denied it vehemently, accused me of making fun of her and ended by showing signs of annoyance.

There it is. I am back in my hotel, so perturbed in mind by the experience that I have not been able to take my luncheon.

19th July

Many persons to whom I have related this incident have laughed at me. What am I to think of it? A wise man would say, "Who knows?"

21st July

I dined at Bougival and finished the evening at a riverside ball. In the last resort, all depends on place and environment. On the *Ile de la Grenouillière* it seems the height of absurdity to believe in the supernatural; but at the top of Mont Saint-Michel? Or in India? We are terribly susceptible to the influence of our surroundings. Next week I shall return to my own house.

30th July

I came home yesterday. All goes well.

2nd August

Nothing of interest. The weather is superb. I pass my days in watching the Seine flow past.

4th August

My servants are quarrelling with each other. They maintain that someone comes by night and breaks the glassware in the cupboards. The valet accuses the cook and the cook accuses the linen-maid, and the linen-maid puts the blame on the other two. Which of them is the culprit? It will take a clever man to discover.

6th August

This time, at least, I am not mad. I have seen. With my own eyes I have seen. I can no longer doubt. I am still chilled to the very finger tips, panic-stricken to the marrow of my bones. I have seen... I have seen... At two o'clock, in broad sunshine, I was walking in my rose garden, between the autumn rose trees which are now coming into bloom. I stopped to admire a *géant des batailles*, which had three magnificent blossoms, and I saw, I saw distinctly, quite close to me, the stalk of one of those roses bent as though by an invisible hand. Then it was broken off, as though ghostly fingers had plucked it. The flower was raised into the air in just such a curve as a hand would have described in carrying it to the lips, and there it remained suspended, without visible support, floating in the clear atmosphere, a terrifying patch of red, only a few feet from my eyes. Aghast,

I sprang forward to seize it. But my fingers encountered nothing. The rose had vanished. I was seized by furious anger against myself. It was beyond all bounds for a serious and rational man to have such hallucinations. But was it really a hallucination? I went back to look at the stalk and found it immediately. It was between the two roses, which still remained on the tree, and it had been freshly broken. At this my mind was convulsed with horror. I am now convinced that I am haunted by an invisible being. I know it, as surely as I know that night follows day. The incubus absorbs water and milk, it can touch things, grasp them and move them from one place to another. Therefore, although invisible, it is material, and it dwells as I do, under this roof.

7th August

I slept well. My mysterious visitor drank the water in my carafe, but did not disturb my sleep. I wonder if I am insane. Walking along the river-bank, in the sunshine, I have felt doubts as to my sanity; not merely those vague suspicions that I used to have, but clearly reasoned doubts. I have seen mad people. There were some, who remained intelligent, lucid, and even unusually shrewd in the affairs of life, save on one point only. They would converse on all subjects with acuteness, subtlety and penetration. Then of a sudden their reason would touch upon the reef of their insanity and be battered to pieces, scattered to the winds. They foundered in that raging and terrifying ocean, full of rolling waves, mists, and sudden gusts of storm; the ocean of dementia. I should have no doubt of my insanity, my absolute insanity, had I not retained full consciousness of my mental plight, had I not probed and analysed it with perfect lucidity. Some unexplained disturbance has taken place within my brain, one of those disturbances which present-day physiologists endeavour to analyse and classify, and this trouble has fixed a deep gulf within my mind and in the logical sequence of my thoughts. Similar phenomena can be noted in dreams, which carry us away into a country of the strangest phantasmagoria, which however, do not astonish us, for this reason that the verifying apparatus, the controlling power in our brains, is in abeyance, whereas the imaginative faculty is wide awake and functioning actively. It is not conceivable that one of the notes of my cerebral keyboard is out of action? As the result of some accident, men sometimes lose a portion of their memory: they are unable to recall proper names, or verbs, or numerals, or possibly, dates. It has been established by recent research that all the several departments of the mind are localized in special portions of the brain. What wonder then if my faculty of controlling these hallucinations of mine, should be temporarily paralysed in me. Such were my reflections during my wanderings on the river-bank.

Everything was bathed in sunshine. The sun glorified the face of the waters: it inspired me with the love of all things, of life, of the swallows, whose darting flight is the delight of my eyes, of the riverside plants, whose quivering in the breeze is music to my ears. In spite of this sense of superficial enjoyment, however, I was penetrated by an inexplicable feeling of uneasiness. I could not rid myself of the conviction that some occult force was numbing my faculties, paralysing my will, curtailing my walks, and even drawing me back to the house. I experienced that distressing impulse to return, which haunts one, when some loved one at home is lying on a bed of sickness, and one has a presentiment that an aggravation of his malady has supervened. I turned homewards convinced that some bad news, a letter or telegram, would be awaiting me. But there was nothing of the sort; and I felt even more discomfited and opressed, than if I had some new and fantastic vision.

8th August

I have had a frightful night. My visitor does nothing definite, but he hangs about me, watching my movements, obsessing me, dominating me. Working in this hidden way he is more terrible than if he manifested his invisible and persistent presence in supernatural phenomena. Still, I had some sleep.

9th August

Nothing happened. But I am afraid.

10th August

Nothing. But what of tomorrow?

11th August

Still nothing. With these fears and thoughts ever torturing my mind, I cannot stay any longer in this house. I am going away.

12 August, 10 p.m.

The whole day long I have been trying to leave home, and I could not do it. I determined to accomplish this act of liberty, so easy, so simple -- to go out of the house, get into my carriage, drive to Rouen. And I found it impossible. Why?

13th August

There are certain maladies that completely destroy the physical elasticity. One's energies are annihilated, one's muscles relaxed, one's bones become as soft as flesh, and one's flesh becomes as fluid as water. Such are the sensations I endure in my moral being, and they work in a strange and devastating fashion. I have lost all strength and courage. I have no dominion over myself; I do not even retain the power of exercising my own faculties. Someone else is in control. I merely carry out his orders.

14th August

I am lost! My mind has become the chattel and serf of some other being; the chattel and serf! There is someone, who orders all my acts, all my movements, all my thoughts. I am reduced to nothing, a servile and terrified spectator of my own actions. If I want to leave the house, I cannot do so, because he will not have it. So I must needs remain at home. He holds me down in my arm-chair! Trembling and distraught, I concentrate on the effort to rise to my feet, so that I am once more my own master. And I cannot do it. I am riveted to my seat, and my seat is riveted to the ground, so that no force can move us. Then all of a sudden I feel a compulsion to go to the end of the garden and pick some strawberries. I eat them. Oh, my God, my God! Is there indeed a God? If there be, deliver me, save me, succour me! Pardon! Pity! Grace! Save me. Save me! Oh, what sufferings I endure, what tortures, what horrors!

15th August

It seems to me clear that my poor cousin was under the same sort of domination and possession, when she came to me to borrow five thousand francs. She was subject to an alien will, which entered into her like a second soul, parasitic and tyrannical. Is the world coming to an end? And the despot, who rules me, who is he? I cannot see him, I can know nothing of this prowling stranger of supernatural origin.

If it be true that invisible beings exist, how is it, that, since the origin of the world, these beings have never yet manifested themselves to others in the same definite manner as they have to me? I have never read anything which suggests the events which have occurred in my house. Oh! -- if I could only

234

leave it, run away from it, escape, and never come back again. That would save me. But I have not the power to do it.

16th August

I managed to escape today for two hours. I was like a prisoner, who discovers that the door of his dungeon is open. I had suddenly the sensation that I was free; that he was far away. I ordered my carriage to be made ready with all speed and I drove to Rouen.

Oh! what a joy it was to be able to tell the coachman to drive to Rouen, and to have the order obeyed. I stopped at the library to borrow Dr. Hermann Herestauss's great treatise on the unknown denizens of the ancient and modern world. And then at the very moment when I was stepping into my carriage, and about to say: "Drive to the station," another order came to my lip, and was forced from me in a cry so loud that the passers-by turned to look at me.

"Home!" I shouted, and crazed with misery, I fell back upon the cushions of my carriage. He had tracked me down; I was again his prisoner.

17th August

Ah! what a night! what a night! And yet it seems to me that I have some cause to rejoice. I was able to read, until one o'clock in the morning. Hermann Herestauss, Doctor of Philosophy and Theogony, deals with the history and manifestations of all the invisible beings who haunt the human race or infest our dreams. He describes their origins, their domain, their powers. But not one of them resembles this incubus of mine. His writings suggest to me that ever since man has been able to think, he has had a terrifying presentiment of the coming of a new being, stronger than himself. This being is to be man's successor upon earth. The human race has felt the approach of its master and, unable to foresee his nature, has in its terror created the whole fantastic world of occult beings, vague phantoms, the offspring of man's fears. Having read Herestauss until one in the morning, I went and sat by my open window, in order to freshen my brain in the cool night breeze. The air was balmy and soothing. In happier circumstances, how I should have enjoyed a night like this.

There was no moon. The stars were twinkling in the depths of the dark firmament. Who were the inhabitants of these worlds, I wondered. What forms, what living creatures, what animals, what plants, would one find there? If there are men with the power of thought in those distant spheres, what knowledge have they that is denied to us? What powers that we do not possess? Can they see objects, of which we do not suspect the existence?

Some day or other, will not one of those beings traverse space, to appear on this earth, to conquer it, as the Normans once upon a time crossed the sea to conquer weaker races? So feeble, so helpless to protect ourselves, so ignorant, so puny, are we who inhabit this particle of mud, revolving in a drop of water. Thus reflecting I fell asleep, with the cool air of night all about me.

I had been sleeping for about forty minutes when I was awakened by strange, confused emotion. Without stirring, I opened my eyes. At first I saw nothing, but suddenly I had an idea that a page of the Herestauss, which I had left on the table, was turning over of its own accord. There was not a breath of air coming in at the window. I watched in amazement. After about four minutes I saw -- yes, with my own eyes I saw -- a second page rise, turn over, subside upon the preceding page, exactly as if a human finger had turned the leaf. My arm-chair was to all appearance empty, but I realized that he was there; he seated in my place, and reading. I made a furious leap, like the spring of a rebellious, wild beast about to disembowel its tamer. I crossed the room; intending to seize him, strangle him; kill him. But before I reached the chair, it was knocked over, as though someone had fled before me. The table rocked, the lamp upset and went out, and the window was closed, as if some robber taken by surprise had hurled himself through it into the darkness, and seizing both sides had slammed them to, behind him.

So then, he had run away. He was afraid, afraid of me. That thing, afraid of me!

Why, then -- why, then -- tomorrow, or some other day, I might perhaps manage to seize him, and dash him to bits on the ground. Dogs have been known to turn on their masters, bite them and worry them to death.

18th August

All day long I have been thinking, and this is the scheme I have devised. I shall continue to obey all his orders, to do as he directs, act as he wills me. I shall show myself humble, submissive, craven. He is stronger than I. But the hour will come...

19th August

Now I know. I know all. I have just read the following paragraph in the Revue du Monde Scientifique:

"We have received a curious communication from Rio de Janeiro. At this moment, in the Province of San Paolo, an epidemic of insanity is raging. It resembles the epidemics of contagious dementia, which afflicted the European peoples in the Middle Ages. The inhabitants, driven to distraction, quit their habitations, desert their villages, abandon their work in the fields, declaring that they are pursued, possessed, and tyrannized over, as if they were cattle. Their tormentors are beings, who are tangible but not visible. They are, seemingly, a species of vampire, which sucks the vitality of its sleeping victim. In addition to this, they drink water and milk, but appears to avoid every other form of nourishment. Professor Don Pedro Henriquez, accomplished by several doctors skilled in research, has left for the Province of San Paolo, in order to study on the spot the origins and manifestations of this amazing mania. He will in due course bring before the Emperor proposals for such measures, as are, in his opinion, calculated to restore the stricken population to reason."

Ah! Ah! Now I remember. I remember that beautiful, Brazilian three-master, which sailed up the Seine on the 8th of May, passing close under my windows. It looked so gay and white and trim. And the Being was on board of her, on his way from Brazil, where his race has its origin. He must have caught sight of me. He must have seen my house, which is white like his ship, and have jumped from the ship on to the bank. Oh, my God! I can now see into the future. The reign of man is over.

He is come; he whom the early and unsophisticated races of the world associated with their first emotions of terror, he, whom anxious priests exorcised, whom sorcerers invoked in the darkness of the night, though unable as yet to compel his appearance; he, whom the anticipation of the temporary masters of the world invented with every conceivable form, whether monstrous or gracious, as gnome, spirit, genie, fairy, or goblin. The gross imaginings of primitive terror having passed away, men of greater perspicacity arrived at a clearer idea. Mesmer divined it, and medical research discovered and established the nature of the new power, ten years before its advent. This mysterious dominion over the human soul, which is thereby reduced to a state of bondage, is the weapon of our future Lord and Master, and the doctors of medicine have been playing with it, calling it magnetism, hypnotism, suggestion, and what not. I have seen them amusing themselves like reckless children with the horrible power. Woe unto us, woe unto mankind! for he has come, the...the what is his name?...the...I have a feeling that he is calling out his name to me and I cannot catch it...yes... he is calling it...I listen...I cannot...say it again...the...Horla...yes...I have heard it...the Horla...it is he, the Horla...he has come.

Alas! the vulture has eaten the dove, the wolf has eaten the sheep, the lion has devoured the sharp-horned buffalo; man has slain the lion with the arrow, sword and powder; but the Horla will treat man, as man has treated the horse and the ox. By the mere exercise of his will-power, he will convert man into his chattel, his slave, his food. Woe unto us!

Sometimes, nevertheless, an animal rebels against his tamer and kills him...that is my own intention...but first I must study him, establish contact with him, see him. Savants say that the eyes of animals are not as ours and

237

that they have a different method of perception. It is true that my eyes cannot distinguish this newcomer, who lords it over me. Why not, I wonder. I recall the words of the monk Mont Saint-Michel. "Do you imagine that we see the hundred-thousandth part of what exists? Consider for example the wind, which is the greatest of the forces of nature. It knocks men down, it demolishes houses, it uproots trees, it stirs up the sea into mountainous waves, it breaks away the cliffs and drives great ships on to the rocks. The wind whistles, groans, bellows, sometimes it even kills. Have you seen it? It exists nevertheless."

And I reflected further. The human eye is so feeble and imperfect that it cannot distinguish even solid bodies, if they happen to be transparent. If a glass without a background of tin-foil happens to be in my way, my eyes will betray me, just as a bird, which has flown into a room, will dash its head against the window panes. There are a thousand things besides, which deceive and delude the sight. What wonder then, if my eyes fail to perceive a new body through which the light passes freely?

A new being? Why not? It was inevitable. And if we are unable to distinguish this new being, just as we failed to discern those who were created before us, the reason is that his nature is more perfect than ours, that his body has finer qualities and is more cunningly contrived. The human frame is such a puny thing. Clumsily conceived, it is one mass of organs that are always jaded, that are always collapsing like unduly complicated springs. We live like plants and beasts, deriving our sustenance laboriously from air, vegetation and flesh. Ours is an animal mechanism, subject to maladies, deformities, putrefaction; we are an inadequate machine, unregulated, childish, grotesque, constructed with perverse ingenuity, a work both clumsy and delicate, a mere embryo of a being that might develop into something intelligent and sublime.

There are a certain number of species on this earth, few enough, to be sure, raging from mollusc to man. Why should not another variation arise after the completion of the period, which separates the successive appearances of the various species? Why not indeed? Why not other trees, with great dazzling blossoms, trees that could fill a whole country-side with their fragrance? Why should there not be other elements, as well as fire, air, earth and water, the parents and fosterers of everything that lives? They are only four in number. What a pity it is! Why should there not be forty, four hundred, four thousand of them?

How poor and paltry and wretched the whole creation! Doled out parsimoniously, contrived without imagination, clumsily constructed. The elephant, the hippopotamus, what grave! The camel, what elegance!

But on the other hand, you will point to the butterfly, that winged blossom. I dream of one as big as a hundred worlds, with wings of such form and beauty, such colour and movement, that I cannot give you even a faint idea of its splendour. But I can see it, as it flits from star to star, while the delicate, rhythmic beating of its pinions diffuses a balmy fragrance. And the dwellers of the stars, in ecstasy and ravishment, watch it fly past.

What has befallen me? It is he, he, it is the Horla who haunts me and fills my mind with these insane imaginings. He lives within me, his soul and my soul are becoming one. But I will kill him.

19th August

I will kill him. I have seen him. I was seated last night by my table, making a pretence of concentrating on what I was writing. I knew that he would come prowling round me, close to me, so close, that I might be able to touch him, or even get him into my clutches. And then I would use every source that a desperate man has at his disposal; hands, knees, chest, head; I would strangle him, crush him, bite and rend him.

With all my senses feverishly excited, I waited and watched. I had lighted two lamps, as well as the eight candles on the mantlepiece, as though the brilliant illumination could reveal him to me. In front of me stood my bed, an old oaken four-poster. On the right was the fireplace, on the left the door, which I had carefully closed, after leaving it open for a sufficient time to attract him to my room. Behind me was a very lofty wardrobe with a glass door. I always shave and dress before the mirror, and lately I had fallen into the habit of stopping whenever I passed it, and examining myself from head to foot.

I knew that the Horla was spying on me, as I on him. To deceive him, I went on making a pretence of writing. Suddenly I became aware, beyond all doubt, that he was looking over my shoulder, reading. I could feel a light contact on my ear.

I rose to my feet and stretched out my hands, turning so quickly that I nearly overbalanced. And what happened then? The room was as bright as daylight. Yet I could not see myself in my mirror. The reflecting surface was blank, clear, deep and shining, but my image was not there, although I was standing right in front of the glass. I scrutinized the gleaming surface from top to bottom. I looked at it aghast. But I durst not go nearer; I feared to make the slightest movement. Although I was conscious that the invisible body, which had annihilated my reflection, was within my reach, I knew that he would again elude my grasp. My terror was indescribable. And then, gradually, my image began to appear within the mirror, as though breaking through the mist that lies upon a sheet of water, drifting slowly from left to right. Every moment my reflection gained in clearness. It was like the passing of an eclipse. This veil that obscured my reflection, had no sharply defined contours; it was vague, semi-opaque and gradually yielded to complete transparency. Presently I was able to distinguish all the details of my person, as clearly as in everyday life.

I had seen the Horla. The terror of that vision abides with me, and I shudder with the horror of it.

20th August

To kill him. Yes. But how, when I cannot lay hands on him? I might try poison, but he would see me mixing it in the water. And in any case, would our poisons take effect on any imperceptible body? None at all, I fear. Is there no other way?

21st August

I have summoned a locksmith from Rouen. I have ordered him to fit the windows of my room with iron shutters, such as you see on the ground floor of private mansions in Paris, to keep out thieves. He is also making an iron door for me. I shall be taken for a coward, but what do I care?

10th September

Hotel Continental, Rouen. It is done. It is done. But have I really killed him? My mind is utterly overwhelmed by the horrors I have witnessed. Yesterday, after the locksmith had put in the iron door and shutters, I left them open until midnight, although it was getting cold. Then I had a sudden conviction of his presence, and I was filled with joy, a delirium of joy. I rose unconcernedly from my chair and walked carelessly about my room. After I kept this up for some time, so as to avoid arousing his suspicions, I calmly removed my boots and put on a pair of old slippers. Then I closed the iron window-shutters, and lounging with assumed nonchalance across the room, I double-locked the iron door. Then I strolled back to the window, fixed a padlock on it, and put the key into my pocket.

At that moment I had the sudden conviction that the Horla was hovering about me in a state of agitation. It was now his turn to be afraid. He was ordering me to open the door and let him out, and I came within an ace of yielding. However, I withstood him manfully, set my back against the panels and opened it just enough to allow myself to slip out backwards. I am very tall, and the crown of my head touched the lintel of the doorway. I was convinced that he had not had a chance of escaping from the room. And I locked him in, all by himself. Imagine my relief! I had him fast! Then I ran downstairs to the drawing-room which was exactly under my bedroom. I took two lamps and emptied the oil all over the carpet and the furniture. Then

I set fire to it, and I escaped from the house, after having double-locked the massive front door. Going to the far end of the garden, I hid myself in a clump of laurels. And then a long time, a very long time elapsed. Everything was dark, silent, motionless. There was not a breath of air, not a star. Overhead were massed great banks of cloud. I could not see them, but I could feel them weighing heavily, heavily, on my soul.

With my eyes fixed on the house, I waited. The delay seemed interminable. By this time I was convinced that the fire had gone out of itself, or that the Horla had extinguished it. At last the fire burst through one of the lower storey windows, and a long tongue of red and yellow flame shot out. Languid, caressing, it glided up the white wall of the house until it licked the roof. The reflection of the flame darted through the tree that shaded the house, illuminating the leaves and the branches, and I will swear that with it came a shudder, a shudder of fear. The birds awoke. A dog began to howl. It was like sunrise.

Presently two other windows fell out, and I could see that the whole lower storey of my house was nothing less than a raging furnace. Then a horrible shrill shriek rent the air, the shriek of a woman. Two attic windows were thrown open. I had forgotten about my servants. I saw their frantic faces, their arms waving for help. Distraught by this horrible spectacle, I ran towards the village, shouting:

"Help, help! Fire, fire!"

Meeting some men, who were already hurrying from the village, I went back with them to the house, which by this time was simply a pyre, magnificent but horrible, a pyre of monstrous size, illuminating the whole earth, a pyre, in which human beings were being consumed. And with them the Horla! The Horla! My prisoner! The new Being! Man's new master! The Horla!

The roof-beams gave way and the whole roof crashed in. A volcano of flame shot up to heaven. Through the hollow window-frames I saw a raging crater of fire. The Horla is there, I thought. He is in that furnace. He is dead.

Dead? Was that so certain? Might it not be that that transparent body of his was invulnerable by forces that are fatal to the human frame? Suppose he had not been destroyed? It may be that time is the only power that can affect him, that has sway over that invisible and terrible Being. Why should he have been endowed with this transparent, mysterious, ethereal body, if there was any need for him to be afraid of illness, wounds, infirmities, or premature destruction?

Premature destruction? All one's fears for humanity are based on that dreadful possibility. After man, the Horla. After man, who may die any day, any hour, any minute, by any sort of accident, comes that Being, who can die only at the appointed day, hour and minute, who can die on this account alone, that his time-limit has run out.

241

No, No. I have not killed him. That is a certainty. And it follows, that there is nothing left for me but to kill myself.

Translated by
Marjorie Laurie

LA-BAS

J.K.Huysmans

...The litanies of lust arise in an atmosphere that is like the wind over a slaughterhouse. The first victim is a very small boy whose name we do not know. Gilles disembowels him, and, cutting off the hands and tearing out the eyes and heart, carries these members into Prelati's chamber. The two men offer them, with passionate objurgations, to the Devil, who holds his peace. Gilles, confounded, flees. Prelati rolls up the poor remains in linen and, trembling, goes out at night to bury them in consecrated ground beside a chapel dedicated to Saint Vincent.

Gilles preserves the blood of this child to write formulas of evocation and conjurements. It manures a horrible crop. Not long afterward the Marshal reaps the most abundant harvest of crimes that has ever been sown.

At dusk, when their senses are phosphorescent, enkindled by inflammatory spiced beverages and by "high" venison, Gilles and his friends retire to a distant chamber of the château. The little boys are brought from their cellar prisons to this room. They are disrobed and gagged. The Marshal fondles them and forces them. Then he hacks them to pieces with a dagger, taking great pleasure in slowly dismembering them. At other times he slashes the boy's chest and drinks the breath from the lungs; sometimes he opens the stomach also, smells it, enlarges the incision with his hands, and seats himself in it. Then while he macerates the warm entrails in ordure, he turns half around and looks over his shoulder to contemplate the supreme convulsions, the last spasms. He himself says afterwards, "I was happier in the enjoyment of tortures, tears, fright, and blood, than in any other pleasure."

Then he becomes weary of these faecal joys...

Soon his furies become aggravated. Until now he has appeased the rage of his senses with living or moribund beings. He wearies of stuprating palpitant flesh and becomes a lover of the dead. A passionate artist, he kisses, with cries of enthusiasm, the well-made limbs of his victims. He establishes sepulchral beauty contests, and whichever of the truncated heads receives the prize he raises by the hair and passionately kisses the cold lips.

Vampirism satisfies him for months. He pollutes dead children, appeasing the fever of his desires in the blood-smeared chill of the tomb. He even goes so far -- one day when his supply of children is exhausted -- as to disembowel a pregnant woman and sport with the foetus...

After these abominable pastimes he may well believe that the art of the charnalist has beneath his fingers expressed its last drop of pus, and in a vaunting cry he says to his troop of parasites, "There is no man on earth who dare do as I have done."

As he can descend no further, he tries returning on the way by which he has come, but now remorse overtakes him, overwhelms him, and wrenches him without respite. His nights are nights of expiation. Besieged by phantoms, he howls like a wounded beast. He is found rushing along the solitary corridors of the château. He weeps, throws himself on his knees, swears to God that he will do penance...

But in this fickle and aberrated mind ideas superpose themselves on each other, then pass away, and those which disappear leave their shadow on those which follow. Abruptly, even while weeping with distress, he precipitates himself into new debauches and, raving with delirium, hurls himself upon the child brought to him, gouges out the eyes, runs his finger around the bloody, milky socket, then he seizes a spiked club and crushes the skull. And while the gurgling blood runs over him, he stands, smeared with spattered brains, and grinds his teeth and laughs. Like a hunted beast he flees into the wood, while his henchmen remove the crimson stains from the ground and dispose prudently of the corpse and the reeking garments.

He wanders in the forest surrounding Tiffauges, dark, impenetrable forests like those which Brittany can still show at Carnöet. He sobs as he walks along. He attempts to thrust aside the phantoms which accost him. Then he looks about him and beholds obscenity in the shapes of the aged trees. It seems that nature perverts itself before him, that his very presence depraves it. For the first time he understands the motionless lubricity of the trees. He discovers priapi in the branches.

Frightful images rise before him. He sees the skin of little boys, the lucid white skin, vellum-like, in the pale, smooth bark of the slender beeches. He recognises the pachydermatous skin of the beggar boys in the dark and wrinkled envelope of the old oaks. Beside the bifurcations of the branches there are yawning holes, puckered orifices in the bark, simulating emunctoria, or the protruding anus of a beast. In the joints of the branches there are other visions, elbows, armpits furred with grey lichens. Even in the trunks there are incisions which spread out into great lips beneath tufts of brown, velvety moss.

244

Everywhere obscene forms rise from the ground and spring, disordered, into a firmament which satanizes. The clouds swell into breasts, divide into buttocks, bulge as if with fecundity, scattering a train of spawn through space. They accord with the sombre bulging of the foliage, in which there are now only images of giant or dwarf hips, feminine triangles, great V's, mouths of Sodom, glowing cicatrices, humid vents. This landscape of abomination changes. Gilles now sees on the trunks frightful cancers and horrible wens. He observes exostoses and ulcers, membranous sores, tubercular chancres, atrocious caries. It is an arboreal lazaret, a venereal clinic.

And there, at a detour of the forest aisle, stands a mottled red beech. Amid the sanguinary falling leaves he feels that he has been spattered by a shower of blood. He goes into a rage. He conceives the delusion that beneath the bark lives a wood nymph, and he would feel with his hands the palpitant flesh of the goddess, he would trucidate the Dryad, violate her in a place unknown to the follies of men.

He is jealous of the woodsman who can murder, can massacre, the trees, and he raves. Tensely he listens and hears in the soughing wind a response to his cries of desire. Overwhelmed, he resumes his walk, weeping, until he arrives at the château and sinks to his bed exhausted, an inert mass.

The phantoms take more definite shape now, now that he sleeps. The lubric enlacements of the branches, dilated crevices and cleft mosses, the coupling of the diverse beings of the wood, disappear; the tears of the leaves whipped by the wind are dried; the white abscesses of the clouds are resorbed into the grey of the sky; and -- in an awful silence -- the incubi and succubi pass.

The corpses of his victims, reduced to ashes and scattered, return to the larva state and attack his lower parts. He writhes, with the blood bursting in his veins. He rebounds in a somersault, then he crawls to the crucifix, like a wolf, on all fours, and howling, strains his lips to the feet of the Christ.

A sudden reaction overwhelms him. He trembles before the image whose convulsed face looks down on him. He adjures Christ to have pity, supplicates Him to spare a sinner, and sobs and weeps, and when, incapable of further effort, he whimpers, he hears, terrified, in his own voice, the lamentations of the children crying for their mothers and pleading for mercy.

Translated
by
Keene Wallace

THE PICTURE OF
DORIAN GRAY

Oscar Wilde

Chapter Twenty

It was a lovely night, so warm that he threw his coat over his arm, and did not even put his silk scarf round his throat. As he strolled home, smoking his cigarette, two young men in evening dress passed him. He heard one of them whisper to the other, "That is Dorian Gray". He remembered how pleased he used to be when he was pointed out, or stared at, or talked about. He was tired of hearing his own name now. Half the charm of the little village where he had been so often lately was that no one knew who he was. He had often told the girl whom he had lured to love him that he was poor, and she had believed him. He had told her once that he was wicked, and she had laughed at him, and answered that wicked people were always very old and ugly. What a laugh she had! -- just like a thrush singing. And how pretty she had been in her cotton dress and her large hats! She knew nothing, but she had everything that he had lost.

When he reached home, he found his servant waiting up for him. He sent him to bed, and threw himself down on the sofa in the library, and began to think over some of the things that Lord Henry had said to him.

Was it really true that one could never change? He felt a wild longing for the unstained purity of his boyhood -- his rose-white boyhood, as Lord Henry had once called it. He knew that he had tarnished himself, filled his mind with corruption, and given horror to his fancy; that he had been an evil influence to others, and had experienced a terrible joy in being so; and that, of the lives that had crossed his own, it had been the fairest and the most full of promise that he had brought to shame. But was it all irretrievable? Was there no hope for him?

Ah! in what a monstrous moment of pride and passion he had prayed that the portrait should bear the burden of his days, and he keep the unsullied splendour of eternal youth! All his failure had been due to that.

Better for him that each sin of his life had brought its sure, swift penalty along with it. There was purification in punishment. Not "Forgive us our sins", but "Smite us for our iniquities" should be the prayer of a man to a just God.

The curiously-carved mirror that Lord Henry had given to him, so many years ago now, was standing on the table, and the white-limbed Cupids laughed round it as of old. He took it up, as he had done on that night of horror, when he first noted the change in the fatal picture, and with wild, tear-dimmed eyes looked into its polished shield. Once, someone who had terribly loved him had written to him a mad letter, ending with these idolatrous words: "The world is changed because you are made of ivory and gold. The curves of your lips rewrite history." The phrases came back to his memory, and he repeated them over and over to himself. Then he loathed his own beauty, and, flinging the mirror on the floor, crushed it into silver splinters beneath his heel. It was his beauty that had ruined him, his beauty and the youth that he had prayed for. But for those two things, his life might have been free from stain. His beauty had been to him but a mask, his youth but a mockery. What was youth at best? A green, an unripe time, a time of shallow moods and sickly thoughts. Why had he worn its livery? Youth had spoiled him.

It was better not to think of the past. Nothing could alter that. It was of himself, and of his own future, that he had to think. James Vane was hidden in a nameless grave in Selby churchyard. Alan Campbell had shot himself one night in his laboratory, but had not revealed the secret that he had been forced to know. The excitement, such as it was, over Basil Hallward's disappearance would soon pass away. It was already waning. He was perfectly safe there. Nor, indeed, was it the death of Basil Hallward that weighted most upon his mind. It was the living death of his own soul that troubled him. Basil had painted the portrait that had marred his life. He could not forgive him that. It was the portrait that had done everything. Basil had said things to him that were unbearable, and that he had yet borne with patience. The murder had been simply the madness of a moment. As for Alan Campbell, his suicide had been his own act. He had chosen to do it. It was nothing to him.

A new life! that was what he wanted. That was what he was waiting for. Surely he had begun it already. He had spared one innocent thing, at any rate. He would never again tempt innocence. He would be good.

As he thought of Hetty Merton, he began to wonder if the portrait in the locked room had changed. Surely it was not still so horrible as it had been? Perhaps if his life became pure, he would be able to expel every sign of evil passion from the face. Perhaps the signs of evil had already gone away. He would go and look.

He took the lamp from the table and crept upstairs. As he unbarred the door a smile of joy flitted across his strangely young-looking face and lingered for a moment about his lips. Yes, he would be good, and the hideous thing that he had hidden away would no longer be a terror to him. He felt as if the load had been lifted from him already.

He went in quietly, locking the door behind him, as was his custom, and dragged the purple hanging from the portrait. A cry of pain and indignation broke from him. He could see no change, save that in the eyes there was a look of cunning, and in the mouth the curved wrinkle of the hypocrite. The thing was still loathsome -- more loathsome, if possible, than before -- and the scarlet dew that spotted the hand seemed brighter, and more like blood newly spilt. Then he trembled. Had it been merely vanity that had made him do his one good deed? Or the desire for a new sensation, as Lord Henry had hinted, with his mocking laugh? Or that passion to act a part that sometimes make us do things finer than we are ourselves? Or, perhaps, all these? And why was the red stain larger than it had been? It seemed to have crept like a horrible disease over the wrinkled fingers. There was blood on the painted feet, as though the thing had dripped -- blood even on the hand that had not held the knife. Confess? Did it mean that he was to confess? To give himself up, and be put to death? He laughed. He felt that the idea was monstrous. Besides, even if he did confess, who would believe him? There was no trace of the murdered man anywhere. Everything belonging to him had been destroyed. He himself had burned what had been below-stairs. The world would simply say that he was mad. They would shut him up if he persisted in his story... Yet it was his duty to confess to suffer public shame, and so to make public atonement. There was a God who called upon men to tell their sins to earth as well as to heaven. Nothing that he could do would cleanse him till he had told his own sin. His sin? He shrugged his shoulders. The death of Basil Hallward seemed very little to him. He was thinking of Hetty Merton. For it was an unjust mirror, this mirror of his soul that he was looking at. Vanity? Curiosity? Hypocrisy? Had there been nothing more in his renunciation than that? There had been something more. At least he thought so. But who could tell?... No. There had been nothing more. Through vanity he had spared her. In hypocrisy he had worn the mask of goodness. For curiosity's sake he had tried the denial of self. He recognized that now.

But this murder -- was it to dog him all his life? Was he always to be burdened by his past? Was he really to confess? Never. There was only one bit of evidence left against him. The picture itself -- that was evidence. He would destroy it. Why had he kept it so long? Once it had given him pleasure to watch it changing and growing old. Of late he had felt no such pleasure. It had kept him awake at night. When he had been away, he had been filled with terror lest other eyes should look upon it. It had brought melancholy across his passions. Its mere memory had marred many moments of joy. It had been like conscience to him. Yes, it had been conscience. He would destroy it.

He looked round, and saw the knife that had stabbed Basil Hallward. He had cleaned it many times, till there was no stain left upon it. It was bright, and glistened. As it had killed the painter, so it would kill the painter's work, and all that that meant. It would kill the past, and when that was dead he would be free. It would kill this monstrous soul-life, and, without its hideous warnings, he would be at peace. He seized the thing, and stabbed the picture with it.

There was a cry heard, and a crash. The cry was so horrible in its agony that the frightened servants woke, and crept out of their rooms. Two gentlemen, who were passing in the Square below, stopped, and looked up at the great house. They walked on till they met a policeman, and brought him back. The man rang the bell several times, but there was no answer. Except for a light in one of the top windows, the house was all dark. After a time, he went away and stood in an adjoining portico and watched.

"Whose house is that, constable?" asked the elder of the two gentlemen.

"Mr Dorian Gray's, sir," answered the policeman.

They looked at each other, as they walked away, and sneered. One of them was Sir Henry Ashton's uncle.

Inside, in the servants' part of the house, the half-clad domestics were talking in low whispers to each other. Old Mrs Leaf was crying and wringing her hands. Francis was as pale as death.

After about a quarter of an hour, he got the coachman and one of the footmen and crept upstairs. They knocked, but there was no reply. They called out. Everything was still. Finally, after vainly trying to force the door, they got on the roof, and dropped down onto the balcony. The windows yielded easily: their bolts were old.

When they entered they found, hanging upon the wall, a splendid portrait of their master as they last seen him, in all the wonder of his exquisite youth and beauty. Lying on the floor was a dead man, in evening dress, with a knife in his heart. He was withered, wrinkled, and loathsome of visage. It was not until they had examined the rings that they recognized who it was.

THE INMOST LIGHT

Arthur Machen

I

One evening in autumn, when the deformities of London were veiled in faint blue mist, and its vistas and far-reaching streets seemed splendid, Mr. Charles Salisbury was slowly pacing down Rupert Street, drawing nearer to his favourite restaurant by slow degrees. His eyes were downcast in study of the pavement, and thus it was that as he passed in at the narrow door a man who had come up from the lower end of the street jostled against him.

"I beg your pardon -- wasn't looking where I was going. Why, it's Dyson!"

"Yes, quite so. How are you, Salisbury?"

"Quite well. But where have you been, Dyson? I don't think I can have seen you for the last five years?"

"No; I dare say not. You remember I was getting rather hard up when you came to my place at Charlotte Street?"

"Perfectly. I think I remember your telling me that you owed five weeks' rent, and that you had parted with your watch for a comparatively small sum."

"My dear Salisbury, your memory is admirable. Yes, I was hard up. But the curious thing is that soon after you saw me I became harder up. My financial state was described by a friend as 'stone broke'. I don't approve of slang, mind you, but such was my condition. But suppose we go in; there might be other people who would like to dine -- it's human weakness, Salisbury."

"Certainly; come along. I was wondering as I walked down whether the corner table were taken. It has a velvet back you know."

"I know the spot; it's vacant. Yes, as I was saying, I became even harder up."

"What did you do then?" asked Salisbury, disposing of his hat, and settling down in the corner of the seat, with a glance of fond anticipation at the menu.

"What did I do? Why, I sat down and reflected. I had a good classical education, and a positive distaste for business of any kind: that was the capital with which I face the world. Do you know, I have heard people describe olives as nasty! What lamentable Philistinism! I have often thought, Salisbury, that I could write genuine poetry under the influence of olives and red wine. Let us have Chianti; it may not be very good, but the flasks are simply charming."

"It is pretty good here. We may as well have a big flask."

"Very good. I reflected, then, on my want of prospects, and I determined to embark in literature."

"Really; that was strange. You seem in pretty comfortable circumstances, though."

"Though! What a satire upon a noble profession. I am afraid, Salisbury, you haven't a proper idea of the dignity of an artist. You see me sitting at my desk -- or at least you can see me if you care to call -- with pen and ink, and simple nothingness before me, and if you come again in a few hours you will (in all probability) find a creation!"

"Yes, quite so. I had an idea that literature was not remunerative."

"You are mistaken; its rewards are great. I may mention, by the way, that shortly after you saw me I succeeded to a small income. An uncle died, and proved unexpectedly generous."

"Ah, I see. That must have been convenient."

"It was pleasant -- undeniably pleasant. I have always considered it in the light of an endowment of my researches. I told you I was a man of letters; it would, perhaps, be more correct to describe myself as a man of science."

"Dear me, Dyson, you have really changed very much in the last few years. I had a notion, don't you know, that you were a sort of idler about town, the kind of man one might meet on the north side of Piccadilly every day from May to July."

"Exactly. I was even then forming myself, though all unconsciously. You know my poor father could not afford to send me to the University. I used to grumble in my ignorance at not having completed my education. That was the folly of youth, Salisbury; my University was Piccadilly. There I began to study the great science which still occupies me."

"What science do you mean?"

"The science of the great city; the physiology of London; literally and metaphysically the greatest subject that the mind of man can conceive. What an admirable salmi this is; undoubtedly the final end of the pheasant. Yet I feel sometimes positively overwhelmed with the thought of the vastness and complexity of London. Paris a man may get to understand thoroughly with a reasonable amount of study; but London is always a mystery. In Paris you may say: 'Here live the actresses, here the Bohemians, and the *Ratés'*; but

252

it is different in London. You may point out a street, correctly enough, as the abode of washerwomen; but, in that second floor, a man may be studying Chaldee roots, and in the garret over the way a forgotten artist is dying by inches."

"I see you are Dyson, unchanged and unchangeable," said Salisbury, slowly sipping his Chianti. "I think you are misled by a too fervid imagination; the mystery of London exists only in your fancy. It seems to me a dull place enough. We seldom hear of a really artistic crime in London, whereas I believe Paris abounds in that sort of thing."

"Give me some more wine. Thanks. You are mistaken, my dear fellow, you are really mistaken. London has nothing to be ashamed of in the way of crime. Where we fail is for want of Homers, not Agamemnons. *Carent quia vate sacro*, you know."

"I recall the quotation. But I don't think I quite follow you."

"Well, in plain language, we have no good writers in London who make a speciality of that kind of thing. Our common reporter is a dull dog; every story that he has to tell is spoilt in the telling. His idea of horror and of what excites horror is so lamentably deficient. Nothing will content the fellow but blood, vulgar red blood, and when he can get it he lays it on thick, and considers that he has produced a telling article. It's a poor notion. And, by some curious fatality, it is the most commonplace and brutal murders which always attract the most attention and get written up the most. For instance, I dare say that you never heard of the Harlesden case?"

"No; no, I don't remember anything about it."

"Of course not. And yet the story is a curious one. I will tell it you over our coffee. Harlesden, you know, or I expect you don't know, is quite on the out-quarters of London; something curiously different from your fine old crusted suburb like Norwood or Hampstead, different as each of these is from the other. Hampstead, I mean, is where you look for the head of your great China house with his three acres of land and pine-houses, though of late there is the artistic substratum; while Norwood is the home of the prosperous middle-class family who took the house 'because it was near the Palace', and sickened of the Palace six months afterwards; but Harlesden is a place of no character. It's too new to have any character as yet. There are the rows of red houses and the rows of white houses and the bright green Venetians, and the blistering doorways, and the little backyards they call gardens, and a few feeble shops, and then, just as you think you're going to grasp the physiognomy of the settlement, it all melts away."

"How the dickens is that? The houses don't tumble down before one's eyes, I suppose!"

"Well, no, not exactly that. But Harlesden as an entity disappears. Your street turns into a quiet lane, and your staring houses into elm trees, and the back-gardens into green meadows. You pass instantly from town to country; there is no transition as in a small country town, no soft gradations of wider lawns and orchards, with houses gradually becoming less dense, but a dead stop. I believe the people who live there mostly go into the City. I have seen once or twice a laden bus bound thitherwards. But however that may be, I can't conceive a greater loneliness in a desert at midnight than there is there at midday. It is like a city of the dead; the streets are glaring and desolate, and as you pass it suddenly strikes you that this too is part of London. Well, a year or two ago there was a doctor living there; he had set up his brass plate and his red lamp at the very end of one of those shining streets, and from the back of the house, the fields stretched away to the north. I don't know what his reason was in settling down in such an out-of-the-way place, perhaps Dr. Black, as we will call him, was a far-seeing man and looked ahead. His relations, so it appeared afterwards, had lost sight of him for many years and didn't even know he was a doctor, much less where he lived. However, there he was settled in Harlesden, with some fragments of a practice, and an uncommonly pretty wife. People used to see them walking out together in the summer evenings soon after they came to Harlesden, and, so far as could be observed, they seemed a very affectionate couple. These walks went on through the autumn, and then ceased, but, of course, as the days grew dark and the weather cold, the lanes near Harlesden might be expected to lose many of their attractions. All through the winter nobody saw anything of Mrs. Black, the doctor used to reply to his patients' inquiries that she was a 'little out of sorts, would be better, no doubt, in the spring'. But the spring came, and the summer, and no Mrs. Black appeared, and at last people began to rumour and talk amongst themselves, and all sorts of queer things were said at 'high teas', which you may possibly have heard are the only form of entertainment known in such suburbs. Dr. Black began to surprise some very odd looks cast in his direction, and the practice, such as it was, fell off before his eyes. In short, when the neighbours whispered about the matter, they whispered that Mrs. Black was dead, and that the doctor had made away with her. But this wasn't the case; Mrs. Black was seen alive in June. It was a Sunday afternoon, one of those few exquisite days that an English climate offers, and half London had strayed out into the fields, north, south, east, and west to smell the scent of the white May, and to see if the wild roses were yet in blossom in the hedges. I had gone out myself early in the morning, and had had a long ramble, and somehow or other as I was steering homeward I found myself in this very Harlesden we have been talking about. To be exact, I had a glass of beer in the General Gordon, the most flourishing house in the neighbourhood, and as I was wandering rather aimlessly about, I saw an uncommonly tempting gap in a hedgerow, and resolved to explore the meadow beyond. Soft grass is very grateful to the feet after the infernal grit strewn on suburban sidewalks, and after walking about for some time I thought I should like to sit down on a bank and have a smoke. While I was getting out my pouch, I looked up in the direction of the houses, and as I looked I felt my breath caught back, and my teeth began to chatter, and the stick I had in one hand snapped in two with the grip I gave it. It was as if I had had an electric current down my spine, and yet for some moment of time which seemed long, but which must have been very short, I caught myself wondering what on earth was the matter. Then I knew what had made my heart shudder and my bones grind together in an agony. As I glanced up I had looked straight towards the last house in the row before me, and in an upper window of that house I had seen for some short fraction of a second a face. It was the face of a woman, and yet it was not human. You and I, Salisbury, have heard in our time, as we sat in out seats in church in sober English fashion, of a lust that cannot be satiated and of a fire that is unquenchable, but few of us have any notion what these words mean. I hope you never may, for as I saw that face at the window, with the blue sky above me and the warm air playing in gusts about me, I knew I had looked into another world -- looked through the window of a commonplace, brand-new house, and seen hell open before me. When the first shock was over, I thought once or twice that I should have fainted; my face streamed with a cold sweat, and my breath came and went in sobs, as if I had been half drowned. I managed to get up at last, and walk round to the street, and there I saw the name *Dr. Black* on the post by the front gate. As fate or luck would have it, the door opened and a man came down the steps as I passed by. I had no doubt it was the doctor himself. He was of a type rather common in London; long and thin, with a pasty face and a dull black moustache. He gave me a look as we passed each other on the pavement, and though it was merely the casual glance which one foot-passenger bestows on another, I felt convinced in my mind that here was an ugly customer to deal with. As you may imagine, I went my way a good deal puzzled and horrified too by what I had seen; for I had paid another visit to the General Gordon, and had got together a good deal of the common gossip of the place about the Blacks. I didn't mention the fact that I had seen a woman's face in the window; but I heard that Mrs. Black had been much admired for her beautiful golden hair, and round what had struck me with such a nameless terror, there was a mist of flowing yellow hair, as it was an aureole of glory round the visage of a satyr. The whole thing bothered me in an indescribable manner; and when I got home I tried my best to think of the impression I had received as an illusion, but it was no use. I knew very well I had seen what I have tried to describe to you, and I was morally certain that I had seen Mrs. Black. And then there was the gossip of the place, the suspicion of foul play, which I knew to be false, and my own conviction that there was some deadly mischief or other going on in that bright red house at the corner of Devon Road: how to construct a theory of a reasonable kind out of these two elements. In short, I found myself in a world of mystery; I puzzled my head over it and filled up my leisure moments by gathering together odd threads of speculation, but I never moved a step towards any real solution, and as the summer days went on the matter seemed to grow misty and indistinct, shadowing some vague terror, like a nightmare of last month. I suppose it would before long have faded into the background of my brain -- I should not have forgotten it, for such a thing could never be forgotten -- but one morning as I was looking over the paper my eye was caught by a heading over some two dozen lines of small type. The words I had seen were simply: 'The Harlesden Case', and I knew what I was going to read. Mrs. Black was dead. Black had called in another medical man to certify as to cause of death, and something or other had aroused the strange doctor's suspicions and there had been an inquest and post-mortem. And the result? That, I will confess, did astonish me considerably; it was the triumph of the unexpected. The two doctors who made the autopsy were obliged to confess that they could not discover the faintest trace of any kind of foul play; their most exquisite tests and reagents failed to detect the presence of poison in the most infinitesimal quantity. Death, they found, had been caused by a somewhat obscure and scientifically interesting form of brain disease. The tissue of the brain and the molecules of the grey matter had undergone a most extraordinary series of changes; and the younger of the two doctors, who has some reputation, I believe, as a specialist in brain trouble, made some remarks in giving his evidence which struck me deeply at the time, though I did not then grasp their full significance. He said: *At the commencement of the examination I was astonished to find appearances of a character entirely new to me, notwithstanding my somewhat large experience. I need not specify these appearances at present, it will be sufficient for me to state that as I proceeded in my task I could scarcely believe that the brain before me was that of a human being at all.* There was some surprise at this statement, as you may imagine, and the coroner asked the doctor if he meant to say that the brain resembled that of an animal. *No*, he replied, *I should not put it in that way. Some of the appearances I noticed seemed to point in that direction, but others, and these were the more surprising, indicated a nervous organization of a wholly different character from either that of man or the lower animals.* It was a curious thing to say, but of course the jury brought in a verdict of death from natural causes, and, so far as the public was concerned, the case came to an end. But after I had read what the doctor said I made up my mind that I should like to know a good deal more, and I set to work on what seemed likely to prove an interesting investigation. I had really a good deal of trouble, but I was successful in a measure. Though why -- my dear fellow, I had no notion of the time. Are you aware that we have been here nearly four hours? The waiters are staring at us. Let's have the bill and be gone."

The two men went out in silence, and stood a moment in the cool air, watching the hurrying traffic of Coventry Street pass before them to the accompaniment of the ringing bells of hansoms and the cries of the newsboys; the deep far murmur of London surging up ever and again from beneath those louder noises.

"It is a strange case, isn't it?" said Dyson at length. "What do you think of it?"

"My dear fellow, I haven't heard the end, so I will reserve my opinion. When will you give me the sequel?"

"Come to my rooms some evening; say next Thursday. Here's the address. Good-night; I want to get down to the Strand." Dyson hailed a passing hansom, and Salisbury turned northward to walk home to his lodgings.

II

Mr. Salisbury, as may have been gathered from the few remarks which he had found it possible to introduce in the course of the evening, was a young gentleman of a peculiarly solid form of intellect, coy and retiring before the mysterious and the uncommon, with a constitutional dislike of paradox. During the restaurant dinner he had been forced to listen in almost absolute silence to a strange tissue of improbabilities strung together with the ingenuity of a born meddler in plots and mysteries, and it was with a feeling of weariness that he crossed Shaftesbury Avenue, and dived into the recesses of Soho, for his lodgings were in a modest neighbourhood to the north of Oxford Street. As he walked he speculated on the probable fate of Dyson, relying on literature, unbefriended by a thoughtful relative, and could not help concluding that so much subtlety united to a too vivid imagination would in all likelihood have been rewarded with a pair of sandwich-boards or a super's banner. Absorbed in this train of thought, and admiring the perverse dexterity which could transmute the face of a sickly woman and a case of brain disease into the crude elements of romance, Salisbury strayed on through the dimly lighted streets, not noticing the gusty wind which drove sharply round corners and whirled the stray rubbish of the pavement into the air in eddies, while black clouds gathered over the sickly yellow moon. Even a stray drop or two of rain blown into his face did not rouse him from his meditations, and it was only when with a sudden rush the storm tore down upon the street that he began to consider the expediency of finding some shelter. The rain, driven by the wind, pelted down with the violence of a thunderstorm, dashing up from the stones and hissing through the air, and soon a perfect torrent of water coursed along the kennels and accumulated in pools over the choked-up drains. The few stray passengers who had been loafing rather than walking about the street had scuttered away, like frightened rabbits, to some invisible places of refuge, and though Salisbury whistled loud and long for a hansom, no hansom appeared. He looked about him, as if to discover how far he might be from the haven of Oxford Street, but strolling carelessly along, he had turned out of his way, and found himself in an unknown region, and one to all appearance devoid even of a public house where shelter could be bought for the modest sum of two pence. The street lamps were few and at long intervals, and burned behind grimy glasses with the sickly light of oil, and by this wavering glimmer Salisbury could make out the shadowy and vast old houses of which the street was composed. As he passed along, hurrying, and shrinking from the full sweep of the rain, he noticed the innumerable bell-handles, with names that seemed about to vanish of old age graven on brass plates beneath them, and here and there a richly carved penthouse overhung the door, blackening with the grime of fifty years. The storm seemed to grow more and more furious; he was wet through, and a new hat had become a ruin, and still Oxford Street seemed as far off as ever; it was with deep relief that the dripping man caught sight of a dark archway which seemed to promise shelter from the rain if not from the wind. Salisbury took up his position in the driest corner and looked about him; he was standing in a kind of passage contrived under part of a house, and behind him stretched a narrow footway leading between blank walls to regions unknown. He had stood there for some time, vainly endeavouring to rid himself of some of his superfluous moisture, and listening for the passing wheels of a hansom, when his attention was aroused by a loud noise coming from the direction of the passage behind, and growing louder as it drew nearer. In a couple of minutes he could make out the shrill, raucous voice of a woman, threatening and renouncing and making the very stones echo with her accents, while now and then a man grumbled and expostulated. Though to all appearance devoid of romance, Salisbury had some relish for street rows, and was, indeed, somewhat of an amateur in the more amusing phases of drunkenness; he therefore composed himself to listen and observe with something of the air of a subscriber to grand opera. To his annoyance, however, the tempest seemed suddenly to be composed, and he could hear nothing but the impatient steps of the woman and the slow lurch of the man as they came towards him. Keeping back in the shadow of the wall, he could see the two drawing nearer; the man was evidently drunk, and had much ado to avoid frequent collision with the wall as he tacked across from one side to the other, like some bark beating up against a wind. The woman was looking straight in front of her, with tears streaming from her blazing eyes, but suddenly as they went by the flame blazed up again, and she burst forth into a torrent of abuse, facing round upon her companion.

"You low rascal, you mean, contemptible cur," she went on, after an incoherent storm of curses, "you think I'm to work and slave for you always, I suppose, while you're after that Green Street girl and drinking every penny you've got? But you're mistaken, Sam -- indeed, I'll bear it no longer. Damn you, you dirty thief, I've done with you and your master too, so you can go your own errands, and I only hope they'll get you into trouble."

The woman tore at the bosom of her dress, and taking something out that looked like paper, crumpled it up and flung it away. It fell at Salisbury's feet. She ran out and disappeared in the darkness, while the man lurched slowly into the street, grumbling indistinctly to himself in a perplexed tone of voice. Salisbury looked out after him, and saw him maundering along the pavement, halting now and then and swaying indecisively, and then starting off at some fresh tangent. The sky had cleared, and white fleecy clouds were fleeting across the moon, high in the heaven. The light came and went by turns, as the clouds passed by, and, turning round as the clear, white rays shone into the passage, Salisbury saw the little ball of crumpled paper which the woman had cast down. Oddly curious to know what it might contain, he picked it up and put it in his pocket, and set out afresh on his journey.

III

Salisbury was a man of habit. When he got home, drenched to the skin, his clothes hanging lank about him, and a ghastly dew besmearing his hat, his only thought was of his health, of which he took studious care. So, after changing his clothes and encasing himself in a warm dressing-gown, he proceeded to prepare a sudorific in the shape of hot gin and water, warming the latter over one of those spirit-lamps which mitigate the austerities of the modern hermit's life. By the time this preparation had been exhibited, and Salisbury's disturbed feelings had been soothed by a pipe of tobacco, he was able to get into bed in a happy state of vacancy, without a thought of his adventure in the dark archway, or of the weird fancies with which Dyson had seasoned his dinner. It was the same at breakfast the next morning, for Salisbury made a point of not thinking of any thing until that meal was over; but when the cup and saucer were cleared away, and the morning pipe was lit, he remembered the little ball of paper, and began fumbling in the pockets of his wet coat. He did not remember into which pocket he had put it, and as he dived now into one and now into another, he experienced a strange feeling of apprehension lest it should not be there at all, though he could not for the life of him have explained the importance he attached to what was in all probability mere rubbish. But he sighed with relief when his fingers touched the crumpled surface in an inside pocket, and he drew it out gently and laid it on the little desk by his easy chair with as much care as if it had been some rare jewel. Salisbury sat smoking and staring at his find for a few minutes, an odd temptation to throw the thing in the fire and have done with it struggling with as odd a speculation as to its possible contents, and as to the reason why the infuriated woman should have flung a bit of paper from her with such vehemence. As might be expected, it was the latter feeling that conquered in the end, and yet it was with something like repugnance that he at last took the paper and unrolled it, and laid it out before him. It was a piece of common dirty paper, to all appearance torn out of a cheap exercise book, and in the middle were a few lines written in a queer cramped hand. Salisbury bent his head and stared eagerly at it for a moment, drawing a long breath, and then fell back in his chair gazing blankly before him, till at last with a sudden revulsion he burst into a peal of laughter, so long and loud and uproarious that the landlady's baby in the floor below awoke from sleep and echoed his mirth with hideous yells. But he laughed again and again, and took the paper up to read a second time what seemed such meaningless nonsense.

"Q. has had to go and see his friends in Paris," it began. "Traverse Handel S. *Once around the grass, and twice around the lass, and thrice around the maple-tree.*"

Salisbury took up the paper and crumpled it as the angry woman had done, and aimed it at the fire. He did not throw it there, however, but tossed it carelessly into the well of the desk, and laughed again. The sheer folly of the thing offended him, and he was ashamed of his own eager speculation, as one who pores over the high-sounding announcements in the agony column of the daily paper, and finds nothing but advertisement and triviality. He walked to the window, and stared out at the languid morning life of his quarter; the maids in slatternly print dresses washing door-steps, the fish-monger and the butcher on their rounds, and the tradesmen standing at the doors of their small shops, drooping for lack of trade and excitement. In the distance a blue haze gave some grandeur to the prospect, but the view as a whole was depressing, and would only have interested a student of the life of London, who finds something rare and choice in its every aspect. Salisbury turned away in disgust, and settled himself in the easy chair, upholstered in a bright shade of green, and decked with yellow gimp, which was the pride and attraction of the apartments. Here he composed himself to his morning's occupation -- the perusal of a novel that dealt with sport and love in a manner that suggested the collaboration of a stud-groom and a ladies' college. In an ordinary way, however, Salisbury would have been carried on by the interest of the story up to lunch time, but this morning he fidgeted in and out of his chair, took the book up and laid it down again, and swore at last to himself and at himself in mere irritation. In point of fact the jingle of the paper found in the archway had "got into his head", and do what he would he could not help muttering over and over, "Once around the grass, and twice around the lass, and thrice around the maple-tree." It became a positive pain, like the foolish burden of a music-hall song, everlastingly quoted, and sung at all hours of the day and night, and treasured by the street boys as an unfailing resource for six months together. He went out into the streets, and tried to forget his enemy in the jostling of the crowds and the roar and clatter of the traffic, but presently he would find himself stealing quietly aside, and pacing some deserted byway, vainly puzzling his brains, and trying to fix some meaning to phrases that were meaningless. It was a positive relief when Thursday came, and he remembered that he had made an appointment to go and see Dyson; the flimsy reveries of the self-styled man of letters appeared entertaining when compared with this ceaseless iteration, this maze of thought from which there seemed no possibility of escape. Dyson's abode was in one of the quietest of the quiet streets that lead down from the Strand to the river, and when Salisbury passed from the narrow stairway into his friend's room, he saw that the uncle had been beneficent indeed. The floor glowed and flamed with all the colours of the East; it was, as Dyson pompously remarked, "a sunset in a dream", and the lamplight, the twilight of London streets, was shut out with strangely worked curtains, glittering here and there with threads of gold. In the shelves of an oak armoire stood jars and plates of old French china, and the black and white of etchings not to be found in the Haymarket or in Bond Street, stood out against the splendour of a Japanese paper. Salisbury sat down on the settle by the hearth, and sniffed and mingled fumes of incense and tobacco, wondering and dumb before all this splendour after the green rep and the oleographs, the gilt-framed mirror, and the lustres of his own apartment.

"I am glad you have come," said Dyson. "Comfortable little room isn't it? But you don't look very well, Salisbury. Nothing disagreed with you, has it?"

"No; but I have been a good deal bothered for the last few days. The fact is I had an odd kind of -- of -- adventure, I suppose I may call it, that night I saw you, and it has worried me a good deal. And the provoking part of it is that it's the merest nonsense -- but, however, I will tell you all about it, by and by. You were going to let me have the rest of that odd story you began at the restaurant."

"Yes. But I am afraid, Salisbury, you are incorrigible. You are a slave to what you call matter of fact. You know perfectly well that in your heart you think the oddness in that case is of my making, and that it is all really as plain as the police reports. However, as I have begun, I will go on. But first we will have something to drink, and you may as well light your pipe."

Dyson went up to the oak cupboard, and drew from its depths a rotund bottle and two little glasses, quaintly gilded.

"It's Benedictine," he said. "You'll have some, won't you?"

Salisbury assented, and the two men sat sipping and smoking reflectively for some minutes before Dyson began.

"Let me see," he said at last, "we were at the inquest, weren't? No, we had done with that. Ah, I remember. I was telling you that on the whole I had been successful in my inquiries, investigation, or whatever you like to call it, into the matter. Wasn't that where I left off?"

"Yes, that was it. To be precise, I think *though* was the last word you said on the matter."

"Exactly. I have been thinking it all over since the other night, and I have come to the conclusion that that *though* is a very big *though* indeed.

Not to put too fine a point on it, I have had to confess that what I found out, or thought I found out, amounts in reality to nothing. I am as far away from the heart of the case as ever. However, I may as well tell you what I do know. You may remember my saying that I was impressed a good deal by some remarks of one of the doctors who gave evidence at the inquest. Well, I determined that my first step must be to try if I could get something more definite and intelligible out of that doctor. Somehow or other I managed to get an introduction to the man, and he gave me an appointment to come and see him. He turned out to be a pleasant, genial fellow; rather young and not in the least like the typical medical man, and he began the conference by offering me whisky and cigars. I didn't think it worth while to beat about the bush, so I began by saying that part of his evidence at the Harlesden inquest struck me as very peculiar, and I gave him the printed report, with the sentences in question underlined. He just glanced at the slip, and gave me a queer look. *It struck you as peculiar, did it?* said he. *Well, you must remember that the Harlesden case was very peculiar. In fact, I think I may safely say that in some features it was unique — quite unique.*

"*Quite so, I replied, and that's exactly why it interests me, and why I want to know more about it. And I thought that if anybody could give me any information it would be you. What is your opinion of the matter?*

"It was a pretty downright sort of question, and my doctor looked rather taken back.

"*Well, he said, as I fancy your motive in inquiring into the question must be mere curiosity, I think I may tell you my opinion with tolerable freedom. So, Mr., Mr. Dyson? if you want to know my theory, it is this: I believe that Dr. Black killed his wife.*

"*But the verdict, I answered, the verdict was given from your own evidence.*

"*Quite so; the verdict was given in accordance with the evidence of my colleague and myself, and, under the circumstances, I think the jury acted very sensibly. In fact, I don't see what else they could have done. But I stick to my opinion, mind you, and I say this also. I don't wonder at Black's doing what I firmly believe he did. I think he was justified.*

"*Justified! How could that be? I asked. I was astonished, as you may imagine, at the answer I had got. The doctor wheeled round his chair and looked steadily at me for a moment before he answered.

"*I suppose you are not a man of science yourself? No; then it would be of no use my going into detail. I have always been firmly opposed myself to any partnership between physiology and psychology. I believe that both are bound to suffer. No one recognizes more decidedly than I do the impassable gulf, the fathomless abyss that separates the world of consciousness from the sphere of matter. We know that every change of consciousness is accompanied by a rearrangement of the molecules in the grey matter; and that is all. What the link between them is, or why they occur together, we* do not know, and most authorities believe that we never can know. Yet, I will tell you that as I did my work, the knife in my hand, I felt convinced, in spite of all theories, that what lay before me was not the brain of a dead woman -- not the brain of a human being at all. Of course I saw the face; but it was quite placid, devoid of all expression. It must have been a beautiful face, no doubt, but I can honestly say that I would not have looked in that face when there was life behind it for a thousand guineas, no, nor for twice that sum.

"My dear sir, I said, you surprise me extremely. You say that it was not the brain of a human being. What was it, then?

"The brain of a devil. He spoke quite coolly, and never moved a muscle. The brain of a devil, he repeated, and I have no doubt that Black found some way of putting an end to it. I don't blame him if he did. Whatever Mrs. Black was, she was not fit to stay in this world. Will you have anything more? No? Good-night, good-night.

"It was a queer sort of opinion to get from a man of science, wasn't it? When he was saying that he would not have looked on that face when alive for a thousand guineas, or two thousand guineas, I was thinking of the face I had seen, but I said nothing. I went again to Harlesden, and passed from one shop to another, making small purchases, and trying to find out whether there was anything about the Blacks which was not already common property, but there was very little to hear. One of the tradesmen to whom I spoke said he had known the dead woman well; she used to buy of him such quantities of grocery as were required for their small household, for they never kept a servant, but had a charwoman in occasionally, and she had not seen Mrs. Black for months before she died. According to this man Mrs. Black was 'a nice lady', always kind and considerate, and so fond of her husband and he of her, as every one thought. And yet, to put the doctor's opinion on one side, I knew what I had seen. And then after thinking it all over, and putting one thing with another, it seemed to me that the only person likely to give me much assistance would be Black himself, and I made up my mind to find him. Of course he wasn't to be found in Harlesden; he had left, I was told, directly after the funeral. Everything in the house had been sold, and one fine day Black got into the train with a small portmanteau, and went, nobody knew where. It was a chance if he were ever heard of again, and it was by a mere chance that I came across him at last. I was walking one day along Gray's Inn Road, not bound for anywhere in particular, but looking about me, as usual, and holding on to my hat, for it was a gusty day in early March, and the wind was making the treetops in the Inn rock and quiver. I had come up from the Holborn end, and I had almost got to Theobald's Road when I noticed a man walking in front of me, leaning on a stick, and to all appearance very feeble. There was something about his look that made me curious, I don't know why, and I began to walk briskly with the idea of overtaking him, when of a sudden his hat blew off and came bounding along the pavement to my feet. Of course I rescued the hat, and gave it a glance as I went towards its owner. It was a biography in itself; a Piccadilly maker's name in the inside, but I don't think a beggar would have picked it out of the gutter. Then I looked up and saw Dr. Black of Harlesden waiting for me. A queer thing, wasn't it? But, Salisbury, what a change! When I saw Dr. Black come down the steps of his house at Harlesden he was an upright man, walking firmly with well-built limbs; a man, I should say, in the prime of his life. And now before me there crouched this wretched creature, bent and feeble, with shrunken cheeks, and hair that was whitening fast, and limbs that trembled and shook together, and misery in his eyes. He thanked me for bringing him his hat, saying, *I don't think I should ever have got it, I can't run much now. A gusty day, sir, isn't it?* and with this he was turning away, but by little and little I contrived to draw him into the current of conversation, and we walked together eastward. I think the man would have been glad to get rid of me; but I didn't intend to let him go, and he stopped at last in front of a miserable house in a miserable street. It was, I verily believe, one of the most wretched quarters I have ever seen: houses that must have been sordid and hideous enough when new, that had gathered foulness with every year, and now seemed to lean and totter to their fall. *I live up there*, said Black, pointing to the tiles, *not in the front -- in the back. I am very quiet there. I won't ask you to come in now, but perhaps some other day --.* I caught him up at that, and told him I should be only too glad to come and see him. He gave me an odd sort of glance, as if he were wondering what on earth I or anybody else could care about him, and I left him fumbling with his latch-key. I think you will say I did pretty well when I tell you that within a few weeks I had made myself an intimate friend of Black's. I shall never forget the first time I went to his room; I hope I shall never see such abject, squalid misery again. The foul paper, from which all pattern or trace of a pattern had long vanished, subdued and penetrated with the grime of the evil street, was hanging in mouldering pennons from the wall. Only at the end of the room was it possible to stand upright, and the sight of the wretched bed and the odour of corruption that pervaded the place made me turn faint and sick. Here I found him munching a piece of bread; he seemed surprised to find that I had kept my promise, but he gave me his chair and sat on the bed while we talked. I used to go to see him often, and we had long conversations together, but he never mentioned Harlesden or his wife. I fancy that he supposed me ignorant of the matter, or thought that if I had heard of it, I should never connect the respectable Dr. Black of Harlesden with a poor garreteer in the backwoods of London. He was a strange man, and as we sat together smoking, I often wondered whether he were mad or sane, for I think the wildest dreams of Paracelsus and the Rosicrucians would appear plain and sober fact compared with the theories I have heard him earnestly advance in that grimy den of his. I once ventured to hint

264

something of the sort to him. I suggested that something he had said was in flat contradiction to all science and all experience. *No, he answered, not all experience, for mine counts for something. I am no dealer in unproved theories; what I say I have proved for myself, and at a terrible cost. There is a region of knowledge which you will never know, which wise men seeing from afar off shun like the plague, as well they may, but into that region I have gone. If you knew, if you could even dream of what may be done, of what one or two men have done in this quiet world of ours, your very soul would shudder and faint within you. What you have heard from me has been but the merest husk and outer covering of true science -- that science which means death, and that which is more awful than death, to those who gain it. No, when men say that there are strange things in the world, they little know the awe and the terror that dwell always with them and about them.* There was a sort of fascination about the man that drew me to him, and I was quite sorry to have to leave London for a month or two; I missed his odd talk. A few days after I came back to town I thought I would look him up, but when I gave the two rings at the bell that used to summon him, there was no answer. I rang and rang again, and was just turning to go away, when the door opened and a dirty woman asked me what I wanted. From her look I fancy she took me for a plain-clothes officer after one of her lodgers, but when I inquired if Mr. Black were in, she gave me a stare of another kind. *There's no Mr. Black lives here,* she said. *He's gone. He's dead this six weeks. I always thought he was a bit queer in his head, or else had been and got into some trouble or other. He used to go out every morning from ten till one, and one Monday morning we heard him come in, and go into his room and shut the door, and a few minutes after, just as we was a-sitting down to our dinner, there was such a scream that I thought I should have gone right off. And then we heard a stamping, and down he came, raging and cursing most dreadful, swearing he had been robbed of something that was worth millions. And then he just dropped down in the passage, and we thought he was dead. We got him up to his room, and put him on his bed, and I just sat there and waited, while my 'usband he went for the doctor. And there was the winder wide open, and a little tin box he had lying on the floor open and empty, but of course nobody could possible have got in at the winder, and as for him having anything that was worth anything, it's nonsense, for he was often weeks and weeks behind with his rent, and my 'usband he threatened often and often to turn him into the street, for, as he said, we've got a living to myke like other people -- and, of course, that's true; but, somehow, I didn't like to do it, though he was an odd kind of a man, and I fancy had been better off. And then the doctor came and looked at him, and said as he couldn't do nothing, and that night he died as I was a-sitting by his bed; and I can tell you that, with one thing and another, we lost money by him, for the few bits of clothes as he had were worth next to nothing when they came to be sold.* I gave the woman half a sovereign for her trouble, and went home thinking of Dr. Black and the epitaph she had made him, and wondering at his strange fancy that he had been robbed. I take it that he had very little to fear on that score, poor fellow; but I suppose that he was really mad, and died in a sudden access of his mania. His landlady said that once or twice when she had had occasion to go into his room (to dun the poor wretch for his rent, most likely), he would keep her at the door for about a minute, and that when she came in she would find him putting away his tin box in the corner by the window; I suppose he had become possessed with the idea of some great treasure, and fancied himself a wealthy man in the midst of all his misery. *Explicit*, my tale is ended, and you see that though I knew Black, I know nothing of his wife or of the history of her death. -- That's the Harlesden case, Salisbury, and I think it interests me all the more deeply because there does not seem the shadow of a possibility that I or any one else will ever know more about it. What do you think of it?"

"Well, Dyson, I must say that I think you have contrived to surround the whole thing with a mystery of your own making. I go for the doctor's solution: Black murdered his wife, being himself in all probability an undeveloped lunatic."

"What? Do you believe, then, that this woman was something too awful, too terrible to be allowed to remain on the earth? You will remember that the doctor said it was the brain of a devil?"

"Yes, yes, but he was speaking, of course, metaphorically. It's really quite a simple matter if you only look at it like that."

"Ah, well, you may be right; but yet I am sure you are not. Well, well, it's no good discussing it any more. A little more Benedictine? That's right; try some of this tobacco. Didn't you say that you had been bothered by something -- something which happened that night we dined together?"

"Yes, I have been worried, Dyson, worried a great deal. I -- But it's such a trivial matter -- indeed, such an absurdity -- that I feel ashamed to trouble you with it."

"Never mind, let's have it, absurd or not."

With many hesitations, and with much inward resentment of the folly of the thing, Salisbury told his tale, and repeated reluctantly the absurd intelligence and the absurder doggerel of the scrap of paper, expecting to hear Dyson burst out into a roar of laughter.

"Isn't it too bad that I should let myself be bothered by such stuff as that?" he asked, when he had stuttered out the jingle of once, and twice, and thrice.

Dyson had listened to it all gravely, even to the end, and meditated for a few minutes in silence.

"Yes," he said at length, "it was a curious chance, your taking shelter in that archway just as those two went by. But I don't know that I should call what was written on the paper nonsense; it is bizarre certainly, but I expect it has meaning for somebody. Just repeat it again, will you, and I will write it down. Perhaps we might find a cipher of some sort, though I hardly think we shall."

Again had the reluctant lips of Salisbury slowly to stammer out the rubbish that he abhorred, while Dyson jotted it down on a slip of paper.

"Look over it, will you?" he said, when it was done; "it may be important that I should have every word in its place. Is that all right?"

"Yes; that is an accurate copy. But I don't think you will get much out of it. Depend upon it, it is mere nonsense, a wanton scribble. I must be going now, Dyson. No, no more; that stuff of yours is pretty strong. Good-night."

"I suppose you would like to hear from me, if I did find out anything?"

"No, not I; I don't want to hear about the thing again. You may regard the discovery, if it is one, as your own."

"Very well. Good-night."

IV

A good many hours after Salisbury had returned to the company of the green rep chairs, Dyson still sat at his desk, itself a Japanese romance, smoking many pipes, and meditating over his friend's story. The bizarre quality of the inscription which had annoyed Salisbury was to him an attraction, and now and again he took it up and scanned thoughtfully what he had written, especially the quaint jingle at the end. It was a token, a symbol, he decided, and not a cipher, and the woman who had flung it away was in all probability entirely ignorant of its meaning; she was but the agent of the "Sam" she had abused and discarded, and he too was again the agent of some one unknown; possibly of the individual styled Q, who had been forced to visit his French friends. But what to make of "Traverse Handel S". Here was the root and source of the enigma, and not all the tobacco of Virginia seemed likely to suggest any clue here. It seemed almost hopeless, but Dyson regarded himself as the Wellington of mysteries, and went to bed feeling assured that sooner or later he would hit upon the right track. For the next few days he was deeply engaged in his literary labours, labours which were a profound mystery even to the most intimate of his friends, who searched the railway bookstalls in vain for the result of so many hours spent at the Japanese bureau in company with strong tobacco and black tea. On this occasion Dyson confined himself to his room for four days, and it was with genuine relief that he laid down his pen and went out into the streets in quest of relaxation and fresh air. The gas-lamps were being lighted, and the fifth edition of the evening papers was being howled through the streets, and Dyson, feeling that he wanted quiet, turned away from the clamorous Strand, and began to trend away to the north-west. Soon he found himself in streets that echoed to his footsteps, and crossing a broad new thoroughfare, and verging still to the west, Dyson discovered that he had penetrated to the depths of Soho. Here again was life; rare vintages of France and Italy, at prices which seemed contemptibly small, allured the passer-by; here were cheeses, vast and rich, here olive oil, and here a grove of Rabelaisian sausages; while in a neighbouring shop the whole press of Paris appeared to be on sale. In the middle of the roadway a strange miscellany of nations sauntered to and fro, for there cab and hansom rarely ventured; and from window over window the inhabitants looked forth in pleased contemplation of the scene. Dyson made his way slowly along, mingling with the crowd on the cobble-stones, listening to the queer babel of French and German, and Italian and English, glancing now and again at the shop windows with their levelled batteries of bottles, and had almost gained the end of the street, when his attention was arrested by a small shop at the corner, a vivid contrast to its neighbours. It was the typical shop of the poor quarter; a shop entirely English. Here were vended tobacco and sweets, cheap pipes of clay and cherry-wood; penny exercise books and penholders jostled for precedence with comic songs, and story papers with appalling cuts showed that romance claimed its place beside the actualities of the evening paper, the bills of which fluttered at the doorway. Dyson glanced up at the name above the door, and stood by the kennel trembling, for a sharp pang, the pang of one who has made a discovery, had for a moment left him incapable of motion. The name over the shop was Travers. Dyson looked up again, this time at the corner of the wall above the lamp-post, and read in white letters on a blue ground the words "Handel Street, W. C." and the legend was repeated in fainter letters just below. He gave a little sigh of satisfaction, and without more ado walked boldly into the shop, and stared full in the face of the fat man who was sitting behind the counter. The fellow rose to his feet, and returned the stare a little curiously, and then began in stereotyped phrase --

"What can I do for you, sir?"

Dyson enjoyed the situation and a dawning perplexity on the man's face. He propped his stick carefully against the counter and leaning over it, said slowly and impressively --

"Once around the grass, and twice around the lass, and thrice around the maple-tree."

Dyson had calculated on his words producing an effect, and he was not disappointed. The vendor of the miscellanies gasped, open-mouthed like a fish, and steadied himself against the counter. When he spoke, after a short interval, it was in a hoarse mutter, tremulous and unsteady.

"Would you mind saying that again, sir? I didn't quite catch it."

"My good man, I shall most certainly do nothing of the kind. You heard what I said perfectly well. You have got a clock in your shop, I see; an admirable timekeeper, I have no doubt. Well, I give you a minute by your own clock."

The man looked about him in a perplexed indecision, and Dyson felt that it was time to be bold.

"Look here, Travers, the time is nearly up. You have heard of Q, I think. Remember, I hold your life in my hands. Now!"

Dyson was shocked at the result of his own audacity. The man shrank and shrivelled in terror, the sweat poured down a face of ashy white, and he held up his hands before him.

"Mr. Davies, Mr. Davies, don't say that -- don't for Heaven's sake. I didn't know you at first, I didn't indeed. Good God! Mr. Davies, you wouldn't ruin me? I'll get it in a moment."

"You had better not lose any more time."

The man slunk piteously out of his own shop, and went into a back parlour. Dyson heard his trembling fingers fumbling with a bunch of keys, and the creak of an opening box. He came back presently with a small package neatly tied up in brown paper in his hands, and still, full of terror, handed it to Dyson.

"I'm glad to be rid of it," he said, "I'll take no more jobs of this sort."

Dyson took the parcel and his stick, and walked out of the shop with a nod, turning around as he passed the door. Travers had sunk into his seat, his face still white with terror, with one hand over his eyes, and Dyson speculated a good deal as he walked rapidly away as to what queer chords those could be on which he had played so roughly. He hailed the first hansom he could see and drove home, and when he had lit his hanging lamp, and laid his parcel on the table, he paused for a moment, wondering on what strange thing the lamp-light would shine. He locked his door, and cut the strings, and unfolded the paper layer after layer, and came at last to a small wooden box, simply but solidly made. There was no lock, and Dyson had simply to raise the lid, and as he did so he drew a long breath and started back. The lamp seemed to glimmer feebly like a single candle, but the whole room blazed with light -- and not with light alone, but with a thousand colours, with all the glories of some painted window; and upon the walls of his room and on the familiar furniture, the glow flamed back and seemed to flow again to its source, the little wooden box. For there upon a bed of soft wool lay the most splendid jewel, a jewel such as Dyson had never dreamed of, and within it shone the blue of far skies, and the green of the sea by the shore, and the red of the ruby, and deep violet rays, and in the middle of all it seemed aflame as if a fountain of fire rose up, and fell, and rose again with sparks like stars for drops. Dyson gave a long deep sigh, and dropped into his chair, and put his hands over his eyes to think. The jewel was like an opal, but from a long experience of the shop windows he knew there was no such thing as an opal one quarter or one eighth of its size. He looked at the stone again, with a feeling that was almost awe, and placed it gently on the table under the lamp, and watched the wonderful flame that shone and sparkled in its centre, and then turned to the box, curious to know whether it might contain other marvels. He lifted the bed of wool on which the opal had reclined, and saw beneath, no more jewels, but a little old pocket-book, worn and shabby with use. Dyson opened it at the first leaf, and dropped the book again appalled. He had read the name of the owner, neatly written in blue ink:

> STEVEN BLACK, M. D.
> Oranmore,
> Devon Road,
> Harlesden.

It was several minutes before Dyson could bring himself to open the book a second time; he remembered the wretched exile in his garret; and his strange talk, and the memory too of the face he had seen at the window, and of what the specialist had said, surged up in his mind, and as he held his finger on the cover, he shivered, dreading what might be written within. When at last he held it in his hand, and turned the pages, he found that the first two leaves were blank, but the third was covered with clear, minute writing, and Dyson began to read with the light of the opal flaming in his eyes.

V

"Ever since I was a young man" - the record began - "I devoted all my leisure and a good deal of time that ought to have been given to other studies to the investigation of curious and obscure branches of knowledge. What are commonly called the pleasures of life had never any attractions for me, and I lived alone in London, avoiding my fellow students, and in my turn avoided by them as a man self-absorbed and unsympathetic. So long as I could gratify my desire of knowledge of a peculiar kind, knowledge of which the very existence is a profound secret to most men, I was intensely happy, and I have often spent whole nights sitting in the darkness of my room, and thinking of the strange world on the brink of which I trod. My professional studies, however, and the necessity of obtaining a degree, for some time forced my more obscure employment into the background, and soon after I had qualified I met Agnes, who became my wife. We took a new house in this remote suburb, and I began the regular routine of a sober practice, and for some months lived happily enough, sharing in the life about me, and only thinking at odd intervals of that occult science which had once fascinated my whole being. I had learnt enough of the paths I had begun to tread to know that they were beyond all expression difficult and dangerous, that to persevere meant in all probability the wreck of a life, and that they led to regions so terrible, that the mind of man shrinks appalled at the very thought. Moreover, the quiet and the peace I had enjoyed since my marriage had wiled me away to a great extent from places where I knew no peace could dwell. But suddenly -- I think indeed it was the work of a single night, as I lay awake on my bed gazing into the darkness -- suddenly, I say, the old desire, the former longing, returned, and returned with a force that had been intensified ten times by its absence; and when the day dawned and I looked out of the window, and saw with haggard eyes the sunrise in the east, I knew that my doom had been pronounced; that as I had gone far, so now I must go farther with unfaltering steps. I turned to the bed where my wife was sleeping peacefully, and lay down again, weeping bitter tears, for the sun had set on our happy life and had risen with a dawn of terror to us both. I will not set down here in minute detail what followed; outwardly I went about the day's labour as before, saying nothing to my wife. But she soon saw that I had changed; I spent my spare time in a room which I had fitted up as a laboratory, and often I crept upstairs in the grey dawn of the morning, when the light of many lamps still glowed over London; and each night I had stolen a step nearer to that great abyss which I was to bridge over, the gulf between the world of consciousness and the world of matter. My experiments were many and complicated in their nature, and it was some months before I realized whither they all pointed, and when this was borne in upon me in a moment's time, I felt my face whiten and my heart still within me. But the power to draw back, the power to stand before the doors that now opened wide before me and not to enter in, had long ago been absent; the way was closed, and I could only pass onward. My position was as utterly hopeless as that of the prisoner in an utter dungeon, whose only light is that of the dungeon above him; the doors were shut and escape was impossible. Experiment after experiment gave the same result, and I knew, and shrank even as the thought passed through my mind, that in the work I had to do there must be elements which no laboratory could furnish, which no scales could ever measure. In that work, from which even I doubted to escape with life, life itself must enter; from some human being there must be drawn that essence which men call the soul, and in its place (for in the scheme of the world there is no vacant chamber) -- in its place would enter in what the lips can hardly utter, what the mind cannot conceive without a horror more awful than the horror of death itself. And when I knew this, I knew also on whom this fate would fall; I looked into my wife's eyes. Even at that hour, if I had gone out and taken a rope and hanged myself, I might have escaped, and she also, but in no other way. At last I told her all. She shuddered, and wept, and called on her dead mother for help, and asked me if I had no mercy, and I could only sigh. I concealed nothing from her; I told her what she would become, and what would enter in where her life had been; I told her of all the shame and of all the horror. You who will read this when I am dead -- if indeed I allow this record to survive -- you who have opened the box and have seen what lies there, if you could understand what lies hidden in that opal! For one night my wife consented to what I asked of her, consented with the tears running down her beautiful face, and hot shame flushing red over her neck and breast, consented to undergo this for me. I threw open the window, and we looked together at the sky and the dark earth for the last time; it was a fine star-light night, and there was a pleasant breeze blowing, and I kissed her on her lips, and her tears ran down upon my face. That night she down came to my laboratory, and there, with shutters bolted and barred down, with curtains drawn thick and close, so that the very stars might be shut out from the sight of that room, while the crucible hissed and boiled over the lamp, I did what had to be done, and led out what was no longer a woman. But on the table the opal flamed and sparkled with such light as no eyes of man have ever gazed on, and the rays of the flame that was within it flashed and glittered, and shone even to my heart. My wife had only asked one thing of me; that when there came at last what I had told her, I would kill her. I have kept that promise."

There was nothing more. Dyson let the little pocket-book fall, and turned and looked again at the opal with its flaming inmost light, and then with unutterable irresistible horror surging up in his heart, grasped the jewel, and flung it on the ground, and trampled it beneath his heel. His face was white with terror as he turned away, and for a moment stood sick and trembling, and then with a start he leapt across the room and steadied himself against the door. There was an angry hiss, as of steam escaping under great pressure, and as he gazed, motionless, a volume of heavy yellow smoke was slowly issuing from the very centre of the jewel, and wreathing itself in snakelike coils above it. And then a thin white flame burst forth from the smoke, and shot up into the air and vanished; and on the ground there lay a thing like a cinder, black and crumbling to the touch.

A TRUE STORY OF
A VAMPIRE

Count Stenbock

Vampire stories are generally located in Styria; mine is also. Styria is by no means the romantic kind of place described by those who have certainly never been there. It is a flat, uninteresting country, only celebrated for its turkeys, its capons, and the stupidity of its inhabitants. Vampires generally arrive at night, in carriages drawn by two black horses.

Our vampire arrived by the commonplace means of the railway train, and in the afternoon. You must think I am joking, or perhaps that by the word "Vampire" I mean a financial vampire. No, I am quite serious. The Vampire of whom I am speaking, who laid waste our hearth and home, was a *real* vampire.

Vampires are generally described as dark, sinister-looking, and singularly handsome. Our Vampire was, on the contrary, rather fair, and certainly was not at first sight sinister-looking, and though decidedly attractive in appearance, not what one would call singularly handsome.

Yes, he desolated our home, killed my brother -- the one object of my adoration -- also my dear father. Yet, at the same time, I must say that I myself came under the spell of his fascination, and, in spite of it all, have no ill-will towards him now.

Doubtless you have read in the papers *passim* of "the Baroness and her beasts". It is to tell how I came to spend most of my useless wealth on an asylum for stray animals that I am writing this.

I am old now; what happened then was when I was a little girl of about thirteen. I will begin by describing our household. We were Poles; our name was Wronski: we lived in Styria, where we had a castle. Our household was very limited. It consisted, with the exclusion of domestics, of only my father, our governess -- a wealthy Belgian named Mademoiselle Vonnaert -- my brother, and myself. Let me begin with my father: he was old and both my brother and I were children of his old age. Of my mother I remember nothing: she died in giving birth to my brother, who was only one year, or not as much, younger than myself. Our father was studious, continually occupied in reading books, chiefly on recondite subjects and in all kinds of unknown languages. He had a long white beard, and wore habitually a black velvet skull-cap.

How kind he was to us! It was more than I could tell. Still it was not I who was the favourite. His whole heart went out to Gabriel -- Gabryel as we spelt it in Polish. He was always called by the Russian abbreviation Gavril - - I mean, of course, my brother, who had a resemblance to the only portrait of my mother, a slight chalk sketch which hung in my father's study. But I was by no means jealous: my brother was and has been the only love of my life. It is for his sake that I am now keeping in Westbourne Park a home for stray cats and dogs.

I was at that time, as I said before, a little girl; my name was Carmela. My long tangled hair was always all over the place, and never would be combed straight. I was not pretty -- at least, looking at a photograph of me at that time, I do not think I could describe myself as such. Yet at the same time, when I look at the photograph, I think my expression may have been pleasing to some people: irregular features, large mouth, and large wild eyes.

I was by way of being naughty -- not so naughty as Gabriel in the opinion of Mlle. Vonnaert. Mlle. Vonnaert, I may intercalate, was a wholly excellent person, middle-aged, who really did speak good French, although she was a Belgian, and could also make herself understood in German, which, as you may or may not know, is the current language of Styria.

I find it difficult to describe my brother Gabriel; there was something about him strange and superhuman, or perhaps I should rather say praeterhuman, something between the animal and the divine. Perhaps the Greek idea of the faun might illustrate what I mean; but that will not do either. He had large, wild, gazelle-like eyes: his hair, like mine, was in a perpetual tangle -- that point he had in common with me, and indeed, as I afterwards heard, our mother having been of gypsy race, it will account for much of the innate wildness there was in our natures. I was wild enough, but Gabriel was much wilder. Nothing would induce him to put on shoes and stockings, except on Sundays -- when he also allowed his hair to be combed, but only by me. How shall I describe the grace of that lovely mouth, shaped verily *"en arc d'amour"*. I always think of the text in the Psalm, "Grace is shed forth on thy lips, therefore has God blessed thee eternally" -- lips that seemed to exhale the very breath of life. then that beautiful, lithe, living, elastic form!

He could run faster than any deer: spring like a squirrel to the topmost branch of a tree: he might have stood for the sign and symbol of vitality itself. But seldom could he be induced by Mlle. Vonnaert to learn lessons; but when he did so, he learned with extraordinary quickness. He would play upon every conceivable instrument, holding a violin here, there, and everywhere except the right place: manufacturing instruments for himself out of reeds -- even sticks. Mlle. Vonnaert made futile efforts to induce him to learn to play the piano. I suppose he was what was called spoilt, though merely in the superficial sense of the word. Our father allowed him to indulge in every caprice.

One of his peculiarities, when quite a little child, was horror at the sight of meat. Nothing on earth would induce him to taste it. Another thing which was particularly remarkable about him was his extraordinary power over animals. Everything seemed to come tame to his hand. Birds would sit on his shoulder. Then sometimes Mlle. Vonnaert and I would lose him in the woods -- he would suddenly dart away. Then we would find him singing softly or whistling to himself, with all manner of woodland creatures around him -- hedgehogs, little foxes, wild rabbits, marmots, squirrels, and such like. He would frequently bring these things home with him and insist on keeping them. This strange menagerie was the terror of poor Mlle. Vonnaert's heart. He chose to live in a little room at the top of a turret; but which, instead of going upstairs, he chose to reach by means of a very tall chestnut-tree, through the window. But in contradiction of all this, it was his custom to serve every Sunday Mass in the parish church, with hair nicely combed and with white surplice and red cassock. He looked as demure and tamed as possible. Then came the element of the divine. What an expression of ecstasy there was in those glorious eyes!

Thus far I have not been speaking about the Vampire. However, let me begin with my narrative at last. One day my father had to go to the neighbouring town -- as he frequently had. This time he returned accompanied by a guest. The gentleman, he said, had missed his train, through the late arrival of another at our station, which was a junction, and he would therefore, as trains were not frequent in our parts, have had to wait there all night. He had joined in conversation with my father in the too-late-arriving train from the town: and had consequently accepted my father's invitation to stay the night at our house. But of course, you know, in those out-of-the-way parts we are almost patriarchal in our hospitality.

He was announced under the name of Count Vardalek -- the name being Hungarian. But he spoke German well enough: not with the monotonous accentuation of Hungarians, but rather, if anything, with a slight Slavonic intonation. His voice was peculiarly soft and insinuating. We soon afterwards found out he could talk Polish, and Mlle. Vonnaert vouched for his good French. Indeed he seemed to know all languages. But let me give my first impressions. He was rather tall with fair wavy hair, rather long, which accentuated a certain effeminacy about his smooth face. His figure had something -- I cannot say what -- serpentine about it. The features were refined; and he had long, slender, subtle, magnetic-looking hands, a somewhat long sinuous nose, a graceful mouth, and an attractive smile, which belied the intense sadness of the expression of the eyes. When he arrived his eyes were half closed -- indeed they were habitually so -- so that I could not decide their colour. He looked worn and wearied. I could not possibly guess his age.

Suddenly Gabriel burst into the room: a yellow butterfly was clinging to his hair. He was carrying in his arms a little squirrel. Of course he was bare-legged as usual. The stranger looked up at his approach; then I noticed his eyes. They were green: they seemed to dilate and grow larger. Gabriel stood stock-still, with a startled look, like that of a bird fascinated by a serpent. But nevertheless he held out his hand to the newcomer. Vardalek, taking his hand -- I don't know why I noticed this trivial thing -- pressed the pulse with his forefinger. Suddenly Gabriel darted from the room and rushed upstairs, going to his turret-room this time by the staircase instead of the tree. I was in terror what the Count might think of him. Great was my relief when he came down in his velvet Sunday suit, and shoes and stockings. I combed his hair, and set him generally right.

When the stranger came down to dinner his appearance had somewhat altered; he looked much younger. There was an elasticity of the skin, combined with a delicate complexion, rarely to be found in a man. Before, he had struck me as being very pale.

Well, at dinner we were all charmed with him, especially my father. He seemed to be thoroughly acquainted with all my father's particular hobbies. Once, when my father was relating some of his military experiences, he said something about a drummer-boy who was wounded in battle. His eyes opened completely again and dilated: this time with a particularly disagreeable expression, dull and dead, yet at the same time animated by some horrible excitement. But this was only momentary.

The chief subject of his conversation with my father was about certain curious mystical books which my father had just lately picked up, and which he could not make out, but Vardalek seemed completely to understand. At dessert-time my father asked him if he were in a great hurry to reach his destination: if not, would he not stay with us a little while: though our place was out of the way, he would find much that would interest him in his library.

He answered, "I am in no hurry. I have no particular reason for going to that place at all, and if I can be of service to you in deciphering these books, I shall be only too glad." He added with a smile which was bitter, very very bitter: "You see I am a cosmopolitan, a wanderer on the face of the earth."

After dinner my father asked him if he played the piano. He said, "Yes, a little," and he sat down at the piano. Then he played a Hungarian csardas -- wild, rhapsodic, wonderful.

That is the music which makes men mad. He went on in the same strain.

Gabriel stood stock-still by the piano, his eyes dilated and fixed, his form quivering. At last he said very slowly, at one particular motif -- for want of

276

a better word you may call it the *relâche* of a csardas, by which I mean that point where the original quasi-slow movement begins again -- "Yes, I think I could play that."

Then he quickly fetched his fiddle and self-made xylophone, and did, actually alternating the instruments, render the same very well indeed.

Vardalek looked at him, and said in a very sad voice, "Poor child! you have the soul of music within you."

I could not understand why he should seem to commiserate instead of congratulate Gabriel on what certainly showed an extraordinary talent.

Gabriel was shy even as the wild animals who were tame to him. Never before had he taken to a stranger. Indeed, as a rule, if any stranger came to the house by any chance, he would hide himself, and I had to bring him up his food to the turret chamber. You may imagine what was my surprise when I saw him walking about hand in hand with Vardalek the next morning, in the garden, talking livelily with him, and showing his collection of pet animals, which he had gathered from the woods, and for which we had had to fit up a regular zoological gardens. He seemed utterly under the domination of Vardalek. What surprised us was (for otherwise we liked the stranger, especially for being kind to him) that he seemed, though not noticeably at first -- except perhaps to me, who noticed everything with regard to him -- to be gradually losing his health and vitality. He did not become pale as yet; but there was a certain languor about his movements which certainly there was by no means before.

My father got more and more devoted to Count Vardalek. He helped him in his studies: and my father would hardly allow him to go away, which he did sometimes -- to Trieste, he said: he always came back, bringing us presents of strange Oriental jewellery or textures.

I knew all kinds of people came to Trieste, Orientals included. Still, there was a strangeness and magnificence about these things which I was sure even then could not possibly have come from such a place as Trieste, memorable chiefly to me for its necktie shops.

When Vardalek was away, Gabriel was continually asking for him and talking about him. Then at the same time he seemed to regain his old vitality and spirits. Vardalek always returned looking much older, wan, and weary. Gabriel would rush to meet him, and kiss him on the mouth. Then he gave a slight shiver: and after a little while began to look quite young again.

Things continued like this for some time. My father would not hear of Vardalek's going away permanently. He came to be an inmate of our house. I indeed, and Mlle. Vonnaert also, could not help noticing what a difference there was altogether about Gabriel. But my father seemed totally blind to it.

One night I had gone downstairs to fetch something which I had left in the drawing-room. As I was going up again I passed Vardalek's room. He was playing on a piano, which had been specially put there for him, one of

Chopin's nocturnes, very beautifully: I stopped, leaning on the banisters to listen.

Something white appeared on the dark staircase. We believed in ghosts in our part. I was transfixed with terror, and clung to the banisters. What was my astonishment to see Gabriel walking slowly down the staircase, his eyes fixed as though in a trance! This terrified me even more than a ghost would. Could I believe my senses? Could that be Gabriel?

I simply could not move. Gabriel, clad in his long white night-shirt, came downstairs and opened the door. He left it open. Vardalek still continued playing, but talked as he played.

He said -- this time speaking in Polish -- *Nie umiem wyrazic jak ciechi kocham* - "My darling, I fain would spare thee; but thy life is my life, and I must live, I who would rather die. Will God not have any mercy on me? Oh! Oh! life; oh, the torture of life!" Here he struck one agonized and strange chord, then continued playing softly, "O Gabriel, my beloved! my life, yes *life* -- oh, why life? I am sure this is but a little that I demand of thee. Surely thy superabundance of life can spare a little to one who is already dead. No, stay," he said now almost harshly, "what must be, must be!"

Gabriel stood there quite still, with the same fixed vacant expression, in the room. He was evidently walking in his sleep. Vardalek played on: then said, "Ah!" with a sign of terrible agony. Then very gently, "Go now, Gabriel; it is enough." And Gabriel went out of the room and ascended the staircase at the same slow pace, with the same unconscious stare. Vardalek struck the piano, and although he did not play loudly, it seemed as though the strings would break. You never heard music so strange and so heart-rending!

I only know I was found by Mlle. Vonnaert in the morning, in an unconscious state, at the foot of the stairs. Was it a dream after all? I am sure now that it was not. I thought then it might be, and said nothing to anyone about it. Indeed, what could I say?

Well, to let me cut a long story short, Gabriel, who had never known a moment's sickness in his life, grew ill: and we had to send to Gratz for a doctor, who could give no explanation of Gabriel's strange illness. Gradual wasting away, he said: absolutely no organic complaint. What could this mean?

My father at last became conscious of the fact that Gabriel was ill. His anxiety was fearful. The last trace of grey faded from his hair, and it became quite white. We sent to Vienna for doctors. But all with the same result.

Gabriel was generally unconscious, and when conscious, only seemed to recognise Vardalek, who sat continually by his bedside, nursing him with the utmost tenderness.

One day I was alone in the room: and Vardalek cried suddenly, almost fiercely, "Send for a priest, at once," he repeated. "It is now almost too late!"

Gabriel stretched out his arms spasmodically, and put them round

Vardalek's neck. This was the only movement he had made for some time. Vardalek bent down and kissed him on the lips. I rushed downstairs: and the priest was sent for. When I came back Vardalek was not there. The priest administered extreme unction. I think Gabriel was already dead, although we did not think so at the time.

Vardalek had utterly disappeared; and when we looked for him he was nowhere to be found; nor have I seen or heard of him since.

My father died very soon afterwards: suddenly aged, and bent down with grief. And so the whole of the Wronski property came into my sole possession. And here I am, an old woman, generally laughed at for keeping, in memory of Gabriel, an asylum for stray animals -- and -- people do not, as a rule, believe in Vampires!

DRACULA

Bram Stoker

(JONATHAN HARKER'S JOURNAL)

16 May

...I was not alone. The room was the same, unchanged in any way since I came into it; I could see along the floor, in the brilliant moonlight, my own footsteps marked where I had disturbed the long accumulation of dust. In the moonlight opposite me were three young women, ladies by their dress and manner. I thought at the time that I must be dreaming when I saw them, for, though the moonlight was behind them, they threw no shadow on the floor. They came close to me and looked at me for some time and then whispered together. Two were dark, and had high aquiline noses, like the Count's, and great dark, piercing eyes, that seemed to be almost red when contrasted with the pale yellow moon. The other was fair, and fair as can be, with great, wavy masses of golden hair and eyes like pale sapphires. I seemed somehow to know her face, and to know it in connection with some dreamy fear, but I could not recollect at the moment how or where. All three had brilliant white teeth, that shone like pearls against the ruby of their voluptuous lips. There was something about them which made me uneasy, some longing and at the same time some deadly fear. I felt in my heart a wicked, burning desire that they would kiss me with those red lips. It is not good to note this down, lest some day it should meet Mina's eyes and cause her pain; but it is the truth. They whispered together, and then they all three laughed -- such a silvery, musical laugh, but as hard as though the sound never could have come through the softness of human lips. It was like the intolerable, tingling sweetness of water-glasses when played on by a cunning hand. The fair girl shook her head coquettishly, and the other two urged her on. One said:--

"Go on! You are first, and we shall follow; yours is the right to begin." The other added:--

"He is young and strong; there are kisses for us all." I lay quiet, looking out under my eyelashes in an agony of delightful anticipation. The fair girl advanced and bent over me till I could feel the movement of her breath upon me. Sweet it was in one sense, honey-sweet, and sent the same tingling through the nerves as her voice, but with a bitter underlying the sweet, a bitter offensiveness, as one smells in blood.

I was afraid to raise my eyelids, but looked out and saw perfectly under the lashes. The fair girl went on her knees and bent over me, fairly gloating. There was a deliberate voluptuousness which was both thrilling and repulsive, and as she arched her neck she actually licked her lips like an animal, till I could see in the moonlight the moisture shining on the scarlet lips and on the red tongue as it lapped the sharp white teeth. Lower and lower went her head as the lips went below the range of my mouth and chin and seemed about to fasten on my throat. Then she paused, and I could hear the churning sound of her tongue as it licked her teeth and lips, and could feel the hot breath on my neck. Then the skin of my throat began to tingle as one's flesh does when the hand that is to tickle it approaches nearer -- nearer. I could feel the soft, shivering touch of the lips on the supersensitive skin of my throat, and the hard dents of two sharp teeth, just touching and pausing there. I closed my eyes in a languorous ecstasy and waited -- waited with beating heart.

(DR. SEWARD'S DIARY)

3 October

...The moonlight was so bright that through the thick yellow blind the room was light enough to see. On the bed beside the window lay Jonathan Harker, his face flushed, and breathing heavily as though in a stupor. Kneeling on the near edge of the bed facing outwards was the white-clad figure of his wife. By her side stood a tall, thin man, clad in black. His face was turned from us, but the instant we saw it we all recognised the Count -- in every way, even to the scar on his forehead. With his left hand he held both Mrs. Harker's hands, keeping them away with her arms at full tension; his right hand gripped her by the back of the neck, forcing her face down on his bosom. Her white night-dress was smeared with blood, and a thin stream trickled down the man's bare breast, which was shown by his torn-open dress. The attitude of the two had a terrible resemblance to a child forcing a kitten's nose into a saucer of milk to compel it to drink. As we burst into the room, the Count turned his face, and the hellish look that I heard described seemed to leap into it. His eyes flamed red with devilish passion; the great nostrils of the white aquiline nose opened wide and quivered at the edges; and the white sharp teeth, behind the full lips of the blood-dripping mouth, champed like those of a wild beast. With a wrench, which threw his victim back upon the bed as though hurled from a height, he turned and sprang at us. But by this time the Professor had gained his feet, and was holding towards him the envelope which contained the Sacred Wafer. The Count suddenly stopped, just as poor Lucy had done outside the tomb, and cowered back. Further and further back he cowered, as we, lifting our crucifixes, advanced. The moonlight suddenly failed, as a great black cloud sailed across the sky; and when the gaslight sprang up under Quincey's match, we saw nothing but a faint vapour.

The editors wish to acknowledge the help of the following
in the preparation of *Blood & Roses*:

Atlas Books
Paul Buck
Dedalus Books
Delectus Books
Alexis Lykiard
Jeremy Reed
Aaron Williamson

The editors found the following books
invaluable to their research:

"The Living Dead"
- A Study of the Vampire in Romantic Literature
James B. Twitchell
(Duke University Press)

"The Vampire in Literature"
- A Critical Bibliography
Margaret L. Carter
(U.M.I. Research Press)

Forthcoming:

THE GREAT GOD PAN
Arthur Machen
Creation Classics IV

First published in 1894, *THE GREAT GOD PAN* is Arthur Machen's first, and greatest, opus of Decadence and Horror. With his singular eye for the bizarre and macabre, Machen unfurls this tale of a young girl cursed by her unnatural parentage.

"Of creators of cosmic fear raised to its most artistic pitch,
few can hope to equal Arthur Machen"
- H. P. Lovecraft.

This new, exclusive edition from Creation Press includes a set of complementary "automatic" drawings by Machen's contemporary and fellow mystic, **Austin Osman Spare,** and a brand new introductory essay on Machen and his works by Iain Smith of the Arthur Machen Society, as well as Machen's own illuminating introduction from the 1914 edition.
Large format, illustrated. £7.95.

Forthcoming:

SALOME
Oscar Wilde
Creation Classics V

Written - and banned - in 1892, **SALOME** is Oscar Wilde's ultimate statement of Decadence, translated from the French by Lord Alfred Douglas.

This brand new edition from Creation Press includes original illustrations drafted by **Aubrey Beardsley** for Lord Douglas' English translation, and also features a 19th Century translation of The Book of Revelation (whence Wilde drew much of the apocalytic imagery in **SALOME**): the book of Armagideon and the Beast 666.

Large format, illustrated. £7.95.

Also available:
CREATION PRESS

"SATANSKIN"   James Havoc
Twenty adult fairy-tales of twisted imagination from the young "madman", disclosing an occult world of graveyard erotica, faecal demonolatry, magick and pansexual lunar mutiny.
In *Devil's Gold*, a transexual pact with excremental demons leads to unexpected metamorphoses; the sorcerer of *White Meat Fever* steals female anatomy to usurp the moon; skinless nuns with *Shadow Sickness* fall prey to a priapic scavenger from Hell; a hapless traveller enters the *Tongue Cathedral* and finds himself inside a vampire's wet-dream; in *The Venus Eye*, an angel wreaks revenge on a paedophiliac butcher from within her coffin; at the throw of bone dice, the *Dogstar Pact* induces lycanthropy in unborn children...
"The adventurousness of language, the compelling imagery, the uncompromising exploration of sexuality, all create a brilliant mosaic...*SATANSKIN* is an extraordinary and fascinating work in the truest sense." - **JEREMY REED**
"*SATANSKIN* shouldn't be missed by anyone with an interest in the unusual."
                              - OUTLOOK
"As a literary bestiary of gratuitous sexual horrors, *SATANSKIN* is up there with *120 Days of Sodom*, genuinely infernal and black." - **DIVINITY**
£5.95

"RAISM - The Songs of Gilles de Rais"   James Havoc and Mike Philbin
Part I: "Meathook Seed"
Havoc's infamous anti-novel, heavily edited and revised to form a graphic novel in 3 parts, plus a brand new fourth and concluding part. Illustrated in finepoint chiaroscuro by Mike Philbin of **"Red Hedz"** notoriety. A surreal, explicit, and deranged work of alchemy and Satanism, unlike any other of its kind.
"...bursting with darkly imaginative, not to say downright revolting, imagery." - **DARKSIDE**
Creation Graphics 1   A4, 32 pages. Full colour cover.
£4.95

"BRIDAL GOWN SHROUD"   Adele Olivia Gladwell
Short fiction, prose-poems and illuminating essays dealing with sexual/textual politics. Using a subversive motif of menstruation, the writer explores the gulf between the symbolic and the imaginary to comment upon the abjection and fragmentation of the misplaced woman. Includes essays on Nick Cave, Religious Ecstasy, Pornography etc.
"The missing link between Lydia Lunch and Julia Kristeva." - **LOADED**
£6.95

"RED HEDZ"   Michael Paul Peter

The hardcore horror classic; an extreme onslaught of shape-shifting, psycho-sexual tyranny and mutation.

"Horror fiction on the edge." - **RAMSEY CAMPBELL**

"Would make a perfect David Cronenberg film if translated to the screen."
         - JORG BUTTGEREIT

"...takes writers like William Burroughs and Clive Barker as merely the starting-point for a mixture of poetry, cut-up fiction, hallucinatory rantings and keenly-observed characterisation." - **SKELETON CREW**

£5.95

"RED STAINS"   Jack Hunter (Ed.)

A lexicon of lesions, bible of blood.

New stories of extreme biological fantasy and the psycho-sexual imagination. A successor to the **"Black Book"**. Authors include: **Ramsey Campbell, Jeremy Reed, Tony Reed, Terence Sellers, James Havoc, Paul Buck, DF Lewis, Michael Paul Peter Philbin, Adele Olivia Gladwell.**

"The most unrelenting collection of sexual horror fiction that I've ever read." - **DIVINITY**

£5.95

"CATHEDRAL LUNG" Aaron Williamson

A volume of ecstatic rage from the explosive writer and performer, who is profoundly deaf.

"Aaron seems to confront his anger by grabbing language by the throat... creates something radically different from most writers." - **SOUNDBARRIER.**

"...a furious gnostic prayer....machine-gunning the page, ricocheting against our smug complacent ears."   - **Brian Catling, poet.**

£4.95

ANNIHILATION PRESS

"RAPID EYE 2"   Simon Dwyer (Ed.)

Latest issue of the leading *occulture* journal. Includes articles on/by **Anton LaVey, Jörg Buttgereit, Timothy Leary, Mondo Movies, Numerology & Serial Killers, Colin Wilson, Genesis P.Orridge, Paul Mayersberg** etc etc.

"...Rapid Eye tells you what is really happening. It tells a wider story of a cultural struggle that will be crucial to the demands of the 90's: the struggle between life and death." - **THE OBSERVER**

"Some of the best pop writing to be found; excellent articles." - **THE FACE**

"Visionary...An intelligent and imaginative journal of what they'd call De-Control. Penetrating....comprehensive...most illuminating." - **NME**

Over 300 pages, with rare photographs.

£9.95